Structural Impediments to Growth in Japan

A National Bureau
of Economic Research
Conference Report

Structural Impediments to Growth in Japan

Edited by **Magnus Blomström, Jennifer Corbett, Fumio Hayashi, and Anil Kashyap**

The University of Chicago Press

Chicago and London

MAGNUS BLOMSTRÖM is professor of economics and president of the European Institute of Japanese Studies, both at the Stockholm School of Economics, and a research associate of the National Bureau of Economic Research. JENNIFER CORBETT is head of the Japan Centre, Faculty of Asian Studies, Australian National University. FUMIO HAYASHI is professor of economics at the University of Tokyo and a research associate of the National Bureau of Economic Research. ANIL KASHYAP is the Edward Eagle Brown Professor of Economics and Finance at the Graduate School of Business, University of Chicago, and a research associate of the National Bureau of Economic Research.

In memory of Albert Ando

The University of Chicago Press, Chicago 60637
The University of Chicago Press, Ltd., London
© 2003 by the National Bureau of Economic Research
All rights reserved. Published 2003
Printed in the United States of America
12 11 10 09 08 07 06 05 04 03   1 2 3 4 5
ISBN: 0-226-06021-7 (cloth)

Library of Congress Cataloging-in-Publication Data

Structural impediments to growth in Japan / edited by Magnus Blomström . . . [et al.].
    p.   cm.
    "A National Bureau of Economic Research conference report."
    Includes bibliographical references (p.) and index.
    ISBN 0-226-06021-7 (acid-free paper)
    1. Japan—Economic conditions—1989– 2. Japan—Economic policy—1989– I. Blomström, Magnus, 1952–

    HC462.95 S78 2003
    330.952—dc21   2003044776

♾ The paper used in this publication meets the minimum requirements of the American National Standard for Information Sciences—Permanence of Paper for Printed Library Materials, ANSI Z39.48-1992.

Relation of the Directors to the Work and Publications of the NBER

1. The object of the NBER is to ascertain and present to the economics profession, and to the public more generally, important economic facts and their interpretation in a scientific manner without policy recommendations. The Board of Directors is charged with the responsibility of ensuring that the work of the NBER is carried on in strict conformity with this object.

2. The President shall establish an internal review process to ensure that book manuscripts proposed for publication DO NOT contain policy recommendations. This shall apply both to the proceedings of conferences and to manuscripts by a single author or by one or more co-authors but shall not apply to authors of comments at NBER conferences who are not NBER affiliates.

3. No book manuscript reporting research shall be published by the NBER until the President has sent to each member of the Board a notice that a manuscript is recommended for publication and that in the President's opinion it is suitable for publication in accordance with the above principles of the NBER. Such notification will include a table of contents and an abstract or summary of the manuscript's content, a list of contributors if applicable, and a response form for use by Directors who desire a copy of the manuscript for review. Each manuscript shall contain a summary drawing attention to the nature and treatment of the problem studied and the main conclusions reached.

4. No volume shall be published until forty-five days have elapsed from the above notification of intention to publish it. During this period a copy shall be sent to any Director requesting it, and if any Director objects to publication on the grounds that the manuscript contains policy recommendations, the objection will be presented to the author(s) or editor(s). In case of dispute, all members of the Board shall be notified, and the President shall appoint an ad hoc committee of the Board to decide the matter; thirty days additional shall be granted for this purpose.

5. The President shall present annually to the Board a report describing the internal manuscript review process, any objections made by Directors before publication or by anyone after publication, any disputes about such matters, and how they were handled.

6. Publications of the NBER issued for informational purposes concerning the work of the Bureau, or issued to inform the public of the activities at the Bureau, including but not limited to the NBER Digest and Reporter, shall be consistent with the object stated in paragraph 1. They shall contain a specific disclaimer noting that they have not passed through the review procedures required in this resolution. The Executive Committee of the Board is charged with the review of all such publications from time to time.

7. NBER working papers and manuscripts distributed on the Bureau's web site are not deemed to be publications for the purpose of this resolution, but they shall be consistent with the object stated in paragraph 1. Working papers shall contain a specific disclaimer noting that they have not passed through the review procedures required in this resolution. The NBER's web site shall contain a similar disclaimer. The President shall establish an internal review process to ensure that the working papers and the web site do not contain policy recommendations, and shall report annually to the Board on this process and any concerns raised in connection with it.

8. Unless otherwise determined by the Board or exempted by the terms of paragraphs 6 and 7, a copy of this resolution shall be printed in each NBER publication as described in paragraph 2 above.

Contents

            Hiroshi Ono and Marcus E. Rebick

9.   **An International Perspective of Corporate Groups
            and Their Prospects**   259
            Yishay Yafeh

            Contributors   285
            Author Index   287
            Subject Index   291

Preface

There has been an immense amount of research on Japan's decade-long economic stagnation. This book differs from most prior work by taking a longer term view of the challenges facing Japan. Some of these, such as the possible impediments associated with business groups and the distribution system, have been discussed for years. Others, such as the Fiscal Investment Loan Program, are only now getting attention. While others, such as the role of women in the workforce and the aging of the population, have been almost pushed off the front pages by the current slowdown. Our goal was to gather all the leading conjectures about what might be relevant over the next decade or so and take a fresh look at them.

We have structured the papers so that they not only provide an introduction to the basic issues and literature associated with each topic, but also offer new analysis that will be relevant for experts on the Japanese economy. There is no simple conclusion that emerges from our work; some of the commonly thought barriers to growth appear to us to be overstated, while others seem to be extremely serious. We believe the standard by which we should be judged is whether our analysis still appears relevant once an economic recovery begins and when the immediate problems strangling the economy have been addressed.

This project could not have been completed without the help of many people and organizations. The idea for the book grew out of the series of annual conference meetings that the editors had organized under the auspices of the National Bureau of Economic Research (NBER), the European Institute of Japanese Studies (EIJS), the Center for International Research on the Japanese Economy (CIRJE), and the Centre for Economic Policy Research. The lively discussion and high quality of the papers being presented led us to believe that a themed book, with submissions invited from among the participants at those meetings, would make a contribution to economic debate in Japan. The authors had planned to gather for a first meeting in Tokyo on September 12, 2001. The tragic events of the day before prevented several people from arriving in Tokyo, but everyone was able to produce first drafts of their papers by the following March, in time for a second workshop in Tokyo. We thank Brett Maranjian at the NBER, Emiko Otsubo at the CIRJE, and Atsushi Hasegawa and Miki Futugawa of the Tokyo office of the EIJS for helping coordinate these meetings.

The Toshiba International Foundation provided critical and timely financial support. The Asian Development Bank Institute and the Swedish Embassy in Tokyo hosted the meetings that preceded the publication. We thank all three of them. The editors also acknowledge the support of their home institutions: the University of Chicago (Kashyap), University of Tokyo (Hayashi), Stockholm School of Economics (Blomström), and the University of Oxford and the Australian National University (Corbett).

The manuscript was copyedited by Larry Meissner. Larry helped bring consistency and clarity to the various chapters. Aileen Teshima at the CIRJE, Luda Mangos at the Asian Studies Faculty of the Australian National University, and Jennifer Williams at the University of Chicago all helped with the production of the final drafts of the chapters.

Finally, we wish to record our debt and gratitude to Albert Ando. This project was inspired by Albert. He was a regular participant in the meetings jointly organized by our four organizations and he encouraged the idea of producing a book bringing together the ideas of the group. Albert was diagnosed with leukemia in August 2002 and died a month later. We all miss him dearly, and we dedicate this book to him.

Introduction

Magnus Blomström, Jennifer Corbett, Fumio Hayashi, and Anil Kashyap

After four decades of rapid economic growth that transformed Japan into a wealthy country at the world's technological frontier, the last decade brought prolonged economic stagnation. Despite the long period of low growth in Japan, there is still little agreement in the universities or amongst policymakers about its causes or cures. This collection of essays by leading scholars from Europe, Japan, and the United States offers a comprehensive assessment of the economic problems facing Japan. Our analysis naturally separates into an investigation of challenges both for government policy and to the private sector. The book is organized around these two areas. The papers are unified by their empirical character. All of the papers present original data analysis, and several uncover new facts that challenge conventional wisdom.

Challenges for Government Policy

The financial crisis is the most commonly cited cause of the prolonged slowdown of the Japanese economy. Yet there is still substantial disagreement over whether the worst is over and whether the current financial difficulties are likely to pose long-run problems. The picture that emerges from our investigation is frightening.

Magnus Blomström is professor of economics and president of the European Institute of Japanese Studies, both at the Stockholm School of Economics, and a research associate of the National Bureau of Economic Research. Jennifer Corbett is head of the Japan Centre, Faculty of Asian Studies, Australian National University. Fumio Hayashi is professor of economics at the University of Tokyo and a research associate of the National Bureau of Economic Research. Anil Kashyap is the Edward Eagle Brown Professor of Economics and Finance at the Graduate School of Business, University of Chicago, and a research associate of the National Bureau of Economic Research.

In the opening essay, Mitsuhiro Fukao assesses the current size of the losses for the insurance companies and banks. Fukao shows that the structural problems in the banking sector are deep. The banks have not made a profit from operations since 1993, and the loan losses continue to accumulate, even though the banks have already written off ¥82 trillion (over 16 percent of the gross domestic product [GDP] through March 2002). He highlights two key problems that underlie the banks inability to make profits. The first is deflation that limits their ability to raise interest rates without crippling their borrowers. The second is the operations of government subsidized financial agencies that often undercut the banks' pricing power. He argues that until both of these conditions are reversed the banks will continue to hemorrhage.

Fukao argues that the insurance companies' problems are slightly different. They have primarily suffered because of overly optimistic promises about how much they would pay to policyholders. Due to deflation, they have been unable to earn the requisite return on assets and hence are losing money on an ongoing basis. It appears that the only way out of this will be a renegotiation of the promised payments to policyholders.

In the meantime, the insurance companies pose another problem because of their interconnections with the banks. The banks have large investments in the insurance companies and the insurers generally are key shareholders of the banks. This "double-gearing" means that losses from one sector may spread to the other.

The picture that emerges is grim. Both the banks and insurance companies are in terrible condition. Fukao estimates that the effective amount of private sector capital in the banking sector was less than ¥5 trillion at March 2002 and that a 10 percent decline in stock prices from the level at that time could wipe out over 75 percent of this capital. Assuming that depositors will be paid in full or nearly so, this means that taxpayers are very close to having to finance all subsequent losses that are uncovered. There is a range of private sector estimates that suggest this could easily amount to another ¥30 trillion.

In the second chapter of the volume, Takero Doi and Takeo Hoshi provide complementary evidence to Fukao by investigating government-sponsored financial institutions more closely. They focus on the question of whether these agencies will be able to repay the loans that they have taken out as part of the fiscal investment loan program (FILP). Historically this program was used to recycle the funds that were deposited in postal savings accounts. The flows involved are large: More than ¥417 trillion (roughly 82 percent of annual GDP) is being lent out each year.

One of their major contributions is identifying the losses that are obscured by various idiosyncrasies of the typical arrangements. They highlight three major features of the system that make the losses much larger than a casual inspection of the agencies' financial statements might suggest. First, the depreciation of assets often has not been recorded in order to allow the agency to book profits. For these agencies if assets were written down to realistic levels they would be insolvent. A second problem is that some agencies have loan losses that they acknowledge exceed their reserves. This is further exacerbated because almost all agencies show very low levels of provisions, so that even small corrections exhaust the reserves. Finally, on a flow basis, most agencies are shown making small profits relative to assets, but the profits often disappear once central government subsidies are taken into account.

Doi and Hoshi suggest conservative estimates indicate that this kind of game playing already is covering up at least ¥35 trillion in losses (over 7 percent of GDP). But these figures take the quality of investments made by the agencies at face value. With reasonable estimates about further undiscovered loan losses, their estimates would be substantially higher.

Doi and Hoshi also explore the losses that are associated with the lending by various government agencies to local governments. These calculations are necessarily more tentative since there are no reliable financial statements for most of the governments, but many of these governments are not running surpluses that are nearly large enough to repay the borrowing that they have undertaken. Projecting current surpluses ahead, their baseline estimates suggest that roughly ¥90 trillion is owed by governments that are likely to have payment problems unless they significantly increase taxes or cut spending. Although this figure varies depending on the exact details of the assumed tax and spending patterns, they consistently find that similarly large amounts of lending are at risk for default or partial default. Their baseline estimate implies that another ¥40 trillion is likely to be lost on these loans.

Collectively these estimates imply that FILP loan losses could be expected to cost taxpayers roughly at least ¥75 trillion (15 percent of current GDP). Together with the losses already identified by Fukao in chapter 1 for the private commercial banks and the likelihood of impending future losses, the Japanese financial crisis is well on the way to being huge in terms of percent of GDP and unprecedented in terms of the absolute size of the losses.

This naturally leads to the question of where government finances are headed in Japan, the topic of Robert Dekle's study (chapter 3). The dismal performance of the Japanese economy in the 1990s brought about reduced tax revenue and increased spending by the government in its attempt to stimulate the economy. As a result, by 2000, Japan had the largest public debt-to-GDP ratio among the Organization for Economic Cooperation and Development (OECD) member countries. (The official figures cover the gross amount of debt issued, and thus ignore the fact that some of the debt was used to purchase assets. However, even once the netting is done, the implied levels are high and rising.) The aging of the population will make Japan's fiscal situation even worse. By 2020, it is estimated that 25 percent of the Japanese population will be older than 65—the current proportion is about 15 percent. This demographic shift will lead to soaring health care expenses and social security payments.

Dekle shows that cost of these payments will require a massive adjustment by the government. His baseline simulation suggests that if current levels of per capita spending are maintained, taxes as a percentage of GDP will have to rise from the current level of 28 percent of GDP to nearly 50 percent by 2040. While this calculation turns on a number of details, the inescapable conclusion of Dekle's chapter is that a huge change in budget policy—either an exorbitant level of taxes or a draconian reform of the social security and health care system—is needed for the Japanese government to remain solvent.

As with the mismeasurement of the size of the public debt, there are concerns that other areas of government statistics do not accurately reflect the seriousness of Japan's current problems. In chapter 4, Kenn Ariga and Kenji Matsui investigate the quality of government statistics. Japanese statistics have been heavily criticized for inaccuracy and sometimes cited as contributing to poor decision making. Ariga and Matsui argue that the reliability of the Consumer Price Index (CPI) could be significantly improved by the simple expedients of increasing the size of the staff working on the index, raising their professional qualifications, and expanding data collection efforts.

Mismeasurement in CPI numbers is obviously important because it leads to an underassessment of the degree of deflation. Ariga and Matsui estimate that the CPI overstates inflation by at least 0.5 percent per year. This makes failure to halt deflation even more costly than conventional estimates suggest. Furthermore it has ramifications for the debate on inflation targeting, where the possibility of effective targeting depends crucially on timely and accurate measurement of inflation, it also affects estimates of GDP since the same retail price data is used in construction of both CPI and GDP. Less obviously, the potential costs of mismeasurement are not limited to policy, but also impact private decision making as well. Financial and consulting sector economists are concerned over noisy and inconsistent data, and frequent, large revisions in data can cause visible swings in financial markets. Chapter 4 concentrates in detail on an investigation of the CPI. However, as the authors point out, the CPI exhibits three of the main problems evident in other heavily criticized statistics: (a) long delays in updating, (b) little interagency coordination in production, and (c) poor documentation.

Changes in consumer behavior are one source of CPI errors identified by Ariga and Matsui. David Flath discusses a related issue, the role of the distribution system, in chapter 5. The service sector in Japan is notorious for its alleged inefficiency. The method by which goods are distributed is widely thought to be a prime contributor to this inefficiency. Most analysts consider these patterns traceable to ill-conceived regulation (such as those that limit the location of large stores).

Simple statistical comparisons confirm that fact that Japan is unusual. For instance, Japan has nearly twice as many stores per inhabitant as the United States and 50 percent more of the workforce in the wholesale sector of the economy, even though the percentage of the workforce in the retail sector is similar. Flath argues, however, that the leap to conclude that Japanese regulation is responsible for these patterns is unwarranted. He shows that distribution patterns across countries (as well as between prefectures in Japan) are well explained by fundamental economic factors, such as the prevalence of car ownership and the average size of homes. Because private car ownership in Japan has been low until recently and houses are small and lack storage space, Japan is a country where transporting and storing goods is not easy for households. Thus, the distribution sector in Japan has been arranged to help with these functions. This may change in the future, as car ownership and suburbanization becomes more common. This chapter draws attention to the fact that not all Japan's problems should be attributed to the public sector. We therefore turn to a consideration of several aspects of private sector behavior.

Challenges to the Private Sector

The second part of the book examines the condition of the private sector of Japan's economy. The valuation of the corporate sector (as reflected in the stock market) is substantially lower than it was through most of the last decade. The issue here is whether there are systemic problems with the way that Japanese corporations and factor markets operate that leave them ill-suited for recovery.

In chapter 6, Albert Ando, Dimitrios Christelis, and Tsutomu Miyagawa study the question of whether Japanese corporations have overinvested and hence are suffering from a glut of excess capacity. Interpreting the data is difficult and Ando, Christelis, and Miyagawa approach the question from a number of different angles. They observe that inconsistencies in valuations derived from different parts of the National Accounts can only be explained if, in fact, the corporate sector has built up a capital stock that is far larger than warranted by the profit-maximization motive. As a result, the rate of return on capital is extremely low. They argue that efficient resource allocation will not occur until this pattern is broken by forcing the corporate sector to pay out more profits via dividends to the household sector. They are not optimistic, however, that this is likely to occur any time soon.

In chapter 7, Lee Branstetter and Yoshiaki Nakamura review the data on research and development (R&D) over two decades, since R&D is one of the main drivers of productivity improvements and thus long-term growth.

Using patent data, the authors demonstrate that from the mid- to late-1980s there is a sharp increase in the productivity of R&D, but by 1990 productivity had reached a plateau and grew little thereafter. Thus, after a decade of convergence between Japanese and U.S. firms, innovation trends diverged sharply in the 1990s.

Interestingly, within Japan, electronics firms' research productivity has held up, while other firms have fared much more poorly. In explaining this pattern, the authors note that because Japanese firms have reached the technology frontier, they have had to reorient their efforts from the application of existing technologies to the creation of fundamental breakthroughs. Branstetter and Nakamura postulate that the shortage of Ph.D.-level engineers, the weakness of academic science, the lack of commercial focus in large, centralized corporate labs, and the absence of a venture capital industry to support start-ups may have created specific difficulties for Japanese firms.

The authors' interviews confirm that firms are in the process of restructuring their R&D operations to correct these problems and that technology alliances with foreign firms are a preferred strategy. They also note some public policy reforms which are addressing the productivity problem, including strengthening the Japanese patent system, increasing public expenditures on research, expanding graduate education, and removing some legal and regulatory barriers to the expansion of venture capital.

Hiroshi Ono and Marcus Rebick follow and probe labor market distortions in chapter 8. Some analysts have identified the long-term aging of the population as foreshadowing a labor shortage. Ono and Rebick examine a number of personnel practices, laws, and regulations that lower the supply of labor in the Japanese economy. They focus on two kinds of impediments: those that restrict the movement of labor between firms and those that discourage women from participating to a greater extent. Using other OECD countries, especially the United States, as a benchmark, they estimate that removal of these barriers would increase the productive labor supply in Japan by some 13 to 18 percent. An increase of this magnitude could raise growth nearly one percent per year for a decade.

Ono and Rebick outline numerous structural impediments that inhibit the mobility of workers between firms, including strong employment protection, pension portability, and the so-called age-limit problem, in which employers refuse to hire persons over the age of forty. Their analysis uncovers a number of social conventions that explain why these personnel practices persist and why their removal is not as easy as some Westerners may think. For example, imposing age limits in hiring remains the number one problem inhibiting the mobility of workers. But the practice is deeply rooted in the Japanese system of seniority, and its ensuing egalitarian pay norms are such that abolishing the practice disrupts the status quo of the current employment system.

Increasing the female labor supply is critical to Japan's economic growth and is often viewed as a viable solution to overcome the foreseeable labor shortage problem, but numerous barriers stand in the way. Ono and Rebick present a list of barriers, such as women's exclusion from the internal labor market, problems in the existing tax and benefit structures, and lack of family-friendly policies. These problems stem from the gender presumptions regarding division of labor in which men are responsible for market activities and women are responsible for nonmarket activities. A typical example of this is shown by the current tax system that was originally intended to foster the greater employment of married women by exempting their income from taxes up to a certain level. The problem is that married women can actually be penalized for providing too much labor if they exceed this level. As it stands, such distortions in the household budget undermine the incentives for Japanese women to work.

The final question in this book is whether the structure of competition in Japan impedes growth. It is often alleged that Japanese corporate groups distort incentives in a variety of ways. Yishay Yafeh analyzes this claim in chapter 9. In doing so, he provides a definitive survey of the role of business groups in Japan. His first important observation is that, while a long list of explanations for group activity have been offered, there is relatively little consistent empirical support for most of the conjectures.

Yafeh compares Japanese business groups to those in other countries. The Japanese groups stand out in several respects. First, Japanese groups, in contrast to the groups in most other countries, lack a centralized decision-making mechanism. Second, the pattern of profits is somewhat unusual. Japanese group members tend to have both lower average profit rates and lower profit volatility. This pattern is not present in many other countries. Third, Japanese groups seem to lack significant political clout. But in most other dimensions (average firm size of members, distribution across industries, and overall prevalence in the economy), Japanese business groups are similar to those found elsewhere.

Yafeh finds no evidence that the group-dominated industries in Japan have evolved any differently from their counterparts in the United States. This observation, along with the fact that the group financial ties seem to have weakened recently, suggests that the presence of groups is not likely to be a factor in the capacity for growth in the future.

In summation, these papers suggest that Japan faces a number of challenges. One message is that fixing the financial system cannot be achieved simply by recapitalizing the commercial banks. Structural problems that prevent the banks from earning normal profits and risky strategies that create fragile linkages between banks and insurance companies must also be addressed. Another message is the need to better understand the investment behavior of the corporate sector. A system that encourages and perpetuates overinvestment by firms also penalizes consumers, creates incentives for excessive savings, and locks resources into unproductive uses. A third problem will be figuring out how to pay for the restructuring needed in light of the growing fiscal problems. To add to these difficulties, inadequate and obscure statistical information makes it more difficult to grasp and tackle the depth of the problem.

At the same time there is some good news. The corporate groups that are often argued to be a serious impediment do not seem to be such a problem looking ahead. Labor market reforms, if properly structured, could generate a significant increase in labor supply. And R&D policies appear to be shifting in response to a recognized problem.

1

Financial Sector Profitability and Double-Gearing

Mitsuhiro Fukao

The Japanese economy's average annual real growth rate was only 0.8 percent from 1991 to 2001. Reflecting the weak economy, Japan has not been able to restore stability in its financial sector even though more than a decade has passed since the 1980s bubble. The Bank of Japan (BOJ) has had a zero nominal interest rate policy most of the time since February 1999, but it has been ineffective because of deflation. By the end of 2001, the gross domestic product (GDP) deflator was about 7 percent below its 1994 peak when adjusted for the 1997 consumption tax hike. The index was falling at annual rate of 1.5 percent at the end of 2001. Given the estimated 6 percent deflationary GDP gap and the near-zero real growth in 2002, deflation is likely to accelerate to more than 2.0 percent by early 2003 (see Japan Center for Economic Research [JCER] 2002, chapter 1).

In this chapter, I show that Japan will not be able to have a viable banking sector without stopping deflation. The banking industry has not shown a profit since fiscal 1993 (ended March 1994) if one excludes capital gains from stock and real estate portfolios. Interest margins have been too low to cover the increase in loan losses brought about by the weak economy.

Banks cannot raise margins for several reasons: competition with subsidized government-sponsored financial institutions (GFIs); intense political pressure, backed by the Financial Services Agency (FSA), to make new loans to small and medium companies; and deflation-weakened borrowers. I expect that the Japanese government will have to nationalize most of the banking sector by 2005. Capital injections will not solve the problems.

Mitsuhiro Fukao is a professor in the faculty of business and commerce at Keio University.
The author would like to thank Professor Anil Kashyap, Larry Meissner, and other conference participants for valuable comments on an earlier draft.

Established Japanese life insurance companies also face a serious situation. In the 1980s and early 1990s they promised high minimum yields on long-term contracts. For whatever reason, the companies did not match these long-term liabilities with long-term fixed-income investments. Under the BOJ zero-interest rate policy, insurers thus are suffering large negative carry. ("Carry" is the industry term for the difference between a product's income and its associated costs).

A complicating factor in this dire picture is banks and life insurance companies providing each other capital—a practice called double-gearing. Weakened banks ask insurance companies to provide equity capital and subordinated loans. In return, the mutual life insurers ask banks to subscribe their surplus notes (similar to nonvoting redeemable preferred shares) and subordinated debt. When Chiyoda Life failed in October 2000, Tokai Bank lost ¥74 billion. The FSA actively encourages this dangerous practice. Thus, Shokichi Takagi, director of FSA's Supervision Department, has publicly stated that double-gearing among financial institutions is highly beneficial to enhance public confidence ("Under-Capitalized Banks Are Not Likely Even after Special Examinations: Interview with Mr. Takagi, Head of Supervision Dept. of FSA," *Nihon Keizai Shinbun,* 27 November 2001, p. 7).

The life insurers' problem is easier to solve than the banks' problem. Using a reorganization procedure, life insurance companies can fail and cut promised interest rates on their policies. On the other hand, bank runs would ensue if the government did not fully pay the depositors of a failed large bank because a large part of the banking sector is either insolvent or very nearly so. In such a situation, the government would have to bear the full brunt of defaulting loans at a time when its own debt to GDP ratio is rising by 10 percentage points a year. If things continue as they are, the Japanese government is unlikely to maintain investment-grade credit ratings on its bonds.

The chapter continues with an analysis of banks' bad loans and their underreserving for them. The deteriorating condition of banks is then considered, and the causes of bank unprofitability examined. As part of this, the effects of deregulation and the role of government-sponsored financial institutions is considered. Turning to life insurance companies, their problems and weak supervision are discussed. The risks of the banks and insurers engaging in double-gearing is then analyzed.

1.1 Banks' Bad Loans

Table 1.1 and table 1.2 show data on problem loans of Japanese banks. Japanese banks have acknowledged ¥82 trillion in losses from bad loans for the ten years through March 2002. In spite of this enormous loss, they still

Table 1.1   Problem Loans of Japanese Banks (¥ billions)

		1993[a]	1994[a]	1995[a]	1996[b]	1997[b]	1998[c]	1999[c]	2000[c]	2001[c]	2002[c]
Specific reserves[d]		945	1,146	1,402	7,087	3,447	8,402	8,118	2,531	2,732	5,196
Write offs[e]		424	2,090	2,808	5,980	4,316	3,993	4,709	3,865	3,072	3,974
Loss from bad loans[f]	A	1,640	3,872	5,332	13,369	7,763	13,258	13,631	6,944	6,108	9,722
Cumulative losses[g]	A'	1,640	5,512	10,744	24,113	31,877	45,135	58,766	65,710	71,818	81,540
Bad loans outstanding[h]	B	12,775	13,576	12,546	28,504	21,789	29,858	29,627	30,366	32,515	42,018
Loan loss reserves	D	3,698	4,547	5,536	13,294	12,334	17,815	14,797	12,230	11,555	13,353

Source: Data are available from the Financial Services Agency web site (http://www.fsa.go.jp).

Notes: Data are for fiscal years ending in March of year shown.

[a]Only major banks disclosed loan loss figures. Bad-loan data are for defaulted loans and loans with arrears.

[b]Bad-loan data are for defaulted loans, loans with arrears for more than six months, and loans with concessional interest rates below the official discount rate of the Bank of Japan.

[c]Bad-loan data are for defaulted loans, loans with arrears for more than ninety days, and loans with concessional terms (similar to U.S. rules).

[d]Defined as the reserves held against individual bad loans.

[e]Includes losses from sale of loans to the CCPC (Cooperative Credit Purchase Corp) and other counterparties.

[f]Sum of the two previous rows.

[g]Cumulative total (beginning with fiscal 1992) of losses from bad loans (in row A).

[h]The series is not consistent because the definition and coverage of bad loans has been broadened twice. See notes a, b, and c. (For a detailed look at how the data have changed, see Hoshi and Kashyap 1999, section 4.)

Table 1.2   Analysis of Japanese Bank Loans, 1997–2002 (¥ billions)

		1997[a]	1998	1999	2000	2001	2002
Normal loans		550,000	544,814	487,500	472,388	470,669	490,537
Classified loans total		76,700	71,700	64,258	63,386	65,671	71,087
Substandard		65,300	65,500	61,024	60,539	63,118	67,787
Doubtful		8,700	6,100	3,160	2,835	2,553	3,300
Estimated loss		2,700	100	74	12	0	0
Required reserves[b]	C	27,350	22,918	19,366	18,828	19,117	20,273
Actual reserves	D	12,334	17,815	14,797	12,230	11,555	13,353
Underreserved (C – D)		15,016	5,103	4,569	6,592	7,562	6,920

Source: Data are available from the Financial Services Agency web site (http://www.fsa.go.jp).
Notes: Data are for fiscal years ending in March of year shown.
[a]Classified loan data are based on Ministry of Finance announcements.
[b]Author's estimates based on 1 percent of normal loans plus 20 percent of substandard loans plus 70 percent of doubtful loans plus 100 percent of estimated loss loans.

have more than ¥42 trillion of disclosed bad loans, about 8 percent of their loan portfolios.

I am one of the many who feel the disclosed figures understate the real situation. The FSA collects data on "classified loans," a broader concept of problem loans, but does not disclose it for individual banks. Under the FSA's *Bank Examination Manual*, banks are required to rate their loans, taking account of default risk and quality of collateral. There are four grades: normal, substandard, doubtful, and estimated-loss loans. The last three are considered classified loans. Banks then estimate their loan-loss reserves and the amount of write-offs. Because of the broader definition, the amount of classified loans is more than twice that of disclosed bad loans. Total classified loans for all banks was ¥71.1 trillion in March 2002.

1.1.1 Underreserving

Total loan loss reserves of Japanese banks have been low relative to those of U.S. banks. While U.S. bad loans declined from 3 percent of total loans in 1992 to 1 percent in 1999, the Japanese ratio rose from 2 percent to 6 percent (fig. 1.1). Loan-loss reserves in the United States have been above 160 percent of bad loans since 1994, while in Japan they have been in the 40 percent to 60 percent range (fig. 1.2). We can clearly see that although the U.S. banking sector recovered quickly from its bad-loan problems in early 1990s, the Japanese situation has been deteriorating even with the 1999 capital injection by the government.

Many analysts of Japanese banks suspect that the banks are not recording enough loan-loss reserves. This problem is exacerbated by the lenient reserving policy stipulated by the FSA *Bank Examination Manual*. Japanese banks usually calculate loan-loss reserves by dividing their loans into

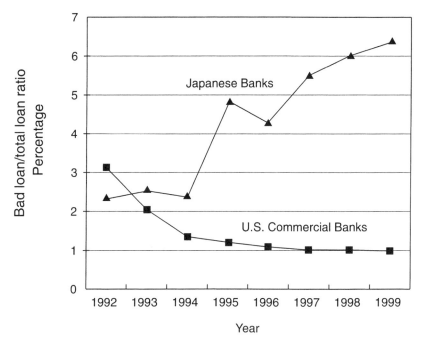

Fig. 1.1   Comparison of the bad loan situation in Japan and the United States
Source: JCER (2001b).

Notes: Japan: fiscal year; United States: calendar year. Figures after fiscal year 1997 do not include data of Hokkaido Takushoku Bank, Tokuyo City Bank, Kyoto Kyoei Bank, Naniwa Bank, Fukutoku Bank, and Midori Bank. Japanese bad loan ratio = Risk control loans/total loans; U.S. bad loan ratio = (loans with arrears for more than 90 days + loans that do not count accrued interest rates as asset + restructured loans)/total loans.

the FSA-mandated categories, then estimated losses for each group using the following time horizons.

1. Normal loans and substandard loans without arrears or reduced interest rates: expected one-year loss rate.

2. Substandard loans with arrears or reduced interest rates and doubtful loans: expected three-year loan loss rate.

Most loans are routinely rolled over, so the one-year figures understate the net present value of future losses over the true life of the loans in category 1. Thus, instead of a one-year rate, banks should reserve using, as a minimum, the three-year cumulative rate for all substandard loans.

To estimate more appropriate reserve figures, I have estimated required loan loss reserves based on FSA data of classified loans. A Bank of Japan (1997) sample study looked at the actual subsequent loan losses of eighteen banks for each category of classified loans on their fiscal 1993 reports (table 1.3). At the end of three years (in March 1997) about 17 percent of

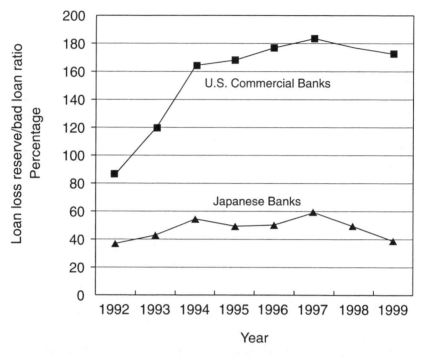

Fig. 1.2   Comparison of the Loan loss provisioning in Japan and the United States
Source: JCER (2001b).
Notes: See figure 1.1 notes.

Table 1.3   **Cumulative Loss Rate**

	Classification of Loan in March 1994 (%)	
Number of Years after Classification	Substandard	Doubtful
March 1995 1	1.7	27.4
March 1996 2	9.8	52.1
March 1997 3	16.7	75.3

Source: BOJ (1997).
Notes: Percentage of loans in the classification in March 1994 that had been written off at the end of each time period. Data are for an eighteen-bank sample.

substandard loans and over 75 percent of doubtful loans had been lost and almost 100 percent of estimated loss loans.

   These figures indicate that banks should keep larger loan loss reserves. I have calculated estimated reserves requirements based on 20 percent of substandard loans, 70 percent of doubtful loans, and 1 percent of normal loans. This last is because of the migration of normal loans to classified loans. The results are in table 1.2, row C.

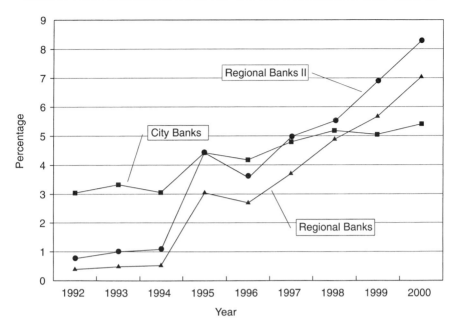

Fig. 1.3   Japanese banks' bad loan–total loan ratios
Source: JCER (2001b).

By comparing rows C and D, we can estimate the lower bound of under-reserving (row C minus row D). Although substantially below the estimated 1997 level, underreserving remains large.

1.2   The Banks' Deteriorating Condition

Figure 1.3 provides further evidence of the deteriorating condition of banks. Although the bad-loan to total-loan ratio has stabilized for city banks, for first- and second-tier regional banks it has been increasing rapidly. The large 1995 increase for regional banks in part reflects changes in disclosure requirements, but the trend since is due primarily to deteriorating loan quality.

Corresponding to the flow (profit) figures, the capital position of Japanese banks has been deteriorating. Under Japanese accounting rules for banks and lenient application by the regulators, Bank for International Settlements (BIS) capital ratios have been manipulated in many ways.

First, banks have underreserved against bad loans, as explained above. This tends to increase bank core capital by the same amount.

Second, banks have large deferred-tax assets on their balance sheets even though they have been losing money continually since 1993 and loss carry-forwards are limited to five years. There is little prospect of utilizing

Table 1.4   **Distribution of Adjusted Capital-Asset Ratios of Major Banks**

Level of Adjusted Capital as % Assets[a]	1998 Mar	1999 Mar	2000 Mar	2000 Sep	2001 Mar	2001 Sep
Less than –2%	2	0	0	0	1	1
–2 to less than 0%	6	2	0	0	0	3
Subtotal, insolvent	8	2	0	0	1	4
0% to less than 2%	8	10	4	5	8	11
2% to less than 4%	3	5	9	10	6	0
4% to less than 6%	0	0	4	0	0	0
Total number of banks	19	17	17	15	15	15
Weighted average %	0.93	2.07	3.48	2.36	1.83	0.86

Source: Updated by the author from JCER (2001).

Notes: Last day of months shown. Fiscal 1997 ended 31 March 1998, and so forth.

[a]Adjusted capital is defined as core capital plus unrealized capital gains and losses plus loan loss reserves minus estimated loan losses minus deferred tax asset. As in table 1.2, estimated loan losses are defined as 1 percent of normal loans plus 20 percent of substandard loans plus 70 percent of doubtful loans plus 100 percent of estimated loss loans. Individual banks do not disclose data on classified loans individually, so I relied on disclosed bad loan data.

the deferred-tax asset by showing genuine profit in the near future, so it should be written off.

Third, most of banks' subordinated loans are held by friendly life insurance companies. The banks, in turn, hold subordinated loans and surplus notes of the life companies. This is double-gearing and the cross-held quasi capital should not be treated as genuine capital for either the banks or the life insurance companies.

Table 1.4 shows core (tier 1) capital adjusted for unrealized capital gains, underreserving, and deferred taxes for major Japanese banks since March 1998. On this calculation, eight banks had negative equity in 1998, but only two were nationalized. The capital ratio recovered in fiscal 1998, part due to the ¥6.2 trillion in capital injected by the government, and rose further as stock prices recovered. But it began deteriorating again in 2000, the result of more loans going bad and stock prices falling. In September 2001 was at 0.86 percent, below where it had been three years earlier.

The capital position of banks is quite sensitive to stock prices. Table 1.5 shows the capital structure of all commercial banks. Core capital based on traditional historical cost accounting is adjusted for unrealized capital gains on stocks, deferred taxes, the public capital injection, and underreserving for loan losses. Although banks show ¥29.3 trillion of capital on their balance sheet at the end of March 2002, this figure is inflated with ¥10.7 trillion of deferred-tax assets (present value of the future tax shelter), ¥6.9 trillion of underreserving, and ¥7.2 trillion of government capital. Removing these amounts, the privately held equity of the banking sector is only ¥4.5 trillion. This is very small compared to their ¥71.8 trillion of problem loans.

Table 1.5 Stock Portfolios and Capital in the Banking Sector (¥ trillions)

	Market Value of Shares (1)	Book Value of Shares (2)	Capital Account (core capital) (3)	Deferred Tax Asset (4)	Estimated Underreserving (5)	Equity Capital Held by Government (6)	Net Capital Account (7)[a]	Nikkei 225 Index (8)
March 1986	*46.9*	*11.9*	12.3	0.0	n.a.	0.0	33.3	15,860
March 1987	*63.7*	*13.4*	13.8	0.0	n.a.	0.0	44.0	21,567
March 1988	*77.6*	*17.6*	17.2	0.0	n.a.	0.0	53.2	26,260
March 1989	*97.1*	*23.2*	22.5	0.0	n.a.	0.0	66.8	32,839
March 1990	88.6	29.7	28.6	0.0	n.a.	0.0	63.9	29,980
March 1991	77.7	33.1	30.2	0.0	n.a.	0.0	57.0	26,292
March 1992	56.4	34.5	31.3	0.0	n.a.	0.0	44.4	19,346
March 1993	56.4	34.5	31.8	0.0	n.a.	0.0	44.9	18,591
March 1994	61.9	36.5	32.3	0.0	n.a.	0.0	47.5	19,112
March 1995	52.0	39.8	32.3	0.0	n.a.	0.0	39.6	15,140
March 1996	64.3	43.0	27.9	0.0	n.a.	0.0	40.7	21,407
March 1997	54.1	42.9	28.5	0.0	15.0	0.0	20.2	18,003
March 1998	50.8	45.7	24.5	0.0	5.1	0.3	22.2	16,527
March 1999	47.1	42.7	33.7	8.4	4.6	6.3	17.1	15,837
March 2000	54.5	44.4	35.2	8.1	6.6	6.9	19.7	20,337
March 2001	44.5	44.3	36.7	7.3	7.6	7.1	14.8	13,000
March 2002	34.4	34.4	29.3	10.7	6.9	7.2	4.5	11,025

Sources: Data from Federation of Bankers Associations of Japan (various issues) and securities reports for individual banks.

Notes: Both market and book values represent listed shares only. The table pertains to banking accounts of all banks in Japan. The market value of stock portfolios was not published prior to March 1990, so we have estimated backwards using the Nikkei 225 share price index from the end of March 1991 (estimates are in italic). However, the tables for 1986–1990 should be discounted, because bank stock portfolios have been gradually increasing, so that values estimated from the end of fiscal 1990 will have an upwards bias the farther back one goes. A 40 percent corporate tax rate is assumed. See table 1.2 for the estimation of underreserving.

[a]Column (3) + (column [1] – column [2]) × 0.6 – column (4) – column (5) – column (6).

Because the ¥34.4 trillion market value of stocks held by banks is about 7.5 times their net capital, a 10 percent fall in the stock price index wipes out about 76 percent of their net capital. In the late 1980s and early 1990s, unrealized capital gains (the difference between columns [1] and [2]) was very large and banks could withstand fluctuations in stock prices. However, in the 1990s, banks sold stock to realize gains to offset huge loan losses. The increase in book value of shares (column [2]) during the 1990s shows the banks were buying back most of the stock they sold.

1.2.1   An Unprofitable Business

Banking in Japan has become an unprofitable, structurally depressed industry. Excluding capital gains realized by selling shares and real estate, Japan's banks as a group have been in the red since the year ended March 1994 (fiscal 1993). The primary cause of this is low interest rates, which are squeezing profits.

Let us look at the profit structure of banks nationwide. Table 1.6 shows the profit-loss accounts of all commercial banks. In the nine years from fiscal 1992 to fiscal 2000, banks made around ¥10 trillion each year as lending margin (row A, defined as interest and dividends earned minus interest paid). Revenue from such sources as bond and currency dealing and service charges were over ¥2 trillion, and ¥3 trillion more recently (row B). This includes all other revenue except capital gains realized on stocks and real estate. Revenues from banks' principal operations therefore amount to roughly ¥12 trillion to ¥13 trillion yen a year (row A + row B).

Total costs—including personnel and other operating expenses—were over ¥7 trillion (row C). Operating costs declined during 1998–2000 because of cost-cutting measures. It is likely to be difficult to continue that pace of cost cutting. Certainly, the banks may cut labor costs further by reducing employment and cutting average compensation. But the banks have to invest heavily in information technology to remain competitive.

In the 1990s the banks stinted on improving systems because of preoccupation with bad-loan problems, and now they have poor quality computer systems. Thus, for example, the *zengin* electronic fund transfer system, which is the main payment system among bank customers, cannot handle two-byte codes, so it cannot send customer names and messages in *kanji* (characters). As a result, more and more payments (especially utility bills) are handled by convenience store chains, which have installed sophisticated terminals.

Since the early 1990s more and more loans held by banks have turned into nonperforming assets. Banks have suffered over ¥6 trillion in loan losses each year since fiscal 1994, and ¥9 trillion in the last year (row E). As a result, banks have not reported positive net operating profit since fiscal 1993 (row F). However, because of occasional realization of capital gains

Table 1.6 Profitability of Japanese Banking Sector (¥ trillions)

		1989	1990	1991	1992	1993	1994	1995	1996	1997	1998	1999	2000	2001
Lending margin	A	7.5	7.1	8.9	9.8	9.2	9.7	10.8	10.7	10.0	9.6	9.7	9.4	9.8
Other revenue[a]	B	2.5	2.6	2.2	2.5	2.8	2.1	3.3	3.7	3.6	3.1	2.5	3.0	3.1
Operating costs	C	6.6	7.1	7.5	7.7	7.7	7.8	7.8	8.0	8.0	7.5	7.3	7.1	7.0
Salaries and wages (part of C)		3.5	3.7	3.9	4.0	4.0	4.0	4.0	4.0	3.6	3.5	3.4	3.2	
Gross profit = A + B − C	D	3.3	2.6	3.5	4.5	4.3	4.0	6.3	6.4	5.6	5.2	4.9	5.3	5.9
Loan losses	E	1.4	0.8	1.0	2.0	4.6	6.2	13.3	7.3	13.5	13.5	6.3	6.6	9.4
Net operating profit = D − E	F	1.9	1.8	2.5	2.5	−0.4	−2.2	−7.0	−1.0	−7.9	−8.3	−1.4	−1.3	−3.5
Realized capital gains[b]	G	2.8	2.0	0.7	0.0	2.0	3.2	4.4	1.2	3.6	1.4	3.8	1.4	−2.4
Net profit = F + G		4.7	3.8	3.3	2.5	1.7	1.0	−2.6	0.2	−4.2	−6.9	2.3	0.1	−5.9
Assets		943.6	927.6	914.4	859.5	849.8	845.0	848.2	856.0	848.0	759.7	737.2	804.3	772.0
Outstanding loans[c]		n.a.	424.3	445.8	460.3	472.3	477.8	482.7	482.3	477.9	472.6	463.4	456.9	465.0

Source: JCER (2001b), updated by the author.

Notes: Financial Statement of All Commercial Banks. Data are for fiscal years, which end in March of following calendar year. n.a. = not available.

[a] Includes all other profit, such as trading for own account and fees, but excludes capital gains realized from stock and real estate sales (which are in row G).

[b] From sale of stocks and real estate.

[c] Domestic banks only.

on stocks and real estate (row G), banks have shown a positive bottom line
(row F + row G).

1.3   Causes of Bank Unprofitability

The profit margin of Japanese banks is too small to cover the increase in
default risk since the bubble burst. Two principal elements of this—the
deregulation that has been going on since the 1980s and competition from
government-sponsored financial institutions—are taken up in the following sections.

The nature of government regulation is a third factor. Thus, under the
terms and condition of the government capital injection in March 1999,
banks are legally required to maintain and increase loans to small and
medium firms. Shinsei Bank, which reduced loans to such firms, was or-
dered by the FSA to increase its lending. Under these conditions, banks often disregard their procedures to make new loans to small companies, at
ultimate cost to the banks and the economy as a whole because of the misallocation of resources.

1.3.1   Effects of Deregulation

The average lending rate of Japanese banks was 1.8 percent in fiscal
2000, while the average funding cost was 0.3 percent and the average intermediation cost was 1.2 percent. Thus, the gross spread was only 0.35 percent (Japanese Bankers Association 2001). The average credit rating of
borrowers from banks is about BB, the annual loan loss rate is well over 1
percent, which means a *negative* margin of 0.65 percent. Part of this is
offset by fees from borrowers and other customers, but a key fact is that the
banks are making losses from lending.

One of the reasons for the small gross spread is the overhang of deposit
interest rate controls until the early 1990s. When the government controlled deposit rates, banks easily made money taking deposits. This is seen
in figure 1.4.

Figure 1.4 decomposes the lending margin (interest earned minus interest paid) into regulatory rent and the true profit margin (the spread between the average lending rate and the market rate). The regulatory rent is
taken as the difference between the banks' funding cost and the risk-free
short-term money market rate. Notice that the true lending margin in
much of the 1980s was negative, which suggests banks passed part of the
rent on to borrowers.

As deposit-rate controls were phased out in the late 1980s and early
1990s, banks tried to keep up profit margins by increasing lending rates relative to short-term market rates.

Although the banks have not raised their profit margin, borrowers are
paying a higher interest rate in relation to the money market rate. Figure 1.5

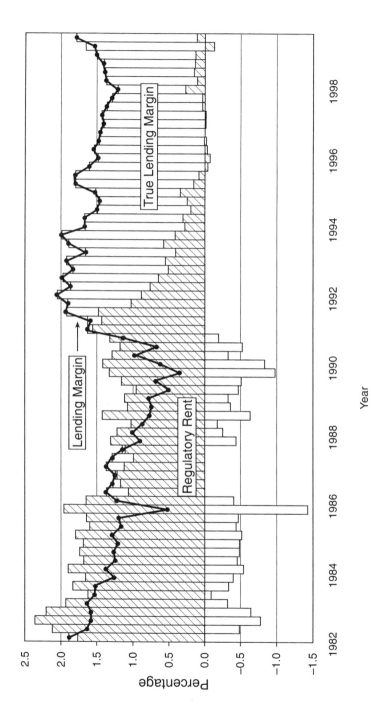

Fig. 1.4 Decomposition of lending margin
Source: Fueda (2000).

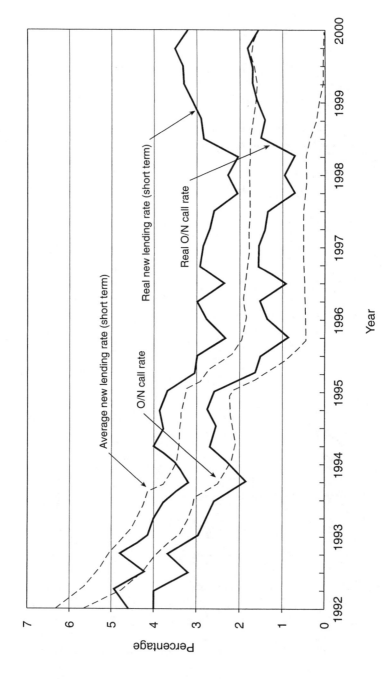

Fig. 1.5 Nominal and real interest rates

Source: JCER (2001b).

Notes: Real interest rates are calculated by subtracting GDP deflator inflation rates from nominal interest rates. The GDP deflator inflation rate is adjusted for changes in consumption tax rates in 1989 and 1997.

Table 1.7 **Size of Government and Private Financial Institutions, 2000**

	Assets		
	As ¥ Trillions	As % of GDP	Market Share (%)
Loans			
Government	163	32	26
Private banks	464	90	74
Total	627	122	—
Deposits			
Postal Savings System	255	50	34
Private banks	486	95	66
Total	741	144	—
Life Insurance			
Postal Life	119	23	40
Private Insurers	180	35	60
Total	299	58	—

Source: Computed by the author from calendar year-end data in BOJ (2001).

shows movements of the average new lending rate, overnight call rate, and the implied ex post real interest rates computed by subtracted the GDP deflator inflation rate. Reflecting the BOJ's loose monetary policy, the real call rate fell from 1991 until 1998. On the other hand, the real rate of new lending has not fallen much because of the increasing gap between the new lending rate and the call rate.

Although the opportunity cost of borrowing for large creditworthy companies is close to the call rate, the cost for small and medium companies is close to the new lending rate. Therefore, smaller companies have been less able than larger ones to enjoy the expansionary effect of loose money. This may have contributed to the relatively weak recovery of the small-business sector in the 1990s.

It was natural for banks to raise lending rates relative to market rates after removal of deposit rate controls. However, banks have not succeeded in obtaining enough of a margin to cover loan losses in a weak economy. At the same time, smaller borrowers have suffered from higher borrowing costs relative to large companies that have access to capital markets.

1.3.2   Government Financial Institutions

In Japanese financial markets, the presence of GFIs is extremely large. Table 1.7 shows the market share of private banks and GFIs at the end of 2000.

In the loan market, the GFI share reaches 30 percent to 40 percent in rural prefectures, although it is only 26 percent overall. GFIs make very long-term loans at about 2 percent. They are especially dominant in housing loans, holding more than half the outstanding balance.

Table 1.8   **Lending Rates of Government Lending Agencies, 9 February 2001**

	Basic Loan Rate (%)	Average Term (years)
Japan Development Bank	2.05	16.7
People's Finance Corp.	2.05	7.3
Japan Finance Corp. for Small Business	2.05	8.9
Japan Finance Corp. for Municipal Enterprises	1.90	n.a.
Housing Loan Corp.	2.70	25.4
Average of all private banks	2.12	<1
Fixed rate housing loan from Fuji Bank	4.65	20

Source: JCER (2001b).

Note: All rates are fixed except the average of all private banks. n.a. = not available.

Table 1.8 shows the base lending rates of GFIs on 9 February 2001. Their rates on new lending are similar to those for short-term loans from private banks, but the average term is much longer.

GFIs obtain subsidies of about ¥1 trillion per year as direct subsidy and indirect subsidy of zero-cost capital. These are estimated to provide a 60 basis point cost advantage relative to private financial institutions. Further, they usually accept prepayment without penalties, so their loans are more attractive to borrowers. As a result, the rates banks can charge are significantly constrained. (See Higo 2001 on the role of GFIs and their institutional details.)

In the deposit market, the Postal Saving System (PSS) is a dominant player. Deposits are fully guaranteed by the government. Rates are set competitively against private deposit-taking institutions. There are more than 24,000 post offices, giving the system a branch network larger than all the city and regional banks combined. The largest private banking group, Mizuho, has only about 600 offices. The PSS does not charge account-maintenance fees, so it is difficult for private banks to charge such fees without alienating a large number of customers.

My calculations indicate banks have to raise their lending margin by 80 to 100 basis points to break even in the current economic environment of deflation and recession.

The loan losses in table 1.6 for 1999 and 2000 understate true losses by some ¥1.5 trillion each year due to underreserving for bad loans. Therefore, banks lost about ¥3 trillion in each of those years before capital gains. Macroeconomic conditions deteriorated in 2001, so banks reported more than ¥9 trillion yen of loan losses in fiscal year 2001 alone, partly recognizing the past understated losses.

By raising lending rates 100 basis points, banks can obtain an additional ¥5 trillion from their ¥500 trillion loan portfolio, which would allow them to write off bad loans as they surface. However, they can neither raise lending rates nor charge higher fees on depositors due to the institutional environment. If the rate of deflation accelerates, banks will run out of capital sooner or later and the government will be forced to take control of the sector.

1.4 Life Insurance Companies

Private life insurers are the second largest part of the financial services industry after commercial banks, with December 2000 total assets of ¥180 trillion, which is about 35 percent of GDP. Limited competition and the robust economy allowed life insurance companies to enjoy fairly high growth and reasonably good profits until the early 1990s. Before the current crisis, there were twenty established companies, almost all organized as mutual companies.

Although the companies are less affected by the bad loan problem than banks, they face a serious problem. In the late 1980s and early 1990s they effectively sold massive amounts of what are forward-rate agreement options. The most important insurance products sold by Japanese companies in the 1980s and early 1990s were whole-life insurance with term rider and long-term annuities. Moreover, most of them are sold as monthly payment plan. These promised high minimum guaranteed returns (*yotei riritsu*) over the life of a policy. As a result, life insurance companies effectively guaranteed high returns on future cash flow. Thus, until 1992, major Japanese life-insurance companies assumed a return on their assets of 5.5 percent or more in designing policies. In 1992, someone buying even a life annuity or whole-life insurance was guaranteed 5.5 percent by all the companies.

The profitability of an annuity to its issuer depends on the difference between assumed and actual results of three factors: return on invested assets, costs, and death rates. For cautious actuaries, assumed death rates and operating costs tend to be higher than actual rates. This provides some cushion for any short-fall in expected investment returns. However, for many insurers, the shortfalls in asset returns were too big to be covered.

Most companies did not match the terms of their assets and liabilities. Generally, the term on the asset side has been about five years, while the average on the liability side has been fifteen to twenty years. When interest rates fell sharply in the 1990s, firms faced massive negative carry. Some companies were operating with little or no equity by the late 1990s. When they finally filed bankruptcy, most were deeply insolvent.

Beginning with the collapse of Nissan Life in April 1997, seven insurers had failed by mid-2002. Together they left ¥2.68 trillion in negative equity. This loss has to be born by policyholders and the Policyholder Protection Fund (PPF) that depends on the contribution by healthier companies. Table 1.9 shows the financial conditions of the failed companies. Although the companies reported fairly high solvency margins just before their fail-

Table 1.9   **Failed Life Insurance Companies: Condition at Time of Bankruptcy**

	Company Name						
	Nissan	Toho	Daihyaku	Taisho	Chiyoda	Kyoei	Tokyo
Legal structure	Mutual	Mutual	Mutual	LLC	Mutual	LLC	Mutual
Date of failure	April 1997	June 1998	May 2000	May 2000	October 2000	October 2000	March 2001
Asset (¥ trillions)	1.82	2.19	1.30	0.15	2.23	3.73	0.69
Equity (¥ trillions)	−0.32	−0.65	−0.32	−0.03	−0.60	−0.69	−0.07
Disclosed solvency margin (SM)	n.a.	154	305	68	263	211	447
Date associated with SM	n.a.	March 1998	March 1999	March 2000	March 2000	March 2000	March 2000
Reduction of reserves by bankruptcy	0%	10%	10%	10%	10%	8%	0%
Average guaranteed return before failure	3.75–5.50%	4.79%	4.46%	4.05%	3.70%	4.00%	4.20%
Guaranteed return after failure	2.75%	1.50%	1.00%	1.00%	1.50%	1.75%	2.60%
Early withdrawal charges (EWC)	15% → 3%	15% → 2%	20% → 2%	15% → 3%	20% → 2%	15% → 2%	20% → 2%
Period of EWC	7 years	8 years	10 years	10 years	10 years	8 years	10 years

Source: JCER (2001a).

Notes: LLC stands for limited liability company. The sliding scale for the early withdrawal charges is described in the text.

Table 1.10   **Solvency Margins of Major Life Insurers**

Company[a]	1998	1999	2000	2001	2002
Toho	154.3	n.a.	n.a.	n.a.	n.a.
Daihyaku	294.6	304.6	n.a.	n.a.	n.a.
Chiyoda	314.2	396.1	263.1	n.a.	n.a.
Kyoei	300.7	343.2	210.6	n.a.	n.a.
Tokyo	431.6	478.7	446.7	n.a.	n.a.
Asahi	654.8	688.8	732.7	543.4	417.6
Daido	1016.8	998.0	1004.2	757.6	772.0
Daiichi	632.1	662.1	858.6	682.3	593.0
Fukoku	722.4	820.6	906.5	779.3	708.2
Meiji	719.9	706.1	731.0	667.2	609.4
Mitsui	491.6	519.6	676.7	492.7	510.7
Nippon	939.9	849.9	1095.8	778.1	714.4
Sumitomo	526.2	589.5	675.7	551.3	534.5
Taiyo	873.0	869.1	1050.3	806.8	768.2
Yasuda	648.1	727.2	808.5	602.6	612.8

Notes: The first five are listed in the order in which they went bankrupt. Others are listed alphabetically. n.a. = not available.
[a]"Life" is the second word in the names of all these companies.

ures, all were found to be insolvent after their bankruptcy. Table 1.10 shows solvency margins. Note that no company has failed since March 2001.

When a life insurance company fails, the court-appointed administrator cuts the liability of the company so as to make the company viable again. Most of the liability of an insurance company is policy reserve that corresponds to the accumulated saving of policyholders. Generally speaking, the surrender value of a policy corresponds to this value. Under the Japanese policyholder protection scheme, the PPF guarantees only 90 percent of the policy reserve and it does not protect guaranteed minimum returns. The PPF can also introduce a cancellation penalty on the policy reserve to reduce the cost of resolution.

As a result, policyholders at bankrupt insurers are hit on three sides. On average, they have lost about 10 percent of their accrued past saving. Guaranteed returns in most cases were cut down to 1 percent to 2 percent. In addition, heavy early-withdrawal charges are levied on cancellations of policies of all types. In the case of Chiyoda Life, a policyholder faces a 20 percent charge for immediate cancellation. This charge declines gradually to two percent in the tenth year. One must wait ten years to cancel without an early cancellation penalty. Because policyholders can realize the surrender value of policies quite easily before a firm fails, companies thought to be weak have faced heavy cancellations.

It is usually better for a healthy person to quickly cancel a cash-value life insurance policy with a failing company and get a new policy elsewhere than to stick to the existing policy. However, getting a new life policy is more expensive, and perhaps not possible, for an unhealthy person. This means the burden of an insurer's failure falls more heavily on those who have become less insurable.

1.4.1 Weak Supervision

The life insurance industry's crisis has been exacerbated by the forbearance policy of its supervisory authorities, the former Ministry of Finance and the FSA. Because of extremely lenient capital requirements and reluctance to close down unhealthy firms, most failed life insurance companies had large negative equity by the time of their formal failure.

The regulatory measure of capital requirements in insurance is the solvency margin, which relates net assets to estimated risk. The net assets are capital + risk reserves + general loan loss reserves + excess reserves over surrender value of policies + future profits + tax effect + subordinated debt. The estimated risk equals $([\text{insurance risk}]^2 + [\text{interest rate risk} + \text{asset value risk}]^2)^{1/2} + \text{management risk}$. The net assets are divided by the estimated risk and multiplied by 200 to obtain the solvency margin. The minimum ratio for sound companies is 200. Below that, regulators are required to take corrective action.

The requirement was imported from the United States, but Japanese regulators have made a number of modifications that weaken the rule considerably, including setting the trigger levels for prompt corrective action much lower. Table 1.11 illustrates the major differences.

For a number of reasons the numerator in Japan is overstated. Especially worrisome is inclusion of a large deferred tax asset and future profits. Moreover, Japan generously includes assets with no liquidation value, although the U.S. standard excludes them. Regarding the denominator side, Japanese risk weights are considerably lower than those of the United States. Thus, for publicly traded corporate equity (stock), the risk weight is about one-third the U.S. level. For real estate and foreign currency assets, the risk weights are one-half the U.S. levels.

The Financial Studies Group of the JCER, which I head, have tried to adjust for the differences in the solvency margin requirements in Japan and the United States. The quality of disclosure by life insurance companies has improved considerably since the mid-1990s, so we can do this from publicly available data. Figure 1.6 shows the results for the end of March 2000.

Based on what they disclose, all the major companies are above the 200 percent level, implying that they are all healthy. We have made three types of adjustments. The first uses U.S. risk weights and adjusts for unrealized capital gains and losses, but allows inclusion of assets with no liquidation value. With these adjustments, two companies are deemed insolvent.

The second is closer to—but still somewhat less stringent than—the U.S.

Table 1.11   **Comparison of U.S. and Japanese Capital Requirements for Life Insurance Companies**

	U.S. RBC regulation	Japanese Solvency Margin Regulation
Assets of no liquidation value in the net asset calculation		
Deferred tax asset	Not allowed	Allowed
Movable property	Not allowed	Allowed
Future profit	Not allowed	One-year profit until March 2000; half-year profit is allowed since then
Unrealized losses		
In domestic bonds	Deducted from asset	Not deducted from assets until March 2001
In foreign securities	Deducted from asset	Not deducted from assets until March 2001
Weights for market risk		
Stocks	22.5–45%	10%
Foreign bonds	10%	5%
Real estates	10%	5%
Trigger levels for the initiation of prompt corrective actions		
No action	More than 250%	More than 200%
Submit plans for improvements	150–250%	100–200%
Stronger intervention	70–150%	0–100%
Authority takes over the control	Less than 70%	Less than 0%

standard. Specifically, we removed assets with no liquidation value. Three companies are insolvent under this definition.

The third approach involves removing subordinated debt from the capital base because its quality as capital is less than that of retained earnings and surplus notes (which are similar to the nonvoting redeemable preferred shares of joint stock companies). Under this measure, four companies were insolvent even when the Nikkei 225 was at 20,337, significantly higher than it is two years later as this is written.

Three companies that had negative adjusted solvency margins failed within a year: Chiyoda Life and Kyoei Life filed bankruptcy in October 2000, as did Tokyo Life in March 2001. The fourth company, Nichidan Life, received a capital injection from Axa, a French insurance company.

Figure 1.7 shows the same picture for March 2002. The disclosed ratios are more than 500 percent except for one company. However, "Adjusted 2" indicates that the FSA should intervene in at least three weaker companies: Mitsui, Asahi, and Sumitomo Life. The Nikkei was 11,025 at that time. We estimated that a 20 percent fall in the index would pull the solvency margin of weaker companies down by about 100 points. Therefore, a Nikkei below 10,000 means three companies probably are critically undercapital-

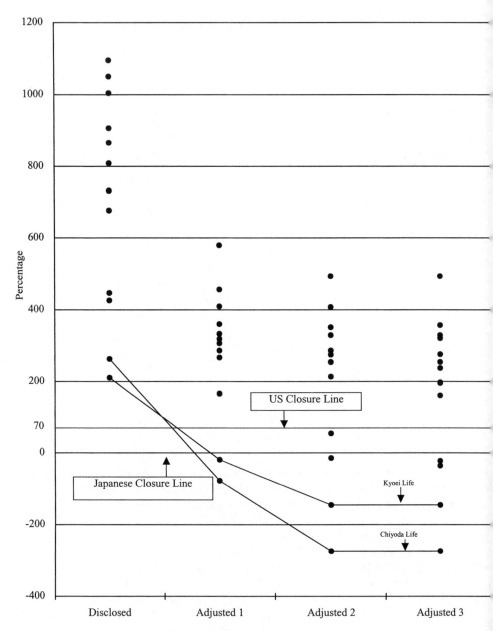

Fig. 1.6   Adjusted solvency margin ratios, March 2000
Source: JCER (2000).

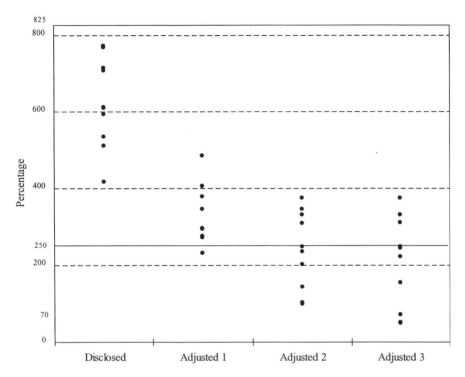

Fig. 1.7   Adjusted solvency margin ratios, March 2002
Source: JCER (2002).

ized and three others would require prompt corrective actions under U.S. standards.

1.5   Increasing Double-Gearing

All the major life insurance companies are mutual companies, so there is no formal cross-holding of shares. However, the insurers are major shareholders of the banks—collectively owning 10 percent or more of each city bank during the 1990s. Moreover, banks and life insurers have relied on each other to raise broadly defined capital. Between March 2000 and March 2001 the bankruptcies of Chiyoda, Kyoei, and Tokyo Life reduced the double-gearing, but it is still significant. At the end of March 2001, seven life insurance companies collectively held ¥5.4 trillion of bank stocks and ¥5.1 trillion of bank subordinated debts. In exchange, banks hold ¥1 trillion of surplus notes and ¥1.2 trillion of subordinated debts of seven life insurance companies.

The double-gearing generates two important problems: poor-quality capital in Japan's financial sector, which increases systemic risk, and a weaker governance structure of banks.

As regards systemic risk, suppose a major life insurer filed for bankruptcy. The banks that hold the company's subordinated loans and surplus notes lose money. The price of the stock of these banks falls to reflect the write-offs, which reduces the assets of insurance companies holding bank stocks. It may even trigger a chain reaction of failures among Japanese financial institutions.

The corporate governance structure of Japan's major life insurance companies is weak. The representative policyholder meeting plays the role a shareholder meeting does for joint stock companies. Each representative policyholder has one vote. They are inevitably chosen by management. Sometimes, they become policyholders only after being asked to be a representative policyholder. In other cases, a manager of a company that borrows from the insurance company is asked.[1]

1.6   Conclusion

Stock prices of listed Japanese banks have been very weak since the end of 2001. I believe that this reflects a number of remaining problems in Japan's financial system. First, profit margins are too small to cover the increased default risk since the bubble burst more than ten years ago. Many firms have not overcome their debt overhang and are surviving on the indulgence of their banks. Banks have not succeeded in increasing their lending margins because of strong competitive pressure from government-backed financial institutions. They also are facing strong political pressure to lend to small and medium firms regardless of merit. More broadly, revisions to the banking law require regulatory approval of new investors, and a condition of approval is that they "fully understand a bank's social responsibilities."

Second, there is massive double-gearing between life insurance companies and banks. Systemic risk remains very high. Financial sector problems can be stabilized by public money; either by injecting capital into the banks or by extending a full government guarantee of deposits, the government can stabilize the fragile financial system. However, a far larger problem will surface in that event: the critical situation of the national debt. Because of deflation and high real interest rates, the Japanese economy is shrinking. Nominal GDP declined 2 percent in 2001 and such negative growth is likely to continue unless there are very strong policy actions.

Table 1.12 shows a simple projection of Japan's budgetary situations under –2 percent nominal growth and an unchanged primary deficit of 6 percent of GDP. I did not take account of the cost of stabilizing the financial system, but I did assume a massive cutting of government expenditures in line with declining tax revenue. The gross debt of the general government will exceed 200 percent of GDP by 2008.

1. See Fukao (1998) for the other weaknesses in the Japanese corporate governance structure.

Table 1.12   Projection for General Government Budget Deficits

Year	Nominal GDP Growth Rate	Primary Surplus to GDP Ratio	General Government Gross Debt to GDP Ratio	General Government Net Debt to GDP Ratio	Effective Interest Rate on Net Debt	Net Interest Cost to GDP Ratio
1999	−0.6	−5.7	120.4	36.0	3.5	1.3
2000	−0.1	−6.8	130.7	43.5	3.3	1.4
2001	−1.9	−5.9	142.0	51.0	2.9	1.5
2002	−2.0	−6.0	150.6	59.6	2.5	1.5
2003	−2.0	−6.0	159.3	68.3	2.1	1.4
2004	−2.0	−6.0	168.1	77.1	2.1	1.6
2005	−2.0	−6.0	177.4	86.4	2.3	2.0
2006	−2.0	−6.0	187.2	96.2	2.7	2.6
2007	−2.0	−6.0	197.8	106.8	3.0	3.2
2008	−2.0	−6.0	209.2	118.2	4.0	4.7
2009	−2.0	−6.0	222.5	131.5	4.0	5.3

Sources: Figures until 2001 are based on the International Monetary Fund (IMF; 2001) and the Organization for Economic Cooperation and Development (OECD; 2001).

Notes: General government gross asset is assumed to be constant after 2001. Sharp downgradings of JGB are assumed after 2005.

If the government cannot stabilize the macro-economy by stopping deflation, I expect Japanese yen government bonds (JGB) to be downgraded to speculative by 2007. (In July 2002 they had the lowest rating among major countries: AA– by Standard & Poor's and A2 by Moody's.) If downgraded further, the government will have to shift to short-term notes to reduce interest costs. However, shortening maturity will increase vulnerability to a sharp rise in interest rates.

A junk bond status of JGB will generate enormous problems for the corporate sector. Sovereign credit usually sets a ceiling for private companies. Japanese banks will not be able to use JGBs as collateral in dealing with foreign banks. Moody's downgraded the major banks' financial strength to its lowest ratings on 2 July 2002. Japanese savers are shifting assets from yen deposits to foreign currency deposits and gold. The relative weakness of the yen in the face of rapidly declining dollar interest rates in 2001 may have indicated a mild form of capital flight.

Massive capital flight will cure Japan's deflation by sharply devaluing the yen. However, other Asian countries will devalue against the dollar to remain competitive. That will export deflation to the rest of the world, including the United States. In that event, the United States may have to follow the Japanese example of a zero interest rate policy.

The end of deflation may trigger a budgetary crisis in Japan. Suppose Japan has 200 percent gross debt, mostly financed by short-term liabilities. Most of its foreign assets are long-term and at fixed interest rates, so the government cannot count on a higher interest income in the short run under increasing interest rates. A 500 basis point rise in interest rates (which would make rates about the same as they were in 1991) will increase interest payments to 10 percent of GDP, ¥50 trillion. This is about the same as total national government tax revenue excluding social security contributions.

Many Japanese policymakers and corporate leaders have spent more than ten years assuming time will solve whatever the problems are with less pain and cost than will aggressive confrontation. Time not only has not solved the problems, it has made many of them worse. I would like to say the scenarios I have depicted are pessimistic assessments, but sadly they are all too possible. The pain and the cost will continue to grow, as the economy stagnates, unless a more immediate, comprehensive, and aggressive attack is made on the known problems.

References

Bank of Japan. 1997. Enhancing the credit risk control with self-classification of bad loans. *Bank of Japan Bulletin* October (Japanese ed.): 2–24.
———. 2001. *Financial and Economic Statistics Monthly* (March).

Federation of Bankers Association of Japan. Various issues. *Analysis of Bank Financial Statements.*

Fueda, Ikuko. 2000. Financial liberalization, asset bubble, and bank behavior (in Japanese). In *Empirical analysis of financial recession*, ed. M. Fukao and Japan Center for Economic Research, 1–32. Tokyo: Nikkei Sinbun Sha.

Fukao, Mitsuhiro. 1995. *Financial integration, corporate governance, and the performance of multinational companies.* Washington, D.C.: Brookings Institution.

———. 1998. Japanese financial instability and weaknesses in the corporate governance structure. *Seoul Journal of Economics* 1 (4): 381–422.

Higo, Masahiro. 2001. The current state of FILP system: The effects of 2001 reform on the functions of the FILP (in Japanese). Bank of Japan Economic Research Department Working Paper no. 01-1. Tokyo: Bank of Japan, March.

Hoshi, Takeo, and Anil Kashyap. 1999. The Japanese banking crisis: Where did it come from and how will it end? In *NBER macroeconomics annual 1999*, ed. Ben S. Bernanke and Julio J. Rotemberg, 129–201. Cambridge: MIT Press.

International Monetary Fund. 2001. *World economic outlook.* Washington, D.C.: IMF, October.

Japanese Bankers Association. 2001. *Analysis of financial statements of all banks, 31 March 2001.* Tokyo: Japanese Bankers Association.

Japan Center for Economic Research (JCER). 2000. *Structural problems of the Japanese financial system* (in Japanese). Tokyo: JCER, October.

———. 2001a. *Deflation and the financial system reform.* Tokyo: JCER, October.

———. 2001b. *Monetary policy under deflation* (in Japanese). Tokyo: JCER, March.

———. 2002. *The weakening Japanese financial system* (in Japanese). Tokyo: JCER, October.

Organization for Economic Cooperation and Development (OECD). 2002. *Economic outlook.* 1(1).

2

Paying for the FILP

Takero Doi and Takeo Hoshi

The Fiscal Investment and Loan Program (FILP) in Japan collects funds through government financial institutions (most notably postal savings) and uses the funds to finance public projects undertaken by government-affiliated corporations or to finance government loans to borrowers in targeted areas (targeted industries, small firms, mortgage borrowers, etc.). Many countries have government-sponsored loan programs: The Japanese program is distinguished by its size. At the end of fiscal 2000 (March 2001), the FILP involved ¥418 trillion, equal to some 82 percent of gross domestic product (GDP), and the program's uses of funds statement totaled more than the GDP. The postal savings system, the most important source of funds for the FILP is the world's largest financial institution. It held ¥250 trillion in deposits (35 percent of total household deposits) at the end of fiscal 2000.

The FILP may promote welfare and economic growth by financing projects that have such large externalities that private institutions would not undertake them. It also may be an impediment to welfare and growth by allowing the government to pursue wasteful projects. Historically the program has ignored market information, and its sheer size makes the cost

Takero Doi is associate professor of economics at Keio University. Takeo Hoshi is the Pacific Economic Cooperation Professor of International Economic Relations at the University of California, San Diego.

The authors thank Albert Ando, Thomas Cargill, Jenny Corbett, Masahiro Higo, Toshihiro Ihori, Yasushi Iwamoto, Anil Kashyap, and Kiyoshi Mitsui, as well as participants of the conference on Structural Impediments to Growth in Japan and a seminar at the Cabinet Office, Government of Japan, for helpful comments. We also thank Masayasu Murakami, Shinobu Shiikawa, and Komako Tanaka for advice on data collection, and Larry Meissner for careful editing. Any remaining errors are our own.

of resource misallocation enormous. This chapter examines the financial condition of the FILP and analyzes reforms begun in April 2001.

The goal of examining the FILP's financial condition is to see if it constitutes a serious impediment to the recovery of the Japanese economy. The FILP's accounts are notoriously opaque. We scrutinize the balance sheets of recipients of FILP funds, including special public corporations (SPCs), central government accounts, and local governments. Through this exercise, we can estimate the amount of financial losses of the FILP either buried in current balance sheets or expected to emerge in the near future.

The data show that existing losses and expected transfers to cover future losses are enormous. These losses are implicit claims on the government (and hence on taxpayers). Together with other implicit claims, such as the cost of cleaning up the financial sector (see chap. 1 of this volume), FILP losses can seriously impede economic recovery.

Because the FILP is supposed to finance socially useful projects that private institutions are unwilling to undertake, it is natural for there to be losses. And, in fact, the central government has been transferring funds from its accounts to numerous FILP agencies in the form of explicit subsidies and capital contributions. The losses may be a result of insufficient past subsidies for social-welfare-increasing (but high-externality) projects. However, any argument that stresses the welfare-enhancing aspects of the FILP must be weighed against the substantial cost. That so little has been done until recently—even by the government—to explore the cost and benefit of projects using FILP funds is telling.

Our second purpose is to describe the reform of the FILP introduced in April 2001 and to evaluate its likely impact. The main stated goal of the reform is the introduction of market discipline in the allocation of funds. Thus, we examine whether reform can be expected to reduce FILP losses in the future.

The work presented here updates and expands that of a number of researchers (primarily available only in Japanese), as outlined in the appendix. The chapter is organized as follows. After briefly describing how the FILP is structured and its size, we begin our investigation of the financial health of FILP agencies. This involves performing a close examination of the balance sheets of the major FILP recipients, correcting for various accounting problems. The financial conditions of local governments, which are also important borrowers of the FILP, are then taken up. This is a topic not covered extensively by other researchers. We then discuss the essence of the FILP reform introduced in April 2001, and evaluate the effects that are observable so far. We conclude by pointing out the direction for future research.

2.1   Background

The FILP is a government-sponsored program that finances government financial institutions and other government-related agencies. It is not just a system of simple financial intermediation because the government and FILP agencies are also linked through flows of direct grants and subsidies. This section presents a brief overview of the structure, size, and history of the FILP.

2.1.1   Structure and Size

Figure 2.1 diagrams the structure of the FILP before the 2001 reform, paying particular attention to the inter-relations between financial intermediation and fiscal transfers. The magnitude of the sums involved is given in table 2.1, sources of funds, and table 2.2, uses of funds.

The Trust Fund Bureau (TFB) Fund is by far the most important source, providing some 83 percent of funds as of the end of March 2001. The majority of the TFB Fund comes from postal savings. Its other major source is pension reserves, which are the difference between the premium receipts

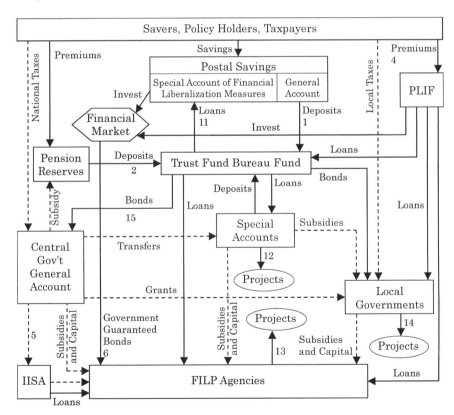

Fig. 2.1   Structure of the FILP before April 2001

Note: IISA = Industrial Investment Special Account. PLIF = Postal Life Insurance Fund. A box represents a sector or an institution involved in the FILP. The arrows indicate the direction of the movement of funds, with solid lines indicating financial transactions and broken lines being fiscal transfers. Numbers next to the lines refer to entries in tables 2.1 and 2.2, which provide the yen amounts represented by the lines.

Table 2.1 **Sources of FILP Funds, March 2001 (¥ billions and %)**

Line	Amount	Share	Source
n.a.	439,663	83.1	TFB fund
4	61,658	11.6	Postal life insurance fund
5	3,383	0.6	Industrial investment SA
6	24,579	4.6	Government-guaranteed bonds
	529,283	100.0	Total
	Components of the TFB Fund[a]		
1	247,008	46.7 (56.2)	Postal savings
2	142,593	26.9 (32.4)	Pension reserves
n.a.	50,062	9.5 (11.4)	Others[b]

Source: Ministry of Finance (2002a).

Note: Line numbers refer to figure 2.1. SA = Special Account. n.a. = not applicable.

[a]Numbers in the parentheses show the shares within the TFB.

[b]Includes postal life insurance premiums collected during the fiscal year (which are deposited into the TFB) and short-term deposits by some special accounts, as well as profits and reserves at the TFB.

Table 2.2 **Uses of FILP Funds, March 2001 (¥ billions and %)**

Line	Amount	Share	Use
10	7,279	1.4	General account (JNR loans)[a]
11	57,350	10.8	Postal savings SA[b]
12	6,298	1.2	Other special accounts
13	259,617	49.0	FILP agencies[c]
14	87,270	16.5	Local government
n.a.	417,814	78.9	FILP Plan total
15	72,682	13.7	Central government bonds[d]
n.a.	38,787	7.3	Other[e]
n.a.	529,283	100.0	Total uses
n.a.	471,993	n.a.	Total excluding Postal Savings SA

Source: Ministry of Finance (2002a).

Note: Line numbers refer to figure 2.1. n.a. = not applicable.

[a]TFB loans to the former JNR and former JNR Settlement Corp (JNRSC), which the government assumed (see box 2.1). Unlike other loans to the general account, these are included in the formal FILP Plan.

[b]Funds the TFB has loaned back to the postal savings system for it to invest directly. These are excluded from the net total.

[c]Includes ¥3,352 billion in contributed capital and ¥256,265 billion in loans.

[d]Including JNR loans (see note a) the central government total is ¥79,961 billion.

[e]Includes short-term loans (mainly to the SA for Grants of Allocation Tax and Transfer Taxes [to local governments]) and certain financial investments with a maturity of less than five years.

Box 2.1   FILP Loan to the General Account

The ¥7.3 trillion FILP loan to the general account relate to privatization of the former JNR. The JNR started to run deficits in 1964, but was allowed to continue operation and to add to its debt. When JNR was privatized in 1987, ¥25.5 trillion of its debt and some JNR assets were transferred to a newly created JNRSC. The remaining debt was assumed by the central government and creditors (including the TFB) received newly issued Japanese government bonds. The JNRSC was supposed to pay down its debt over ten years using proceeds from sales of the assets it received. Assets sales stalled and the amount of liabilities actually increased. When the statute establishing JNRSC expired in 1997, the government assumed almost all of its ¥28.3 trillion debt. Thus, the ¥7.3 trillion loan from the FILP should be considered a loan to these already-failed corporations.

---

and pension payouts of the public pension system during the current fiscal year.

Uses of FILP funds are grouped into seven categories, as shown in table 2.2. Box 2.1 explains the FILP loan to the general account.

The first five uses are formally put in the FILP Plan every year and submitted to the Diet as an attachment to the budget bill. Thus, the size of the FILP Plan (¥418 trillion for the end of March 2001) is smaller than the total size of the FILP. This is because the total program includes the TFB's holding of government bonds and other financial assets.

The FILP Plan disburses funds to many local governments, which account for 24 percent of net FILP loans, and fifty-seven other entities. Of the latter, eleven are central government accounts (Postal Savings Special Account, nine other special accounts, and Japan National Railroads [JNR] loans) and forty-six are FILP agencies (eight government financial institutions, twenty-seven SPCs, and eleven special firms).

Table 2.3 summarizes data on the fifty-eight entities that had outstanding FILP loans or government-guaranteed bonds (which are held by the public but considered a part of the FILP) at the end of March 2001. The total was ¥414 trillion, or ¥357 trillion net of ¥57 trillion loaned back to the postal savings system.

2.1.2   Historical Development

When the FILP started in the 1950s, financing economic recovery was the most important goal. Hence, the FILP heavily targeted industrial fi-

Table 2.3	FILP Loans and Bond Guarantees, 31 March 2001 (¥ billions)	
Number of Recipients[a]	Amount	Originating Lending Source
47	270,844	Trust Fund Bureau[b]
32	61,658	Postal Life Insurance
3	31	Industrial Investment SA
51	332,533	Net total FILP loans[b]
24	24,579	Government-guaranteed bonds
57	357,112	Total
1	57,350	Postal Savings SA loans
58	414,462	Total FILP funds[c]

Source: This table is the column totals of supplemental table 1, which provides data (from Ministry of Finance 2002a) on each of the fifty-eight recipients. It is available on our web site (http://www.econ.keio.ac.jp/staff/tdoi/ and http://www2-irps.ucsd.edu/faculty/thoshi/) and the NBER web site (http://www.nber.org/data/).

[a]Number of recipients, counting local governments (which have TFB and Postal Life Insurance [PLI] loans) as one. Not counting local governments and the Postal Savings SA (see note [b]), there are fifty recipients of FILP loans and an additional six have bond guarantees but no loans.

[b]Excludes funds the TFB has loaned back to the postal savings system for it to invest directly. With them, loans from the TFB total ¥328,194 and total loans are ¥389,883.

[c]Adding ¥3,352 in capital contributions to this yields the ¥417,814 FILP Plan total in table 2.2.

nancing through the Japan Development Bank (JDB; predecessor of the present Development Bank of Japan) and other government financial institutions. When the economy recovered and started to grow rapidly, the focus gradually shifted to housing (including mortgage lending) and projects to improve living standards (such as building sewer systems). Providing assistance to small businesses also became an important goal. Financing industrial development does not constitute a large area for the FILP Plan any more: Only 1 percent of new funds are used for this purpose. Table 2.4 provides a breakdown of the FILP Plan for fiscal 2001 by target areas.

2.2   Financial Condition of FILP Agencies

In this and the next five sections, we examine the financial condition of the FILP recipients other than the local governments, which collectively receive 76 percent of the total net FILP loans. The financial condition of the local governments is examined in section 2.8.

The first step in analyzing the financial condition of the FILP recipients is to look at the self-reported accounting information. By their own accounts, nine recipients of FILP funds are insolvent. That is only a very partial picture, however. The publicly disclosed accounting statements of FILP recipients exhibit serious problems, which make it hard to assess their financial conditions.

To provide a more accurate list of insolvent agencies and estimate the

Table 2.4   Distribution of FILP Plan by Target Area, Fiscal 2001

Percents	Target Areas
29.9	Housing
19.9	Living environment
16.1	Small and medium businesses
11.2	Road construction
4.8	Trade and economic cooperation
3.9	Social welfare
3.4	Regional development
2.8	Education
2.4	Agriculture[a]
2.3	National land preservation[b]
2.3	Transport and communication
1.0	Industry and technology

Source: Ministry of Finance (2002a).

Note: The FILP plan total for the year was ¥32.5 trillion. For further information, see Cargill and Yoshino (2000, table 8.3), who show the uses of FILP funds by target areas from 1955 to 1998.

[a]Includes forestry and fisheries.
[b]Includes reconstruction in the event of disaster.

cost to taxpayers of the FILP, in each of the next four sections we look at a problem area and make adjustments to provide a more accurate assessment. The first three areas involve financial losses already accumulated. The losses already made come from two principal sources: underreserving for bad loans and overvaluing assets. In addition, other adjustments need to be made to the stated capital (reserves) of many FILP participants. Our analysis of these areas involves examining the balance sheets of FILP participants.[1] The fourth area is the present value of the cost of covering expected future losses that will arise if FILP agencies continue to operate. To estimate this, we rely on projections made by the agencies themselves.

2.3   Capital (Reserves)

In assessing financial condition, we have paid special attention to the amount of capital (usually called reserves in public corporation accounting). The amount of capital measures how much loss the entity can sustain without requiring additional resources from the government. Negative capital means de facto insolvency. Because the government is both a large

1. Five special accounts and one special firm do not publish balance sheets regularly, so they are excluded from our analysis. Fortunately, the ¥4.5 trillion in FILP loans to them amounts to just 1.3 percent of net FILP loans. The six are noted on supplemental table 1, which is available on our web sites and the NBER web site (see note 2). Also available on our web sites are the balance sheets and income statements included in the administrative cost statements compiled by the SPCs studied here.

creditor and the equity holder of public corporations, insolvency implies future losses for the government, and hence for taxpayers. If the capital is positive but very small, taxpayers are risk for providing more money if even small losses occur. We will see that this is a pervasive problem.

The amount of capital falls for many corporations when they restate their balance sheets based on accounting standards for the private sector. By their own accounts, nine agencies are insolvent—that is, they have negative capital ratios. (As an example of how labyrinthine FILP accounting is, a tenth agency is insolvent on its original balance sheet but manages to become solvent using private sector standards!)

Data on capital are included in table 2.5 as column (5). Supplemental table 2[2] lists the amount of capital for each government account and public corporation as reported on its original balance sheet (that is, using accounting standards for public corporations) and on its administrative cost statement (using standards for private sector firms), as well as the capital ratio.

There is a quite serious accounting problem regarding the largest recipient of FILP funds, Government Housing Loan Corporation (GHLC), and two small special accounts. Their balance sheets list cumulative losses on the *asset* side. The losses are to be paid off over time by gradually reducing capital. Because the losses have been identified already and are not likely to be eliminated (without a corresponding reduction of the capital or infusion of new capital), it is necessary to subtract these items from capital immediately to get an unbiased picture of their current financial condition. In our analysis, the cumulative losses are subtracted from assets in calculating these agencies' capital. Such losses amount to ¥518.6 billion in total.

2.4   Nonperforming Loans

Disclosed nonperforming loans totaled ¥5.6 trillion in March 2001, which is 3.2 percent of total loans made by the institutions. This is a lower bound for the level of bad loans. Although reporting of nonperforming loans may be better than before, the small loan-loss reserves of many institutions suggest serious underreserving. Table 2.6, column (1), summarizes the amount of bad loans disclosed in the administrative cost statements. (Supplemental table 3[3] has data for each agency.)

Bad loans on the administrative cost statements of government financial institutions are risk management loans, defined in the same way as for private sector banks. These are loans to failed enterprises, loans more than

---

2. See our websites (http://www.econ.keio.ac.jp/staff/tdoi/ and http://www2-irps.ucsd.edu/faculty/thoshi/) and the NBER website (http://www.nber.org/data/).
3. See note 2.

Table 2.5   Total Financial losses of the FILP and Net Capital of FILP Agencies, 31 March 2001 (¥ billions)

Underreserved Loans[a]	Overvalued Assets[b]	Policy Costs[c]	Total Losses[d]	Gross Capital[e]	Net Capital[f]	Agency
Government Financial Institutions						
1,356.7	n.a.	−154.9	1,201.8	−188.8	−1,390.6	Government Housing Loan Corp.
500.9	n.a.	43.6	544.5	−180.1	−724.6	National Life Finance Corp.
179.3	n.a.	88.7	268.0	155.2	−112.8	Japan Finance Corp. for Small Business
149.5	n.a.	499.0	648.5	244.8	−403.7	Agriculture Forestry & Fisheries Finance Corp.
5,072.5	n.a.	9.3	5,081.8	1,324.7	−3,757.1	Japan Finance Corp. for Municipal Enterprises
134.5	n.a.	5.0	139.5	49.3	−90.2	Okinawa Development Finance Corp.
273.3	n.a.	128.2	401.5	1,616.2	1,214.7	Development Bank of Japan
281.2	n.a.	723.1	1,004.3	7,338.2	6,333.9	Japan Bank for International Cooperation
Special Public Corporations						
40.3	1,199.4	1,234.2	2,473.9	417.4	−2,056.5	Urban Development Corp.
29.6	n.a.	325.7	355.3	−819.8	−1,175.1	Pension Welfare Service Public Corp.
10.1	n.a.	n.a.	10.1	1,508.9	1,498.8	Employment & Human Resources Development Org.
0.0	165.2	36.5	201.7	−15.8	−217.5	Japan Environment Corp.
n.a.	43.1	−10.7	32.4	107.7	75.3	Teito Rapid Transit Authority
5.3	n.a.	78.7	84.0	134.8	50.8	Japan Regional Development Corp.
n.a.	37.0	74.7	111.7	−7.4	−119.1	Japan Sewage Works Agency
16.2	n.a.	69.6	85.8	297.8	212.0	Social Welfare & Medical Service Corp.
5.4	n.a.	4.9	10.3	3,315.2	3,304.9	Promotion & Mutual Aid Corp. for Private Schools of Japan
9.7	n.a.	104.9	114.6	−77.8	−192.4	Japan Scholarship Foundation
0.1	n.a.	1,374.3	1,374.4	686.1	−688.3	Japan Green Resources Corp.
4.7	n.a.	n.a.	4.7	107.4	102.7	Japan International Cooperation Agency
n.a.	4,445.1	3,461.5	7,906.6	6,109.1	−1,797.5	Japan Highway Public Corp.
n.a.	1,107.2	371.2	1,478.4	994.8	−483.6	Metropolitan Expressway Public Corp.
n.a.	475.6	270.9	746.5	187.1	−559.4	Hanshin Expressway Public Corp.

(continued)

Table 2.5 (continued)

Underreserved Loans[a]	Overvalued Assets[b]	Policy Costs[c]	Total Losses[d]	Gross Capital[e]	Net Capital[f]	Agency
n.a.	648.4	630.6	1,279.0	−623.0	−1,902.0	Honshu-Shikoku Bridge Authority
0.0	2,553.4	2.0	2,555.4	−645.8	−3,201.2	Japan Railway Construction Public Corp.
n.a.	218.6	−62.0	156.6	282.9	126.3	New Tokyo International Airport Authority
6.7	n.a.	3.3	10.0	962.8	952.8	Corp. for Advanced Transport & Technology
n.a.	464.0	235.4	699.4	42.3	−657.1	Water Resources Development Public Corp.
4.2	n.a.	n.a.	4.2	10.9	6.7	Fund for the Promotion & Development of the Amami Isles
1.5	n.a.	0.6	2.1	25.5	23.4	Metal Mining Agency of Japan
100.2	n.a.	1,824.2	1,924.4	1,474.9	−449.5	Japan National Oil Corp.
n.a.	n.a.	n.a.	n.a.	−3,489.0	−3,489.0	Postal Life Insurance Welfare Corp.
						Special Firms
69.3	n.a.	53.2	122.5	608.5	486.0	Shoko Chukin Bank
n.a.	n.a.	2.2	2.2	419.1	416.9	Kansai International Airport Co. Ltd.
n.a.	n.a.	1.3	1.3	26.3	25.0	Org. for Promoting Urban Development
8,251.3	11,357.0	11,429.2[g]	31,037.4	−6,047.5	−23,467.2	Total
—	—	—	—	—	—	Total for negative capital

Note: Five special accounts and one special firm do not publish balance sheets regularly, so they are excluded from our analysis. These are noted on supplement table 1. Supplemental Tables are available on our web sites (see table 2.3). n.a. = not available, and the dashes indicate "not applicable."

[a]Underreserved bad loans are from supplemental table 3, column (1) minus column (3). An entry of 0.0 means the agency's nonperforming loans were found by our analysis to be fully reserved.

[b]Over-valued assets are from supplemental table 4, column (2) minus column (3).

[c]Policy costs numbers are found in Ministry of Finance (2002b).

[d]Total losses are the sum of the first three columns.

[e]Gross capital is from the agency's administrative cost statement where available, otherwise from its original balance sheet. These are reported on supplemental table 2.

[f]Net capital is gross capital minus total losses.

[g]Composed of ¥11,656.8 in policy costs from twenty-eight agencies and ¥227.6 in policy benefits from three agencies.

Table 2.6   **Disclosed Bad Loans of FILP Agencies, 31 March 2001**

Bad Loan		Loan Loss Reserve		
¥ Billions[a]	As % of All Loans[b]	¥ Billions	As % of Bad Loans[a]	Name or Type of Agency and Number of Agencies[d]
1,398	1.8	41	2.9	Government Housing Loan Corp
3,148	5.0	1,629	51.8	Other government financial institutions (6)
519	2.3	354	41.6	SPCs (18)
534	4.9	465	87.0	Shoko Chukin Bank
5,599	3.2	2,489	44.5	Total for all agencies
5,441	3.2	2,262	41.6	Total for underreserved agencies (21)

Source: Summarized from supplemental table 3, which provides data specific to each agency. It is available on our web sites and the NBER web site (see table 2.3).

Note: The absolute amount of underreserving for each agency is included in table 2.5. Total underreserving (the difference between bad loans in column [1] and reserves in column [3]) is ¥3,179 billion for underreserved agencies. Including JFM (see box 2.2), the total is ¥8,251 billion.

[a]For government financial institutions and Shoko Chukin Bank, entries are for risk-management loans. SPCs are allowed to use a less strict definition. For them, the figures show amounts of loans past-due six months or more or loans to bankrupt entities that they report with their balance sheets.

[b]Bad loans as a percentage of total loans made.

[c]An entry under 100 percent means the agency is underreserved.

[d]Only agencies that disclose nonperforming loans are included.

three months past due, and restructured loans (i.e., loans that have relaxed conditions). Note that loans clearly headed for trouble, but technically still performing, do not need to be included. Nonfinancial SPCs must disclose only loans that are past due more than six months; They hold 6.4 percent of the bad loans in the table.

In determining underreserving, we assume 100 percent of reported bad loans will be lost eventually. The 100 percent loss rate may seem extreme, but the late 1990s experience of private sector banks shows this actually is a rather conservative assumption. At the end of March 1996, the first time that all banks in the private sector disclosed risk-management loans, the total was ¥28.5 trillion. Disposal of bad loans cost banks ¥34.7 trillion in the following three years. Despite writing off 122 percent of the starting level, total risk-management loans at the end of March 1999 stood at ¥29.6 trillion, slightly higher than the initial level! This suggests risk-management loans at the end of March 1996 were severely underreported. It seems reasonable to expect a similar magnitude of underreporting by FILP agencies.

Of the twenty-six agencies covered, only five have reserves equal to or in excess of their bad loans. For the twenty-one agencies that are underreserved, estimated underreserving is ¥3.2 trillion. One agency, Japan Finance Corporation for Municipal Enterprises (JFM), does not have any loan loss reserves on its balance sheet, but it should (box 2.2). Total un-

Box 2.2

Table 2.6 and supplemental table 3 do not list JFM, which raises fund by issuing government-guaranteed bonds and lends to local governments and public corporations owned by local governments, because it claims to have no risk management loans. Because we have budget data for local governments, we could estimate JFM underreservation in the same way we estimate expected losses on FILP funds lent to local governments. The details are reported later, but the calculation suggests that ¥5,072.5 billion of JFM loans is likely to be uncollectible, and thus the amount of underreservation also is ¥5,072.5 billion.

derreserving including JFM reaches ¥8.3 trillion. Table 2.6 summarizes loan loss reserves and reserves as a percentage of bad loans.

2.5 Valuation of Physical Assets

The value of physical assets reported on balance sheets of SPCs may not reflect the true value of the assets, primarily because they are not properly depreciated, and also because assets are not marked-to-market.

When book value (original cost) is used for land purchased a long time ago, its actual value can be significantly understated. On the other hand, if a corporation has assets that have lost value (such as land purchased in the late 1980s), book value may overstate the true value.

Improper depreciation of physical assets is a more serious problem and it tends to overstate the level of existing assets. For example, Iwamoto (1998a, 166) reports that Japan Highway Public Corporation is allowed to (and actually does) accumulate reserves for depreciation out of profits whenever it feels it is convenient, rather than charging depreciation every year. Hence the assets figures on its balance sheet are gross capital numbers, which include past depreciation. To get net numbers, one has to subtract cumulative reserves (for future redemption of loans) from the capital. Capital calculated in this way still suffers from the problem of underreporting of depreciation, because the corporation charges depreciation only when a sufficient amount of profit is realized.

2.5.1 Revaluing Assets

For twelve corporations that carry large amounts of physical assets on their books, we have revalued their assets to reflect market value changes and proper depreciation. All are involved in urban development or providing infrastructure.

Comparing the amounts reported on their original balance sheets to those reported in their administrative cost statements, some public corporations adjusted their assets figures substantially downward. Still, our calculations suggest the official numbers remain overstated for many agencies, and the level of misvaluation varies significantly. For the eleven with overvaluations, the total is ¥11.4 trillion.[4]

2.6 Future Losses

In addition to the losses already incurred, some FILP agencies are expected to generate more financial losses if they continue to operate. Carefully estimating the size of such future losses is beyond the scope of this chapter. Instead, we rely on the policy cost analysis conducted by each FILP agency.

The analysis, which calculates a present discounted value of estimated government subsidies needed to cover the difference between revenues from FILP projects and their costs, started in fiscal 1999. That year, the analysis was applied to five agencies. In fiscal 2000, coverage was extended to fourteen agencies, and with fiscal 2001, all thirty-three agencies that receive new funds from the FILP were required to publish a policy cost analysis. Kikkawa, Sakai, and Miyagawa (2000) have found that the published policy cost analyses often seriously overestimate future revenues, and hence underestimate the policy cost. Thus, the published data should be taken as a lower bound for expected future losses.

Projects are expected to generate more revenue than costs at five agencies. For the twenty-eight agencies expecting policy costs, the total as of March 2001 is ¥11.7 trillion; for all thirty-three agencies the projected cost is ¥11.4 trillion. (The estimate made by each agency is in table 2.5 column [3].)

2.7 FILP Agency Losses

Table 2.8 summarizes and totals the financial losses revealed by our analysis in the previous sections. At March 2001, for the thirty-four FILP agencies for which we estimate losses the total was ¥31.0 trillion. These losses reduce the agencies' net capital, in some cases giving them negative net capital.

Our analysis finds twenty FILP agencies that are insolvent (have negative net capital) including projected policy costs. Of these, nine are admit-

---

4. The Supplemental Appendix A describes the revaluation method in detail and discusses the depreciation rates and land price series used for each corporation. Data are in supplemental table 4. These are available on our web sites and the NBER web site. Two other agencies report significant physical assets, but we are unable to revalue their assets because changes in accounting rules in 1986 prevent a consistent time series.

Table 2.7   Government Capital and Public Funds Already Lost, 31 March 2001 (¥ billions)

	Government capital		Public loss of		
%[a]	¥[b]	Original Capital[c]	Other[d]	Total	Agency
			Government Financial Institutions		
100.0	166.2	166.2*	1,390.6	1,566.8	Government Housing Loan Corp.
100.0	321.9	321.9*	724.6	1,046.5	National Life Finance Corp.
100.0	410.9	410.9*	112.8	523.7	Japan Finance Corp. for Small Business
100.0	311.1	311.1*	403.7	714.8	Agriculture Forestry & Fisheries Finance Corp.
100.0	16.6	16.6*	3,757.1	3,773.7	Japan Finance Corp. for Municipal Enterprises
100.0	63.2	63.2*	90.2	153.4	Okinawa Development Finance Corp.
100.0	1,039.4	0.0	0.0	0.0	Development Bank of Japan
100.0	6,986.2	652.3	0.0	652.3	Japan Bank for International Cooperation
			Special Public Corporations		
99.3	683.0	683.0*	2,056.5	2,739.5	Urban Development Corp.
100.0	1,075.4	1,075.4*	1,175.1	2,250.5	Pension Welfare Service Public Corp.
100.0	2,118.4	620.2	0.0	620.2	Employment & Human Resources Development Org.
78.8	15.6	15.6*	217.5	233.1	Japan Environment Corp.
53.4	31.0	0.0	0.0	0.0	Teito Rapid Transit Authority
100.0	135.8	85.0	0.0	85.0	Japan Regional Development Corp.
55.4	1.5	1.5*	119.1	120.6	Japan Sewage Works Agency
100.0	292.6	80.6	0.0	80.6	Social Welfare & Medical Service Corp.
100.0	723.1	371.9	0.0	371.9	Labor Welfare Corp.
95.4	51.5	30.9	0.0	30.9	Org. for Pharmaceutical Safety & Research
100.0	48.7	0.0	0.0	0.0	Promotion & Mutual Aid Corp. for Private Schools of Japan
100.0	3.7	3.7*	192.4	196.1	Japan Scholarship Foundation
99.9	1,257.7	110.2	0.0	110.2	Japan Small & Medium Enterprise Corp.
100.0	675.9	675.9*	688.3	1,364.2	Japan Green Resources Corp.
100.0	132.6	29.9	0.0	29.9	Japan Intl Cooperation Agency
92.8	70.3	49.6	0.0	49.6	Bio-oriented Technology Research Advancement Institution
100.0	1,980.1	1,980.1*	1,797.5	3,777.6	Japan Highway Public Corp.
50.0	298.5	298.5*	483.6	782.1	Metropolitan Expressway Public Corp.
50.0	235.1	235.1*	559.4	794.5	Hanshin Expressway Public Corp.

a					
67.5	516.9	516.9*	1,902.0	2,418.9	Honshu-Shikoku Bridge Authority
99.5	64.2	64.2*	3,201.2	3,265.4	Japan Railway Construction Public Corp.
100.0	284.7	158.4	0.0	158.4	New Tokyo International Airport Authority
88.1	20.8	0.0	0.0	0.0	Corp. for Advanced Transport & Technology
99.1	382.5	217.9	0.0	217.9	Telecommunications Advancement Org. of Japan
100.0	2.4	2.4*	657.1	659.5	Water Resources Development Public Corp.
63.1	7.2	3.0	0.0	3.0	Fund for Promotion & Development of the Amami Isles
100.0	23.7	0.3	0.0	0.3	Metal Mining Agency of Japan
84.9	1,636.8	1,636.8*	449.5	2,086.3	Japan National Oil Corp.
99.98	548.3	384.7	0.0	384.7	Japan Science & Technology Corp.
96.9	319.9	265.9	0.0	265.9	Information-Technology Promotion Agency
94.5	305.6	252.2	0.0	252.2	Japan Key Technology Center
56.7	57.6	1.0	0.0	1.0	Industrial Structure Improvement Fund
72.4	9.5	0.2	0.0	0.2	New Energy & Industrial Technology Development
100.0	442.2	442.2*	3,489.0	3,931.2	Postal Life Insurance Welfare Corp.
			Special Firms		
79.8	394.1	6.3	0.0	6.3	Shoko Chukin Bank
66.7	394.7	116.6	0.0	116.6	Kansai International Airport Co. Ltd.
	12,358.4	12,358.4	23,467.2	35,825.6	Totals

Note: Not all institutions with government capital contributions are FILP agencies. This table covers only FILP agencies.

aGovernment's percentage share of paid-in (contributed) capital.

bAmount of government contribution on the agency's balance sheet. This includes any contributions through the Industrial Investment Special Account (IISA), which are included in the formal FILP plan, as well as 95 contributions directly from the general account and from other special accounts, which are not included in the FILP plan.

cGovernment's loss of its original capital. If net capital (table 2.5, column [6]) is negative (as is the case for twenty agencies), all the government contribution to the corporation is considered lost. These cases are indicated by an *. If net capital is positive but smaller than the government contribution (as is the case for twenty agencies), the net loss is the amount by which the government's share of net capital is less than its contribution (column [4]). The government's share of net capital is column (1) (as a decimal) multiplied by table 2.5, column (6). In seven cases, the government did not provide 100 percent of capital.

dGovernment's share of losses that exceed its original capital contribution. The assumption is that all loans to insolvent FILP recipients eventually will be taken over by the government (as has already happened for the former JNR), while nongovernmental contributors of capital will lose no more than their original capital. For insolvent corporations (marked with *), the additional loss is the amount of negative net capital from table 2.5, column (6). For solvent corporations, it is zero.

Table 2.8   **Total Financial Losses of FILP Agencies with Losses, 31 March 2001 (¥ billions)**

Number of Agencies with Each type of Loss	Amount of Loss	Source of Loss
22	8,251	Underreserving of bad loans
11	11,357	Overvaluing of assets
28	11,657	Policy costs
3	−228	Policy gains offsetting other losses
34	31,037	Total

Source: Table 2.5, which gives data by agency.
Note: The total amount (¥31.0 trillion) is about 6 percent of GDP.

tedly insolvent (have negative capital on their administrative statements), and another eleven are shown to be insolvent after adjustments for the accounting problems we have outlined. Data are in table 2.5.

The twenty insolvent agencies represent more than 60 percent (¥217 trillion) of net FILP fund loans. Not all of the bad loans have been, or will be, truly lost to the FILP. Indeed, because the borrowers are all government or quasi-governmental institutions, we expect all FILP loans to be paid in full eventually. Taxpayer money will be used if necessary, as has already happened for the former JNR. That means the funds the agencies receive to pay back FILP loans should be considered a cost of the FILP, one that will be borne by future taxpayers.

Thus, a comprehensive approach to the FILP's cost to the public is to estimate what it would take to bail-out all FILP agencies. This involves computing the amount of capital originally contributed by the government that has already been lost and the cumulative losses that exceed the government's original capital. Data for forty-four agencies are in table 2.7.

The government has lost all or part of its capital in forty agencies, a total of almost ¥12.4 trillion. Losses that exceed original capital add another ¥23.4 trillion, for a total loss of ¥35.8 trillion.

2.8   Local Governments

Of ¥357 trillion of net FILP funds outstanding at the end of March 2001, ¥87 trillion (24.4 percent) were loans directly to local governments and public enterprises owned by local governments. These entities also borrow from the JFM, which is a large recipient of FILP funds. Thus, the solvency of local governments is an important determinant of the financial health of the FILP.

The amount of FILP loans to local governments each year is determined in a process that is led by the Ministry of Public Management, Home Affairs, Posts and Telecommunications (Ministry of Home Affairs before the government restructuring in January 2001). The process requires any local government planning a bond issue to obtain the Ministry's permission in advance. When permission is granted, the Ministry also decides how much of the bonds will be bought by the TFB Fund and Postal Life Insurance Fund.

There is no mechanism ensuring FILP loans go only to financially healthy entities. Indeed, loans are routinely used by the Ministry to distribute funds to financially troubled local governments and may even be skewed toward such governments. Doi (2002) found that a local government that depends heavily on FILP loans tends to have low tax revenues and a large amount of local-allocation tax grants (lump-sum grants distributed by the central government to make up for shortages in local tax revenues.)

Thus, one would suspect that many local governments with high debts are servicing the debts using funds provided by the central government. If this is the case, we would find a substantial amount of nonperforming FILP loans to local governments.

Local governments are not required to prepare balance sheets, which prevents us from applying the approach used for FILP agencies. So, in this section, we focus on the ability for a local government to pay off its current outstanding bonds.

2.8.1   Local Government Solvency and Losses

For each local government, we calculate debt capacity defined as the present discounted value of future expected primary surpluses (revenues minus noninterest expenditures). If the current local government debt exceeds the calculated debt capacity, we conclude the local government is de facto insolvent.

Budget data for fiscal 1997 through 2000 are used. A lack of budget data prevents including public enterprises owned by local governments. Thus, the estimates reported are a lower bound for the losses expected in FILP loans to local governments and local public enterprises. We start by estimating future primary surpluses for each local government, using six different scenarios.

Estimating Procedure

Letting S_i denote the expected primary surplus for the local government i, we can calculate the debt capacity of the government, denoted by B_i^*, as

$$(1) \qquad B_i^* = \max\left\{\frac{S_i}{r}, 0\right\},$$

where r is the constant discount rate, assumed to be 4 percent. Note that we assume debt capacity cannot be below zero. Thus, if a local government runs a primary deficit, its debt capacity is defined as zero.

By comparing B_i^* to the outstanding debt as of the end of March 2001, denoted by $B_{i,2001}$, we can calculate the amount of debt that is not likely to be paid off. Let us define $DF_{i,2000}$ as

(2) $$DF_{i,2001} = \max\{B_{i,2000} - B_i^*, 0\}.$$

If $DF_{i,2000}$ is strictly positive, we say the local government is de facto insolvent and the size of $DF_{i,2000}$ shows the magnitude of insolvency. The result, of course, depends critically on the estimated level of S_i.

The Scenarios

In the baseline case (scenario 1), we assume this is constant and equal to the simple average of the primary surpluses in fiscal 1997–2000.

Because we estimate the future primary surplus from data for four years when the economy was stagnating (April 1997 through March 2001), it might be lower than the long-run level after the economy recovers. To address this, we consider scenario 2, which assumes general revenue (tax revenue, local transfer taxes, and local-allocation tax) jumps 20 percent in the first year and stays there.

Another assumption in the baseline case is that the future primary surplus does not grow. Scenario 3 considers an alternative where the surplus grows 2 percent each year.

In the first three scenarios, we assume the local governments can continue to rely on local-allocation tax grants from the central government. That system, however, is likely to change in the near future. Its overhaul is an important part of the fiscal decentralization that the government has been deliberating since the mid 1990s.

A Decentralization Promotion Committee was created within the Prime Minister's Office in 1995, and started drafting a decentralization plan. The committee published its final report in June 2001. On the issue of local-allocation tax grants, the committee argues that there should be a transfer of tax bases from the central government to local governments to improve the fiscal condition of local governments and that the local-allocation tax grants should be reduced so that the transfer of tax bases is neutral to the total tax revenue of the central and local governments (see Decentralization Promotion Committee 2001, chap. 3, section 1).

In scenarios 4, 5, and 6, we consider the case where the tax base for local-allocation tax grants is assumed to be transferred to local governments according to the current size of their own tax revenues, and local-allocation tax grants become zero. Scenario 4 assumes the expected future primary surplus is given by the average for fiscal 1997–2000. Scenario 5 assumes general tax revenue increases 20 percent in the first year and then stays constant. Scenario 6 assumes the future primary surplus grows 2 percent annually.

Results

Table 2.9 summarizes the results of our calculation. At the end of fiscal 2000, total debts outstanding for forty-seven prefectures, 693 cities (and wards in Tokyo), and 2,557 towns and villages amounted to ¥125.5 trillion, of which ¥55.0 trillion was owed to the FILP fund and ¥8.2 trillion was owed to the JFM. These are amounts in the ordinary accounts of local governments, and do not include debts in enterprise accounts and of public corporations owned by the local governments.

Table 2.9   Expected Insolvency of Local Governments, 31 March 2001 (¥ billions)

JFM[a]	FILP	Total[b]	Prefectures	Cities & Wards	Towns & Villages	
	Source of Funds			Borrower, By Type		
n.a.	n.a.	n.a.	47	693	2,557	Number
8,246.4	54,999.5	n.a.	n.a.	n.a.	n.a.	Total loaned
n.a.	n.a.	124,760.7	72,326.3	41,831.4	10,603.0	Total debt[b]
		Loans to Insolvent Entities[c]				
						Scenario
6,160.4	42,331.1[d]	105,775.5	69,546.4	29,767.3	6,461.8	1
1,443.6	10,964.1	30,150.5	25,622.9	3,665.3	862.2	2
5,207.6	36,199.1	94,659.8	66,656.9	23,244.4	4,758.5	3
5,803.0	39,553.1	85,463.4	52,475.8	22,737.7	10,249.9	4
4,389.8	31,785.9	64,891.2	46,115.2	9,135.7	9,640.2	5
5,718.6	39,171.5	84,762.0	52,475.8	22,158.7	10,127.4	6
		Expected Default[e]				
5,072.5	35,201.8[f]	89,517.4	61,862.5	22,633.4	5,021.5	1
462.7	3,494.4	9,374.4	5,943.1	2,929.2	502.1	2
4,397.3	30,317.1	76,342.5	53,983.2	18,316.4	4,042.8	3
5,679.1	38,925.9	84,282.2	52,475.8	21,558.1	10,248.2	4
4,263.1	31,178.8	63,617.2	46,089.4	7,931.4	9,596.3	5
5,582.8	38,384.2	83,118.6	52,475.8	20,472.1	10,170.7	6

Source: Authors' calculations.

Note: The scenarios are explained in the text. The analysis excludes local public enterprises because of a lack of data. These enterprises have losses, so the estimates here are lower bounds. n.a. = not applicable.

[a]JFM is the Japan Finance Corporation for Municipal Enterprises.

[b]Total debt outstanding, defined as local bonds plus contract-authorized liabilities minus reserve minus net excess of revenue at the end of fiscal year 2000.

[c]Sum of the debts of insolvent local governments, where insolvency is defined as debts exceeding debt capacity. Debt capacity is the present discounted value of the expected level of primary surplus, as explained in the text. A 4 percent discount rate is assumed.

[d]Value for "Loans to Insolvent local goverments" used in table 2.10.

[e]Sum of the differences between total debts and debt capacities under each scenario. The seniority of FILP and JFM loans are assumed to be the same as other liabilities.

[f]Value for "Expected Default of local government debt" used in table 2.11.

If the current system of local-allocation tax grants continues and if the primary surpluses of local governments do not improve (scenario 1, the baseline case), the current level of local debts is estimated to exceed the debt capacity for all forty-seven prefectures, 326 out of 693 cities, and 1,240 of 2,557 towns and villages. The total size of the insolvency is ¥89.5 trillion. In other words, these entities have borrowed almost ¥90 trillion more than we expect them to be able to repay based on their current tax and spending patterns. Assuming that the insolvency is addressed by defaulting on the loans (rather than raising taxes or cutting spending) and that FILP loans and JFM loans have the same seniority as other debts, 64 percent (¥35.2 trillion) of the outstanding FILP loans to local governments and 62 percent (¥5.1 trillion) of the outstanding JFM loans to local governments will be defaulted.

When we assume the system of local-allocation tax grants is decentralized (scenario 4), debt capacity improves for some prefectures and cities, while the capacity of many towns and villages declines. This is because the current allocation of tax grants is skewed in favor of financially poor local governments, which include many towns and villages.

Scenarios 2 and 5, which assume an economic recovery that increases general revenue 20 percent, of course produce much smaller losses. Comparing scenarios 2 and 5 suggests that the increased debt capacity of local governments in scenario 2 mostly results from increased local-allocation tax grants at local governments already receiving disproportionately large allocations. When the system of grants is decentralized (scenario 5), these governments lose the extra-large allocations. The result suggests that many such local governments would not be able to meet the debt payments without redistribution through grants at the current level.

Scenarios 3 and 6, which have 2 percent annual growth in the primary surplus, see enhanced debt capacities of some local governments, but the expected amount of insolvency are not much different from the baselines (scenarios 1 and 4).

2.9   Overall Cost to Taxpayers

Table 2.10 summarizes total bad loans. Of the ¥357 trillion of net FILP funds, 75 percent (¥267 trillion) can be considered bad loans.

Our estimate of the total cost to taxpayers to bail-out and recapitalize public corporations, cover local-government defaults, and retire former JNR–related debt is ¥78.3 trillion, which amounts to over 15 percent of fiscal 2000 GDP (table 2.11). As discussed previously, we consider this a lower bound.

2.10   Fundamental Reform

A government study in the late 1990s found three shortcomings in the FILP that have motivated change (Ministry of Finance 2001, 24). First, the

Table 2.10   **Bad Loans in the FILP, 31 March 2001 (¥ trillions)**

Amount	Borrower
7.3	JNR-related debt (box 2.1)
217.0	Insolvent agencies[a]
42.3	Insolvent local governments (table 2.9)
266.6	Total

[a]Insolvent agencies (that is, agencies with negative net capital) are listed in table 2.5. Their debt is included with their entries in supplement table 1, which is available on our web sites and the NBER web site (see table 2.3).

Table 2.11   **Expected Cost to Taxpayers, 31 March 2001 (¥ trillions)**

Amount	Source
7.3	JNR-related debt (box 2.1)
35.8	Cost to restore capital of FILP agencies (table 2.7), composed of
12.4	Lost original capital
23.5	Cumulative operating losses in excess of original capital
35.2	Expected default of local government debt (table 2.9)
78.3	Total

Note: The cost to restore capital of FILP agencies (¥35.8 trillion) in this table differs from the total financial losses reported in table 5.8 (¥31.0 trillion) because the figure in this table includes the losses that are already reported on the agencies' original balance sheets even before we estimate the additional losses in table 2.8.

TFB, which handled all the deposits from postal savings and pension reserves, may have become too big to be efficient. Second, too much consideration for TFB depositors (that is, the pension funds and postal savings) may have been keeping the cost of FILP funds too high. Third, the opaque nature of the FILP's subsidy component may have been hiding substantial future burdens on taxpayers.

To address these issues, effective 1 April 2001, the FILP went through a fundamental reform. Figure 2.2 shows how the FILP system will look when the transition is complete.

The TFB has been abolished. Its personnel and assets have been inherited by the Fiscal Loan Fund (FLF). Postal savings and pension reserves are not automatically deposited into the FLF. Instead, the funds are invested in the financial market at the discretion of the postal savings and pension systems, as was the case already for a small share of the funds.

The way FILP agencies raise their funds also has changed. Under the new FILP, the agencies raise funds in three ways. The preferred way is for an agency to issue its own bonds in the financial market. The Framework of the Fundamental Reform declares that each agency should "make utmost effort to issue FILP agency bonds" (Ministry of Finance 2001, 28).

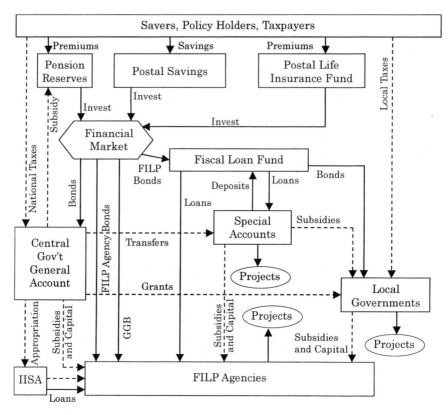

Fig. 2.2   Structure of the new FILP after April 2001
Note: A box represents a sector or an institution involved in the FILP. The arrows indicate the direction of the movement of funds, with solid lines indicating financial transactions and broken lines being fiscal transfers. The postal savings and the postal life insurance fund plan to buy bonds directly from local governments, because most of the local governments would have trouble floating their bonds in the market. The purchases of local bonds are not included in this figure.

Agencies not healthy enough to place bonds in the open market will be allowed to issue bonds with a government guarantee. Finally, agencies can tap funds raised collectively through the issuance of FILP bonds by the FLF.

2.10.1   Intended Results of the Reform

Use of FILP agency bonds rather than TFB funds can potentially eliminate the problem of fund costs, if some FILP agencies can issue bonds at lower yields than they have been paying the TFB for funds.

Nontransparency is addressed by requiring further disclosure of FILP agencies and the FILP system as a whole. Two specific measures have been implemented.

First, starting with fiscal 1999, the government began calculating the policy cost for each FILP agency and publishing the result. Policy cost is defined as the present discounted value of the stream of net transfers from the government to an agency. This measure reveals the expected cost to the government (thus, taxpayers) to sustaining operation of an agency.

Second, in June 2001, the Fiscal System Council of the Ministry of Finance came up with a recommendation on accounting disclosures for SPCs. As a result, all SPCs (many of which are FILP agencies) were required to publish "administrative cost statements" for fiscal 2000 by the end of September 2001. These are discussed in the next section.

2.10.2   Administrative Cost Statements

SPCs are required to publish balance sheets and income statements using the accounting standards of private sector firms beginning with the fiscal 2000 (which ended March 2001). The opportunity cost of government funds used as capital for the agency also is calculated. Adding that to the loss shown on the income statement yields the "administrative cost statement" (*gyosei cost keisansho*). (The importance of including the opportunity cost of government funds was first pointed out by Fukao 1998.)

The statements are supposed to be free from the accounting problems identified in earlier sections. For example, the Fiscal System Council's guideline requires SPCs to adjust depreciable assets for depreciation. They also require government financial institutions (but not SPCs) to disclose nonperforming loans using the same criteria as private sector financial institutions.

Although the reform was launched on 1 April 2001, implementation is planned to be gradual and many transitional measures are provided. For example, postal savings and the pension reserves are committed to buy a substantial amount of FILP bonds until the market for the bonds fully develops. Moreover, the postal savings and the postal life insurance fund plan to buy bonds directly from local governments, because most local governments would have trouble floating bonds in the market. Thus, the discretion that the postal savings and other funds are supposed to enjoy is seriously limited during the transition period.

2.10.3   Actual Substantive Change is Not Assured

A comparison of the old and new systems reveals the possibility that, the government's claim that the reform is fundamental notwithstanding, the new system may in practice not differ substantially from the old after all. It is possible for the new system to replicate the financial flows of the old system even after the transitional measures expire. For example, postal savings may continue to buy FILP bonds, and FILP agencies may continue to borrow from the FLF. Then, although the name of the intermediary is different, the flow of funds would be exactly the same as under the old system. Moreover, local governments will not be required to issue bonds in the financial market and can continue to depend on the FLF.[5]

The introduction of FILP agency bonds, which are supposed to be without government guarantees, may not change the situation much, either. The market may continue to believe FILP agency bonds are implicitly guaranteed by the government. Wallison (2001) makes an interesting comparison between FILP agency bonds and bonds issued by government-sponsored enterprises (GSEs), such as Federal National Mortgage Association (FNMA, or Fannie Mae) in the United States. He points out that even though U.S. legislation explicitly states that Fannie Mae securities are not government guaranteed, yields on its securities are only slightly higher than on U.S. Treasury bonds. Thus, he is skeptical of the idea of market discipline from FILP agency bonds.

2.11   Effects of Reform

Reform does not change losses that the FILP has already sustained, but it may prevent FILP agencies from accumulating further losses. After the reform, public corporations are supposed to raise funds from the financial market. The postal savings and pension reserve funds, which used to fund them automatically through the TFB now can invest in the financial market, without necessarily buying the FILP bonds or FILP agency bonds.

The changes are intended to expose public corporations to market monitoring. A loss-accumulating corporation may have difficulty raising funds and may be forced to restructure its operation. Or, the central government may be forced to subsidize a corporation explicitly so that it can continue its loss-making but socially beneficial activities.

Writing fourteen months from the start of the reform, we can examine some early data to see whether the reform looks promising. First, we look at how uses of postal savings funds and the sources of funds used by FILP agencies have changed. Second, we study the secondary market pricing of the limited number of FILP agency bonds being traded.

2.11.1   Flow of Funds

Financial flows in the FILP need to change substantially to make FILP agencies subject to the market discipline. However, the reform may not necessarily change the flow of funds: If the postal savings system chooses to buy FILP agency bonds, FILP bonds, and local government bonds, flows in the reformed FILP will replicate those of the old FILP.

Table 2.12 shows planned uses of postal savings funds for the first two

5. Several local governments—including Tokyo Metropolitan and Osaka City—were issuing bonds in the financial market before the reform. However, the amount of outstanding local bonds so issued is a little less than 10 percent of total local bonds outstanding. In the first year since the reform, the issuance amount has hardly changed.

Table 2.12   Sources and Uses of New Postal Savings Funds (¥ billions)

FY 2001[a]	FY 2002[b]	
		Sources of Funds
32,297	23,723	Matured TFB deposits
8,223	15,393	Other[c]
−16,019	−3,848	Reduction in deposits[d]
24,501	35,267	Total
		Uses of Funds
15,800	13,600	FILP bonds
1,200	7,950	Other JGB[e]
450	450	Public corporation bonds
550	550	Local government bonds
1,000	980	Local government loans
934	713	Loans to depositors
400	400	Corporate bonds
50	50	Foreign bonds
750	2,350	Money trust[f]
3,367	8,224	Short-term securities

Sources: Ministry of Posts and Telecommunications (2000) and Postal Services Agency (2001).
[a]Fiscal year ending 31 March 2002.
[b]Fiscal year ending 31 March 2003.
[c]Income from the investments made by postal savings on its own account.
[d]Expected net withdrawals by depositors in the postal savings system.
[e]Japanese government bonds.
[f]This relates to the Postal Life Insurance Welfare Corp.

Table 2.13   Use of FILP Agency Bonds (¥ billions)

FY 2001	FY 2002	
22,759	1,749	New FILP loans[a]
1,006	2,487	New issues of FILP agency bonds
4.4	14.3	Agency bonds as % of loans

Source: Ministry of Finance (2002a).
[a]Does not include loans to the central government or to local governments. FY = fiscal year.

years after the FILP reform (fiscal 2001 and 2002). There are no substantial changes: The majority of available funds are to be invested in the FILP and most of the rest is to be invested much as it was by the TFB. The optimistic interpretation is that the allocation of postal savings so far has been heavily constrained by transitional measures that require postal savings to absorb a substantial amount of FILP bonds.

The sources of funds for FILP agencies also show little change. Table 2.13 gives the amount of the FILP loans to public corporations in the FILP plans for fiscal 2001 and 2002 and compares those to the size of FILP agency bond issues. The introduction of FILP agency bonds is perhaps the most important aspect of the reform, but they have not become a major source of funds. Although for fiscal 2002 the ratio of bonds to loans is planned to slightly exceed 14 percent, it will take a long time for the total outstanding amount of bonds to approach the level of loans.

2.12   The Market's View of Agency Bonds

A key question is whether the market sees these bonds as having implicit government guarantees. If it does, market discipline will be absent, as there is no incentive to monitor and evaluate the agencies. To find the market's view, this section looks at ratings and spreads between agency bonds and JGBs.

2.12.1   Ratings

Table 2.14 shows the bond ratings for FILP agencies granted by major rating agencies. Tokyo-based R&I (Rating & Investment Information Inc.) has the most extensive coverage of the three major rating agencies, assessing bonds issued by fifteen FILP agencies. The Japanese branches of Moody's and Standard & Poors rate far fewer, and add only two. Thus, seventeen FILP agencies are rated by at least one rating agency.

The R&I seems to distinguish among FILP agencies, and this suggests it

Table 2.14   **Ratings of FILP Agency Bonds (May 2002)**

S&P	Moody	R&I	Agency
AA–	Aa1	AAA	Japanese government bonds (JGB)
AA–	Aa1	AAA	Japan Finance Corp. for Municipal Enterprises
AA–	Aa1	AAA	Development Bank of Japan
AA–	Aa1	AAA	Japan Bank for International Cooperation
A+	Aa1	n.a.	Japan Highway Public Corp.
n.a.	Aa3	n.a.	Hanshin Expressway Public Corp.
n.a.	n.a.	AA+	Japan Finance Corp. for Small Business
n.a.	n.a.	AA+	National Life Finance Corp.
n.a.	n.a.	AA	Agriculture, Forestry & Fisheries Finance Corp.
n.a.	n.a.	AA	Japan Railway Construction Public Corp.
n.a.	n.a.	AA	Metropolitan Expressway Public Corp.
n.a.	n.a.	AA	Promotion & Mutual Aid Corp. for Private Schools
n.a.	n.a.	AA	Social Welfare & Medical Service Corp.
n.a.	n.a.	AA	Water Resources Development Public Corp.
n.a.	n.a.	AA–	Corp. for Advanced Transport & Technology
n.a.	n.a.	AA–	Japan Scholarship Foundation
n.a.	n.a.	AA–	New Tokyo International Airport Authority
n.a.	n.a.	A+	Urban Development Corp.

Sources: Moody's Japan (http://www.moodys.co.jp), Standard & Poor's (http://www.standardpoors.com/japan). Rating & Investment Information (R&I; http://www.r-i.co.jp).

does not see all the bonds as government guaranteed. Three government financial institutions are rated as high as Japanese government bonds (JGBs) were in May 2002. Most of the fourteen others were one notch below. Moody's and S&P rank the same three agencies on par with JGBs, as does R&I. The numbers of FILP agencies that Moody's and S&P rate are so small that it is hard to judge if they are carefully distinguishing between FILP agency bonds issued by different agencies.

2.12.2   Spreads

By comparing yields on FILP agency bonds to those on JGBs or government-guaranteed bonds (also issued by public corporations), we can see if the market views FILP agency bonds as implicitly guaranteed. As of May 2002, twenty-eight bonds issued by seventeen FILP agencies have sufficient secondary-market data.

Figure 2.3 plots the yields of FILP agency bonds and JGBs against maturities. Agency bonds are all above the yield curve of JGBs, with the premium exceeding 80 basis points for some issues. Thus, the market seems to view FILP agency bonds as significantly more risky than JGBs.

Figure 2.4 compares FILP agency bonds to government-guaranteed bonds (many issued by the agencies). The market clearly distinguishes FILP agency bonds from government-guaranteed bonds issued by the same agencies.

Looking at the yield spreads between the twenty-eight bonds and comparable JGBs shows substantial differences from one agency to another. The spreads for bonds issued by Japan Bank for International Cooperation (JBIC) and Development Bank of Japan, which are healthier than

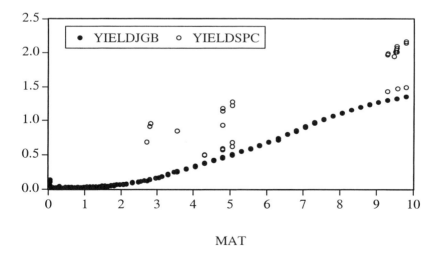

MAT

Fig. 2.3   Yields on FILP agency bonds and JGBs (%; 30 May 2002)

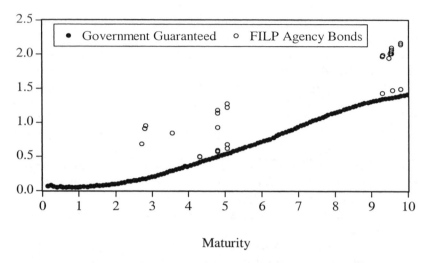

Fig. 2.4   Yields of FILP agency bonds and government-guaranteed public corporation bonds (%; 30 May 2002)

the other agencies in our analysis and are rated the same as JGBs by all three rating agencies, have been relatively small (11 to 14 basis points). Agencies with high estimated financial losses, tend to have high spreads (68 to 82 basis points). At 30 May 2002, Urban Development Corporation, lowest-rated of the agencies reviewed by R&I and de facto insolvent based on our accounting, had a spread of 77.7 basis points. The widest spread was 81.8 basis points for an unrated issue of Japan Regional Development Corporation, although it is solvent even after accounting adjustments.[6]

The gap between low-spread agencies and high-spread agencies seems to have widened after April 2002. This may suggest that the financial market for FILP agency bond is getting better at discriminating between bonds issued by different agencies.

Although the FILP reform talked about using FILP agency bonds as a device to apply market discipline on public corporations, it is not clear how that will work in the extreme. There is no transparent mechanism to deal with failures of public corporations and defaults of FILP agency bonds. Indeed, there is no legal procedure for closing a poorly performing public corporation.

Thus, although our review suggests an emergence of market signals on the quality of specific FILP agency bonds, it is not clear how useful this will be in improving the allocation of funds.

---

6. Supplemental table 5 provides data on the spreads of each issue. It is available on our web sites and the NBER web site. The Japan Securities Dealers Association our original source, posts secondary market quotes (in Japanese) on its web site: http://www.jsda.or.jp.

2.13   Conclusions

This chapter has examined the financial cost that FILP has imposed on taxpayers by studying the financial condition of recipients of FILP loans: mainly public corporations and local governments. Many FILP recipients are de facto insolvent. Of the ¥357 trillion of the net FILP funds, about ¥267 trillion is loaned to insolvent recipients. The cost to taxpayers to clean up the expected FILP loss is estimated to be at least ¥78 trillion, over 15 percent of 2001 GDP.

Together with the massive cost of cleaning up the financial sector (chap. 1 in this volume) and the increasing burden of the social security system (chap. 3 in this volume), the losses in the FILP constitute a serious impediment to recovery of the Japanese economy. To the extent that funds have been misallocated to projects with low returns or that losses have resulted from inefficient use of funds, this chapter provides evidence that the FILP has hurt economic growth, at least since the late 1990s.

Regarding the FILP reforms introduced in April 2001, we found the pattern of financial flows in the FILP has hardly changed. Some good news is that the financial market distinguishes FILP agency bonds from government-guaranteed bonds, which is essential if the use of FILP agency bonds is to introduce market discipline on their issuers. It is too early to tell, however, whether the bonds will be an effective disciplinary device.

2.13.1   Other Issues

There are four major issues about the FILP and its future that this chapter did not examine thoroughly. These are left for future research.

First, nothing is said about the welfare aspects of the FILP. If foregone opportunities from resource misallocation are taken into account, the welfare cost of the FILP might turn out to be even larger than our estimate of financial losses suggests. On the other hand, some loss-making agencies may be providing welfare-enhancing services that offset the financial losses. Examining welfare aspects of the FILP is an important future research topic.

Second, we relied on estimates of policy cost published by each FILP agency. As Kikkawa, Sakai, and Miyagawa (2000) show, for several FILP agencies, this most likely understates the true magnitude of the cost. Studies to improve the estimates of future losses are needed.

Third, empirical analysis of the new FILP is limited by the amount of data, because the new regime started just fourteen months ago. It is important to continue monitoring changes in the pattern of financial flows and development of the market for FILP agency bonds.

Finally, the lack of a clear mechanism to close down poorly performing public corporations is an important shortcoming of the 2001 FILP reform. Such a mechanism is a necessary condition for disciplining through FILP agency bonds. Absent a strong government commitment not to bail out public corporations, and a credible mechanism to prevent bail-outs, market discipline will not develop (see Iwamoto 1998b).

Such a mechanism is also necessary to deal with the losses that have already been incurred by the FILP. It is important to recognize the losses as soon as possible and to decide on the loss-sharing mechanism. Without a clear loss-sharing mechanism, negotiations between stakeholders will lead to delay. Delay increases the losses. Serious research on efficient closure rules for nonperforming FILP agencies is an urgent task.

Appendix

Literature Review

Good descriptions of the FILP and the postal savings system in English are Cargill and Yoshino (2000, 2003). Bayoumi (1998) is a nice introduction to the FILP and the Japanese fiscal system in general.

The FILP Report, an annual publication available on the Ministry of Finance's web site (http://www.mof.go.jp/english), is an official guide to the FILP. The description is often self-congratulatory, but it provides basic information.

Kikkawa, Sakai, and Miyagawa (2000) examine the financial health of selected FILP agencies. Their study focuses on the future expected cash flows of the agencies. They estimate the present value of the future losses (negative cash flows) of FILP agencies to be much higher than the estimates published by the Ministry of Finance. In this chapter, we do not estimate future cash flows for each agency. Instead, we use the Ministry of Finance estimates. The results in Kikkawa suggest that our estimates of total losses are most likely the lower bound of the true amount.

Wallison (2001) discusses the FILP reform of 2001 and argues that the attempt to rely on the market to discipline FILP agencies without privatizing them is likely to fail. Iwamoto (2002) argues that the reform has failed to force the government to reevaluate the role of SPCs and to close down the ones that have ceased to be useful.

In Japanese, a comprehensive survey of the huge body of research is provided by Iwamoto (2001). Most of it examines government financial institutions in the FILP, such as the JDB and the GHLC.

Matsuura (1990), Kono (1993), and Fukao (1998) are among several papers that seek to provide a comprehensive picture on how the FILP works. They carefully disentangle the complex flow of funds and subsidies among the central government, public corporations, and local governments in the FILP.

The work most closely related to this essay are Iwata (1998) and Doi and Mori (2003). Iwata finds serious undercapitalization, a substantial amount of bad loans, and significant underreporting of depreciation for selected FILP agencies. Doi and Mori find similar problems for a wider set of FILP agencies. This essay complements their analyses by using more recent data. Most importantly, we use the financial statements of public corporations based on private-sector accounting standards, which were first published 2001. The problems Iwata and Doi and Mori identified are still found even with supposedly better accounting.

Yoshida and Konishi (1996) was the first comprehensive analysis of the financial condition of the FILP agencies. Perhaps hindered by incomplete disclosure and improper accounting, they failed to recognize the serious financial problem hidden in the FILP. It is also possible that the magnitude of the problem was smaller then. In any case, using more recent data, we find much a larger problem than they did.

Higo (2001) provides a very useful description of the FILP reform of April 2001.

Noguchi and Sasaki (1999) examined yield spreads between government-guaranteed bonds and a few non–government-guaranteed bonds issued by FILP agencies before the 2001 FILP reform. They found the spreads were at most 15 basis points, suggesting the financial markets considered the bonds implicitly government-guaranteed. We find more substantial spreads between FILP agency bonds and government-guaranteed bonds since the FILP reform.

We go beyond a descriptive analysis of the reform and try to examine its impact empirically. This chapter also examines the financial health of local governments, something the works cited generally give little, if any, attention.

References

Bayoumi, Tamim. 1998. The Japanese fiscal system and fiscal transparency. In *Structural change in Japan: macroeconomic impact and policy challenges*, ed. Bijan B. Aghevli, Tamim Bayoumi, and Guy Meredith 177–212. Washington, D.C.: International Monetary Fund.

Cargill, Thomas F., and Naoyuki Yoshino. 2000. The Postal Savings System, Fiscal Investment and Loan Program, and modernization of Japan's financial system. In *Crisis and change in the Japanese financial system*, ed. Takeo Hoshi and Hugh Patrick, 201–30. Boston: Kluwer Academic Publishers.

———. 2003. *The Postal Savings System and Fiscal Investment and Loan Program in Japan: Financial liberalization, dilemmas, and solutions.* Oxford: Oxford University Press.

Decentralization Promotion Committee, Prime Minister's Office. 2001. *Final report* (in Japanese). http://www8.cao.go.jp/bunken/bunken-iinkai/saisyu.

Doi, Takero. 2002. System and role of local bonds permits in Japan. In *Government deficit and fiscal reform in Japan*, ed. Toshihiro Ihori and Masakazu Sato, 121–51. Boston: Kluwer Academic Publishers.

Doi, Takero, and Takeo Hoshi. 2002. Paying for the FILP. NBER Working Paper no. 9385. Cambridge, Mass.: National Bureau of Economic Research.

Doi, Takero, and Koichiro Mori. 2003. *Koteki nenkin tsumitatekin no keizai bunseki* (Economic analysis of public pension reserves). Tokyo: Nihon Hyoron-sha.

Economic Planning Agency. 1998. *Nihon no shakai shihon* (Social infrastructure of Japan). Tokyo: Toyo Keizai Shimpo-sha.

Fukao, Mitsuhiro. 1998. Zaisei toyushi seido no gaikan to mondai no shozai (Fiscal Investment and Loan Program: An overview and problems). In *Zaisei toyushi no keizai bunseki* (Economic analysis of the Fiscal Investment and Loan Program), ed. Kazumasa Iwata and Mitsuhiro Fukao, 1–23. Tokyo: Nihon Keizai Shimbun-sha.

Higo, Masahiro. 2001. Zaisei toyushi no genjo to kadai: 2001 nendo kaikaku ga zaito no kino ni ataeru eikyo (Status quo and problems of Fiscal Investment and Loan Program: Effects of the FILP reform in FY 2001). Working Paper Series no. 01-1. Tokyo: Research and Statistics Department, Bank of Japan.

Hoshi, Takeo, and Anil Kashyap. 2001. *Corporate financing and governance in Japan: The road to the future.* Cambridge, Mass.: MIT Press.

Iwamoto, Yasushi. 1998a. Zaisei toyushi to shakai shihon seibi (Fiscal Investment and Loan Program and infrastructure investment). In *Zaisei toyushi no keizai bunseki* (Economic analysis of the Fiscal Investment and Loan Program), ed. Kazumasa Iwata and Mitsuhiro Fukao, 147–74. Tokyo: Nihon Keizai Shimbun-sha.

———. 1998. Zaito sai to zaito kikan sai (FILP bonds and FILP agency bonds). *Financial Review* 47:134–53.

———. 2001. Nihon no zaisei toyushi (Fiscal Investment and Loan Program: A perspective on government interventions in the Japanese financial sector). *Economic Review* 52 (1): 2–15.

———. 2002. The Fiscal Investment and Loan Program in transition. *Journal of the Japanese and International Economies* 16 (4): 583–604.

Iwata, Kazumasa. 1998. Zaisei toyushi no shorai (The future of the Fiscal Investment and Loan Program). In *Zaisei toyushi no keizai bunseki* (Economic analysis of the Fiscal Investment and Loan Program), ed. Kazumasa Iwata and Mitsuhiro Fukao, 245–97. Tokyo: Nihon Keizai Shimbun-sha.

Kikkawa, Masahiro, Takeshi Sakai, and Hiroyuki Miyagawa. 2000. Soundness of the Fiscal Investment and Loan Program. In *Structural problems of the Japanese financial system*, ed. Mitsuhiro Fukao, 41–59. Tokyo: Japan Center for Economic Research.

Kono, Koretaka. 1993. *Zaisei toyushi no kenkyu* (Research on the Fiscal Investment and Loan Program). Tokyo: Zeimu Keiri Kyokai.

Matsuura, Katsumi. 1990. Zaisei toyushi—Koteki kin'yu—no kenkyu (Analysis of Fiscal Investment and Loan Program). *Keizai Bunseki* (*Economic Analysis*) 119:1–80.

Ministry of Finance. 2001. *FILP report 2000.* http://www.mof.go.jp/zaito/zaito00e.html.

———. 2002a. *FILP report 2001.* http://www.mof.go.jp./zaito/zaito2001e/zaito 2001e.htm.

———. 2002b. *FILP report 2001 extension volume: Policy cost analysis of FILP projects FY2001.* http://www.mof.go.jp.english/zaito/zaito2001e-exv/exv-index.htm.

―――. 2002c. *Heisei 14 nendo zaisei toyushi keikaku* (Fiscal 2002 FILP plan). http://www.mof.go.jp/english/zaito/za2002.pdf.

Ministry of Posts and Telecommunications. 2000. *Heisei 13 nendo ni okeru yubin chokin shikin unyo keikaku* (Postal Savings Fund investment plan for fiscal 2001). http://www.yusei.go.jp/pressrelease/japanese/kawase/01224j301.html (posted 24 December 2000).

Noguchi, Taku, and Hiroo Sasaki. 1999. Tokushu hojin to ga hakkosuru hi-seifu-hosho-sai no "amnoku no seifu hosho" ni tsuite no ichi kosatsu (A study of "implicit government guarantee" of non-government-guaranteed bonds issued by special public corporations). *Financial Review* 49:167–88.

Postal Services Agency. 2001. *Heisei 14 nendo ni okeru yubin chokin shikin unyo keikaku* (Postal Savings Fund investment plan for fiscal 2002). http://www.yusei.go.jp/pressrelease/japanese/kawase/011224j301.html (posted 24 December 2001).

Wallison, Peter J. 2001. An American looks at FILP. Washington, D.C.: American Enterprise Institute. Manuscript.

Yoshida, Kazuo, and Sachio Konishi. 1996. *Tenkanki no zaisei toyushi* (Fiscal Investment and Loan Program in transition). Tokyo: Yuhikaku.

3

The Deteriorating Fiscal Situation and an Aging Population

Robert Dekle

Japan's deteriorating fiscal situation has attracted worldwide attention. If the situation does not improve, the resulting huge public debt is expected to sharply increase Japanese interest rates, lower Japan's international creditworthiness, and adversely affect the welfare of future generations. In this chapter, I assess what current Japanese government fiscal policies mean for the future of public debt and the economy in general, given the inevitable aging of the population.

Owing to a very weak domestic economy, which lowered tax revenues and raised government spending, Japan's fiscal balance has deteriorated dramatically. The budget, in surplus until 1992, turned negative in 1993, and the deficits have continued to worsen, reaching almost 11 percent of gross domestic product (GDP) in 1998. Debt ballooned: The government debt-GDP ratio increased by almost half from 1991 to 1997 and by another quarter in the two years after that. By 2000, Japan had the largest ratio among the Organization for Economic Co-operation and Development (OECD) member countries.

Japan's fiscal situation continues to look grim, especially given the demographic situation. Population aging is expected to slow economic growth and raise future government health care and social security expenditures. Projections of the country's population and the percentage of the total population that is elderly are plotted in figure 3.1 (Ministry of Health and Welfare 1998).

Robert Dekle is associate professor of economics at the University of Southern California.

I thank Magnus Blomström, Jennifer Corbett, Fumio Hayashi, Anil Kashyap, and other National Bureau of Economic Research (NBER) conference participants for helpful comments. I also thank Mr. Akira Furukawa for advice on data collection, and Larry Meissner for editing the manuscript. Any remaining errors are my own.

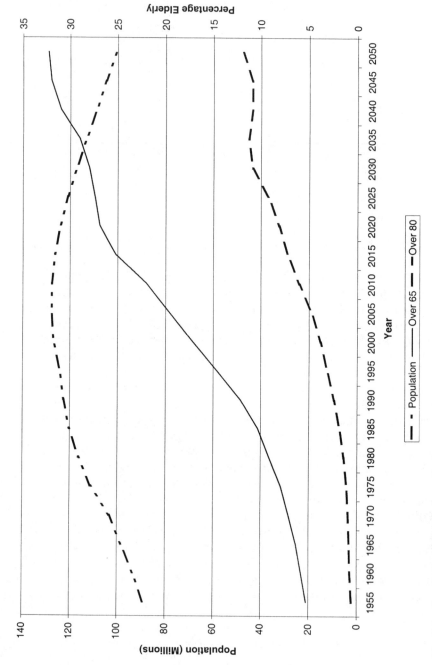

Fig. 3.1 Population and elderly projections

The population over sixty-five has grown rapidly and now stands at about 15 percent. By 2020, its percentage is expected to approach 25 percent, and by 2050, 33 percent. These rates of aging are much higher than for example in the United States, where only about 15 percent of the population will be over sixty-five by 2025.

This chapter first reviews how Japan got into its current fiscal mess during the 1990s. This is followed by an analysis of debt dynamics. With unchanged fiscal policies, Japan's public debt will rise to between 260 percent and 380 percent of GDP in 2020, and to between 700 percent and 1,300 percent in 2040—clearly unsustainable levels. For the debt to be sustainable, significant increases in taxes or cuts in government spending are necessary.

Next, the government's fiscal agendas are briefly discussed. The focus has been on spending cuts rather than tax increases. However, most of the proposed cuts were postponed or abandoned as the government sought to stimulate demand in light of the very weak domestic economy. The results of a simulation exercise that explicitly incorporates the effects of an aging Japanese population are then presented. In the simulation, I explicitly model the interplay between government fiscal policies and household and corporate behaviors. This is important, because fiscal policies clearly can affect private behavior, and these changes in private behavior may, in turn, influence the dynamics of government debt. The simulation shows that, absent cuts in government spending, for the government debt to be sustainable, taxes would need to increase from the current 28 percent of GDP to over 40 percent by 2020. The tax increases and the inevitable aging of the population are projected to sharply reduce household saving rates. As the labor force declines and the need to equip workers with capital decreases, corporate investment rates also are projected to fall.

3.1 The Current Japanese Fiscal Situation

Government saving declined and public investment rose in the 1990s (table 3.1). These trends were caused by the recession, as well as by structural changes. The recession and the decline in the rate of economic growth lowered tax revenues. Structural changes that worsened government saving included tax reforms that lowered tax elasticities and thus tax revenues, and the aging of the population, which raised social security and health care expenditures. In the 1990s the government also boosted public investment in an attempt to stimulate aggregate demand. These changes in government saving and public investment led to a sharp deterioration in government finances. The resulting increase in outstanding bonds has raised concerns about fiscal sustainability and calls for fiscal reform.

Table 3.1   Japanese Private and Government Saving, Investment, and Net Exports (% of GDP)

	Private Saving	Government Saving[a]	Private Investment[b]	Public Investment	Net Export Surplus
1955–1973	13.5	9.5	17.3	7.3	−1.5
1974–1979	26.3	3.1	20.7	9.2	−0.6
1980–1990	26.0	4.5	20.7	7.4	2.4
1991–1995	26.0	5.2	21.5	7.7	1.9
1996–1999	28.4	1.6	20.3	8.0	1.8

Source: Economic and Social Research Institute (1999, 2001).
[a]Includes net social security surplus.
[b]Includes plant and equipment, housing, and inventory investment.

3.1.1   Government Saving

Government saving can be divided into full-employment and cyclical components. In a recessionary environment, government spending usually increases because of higher unemployment and social welfare benefits. However, owing to the low cyclical variability of Japanese unemployment and social welfare benefits, government spending increases in Japan during the 1990s recession were capped. Also during recessions, tax revenues can decline because of lowered incomes. I estimate that during 1990–1999, Japan's full-employment government saving was about 2.6 percent of GDP, compared to an actual level of 2.0 percent, making the cyclical component −0.6 percent. Thus, much of the decline in government saving in the late 1990s was from structural factors, such as tax reductions, rather than from automatic stabilizers.[1]

Government saving also can be broken down into the social security surplus, the surplus in other categories, and health care expenditures (table 3.2). The social security surplus (benefits minus contributions) fell from about 1.3 percent of GDP in the early 1990s to about 0.4 percent in 1999 because of the recession (lowering contributions) and increase in the number of elderly (raising benefits). Government health care expenditures rose from about 3.6 percent of GDP in the early 1990s to about 4.3 percent in

---

1. I estimate full-employment government saving by regressing government saving on the output gap and a constant, using quarterly data from 1990 to 1999. I interpret the estimated value of the constant—which is the government saving rate when the output gap is equal to zero—as full-employment government saving. The estimated value of the constant equaled 2.6 percent.

Ihori, Nakazato, and Kawade (2002) also show that the acyclical component of government saving was small. They find that much of the decline in government saving can be attributed to the decline in trend output, rather than to the decline in acyclical output. The low cyclical variability of government saving is corroborated in an International Monetary Fund (IMF) study showing that a 1 percentage point increase in the output gap translated into an increase of the cyclical deficit by about 0.33 percent of GDP, which is about half of the deficit response in other OECD countries (Muhleisen 2000).

Table 3.2   **Overview of Government Finances (% of GDP)**

	1990	1991	1992	1993	1994	1995	1996	1997	1998	1999
Fiscal balance[a]	1.9	1.8	0.8	−2.4	−2.8	−4.1	−4.9	−3.7	−10.7	−7.0
Government saving	7.2	7.2	6.7	4.7	4.2	2.9	2.6	2.6	1.2	0.0
Social security surplus	1.3	1.7	1.6	1.4	1.2	1.2	1.1	1.2	0.8	0.4
Healthcare	−3.6	−3.5	−3.7	−3.8	−3.9	−4.1	−4.2	−4.1	−4.2	−4.3
Other surplus	9.5	9.0	8.8	7.1	7.0	5.9	5.6	5.5	4.6	3.9
Gross debt	65.1	64.7	67.6	72.7	78.4	85.4	91.8	97.5	108.5	120.5
Net debt A[b]	7.3	6.4	12.3	10.1	12.1	16.9	21.6	27.9	38.0	44.4
Net debt B[a]	35.4	35.5	42.9	42.8	46.6	52.5	57.7	64.6	75.9	84.9

Source: Economic and Social Research Institute (2001).

[a]Government saving plus net land purchases and net gift and inheritance taxes minus public investment.

[b]Including social security system assets.

[c]Excluding social security system assets.

1999, mainly owing to the increase in the elderly, who use most of the hospital services. However, the health care expenditure-GDP ratio in Japan is still smaller than in the United States (6.6 percent) and Germany (7.7 percent). The remaining category of government saving includes such items as education, defense, and policing and firefighting. Saving in this category declined sharply from 9.5 percent of GDP to 3.9 percent because of the fall in income and consumption tax revenues.

3.1.2   Public Investment

During the 1990s, the Japanese government passed ten stimulus packages in an attempt to jump-start the stalled economy. The most important component of these packages was public works, which are included in public investment. However, the actual increases in the late 1990s were rather moderate compared to the prominent and headline grabbing role of public works in the stimulus packages.

There are two reasons actual public works fell short of announced levels. First, the central government assigned roughly two-thirds of the increased public works spending to local governments without providing a commensurate increase in funding. The capacity of local governments to expand public investment was affected by their poor financial situation, and the continued rise in public investment has increasingly been financed through local bond issues. The amount of outstanding local government bonds increased from 12 percent of GDP in 1990 to 22 percent in 1997. Many local governments surpassed the legally allowed threshold of bonds outstanding and were put under bond issuance restrictions by the central government. Second, some of the public investment funds provided by the stimulus packages remained unused because of poor project implementation. Ishii and Wada (1998) calculated that only 60 percent to 70 percent of the packages' public works had been translated into additional demand by the during late 1990s.[2]

3.1.3 Government Debt and Liabilities

The late 1990s decline in government saving and rise in public investment led to a surge in government debt, as shown in table 3.2. The fiscal surplus declined almost continuously in the 1990s until reaching about minus 11 percent in 1998. The 1999 improvement has not carried over in the 2000s. Correspondingly, the ratio of debt to GDP has risen sharply. By international standards, Japan's *gross* debt-GDP in 1999 was the highest among the Group of Seven (G7) countries—Italy's was 115 percent and the United States' was 62 percent.

The fiscal balance as a percentage of GDP is less than the difference between the government saving ratio and the public investment ratio (table 3.1, column [2] minus column [4]) by about two percentage points, mainly because of the inclusion of net government land purchases in the fiscal balance. During the 1990s, the government bought significant amounts of land from the private sector to prop up land prices.

Because of the partly funded nature of the Japanese pension system, as well as the government's major role in financial intermediation, the Japanese government holds significant assets, keeping *net* debt-GDP at a moderate level and lower than in other G7 countries. However, the assets of the social security system are more than offset by future pension obligations. Therefore, some, including the OECD and the IMF, exclude social security net assets when assessing Japan's debt situation. As a result, Japan's *net* debt *excluding social security net assets*, at 85 percent, is significantly higher than the United States' 60 percent, and Germany's 53 percent.

3.2 Projecting the Debt Burden

Table 3.3 depicts the dynamics of the debt-GDP ratio under three scenarios about tax, public investment, and spending policies and two assumptions regarding real interest rates. In scenario 1, current policies continue and the debt dynamics are clearly unsustainable: Even under optimistic interest rate expectations, debt exceeds 250 percent of GDP by 2015. (I define "unsustainable" as meaning that the debt-GDP ratio goes to infinity.) Scenario 2, like scenario 1, assumes government spending and public investment policies remain unchanged, but also assumes the government sufficiently raises taxes so that the debt-GDP ratio stabilizes and

---

2. Tracking public works budgets in Japan is tricky because so much of the spending is outside the regular budget of the central government. Thus, looking just at the general expenditures data there actually were declines each year from fiscal 1994 to 1999.

Table 3.3 **Debt-to-GDP Ratio Dynamics (% of GDP)**

Year	Taxes	Public Investment	Government Spending	Debt If 3%[a]	Debt If 6%[b]
			Scenario 1: Unchanged Government Policies		
2000	28	8	25	45	45
2005	28	8	26	80	91
2010	28	8	28	127	157
2015	28	8	28	191	257
2020	28	8	26	262	381
2025	28	8	27	337	508
2030	28	8	27	428	715
2035	28	8	33	540	949
2040	28	8	30	690	1263

Year	Public Investment	Government Spending	Taxes If 3%[a]	Debt If 3%[b]	Taxes If 6%[b]	Debt If 6%[b]
			Scenario 2: Increased Taxes			
2000	8	25	28	45	28	45
2005	8	26	31	81	31	91
2010	8	28	34	111	34	140
2015	8	28	39	141	47	200
2020	8	26	40	149	49	202
2025	8	27	41	141	50	186
2030	8	27	41	134	50	166
2035	8	33	44	130	51	143
2040	8	30	44	129	53	129

Year	Taxes	Public Investment	Government Spending	Debt If 3%[a]	Debt If 6%[b]
			Scenario 3: Cuts in Spending and Investment		
2000	28	8	25	45	45
2005	28	3	22	71	81
2010	28	3	24	67	92
2015	28	3	24	72	116
2020	28	3	22	74	145
2025	28	3	23	70	175
2030	28	3	23	69	213
2035	28	3	27	72	264
2040	28	3	25	93	346

[a]Assuming a 3 percent real interest rate on government debt.
[b]Assuming a 6 percent real interest rate on government debt.

eventually declines. Stabilization with 3 percent interest rates comes around 2015–2025, at 140 percent to 150 percent, and with 6 percent interest is at just over 200 percent in the 2010s.

As described later, the government is undertaking fiscal reform, and is planning deep cuts in spending and public investment. Scenario 3 assumes the reforms are carried out. This leads to dramatically improved debt dynamics. Still, the debt-GDP ratio continues to grow, albeit significantly more slowly than in scenario 1, as taxes are not sufficient to cover the government's total expenditures (including the interest payments on the outstanding debt). Note that at 6 percent interest the debt ratio increases steadily but at 3 percent it is fairly stable during 2005–2035. This is because at 6 percent interest, debt grows much faster than GDP.

At 3 percent interest rates, spending cuts (scenario 3) produce lower ratios than increased taxes (scenario 2) but, at 6 percent rates, the ratio in scenario 3 is higher by 2030. The remainder of this section more fully explains the scenarios.

3.2.1   Assumptions

Because unfunded future social security liabilities are already accounted for in the scenarios, the *net* figure of 45 percent is taken as the initial ratio of debt to GDP. The dynamics of the debt-GDP ratio are highly sensitive to assumptions regarding the real interest rate and the real GDP growth rate. Other things being equal, the higher the real interest rate, the higher the ratio; and, the higher the real GDP growth rate, the lower the ratio. Consistent with most forecasters' projections of real GDP growth for the next twenty years of between 1 percent and 1.5 percent annually (Japan Center of Economic Research [JCER] 2001), the analysis here assumes an average of 1.2 percent annually between 2000 and 2040.

There are two real interest rate assumptions. The first is 3 percent because, since the early 1980s, Japanese real interest rates have averaged about 3 percent and that rate is used in other studies to project the path of future Japanese government deficits (IMF 2000; Jinno and Kaneko 2000). However, in the future, the Japanese government may no longer be able to borrow at such a low rate and may have to borrow at higher international real rates. Thus, the second assumption is 6 percent, which reflects the average real cost of borrowing in international financial markets in the 1990s. Note that since 2000, the nominal interest rate on five- to six-year maturity Japanese Government Bonds (JGBs) has been close to 4 percent. Because inflation rates are essentially zero, the real rate on Japanese government borrowing is now close to 4 percent.

3.2.2   The Scenarios

Scenario 1, the baseline, is that future government policies essentially remain unchanged. With regards to tax and public investment policies, the

Table 3.4   Projected Government Spending, 2000–2040

	1995 ¥ Billions			% of GDP[a]			
	Social Security	Health Care	Education	Social Security	Health Care	Education	Total[b]
2000	57,667	27,271	16,327	10.7	5.3	3.2	24.8
2005	65,265	28,471	15,634	11.9	5.4	2.9	25.8
2010	74,032	29,462	15,445	13.9	5.7	3.1	28.2
2015	78,318	30,550	15,067	14.1	5.7	2.8	28.2
2020	78,903	30,659	14,689	13.2	5.1	2.4	26.3
2025	79,098	30,089	13,680	14.2	5.2	2.3	27.3
2030	79,683	29,392	12,923	14.2	5.2	2.3	27.3
2035	81,630	28,764	12,167	18.3	6.3	2.7	32.9
2040	81,046	28,407	11,915	16.1	5.7	2.4	29.8

[a]The GDP projections are from the simulation model in Dekle (2002).
[b]Includes 5.6 percent each year for "other spending" (i.e., for defense, policing, administration, etc.).

assumption is that the government keeps the tax-GDP and public investment-GDP ratios at current (average 1996–1999) levels. With regards to government spending policies, projections are more complicated, as population aging affects future government social security and health care expenditures. It is assumed that the government keeps age-specific expenditure patterns for social security, health care, and education constant at current (average 1996–1999) real levels. That is, if the average sixty-seven-year old receives ¥190,000 in government health care in 2000, the average sixty-seven-year old in 2035 will receive the same inflation-adjusted amount. In addition, it is assumed that eligibility for social security remains at sixty, and for old age health care benefits remains at seventy. Other government spending, mainly defense, policing, and administration, are assumed to always equal the average 1996–1999 ratio to GDP of 5.6 percent.[3]

Under these spending assumptions, table 3.4 shows the projections of total government spending in 1995 yen and as a share of projected GDP. The shift in the age distribution towards the elderly significantly raises government spending. In particular, in 2035 the population over sixty-five increases significantly, leading to a spike in social security and health care spending. These spending projections (after rounding) are used directly in scenarios 1 and 2.

3. For social security, I divided average social security expenditures in 1996–1999 by the population over age sixty. For health care, I allocate average health care spending in 1996–1999 to different ages, using the age-specific expenditure patterns reported by in Ishi (2000). For education, I divide average education spending in 1996–1999 by the population aged five to twenty.

In scenario 3, in 2015, the age of eligibility for social security is raised to sixty-five and for old-age health care benefits, to seventy-five. Other spending is reduced by 10 percent in 2005. These changes in social security and in old-age health care correspond roughly to what are actually included in the fiscal reform agendas. Public investment is cut especially sharply to 3 percent of GDP by 2005—the level prevailing in the United States (Muhleisen 2000).

3.3   The True Size of Government Liabilities

Because of unfunded liabilities, the government's true net obligations today may be substantially higher than the reported 45 percent of GDP. In addition to unfunded social security obligations, there are three main sources of unfunded liabilities. These are potential losses on government assets, explicit government guarantees of private sector lending, and *implicitly* guaranteed private sector loans.

Potential losses on government assets are significant. A portion of the government's assets represent soft loans that may not be repaid. Many large public or joint public-private infrastructure projects financed from Fiscal Investment and Loan Program (FILP) loans generate less revenue than budgeted, which may imply significant contingent liabilities of the government. Doi and Hoshi (chapter two of this volume) show that many public corporations and local governments carrying out infrastructure projects are essentially insolvent. They estimate the amount of potential government bailout of the FILP and the local governments as over 15 percent of the 2000 GDP.

The second source of unfunded liabilities is explicit government guarantees of private sector lending. Explicit guarantees are extended by the FILP and other government entities to encourage lending by private financial institutions. Examples are guarantees of bank deposits by the Deposit Insurance Corporation and of lending by credit cooperatives to small- and medium-enterprises. Although these do not entail fresh government lending, should the guaranteed loans not be repaid, the government must cover them from its budget. The total amount of outstanding government-guaranteed bonds and loans amounted to about 10 percent of GDP in 2000. Although historically only about 1 percent of such loans are never repaid, the percentage could soar if the Japanese economy worsens (Bayoumi 1998).

In addition to explicit government guarantees, there are *implicitly* guaranteed private sector loans. Historically, the Japanese government has shown a willingness to make good the irrecoverable loans of private financial institutions. In 2000, public funds spent recapitalizing the banking system and included in government spending totaled about ¥8 trillion (2 percent of GDP). This willingness represents implicit guarantees, and these guarantees are (unfunded) contingent liabilities of the government. Despite the large amount of public funds already spent, Fukao (chapter one of this volume) argues that the Japanese government may have to expend additional funds to recapitalize the private banking system within the next two or three years. In that case, the cost to taxpayers would be equal to the estimated losses on problem loans minus the loan loss reserves of the banking sector. Fukao calculates that this cost to taxpayers would be about 2 percent of GDP (¥7.6 trillion at March 2001).

3.4 Fiscal Reform Measures

To restrain future increases in the government's debt and in other liabilities, the government proposed several fiscal reform measures in the 1990s. However, most of the measures were postponed or abandoned as the government sought to stimulate demand in light of the very weak domestic economy. The 1997 Fiscal Structural Reform Law, with its goal of eliminating fiscal deficits by 2003, is the most significant measure.

The main instruments in the 1997 law were cuts in government consumption and investment, rather than tax increases. Public investment spending was to be cut by 7 percent in 1998, with zero nominal growth until 2001; and energy, education, and overseas development assistance were to be cut by 10 percent in 1998, with annual reductions until 2001 (Ishi 2000, 149). However, with the severe recession of 1997, fiscal consolidation was put on hold, and a wide range of pump-priming measures were introduced. In particular, rather than declining, public investment for 1998 was increased by over 10 percent.

Health care and social security were areas where the 1997 law had an effect. In 1997, the contribution rate and copayments by patients for government health insurance schemes were increased sharply (Ishi 2000). In particular, patients aged seventy and above are required to pay a fixed proportion (10 percent) of their medical costs. The government also capped prescription drug prices, which are very high in Japan.

In 2000, a social security reform bill based on the 1997 law passed the Diet. The bill contains provisions to cut lifetime benefits by about 20 percent. Specifically, benefits for new retirees will be cut by 5 percent; beginning in 2013, the age of eligibility will be raised gradually from sixty to sixty-five; and benefits will be subject to an earnings test. Analysts have estimated that these reforms will reduce government unfunded social security liabilities from the current 60 percent of GDP to 30 percent of GDP (IMF 2000).

The government is planning to implement further cuts once the economy recovers fully. A political commitment has been made to cap government deficit bond issues at ¥30 trillion (6 percent) of GDP in 2002. Although deficit bonds reflect only a portion of total government borrowing, this ceiling should help lower future fiscal deficits.

As stipulated in the 1997 law, public investment is due for further cuts. Criticism has been directed at the economic value of public works projects, as well as contracting procedures. To address the efficiency issues, new cost-benefit guidelines for reviewing projects were announced. Contracting procedures also have been reformed. Public works projects in fiscal 2002 (ends March 2003) were scheduled to be cut by 10 percent, although it is unclear if the cuts will materialize. The government intends to change the form of public works from traditional construction projects to broader social infrastructure investment. This includes environmental and energy-related projects, telecommunications networks, scientific research, nursing homes, and the like.

With regards to health care, contribution rates and copayments, especially by the elderly, are to increase further. The stated goal is to restrict the growth of medical costs of the elderly to no more than the rate of inflation. In this regard, the Diet has just passed a law to increase the health care copayment ratio from 20 percent to 30 percent. The age of eligibility for elderly medical care eventually will also be raised from seventy to seventy-five. Further cuts are also planned in social security. There are even suggestions that average benefits be reduced by another 40 percent to avoid large increases in future contribution rates (Sakurai 1998).

3.5   Interaction with Private Behavior

The calculations of Japanese government debt reported in table 3.3 implicitly assume that private behavior is unaffected by government fiscal policies. However, in reality, fiscal policies clearly influence private behavior, and changes in private behavior may, in turn, affect the dynamics of government debt. For example, government taxation can alter the path of household saving and corporate investment that, in turn, can change tax collections. To better project the dynamics of government debt under an aging population, the interplay between fiscal policy and household and corporate behavior should be accounted for. To this end, I have constructed a simulation model.

3.5.1   A Simulation Model

In Dekle (2002), I projected the path of the government budget, together with the path of private saving and investment in Japan, using a formal dynamic economic growth model. Admittedly, the assumptions underlying the model's projections are somewhat special, but they are plausible and provide a fairly rigorous basis for analyzing policy implications.

Specifically, I closely followed Cutler et al. (1990) in examining the impact of changing demographics on government debt, private investment, and saving. I simulated the growth model using the future path of demographics, summarized by the support ratio, which is the ratio of the labor force to the total population. The support ratio is projected to fall by 20 percent in the next fifty years.[4]

In the model, firms maximize profits using labor, private capital, and public capital as inputs to produce output (GDP). Firms are blessed with technical progress that raises the efficiency of labor by 1.2 percent a year. Private capital can be loaned or borrowed at a constant international rental (real interest) rate of 6 percent.

I show that, if the support ratio is constant, output per capita grows at 1.2 percent per year. A declining support ratio, however, implies output per capita growth of less than 1.2 percent, as there are fewer workers to support the population.

Households are assumed to maximize not only their own welfare, but also the welfare of their children. Preferences are such that households desire to keep consumption per capita growing at a constant rate (consumption smoothing). The model shows that, by borrowing from international capital markets, households can indefinitely maintain growth in consumption per capita of 1.2 percent. Thus, although consumption per capita grows at 1.2 percent, output per capita grows at less than 1.2 percent when the support ratio is declining. Thus, a declining support ratio raises the ratio of consumption to output and lowers the private saving rate.

In the model, the government performs three actions, always taking into account the effect of these actions on private behavior. First, it supplies goods and services to households in the form of social security benefits, health care, and other services. Government expenditures of this form are assumed to be determined by the age structure of the population, and the time path of these expenditures is taken as given (from table 3.4).

Second, the government carries out public investment to supply public capital to firms. The government is assumed to choose the time path of public capital optimally, taking into account the offsetting effects of this public capital on GDP growth and on the public debt burden.

Third, the government levies a tax on households to pay for its spending and public investment, and this tax imposes efficiency losses on households. Given these efficiency losses, the model shows that the government will choose to levy a tax that is not fluctuating and is growing at the same 1.2 percent annual rate as consumption (tax smoothing). For the government to remain solvent, the present value of these taxes must be at least as large as the current stock of public debt plus the present value of all future government spending and public investment. That is, if government tax revenues are insufficient to cover government spending today, then tax revenues must exceed government spending in the future.

---

4. That is, LF /POP $= \sum_{i=20}^{64} N_i / \sum_{i=1}^{99} N_i$, where N_i is the number of people of age i, LF is the labor force, and POP is the total population. Dekle (2002) can be downloaded from my web site: http://www.usc.edu/dept/LAS/economics/Pages/faculty/fac_pages/web_dekle.htm.

3.6   Projections of Government Debt

The path of government debt and of private saving and investment from 2000 to 2040 are presented in table 3.5, using the results of the model. Under tax smoothing, taxes per capita increase at a constant rate, while output per capita grows at a slower rate; thus, the tax-GDP ratio rises over time. However, the actual tax rate (28 percent of GDP) in the starting year (2000) is lower than the 33 percent necessitated by tax smoothing and the requirement that the government be solvent. To satisfy the government's solvency constraint, taxes per capita are allowed to increase more rapidly between 2000 and 2015, and then increases in taxes per capita are smoothed from 2015 onward. By 2040, tax rates need to increase to almost 50 percent of GDP for the government to recoup its current outstanding debt, projected future spending (from table 3.4), and projected future public investment (table 3.5).

Government saving rates rise from about 1 percent to 2 percent of GDP in 2000 to about 10 percent in 2020, owing to the increased tax receipts. Government saving rates decline somewhat in 2035 because of increases in social security and health care spending caused by the spike in the over-sixty-five population in 2035. Because of falling public investment and high government saving, the fiscal surplus (government saving minus public investment) turns positive after 2020, and rises thereafter. Thus, the decline in the government net debt-GDP ratio is fairly rapid between 2020 and 2040.

Private saving rates are projected to fall a few percentage points until 2010, and then fall rapidly from 2010 to 2040. This pattern is a result of declines in the support ratio and increases in tax rates, which reduces dispos-

Table 3.5   Projections of Government Debt and of Private Saving and Investment Rates (% of GDP)

Year	Support Ratio[a]	Net Debt	Government Tax Rate	Government Saving	Private Saving	Private Investment	Government Investment
2000	0.63	45	28	1	28	20	8
2005	0.61	88	31	0	28	20	8
2010	0.59	128	38	2	26	19	7
2015	0.57	153	43	6	18	18	7
2020	0.56	155	45	10	15	18	7
2025	0.55	140	45	9	13	17	6
2030	0.54	122	46	10	11	17	6
2035	0.54	102	47	7	12	16	6
2040	0.52	89	49	13	6	16	6

Source: Dekle (2002).
[a]Ratio of labor force to total population, from Japanese government estimates (Ministry of Health and Welfare 1998).

able income. Although consumption per capita grows at a constant 1.2 percent, output per capita grows at a slower rate (as the support ratio declines), thus lowering saving rates. In effect, consumers are seeking to smooth their consumption when income is growing very slowly by lowering their saving rates.

As the labor force shrinks, the need to equip workers with capital equipment decreases, and both private and public investment rates decline. The private investment rate declines from 20 percent today to about 16 percent in 2040; the public investment rate declines from 8 percent today to about 6 percent in 2040.

3.6.1 Comparison with Earlier Projections

Only a few studies have examined the interplay between fiscal policy and private saving and investment in Japan. As in my model, these earlier studies generally predict worsening government budget deficits unless there is significant fiscal reform, and declining saving and investment rates as the Japanese population ages. These studies start from the premise that the future path of Japanese government debt is unsustainable unless there is significant fiscal reform. Their reform scenarios are shown in table 3.6.

The Economic Planning Agency (1998) study envisages significant cuts in future social security benefits and moderate increases in payroll taxes. Consequently, government saving rises, while private saving falls sharply as a result of the population aging. The IMF (2000) study envisages reductions in social security benefits, sharp cuts in public investment, and in-

Table 3.6   **Earlier Projections of Japanese Government Debt and Saving and Investment Fiscal Reform Scenarios (% of GDP)**

	2005	2010	2025	2050
Economic Planning Agency (1998)				
Government saving	−1.1	n.a.	−0.5	0.3
Tax rate	32.6	n.a.	34.5	35.4
Private saving	31.5	n.a.	22.6	15.2
Total investment	32.8	n.a.	25.0	20.2
International Monetary Fund (2000)				
Net government debt[a]	62.0	62.0	50.0	30.0
Fiscal balance[b]	−6.0	2.0	3.0	0.0
Private saving	22.0	23.0	22.0	22.0
Japan Center for Economic Research (2001)				
Gross debt	149	163	187	n.a.
Fiscal balance	−6.0	−5.0	−2.1	n.a.
Tax rate	46.0	47.3	49.9	n.a.

Note: n.a. = not available.

[a]Government gross debt minus gross assets.

[b]Government saving minus public investment.

creases in payroll and consumption taxes. Consequently, fiscal balances improve dramatically and the debt-GDP ratio first stabilizes, then plummets. A special feature of the IMF model is that, even when income declines, households do not decumulate their assets; thus, the fall in private saving is moderated. Finally, the Japan Center for Economic Research (JCER; 2001) envisages sharp increases in taxes and cuts in public investment. Consequently, fiscal balance improves, although debt-GDP continues to increase slightly, owing to sluggish GDP growth.

3.7   Conclusion

The prospects for improvements in the Japanese fiscal situation are grim unless the government carries out significant fiscal reform. For example, under unchanged spending policies, taxes would need to increase from the current 28 percent of GDP to over 40 percent by 2020 for the government to be solvent. Japanese citizens should brace themselves for painful adjustments in the near future, in the form of lower public services and higher taxes.

A resumption of strong growth in real GDP would reduce the need for spending and tax adjustments. For example, if real interest rates are 3 percent, a real GDP growth rate of slightly in excess of 3 percent can imply falling debt-GDP ratios. The analysis here has assumed that real growth averages just 1.2 percent per year form 2000 to 2040. This assumes labor-augmenting technical progress of about 1.2 percent per year, or total factor productivity growth (TFP) growth of 2.0 percent per year. A TFP growth of 2.0 percent is actually an assumption on the high side, as it is about equal to Japan's average TFP growth between 1970 and 1990, and Japan has not been as innovative it was then (Branstetter and Nakamura, chapter seven of this volume). The dramatic 0.8 percent annual decline in the labor force caused by the aging of the population is what lowers GDP growth from 2.0 percent to 1.2 percent.

Thus, one way to increase GDP growth is to raise the labor supply. Ono and Rebick (chapter eight of this volume) argue for removals of structural impediments that restrict the movement of labor between firms and discourage women from participating to a greater extent. Another possibility that has received scant attention until now is to promote immigration into Japan. Further studies on the impact of increased foreign immigration on Japanese growth, saving, and the government debt are of high priority.

An aging population does not necessarily mean that Japan will sink into international oblivion. Certainly, Japanese policymakers are aware not only of the problems associated with aging, but also of a slew of proposals to address the problems, both directly and indirectly, through removing the other impediments to growth discussed in this volume and elsewhere.

References

Bayoumi, Tamin. 1998. The Japanese fiscal system and fiscal transparency. In *Structural change in Japan,* ed. B. Aghevli, Guy Meredith, and Tamin Bayoumi, 164–91. Washington, D.C.: International Monetary Fund.

Cutler, David, James Poterba, Loise Sheiner, and Lawrence Summers. 1990. An aging society: Opportunity or challenge? *Brookings Papers on Economic Activity,* Issue no. 1:1–55. Washington, D.C.: Brookings Institution.

Dekle, Robert. 2002. A population aging in Japan: Its impact on future saving, investment, and budget deficits. University of Southern California, Department of Economics. Working Paper. Available at http://www.usc.edu/dept/LAS/economics/Pages/faculty/fac_pages/web_dekle.htm.

Economic and Social Research Institute, Government of Japan. 1999. *Annual report on the National Accounts.* Tokyo: Ministry of Finance Printing Office.

———. 2001. *Annual report on the National Accounts.* Tokyo: Ministry of Finance Printing Office.

———. 2002. *Annual report on the National Accounts.* Tokyo: Ministry of Finance Printing Office.

Economic Planning Agency. 1998. An economic analysis of Japan's aging society. *Keizai Bunseki* 24 (September): 138–147.

Ihori, Toshihiko, Toru Nakazato, and Masumi Kawade. 2002. Japan's fiscal policies in the 1990s. University of Tokyo, Department of Economics. Mimeograph.

International Monetary Fund (IMF). 2000. *World Economic Outlook.* Washington, D.C.: IMF.

Ishi, Hiromitsu. 2000. *Making fiscal policy in Japan.* Oxford: Oxford University Press.

Ishii, Hiroko, and Erica Wada. 1998. *Local government spending: Solving the mystery of Japanese fiscal packages.* Institute for International Economics Working Paper no. 98-5.

Japan Center for Economic Research (JCER). 2001. *Long-run forecasts of the Japanese economy.* Tokyo: JCER.

Jinno, Naohiko, and Masaru Kaneko. 2000. *Zaisei hakai o kuitomeru* (Stopping the deterioration in fiscal budgets). Tokyo: Iwanami.

Ministry of Health and Welfare. 1998. *Population projections for Japan, medium variant.* Tokyo: Ministry of Finance Printing Office.

Muhleisen, Martin. 2000. Sustainable fiscal policies for an aging population. In *Selected issues, Japan,* ed. Charles Collyns and Tamin Bayoumi, 134–162. Washington, D.C.: International Monetary Fund.

Sakurai, Yoshiko. 1998. *Nihon no kiki* (Japan's crisis). Tokyo: Shinchosha.

4

Mismeasurement of the CPI

Kenn Ariga and Kenji Matsui

As the Japanese economy continues to experience negative or near-zero growth under weak demand, many economists and policy makers are increasingly concerned over the accuracy of many key economic statistics. In particular, the accuracy of the consumer price index (CPI) has become a central issue.

The annual CPI registered declines in 1998 through 2001. In early 2002, the data indicate the possibility that deflation might be somewhat accelerating. While the economy seems to be floating at the edge of a deflationary spiral, many suspect and are worried that prices are falling faster than CPI statistics suggest. Supporting these concerns are such things as Seiyu, a large supermarket chain, publishing an index showing how its own prices had fallen much faster than the official CPI.

If CPI data contain significant measurement errors, such that the downward trend is not measured with accuracy, the cost of such bias can be substantial. Consider, for example, potential ramifications on the heated debate over monetary policy, especially inflation targeting. The very idea of

Kenn Ariga is professor of economics at the Kyoto Institute of Economic Research. Kenji Matsui is associate professor of business administration at Yokohama National University.

The authors benefited greatly from valuable comments and suggestions by Albert Ando, Jenny Corbett, David Flath, Fumio Hayashi, Yasushi Iwamoto, Anil Kashyap, Robert Lipsey, Shigenori Shiratsuka, and other participants in the National Bureau of Economic Research (NBER) Japan Project. We also wish to thank Albert Ando and Robert Lipsey, as well as Ignazio Visco and Enrico Giovanni at the Organization for Economic Co-operation and Development (OECD) for helping locate data on statistical programs of OECD countries. Special thanks are due Mr. Masato Aida and others at Japan's Statistics Bureau for their replies to our queries regarding the price survey procedures used in the consumer price index (CPI) and for data on the educational background of statistical staff. Finally, Larry Meisner's superb professional editing has made the presentation in the final version far clearer. The authors are of course responsible for any errors in the paper.

inflation targeting hinges critically on timely and accurate measurement of the inflation rate. Because retail price data collected by Sōmusho (Ministry of Public Management, Home Affairs, Posts, and Telecommunications) for the CPI are also used for the national income statistics, mismeasurements in the CPI can lead to serious errors in gross domestic product (GDP) statistics as well.

In general, the potential cost of incorrect or absent measurements in official statistics can be substantial and are not limited to affecting policy making. Many economists in the financial sector and consulting firms have voiced concern over the noise and inconsistency in the quarterly GDP estimates. The discrepancy between preliminary and final GDP figures is suspected to originate in the inconsistency in several dimensions of the methodologies employed in the two estimates.[1]

Given the critical role of key economic indicators such as GDP and CPI, it is not surprising that large and frequent swings in official statistics can create visible commotions in financial markets and other sectors of the economy. The potential costs due to problems in the official statistics are widespread and far reaching. For example, a key part of the structural reform advanced by the Koizumi government is job creation in services and information technologies (IT). However, there are no official statistics to guide such policy, as none of the published data report job creation by start-ups or job destruction from closing of establishments.

To be fair, there are many good, even wonderful, things to say about economic statistics in Japan. There is extensive and comprehensive coverage on a wide spectrum of topics, especially those collected on an establishment basis. Some are quite exotic and probably not available anywhere else in the world; many are collected by nongovernment institutions. Moreover, data are comprehensive, geographically and otherwise. Although the country consists of many small islands, most government statistics cover virtually the entire population.

There are problems, of course, some rather serious in nature and quantitatively important. In this paper, we point out several underlying factors responsible for the problems in official statistics in Japan. In doing this, however, the focus is on the CPI. Most of the problems raised by the Boskin Commission for the U.S. CPI are found in Japan's CPI. In many areas, the potential ramifications seem even more important in Japan.

The CPI is an important and popular statistic and is used for many different purposes. The CPI inflation rate is one of the key indicators for cyclical fluctuations of the economy. The CPI also is used as the bench-

---

1. For example, in the preliminary GDP figures, private fixed investment growth for the year 2000 initially was reported as 4.6 percent, this became 9.3 percent in the final figure. For a brief review of the quality-of-statistics issue and a response by the Economic and Social Research Institute, Cabinet Office, see the website http://www5.cao.go.jp/2000/g/0602g-gdpcoments.html.

mark in many wage-setting negotiations and public pensions are linked to it. (Although, for political reasons, the pensions have not been adjusted downward to reflect the sizable decline in the CPI.) Recent macroeconomic developments in Japan also add to the significance of studying potential mismeasurements in CPI in that the stagnant economy has been experiencing zero or negative inflation rates for prolonged periods, an experience that is rather unique and which might shed new light on issues of measurement biases in CPI.

The choice of the CPI is partly because of the authors' background: In past research we have used disaggregated price data as well as price indices such as CPI or wholesale price index (WPI) and therefore we are concerned about their accuracy. More important is the depth of the analysis that can be achieved. Although GDP is by far the most popular and important statistic, it is a secondary one based on a large variety of primary statistics. That means the potential sources of biases and other problems are simply too great to be thoroughly analyzed in a single paper.[2]

Moreover, the CPI shares with other major official statistics the underlying causes of the problems in the Japanese official statistics system. We hope this investigation of the CPI helps elucidate the nature of the problems commonly found in many important official economic statistics of Japan.

The paper is organized as follows: First we offer an overview of official statistics in Japan, point out several important deficiencies, and then review key issues in the CPI. Using this background, we investigate potential problems in several major aspects of the CPI. These include data collection procedures (including how discounted prices are handled), services, quality change and new products, and aggregation issues (substitution across time, brands, and stores). We then look at a discrepancy between CPI and WPI that probably relates to differences in how quality adjustments are made and some hitherto neglected aspects of the measurement problem, relating to shopping and storage behaviors. From this analysis we offer a tentative assessment of the magnitude of the CPI inflation rate bias and draw some suggestions for improving the statistics in general and the CPI in particular.

A cautionary note on the distinction between potential measurement errors in general and bias in the inflation rate: Measurement errors contaminate the CPI, but they do not imply systematic bias in the measured inflation rate, or changes in the cost-of-living index. For example, consider medical and health care services. Although we believe there are serious

---

2. For the revised System of National Account (SNA) in Japan, see the website http://www.esri.cao.go.jp/en/sna/020612/outline.pdf. Ando (2002) explains in great detail the problems he encountered in SNA data as he investigated the cause of the long stagnation of the Japanese economy. For those not familiar with Japanese economic statistics, Matsuoka and Rose (1994) provide a gateway into major economic statistics in Japan.

measurement errors and under-representation problems, it is unclear if and in which direction they affect the measured inflation rate. Indeed, several indices shown in Iwamoto (2000) indicate higher, and others, lower, inflation in medical expenditure than does the CPI.

4.1 Overview of Official Statistics

Japanese official statistics fall into three broad groups based on how they are created. Primary statistics collected for specific purposes (*chōsa-tōkei*), primary statistics collected as part of the regular tasks of governmental offices (*gyōmu-tōkei*), and processed statistics derived from primary data. Primary data on exports and imports (Custom Clearance Statistics) compiled by the Ministry of Finance (MOF) is an important example of the second group. The National Accounts are by the far the most well known of the last group.

A more important distinction among *chōsa-tōkei* is based on legal status. The core series of official statistics are called designated statistics (*shitei-tōkei*). There also are approved statistics, so named because they are approved by the Minister of Sōmusho.

Designated and approved statistics have special status in the law. Specifically, the law stipulates clearly that government bodies collecting these statistics are endowed with authority to request and enforce proper cooperation from the public chosen to be surveyed. At the same time, the law sets rather rigid restrictions on the use and dissemination of information so obtained. This allows the data collection agency to conduct surveys and census in a way that private bodies without such authorization cannot hope to accomplish. In short, compared to other official statistics, these two types of statistics are given priority in data collection and a more stringent set of rules governs their use and dissemination. Table 4.1 lists the number of designated and approved statistics by the ministry responsible for collecting them along with that ministry's staff and budget for statistics.

4.1.1   Staffing and Collecting

Officially, the Statistics Bureau of Sōmusho is responsible for coordinating the activities of the statistics sections of all ministries. It is apparent, however, that the system is highly decentralized and each ministry seems to act on its own in creating, collecting, abandoning, and publishing data. Which ministry is responsible for a series often is a historical accident, but ministries seem unwilling to reshuffle assignments. For example, Sōmusho conducts the Survey of Research and Development, the National Tax Agency collects data on salaries in the private sector, and the Bank of Japan (technically not even a part of the government) compiles the WPI and corporate service price index (CSPI).

Table 4.2 displays data for the U.S. federal government comparable to

Table 4.1   **Major Official Statistical Series, 2000**

Ministry	Designated[a]	Approved[b]	1999 Budget (¥ millions)[c]	Staff
Agriculture	8	119	13,032	5,979[d]
Education	4	50	256	102
Finance	2	8	144	86
Health and labor	8	102	5,758	465
Land and transport	7	68	4,169	124
Public management (Sōmusho)	14	59	14,494	1,617
Trade and industry	17	47	5,867	381
Others	0	27	1,360	50
Total	62	480	45,080	8,804[e]

Source: Sōmusho (1999, 2000b).

[a]We include only those designated statistical series that are currently collected on a periodic basis, thus excluding those for which new data collection has been stopped. In effect, the latter series are no longer used, primarily because of the lack of interest (they retain the special status only because the use of the original data is still tightly controlled by law).

[b]The number of approved series collected in each year at each ministry varies widely, but the total number has been stable between 400 and 500 since the mid-1990s. Unlike the designated series, many of these statistics are collected once and only.

[c]In ¥ millions for fiscal 1999, which ended 31 March 2000. This is roughly 0.06 percent of the central government budget. The budget has been in a ¥40–50 billion range since the early 1990s, except when there is a population census (years ending in 0 and 5). Thus, the total fiscal 2000 budget was ¥98.6 billion, with ¥75.9 billion allocated to Sōmusho, which conducts the census.

[d]This is 68 percent of the total. Most of them are at regional offices of the ministry.

[e]The total given is 2.2 percent of total central government administrative staff, 398,000.

Table 4.2   **U.S. Statistical Staff and Budget**

	2002 Budget ($ millions)[a]	Permanent Staff Total	Permanent Staff Statisticians
Agriculture	366.6	1,595	33
Commerce, except census	143.1	4,154	1,403
Census Bureau	563.4	3,708	1,398
Education	198.0	127	78
Health, "Homeland Security"	1,260.6	606	212
Justice	57.4	67	42
Labor	655.4	2,792	179
Transportation	122.3	162	54
Other	686.3	374	55
Total	4,110.5	9,877	2,056
Total[b]	3,906.3	6,169	658

Source: U.S. Executive Office of the President, Office of Management and Budget (2002).

[a]Estimate for fiscal year ending 30 September 2003.

[b]Excludes the 2000 census, entities spending less than $0.5 million, and statistics collection in conjunction with other major activities.

table 4.1. Its budget in 2002 was roughly ten times that of Japan in absolute terms and over three times in share terms. Although total staff is similar, this is only because of the large number employed at Japan's Ministry of Agriculture, Forestry, and Fishery.

Composition of staff in Japan is problematic. As far as is known, only a very few workers actually have advanced degrees in statistics, and virtually no one does in economics. Based upon information from Sōmusho, Statistics Bureau, perhaps 10 (out of 384 full time staff) have an M.S. in statistics, and no one had an M.A. or Ph.D. in economics.[3] In contrast, the U.S. federal government employs more than 2,000 professional statisticians on a full-time permanent basis. It is not clear, however, how many of them have advanced degrees in statistics or economics. In any case, we are certain that U.S. government professional staff with advanced degrees far outnumbers the Japanese counterpart.

4.2   General Data Problems

Japanese statistics have several broad problems in addition to the absence of statistical professionals among the staff mentioned above. These include long lead times, coordination among agencies, appropriateness of the data collected, access to raw data, and information on how data are processed.

4.2.1   Long Delays in Adjustments

Titles of the designated statistics indicate that their coverage is far from being well balanced. Although each series differs in scope and size, table 4.1 is at least suggestive of the imbalance between the coverage of official statistics and the relative importance of subjects covered. This reflects slowness in changing the data collected to reflect changes in the economy. The imbalance is particularly noticeable in agriculture and fishery. In 1999, the Ministry of Agriculture, Forestry, and Fisheries spent 29 percent of the total budget and employed 68 percent of staff devoted to statistics collection and compilation, but all primary industries combined provide less than 2 percent of GDP.

For example, domestic production and usage of coal is a designated series even though only 1.9 percent of total coal consumption is produced domestically and only 12 percent of total energy consumptions is coal. There are three designated statistics on shipping and sailors, although Japanese commercial ships long ago replaced Japanese crew with foreigners. Even though the industry was all but extinct years earlier, production of silk and silk worms was a designated statistic until the end of fiscal 2002.

On the other hand, surprisingly few resources are allocated for data on

3. We are grateful to Mr. Masato Aida at Sōmusho for this information.

tertiary industries, especially services. There is only one designated series that covers the service industry on an annual basis, offering basic data on production, employment, firm size, and so forth. Even this statistic rotates among subsectors on a three-year cycle so that the data for each subsector is available only every third year. There is only one other designated series that covers the service industry, but this survey is conducted every five years and it covers only those not covered in the first survey.

As we see more closely later, the weights attached to items in the CPI are based on the FIES (Family Income and Expenditure Survey), and it is fixed for a five-year period, even though the FIES is conducted monthly. Japan is not unique in this, other countries also have similar delays in adjusting coverage and weights. In the U.S. CPI, 1982–1984 weights were used until 1996, finally being replaced by 1993–1995 weights.

Especially for GDP statistics, long lead times are a problem. Preliminary figures are not announced until three months after the end of a quarter. These are revised three months later. The final figure is made available in December of the next year. Moreover, the inconsistency between quarterly estimates and the final figures reflects underlying differences in the estimation procedure. The inconsistency and long lead times in GDP statistics have been known for quite some time, but there seems little hope that any fundamental measures will be taken to rectify the situation. In the United States, preliminary quarterly GDP data are announced in eight weeks, and the final figure is available in about thirteen weeks. In other words, by the time the preliminary Japanese figures are announced, the final U.S. figure has already been announced. The release of the latest CPI figures is far more timely. The most recent month's figure is released on the Friday of the last week of each month, whereas in the second ten days of the current month the CPI for metropolitan Tokyo area is released on the same day.

4.2.2   Lack of Proper Coordination

There is a lack of proper coordination among different bodies of government and coordination with nongovernmental institutions is uncommon. As a result, different bodies collect similar, if not duplicate, sets of data. At the same time, in many important areas there is a lack of proper official statistics, due mainly to the fact that the area falls under more than one ministry's responsibility. This is especially true in the areas of information and communication: Subsets of these are covered rather independently by sections of Sōmusho and the Ministry of Economy, Trade, and Industry (formerly, the Ministry of Trade and Industry [MITI]).

Inadequate coordination creates difficulties in combining sets of statistics. For example, many statistics on private enterprises and establishments cover essentially the same universe of firms, yet each series employs its own coding method, sample selection methodology, and so forth, with the result that none of these statistics can be integrated to form a unified series.

In other cases, the series employ unique geographical grids, strata, or categories, which means cross-referencing is often difficult and may lead to erroneous conclusions. The best known example is the apparent inconsistency in personal savings rates in the National Accounts and the *Household Saving and Expenditure Survey*.

Lack of coordination places a heavy burden on sample respondents, especially the large firms that are included in most enterprise-based statistics. In 1993, more than 25 percent of polled firms listed on the Tokyo Stock Exchange said they had to reply to more than 100 different central and local government surveys each year.[4]

Rectifying the situation is straightforward in some cases. For example, many establishment-based surveys cover 100 percent of firms (their establishments) with more than ¥1 billion paid capital. It would be easy to use the same identification code for these firms to facilitate cross-referencing of a large variety of statistics.

4.2.3   Inadequate Disclosure

Inadequate disclosure of information is especially troublesome in two ways. First, many published statistics are processed using one or more primary statistical series, but details of the procedure generally are not available. The disclosure problem is extremely severe for most of the National Accounts data, as they incorporate so many different statistics. (See Ando 2002 for the problems he faced in his exploration of the measurement errors in savings rate.)

In GDP statistics, the corporate sector includes not only privately incorporated enterprises, but also the portion of central and regional governmental activities conducted by specific agencies (such as the postal system). There is no precise and reliable information on how to identify which part of the government activities are included. The problem is not limited to secondary statistics. The CPI is based on surveys of prices at sample retail stores, but original results are not available. For example, it is consequently not known how adjustment is made for quality change and by how much. The same problems exist for the WPI.

For economists, an equally, if not more, important problem is government unwillingness to make original microdata available to outside researchers. The law explicitly and categorically prohibits use of official statistics for purposes other than the ones specified in the law establishing each statistical series or the corresponding ministerial orders. Thus, to obtain original data for designated statistics, one must file a petition for special exclusion. This is a complicated, time-consuming process with no

---

4. The preceding results cited are taken from the following survey: *Tokeichōsa Hōkoku To no Kinyūni Kansuru Jittai Chōsa* (*Survey on the Burden of Respondents in Official Surveys and Statistics*, by Sōmucho (1994; to become Sōmusho in 2001), summary available at http://www.stat.go.jp/info/seido/6-1-2.htm.

guarantee that permission will be granted (see Matsuda, Hamasura, and Mori 2000 for details).

The difficulty in obtaining original data places severe constraints on outside observers, making it difficult even to point out with any reasonable accuracy where problems may be. Concern over the accuracy of CPI arose partly because many retail firms started publishing their own price data to argue that the CPI contains sizable upward bias (see, e.g., Sezon Research Institute [SRI] 2000). The resulting debate ultimately was unproductive in part because Sōmusho would not disclose data comparable to those covered by the retailers.

4.3   CPI Statistics

Japan's CPI is collected and published by Sōmusho Tōkeikyoku (Statistics Bureau and Center, Ministry of Public Management, Home Affairs, Posts and Telecommunications). Japan's CPI is by and large typical of CPIs collected in most countries. It is essentially a fixed-weight Laspeyres index with weights taken from FIES, which also is conducted by Sōmusho. The weights are revised every five years, incorporating the latest FIES.

Especially since the late 1990s when deflationary pressure became apparent, the CPI index has been criticized for its apparent failure to register the impact of rapidly declining retail prices as reported in the media and by some of the largest national general merchandise stores (GMSs).[5]

Compared to the CPI in the United States, there are several notable differences in data-collection procedures and lower-level aggregations. The Japanese CPI includes a larger number of individual items (roughly 600 compared to about 200 in the United States). For each item, Japan uses a single brand and a single retail outlet within each designated area to survey prices. Both the outlets and items used are rotated in the United States.

Surveys are prices on specific days of each month rather than averages over period or brands, as in the United States. Arithmetic means are used in every stage of aggregation, rather than geometric means. (The United States converted to geometric for lower-level aggregation in January 1999, as recommended by the 1996 Boskin Commission Report.)

4.3.1   Alternative Inflation Measures

If the CPI inflation rate is so problematic, why not use some other measures such as the GDP deflator or WPI? In fact, all of these are used to measure inflation, and many view the GDP deflator as a better indicator than the CPI. However, the same primary price survey data are used to estimate

---

5. The most comprehensive study is Shiratsuka (1997). Shiratsuka (1999) offers a review of his 1997 monograph and other major studies in English. Sōmusho posts various documents prepared by the Ministry on this issue at http://www.stat.go.jp/data/cpi/8.html.

Table 4.3   Annual Inflation Rates, 1900–2000 (%)

Period	CPI	WPI[a]	GDP[b]
1990–2000	1.64	−0.55	0.49
1995–2000	0.30	−0.76	−0.32

[a]For final consumption goods.
[b]Deflator for household final consumption. This is a Paasche index using current weights from FIES. Both factors tend to generate a lower inflation rate than the CPI.

GDP deflators as to estimate CPI and WPI. So, if CPI and WPI data contain measurement errors, they will also appear in other processed statistics such as the GDP deflator.

Moreover, the CPI is a more appropriate measure of overall changes in the cost of living. In contrast, changes in the GDP deflator reflect overall changes in the prices of goods and services produced in the country, not necessarily those consumed. The difference can be large and important when events, such as large increases in crude oil, give rise to major swings in the final price.

Table 4.3 shows the CPI, WPI for final consumption demand, and the GDP deflator for household final consumption. The CPI and WPI are both Laspeyres indexes with weights fixed for five-year periods, whereas the GDP deflator is a Paasche index with weights given by current-year expenditure shares. By construction, inflation in the GDP deflator has a downward bias, as opposed to an upward bias in CPI and WPI.

4.3.2   The CPI as the Cost of Living Index, the CPI as the Cost of Goods Index

From the viewpoint of standard microeconomic theory, the principal objective of a CPI is to provide a benchmark for the cost of living index (COLI). However, as is the official view in most other countries, the Statistics Bureau of Sōmusho clearly states that the CPI should be viewed as the index of the specific basket of goods it contains—that is, the cost of goods index (COGI). It does not subscribe to the view that the CPI should be the best estimate of the COLI. (See Schultz and Mackie, forthcoming, for a discussion of this incorporating the Boskin report.) Box 4.1 discusses the CPI as a COLI.

Even though we concur with the majority view among economists that CPI should serve as a measure of COLI, we also think that COGI, as it is constructed as an index representing a fixed basket of consumption goods, has its own merits. Especially as a macroeconomic indicator, the inflation rate measured in terms of changes in COGI is important, given the crucial role played by the private and social costs of changing nominal prices. Unlike COGI, a properly defined COLI can change without any accompanying change in nominal prices (for example, due to changes in quality). This

Box 4.1   CPI as a COLI

Under certain strict conditions, we can derive a group of price indexes called superlative price indexes (see Diewart [1976] and Caves, Christensen, and Diewert [1982]) that approximate the true COLI up to the second order. One index among the group is the Tornqvist price index (TR) and it is given by

$$\log P_{0t}^{\mathrm{TR}} = \sum_{i=1}^{n} \frac{1}{2}(\omega_0^i + \omega_t^i)(\log p_t^i - \log p_0^i)$$

where 0 denotes the reference period, i is the index for the goods and services, ω is the expenditure share, P is the price index, and p is individual prices. The Laspeyres index, on the other hand, is given by

$$P_{0t}^{L} = \sum_{i=1}^{n} \omega_0^i \frac{p_t^i}{p_0^i}.$$

The major advantage of a superlative price index, including the Tornqvist, is that the index properly incorporates substitutions among goods and services in response to changes in relative prices, among other things. Neither Laspeyres (reference-period fixed weights), nor Paasche indices (current-period fixed weights) incorporate substitutions. The most serious problem with Laspeyres as an approximation of a COLI is that the index tends to overrepresent prices that have risen from the reference period, thus overstating the impact of price increases. By the same token, the index underrepresents the impact of price declines. The magnitude of the bias depends crucially on two factors: relative prices and the degree of substitution across goods and services.

The practical difficulty in using Tornqvist or Fischer (geometric mean of Laspeyres and Paasche) indexes is that they require current data on expenditure shares. If expenditure shares are continuously available, one can construct corresponding chained indexes.

$$\log P_{0t}^{\mathrm{TRC}} = \prod_{s=0}^{t-1} \sum_{i=1}^{n} \frac{1}{2}(\omega_s^i + \omega_{s+1}^i)(\log p_{s+1}^i - \log p_s^i)$$

$$P_{0t}^{\mathrm{LC}} = \prod_{s=0}^{t-1} \sum_{i=1}^{n} \omega_s^i \frac{p_{s+1}^i}{p_s^i}$$

The important drawback of chained indexes is path dependence. That is, the same magnitude of total price changes results in different price index values, depending on the sequence in which the changes take place. The problem is quantitatively important in high-frequency data (See Feenstra and Shapiro 2001 on such bias).

can be misleading, especially when quality unadjusted indexes are not available.

In relation to other price indices, such as WPI, CSPI, and various wage indices, the COGI is also important in monitoring the dynamics of vertical price formation. Thus, we agree that the CPI should continue to serve as a COGI, providing an aggregate measure of nominal price changes.

Even as a COGI, however, the CPI should perform better by incorporating lower-level substitution more explicitly. Accordingly, there is strong evidence that consumers substitute brands, shop around, and continue to shift toward mass retailers with lower prices. Moreover, unless one subscribes to an extremely narrow and rigid definition of a fixed basket (i.e., fixed brand purchased at fixed set of retailers), CPI should move in the direction of COLI at least in these dimensions.

We believe the CPI should serve both COLI and COGI purposes. Whenever an important difference arises between the purposes, separate COLI and COGI series can be compiled. There is no practical or theoretical difficulty in this. As a matter of fact, the additional cost of preparing a separate COLI for different groups of households is relatively small, and the current CPI does include such series. We suspect, however, that the relevant COLIs for different groups differ substantially, once proper attention is paid to shopping behavior. To incorporate shopping behavior into the COLI, it is essential that information be collected at the household level.

Whether the CPI is viewed as strictly a COGI or also serves as a COLI, it is crucial to disclose details of the compilation processes, such as quality adjustments and brand and sample-store replacements. Without full and timely disclosure of these details and the original survey results, the extent to which external monitoring can check potential problems is limited.

4.4   Major Sources of CPI Bias

There are several fairly well-known, if not well-established, sources of problems in the Japanese CPI, and all are considered sources of upward bias. One set relates to aggregation procedures and the second to lower-level data collection procedures (including how discounted prices are handled). Collection procedures, services, quality change, and new products are covered in this section. Aggregation issues are taken up in later sections.

4.4.1   Lower-Level Data Collection Procedures

Under current procedures, prices for each item are collected first by specifying the most representative brand for each item, then by selecting the most representative sample store (usually the one with the largest sales volume of the item) within each precinct.

The brand selection procedure is problematic. Setting aside the problem of changes in the leading brand over time, fixing a particular brand in itself creates upward bias because many people are largely indifferent among brands and thus will substitute among brands, especially when one is temporarily discounted. Fixing a particular brand gives unbiased COLI data if and only if all consumers are completely brand loyal or retail prices of different brands all move together. Sōmusho does not release data on how many or how often brand replacements occur, but states that it checks the selection of specific brands every half year and replaces brands whenever appropriate.

In the United States, CPI does not fix any particular brand and different brands rotate in each price survey. The U.S. procedure is superior because the procedure avoids the inherent bias associated with fixing particular brands. On the other hand, Shapiro and Wilcox (1996) contend that brand turnover is closely related to CPI inflation in the United States because the bulk of the inflation rate is attributable to the imputed price increase registered for newly surveyed brands and entry-level (new) items when the sample is changed. That is, if brand A is substituted for brand B in the sample, the price difference between the two will be recorded as a price change affecting the CPI whether or not there is an actual change in the price of either brand between sample periods.

Selection of a single store within each sample precinct also is problematic because consumers substitute among shopping outlets. Neglecting store substitution also tends to introduce upward bias.

Discount prices or specials are another issue. Each month the survey collects prices on the Wednesday, Thursday, or Friday of the week that includes the 12th of the month. If the price is a discount price, the sample is void unless the price has been quoted for at least eight days at the time of the survey. It is not clear how regular and discount prices are defined. In most cases, the highest selling price seems to be the one defined as the regular price. It is unclear if the regular price ever changes at each store and, if so, how often—even though actual prices change quite frequently.

The current procedure thus tends to ignore almost all discount prices of short duration. However, the bulk of sales of many products, especially ones easily stored, are concentrated in short periods when prices are discounted.

The extent to which discount sales are used differs systematically across items, brands, and types of retail outlets. Discounts are widespread and routinely used by national brands, whereas most generic commodities without strong brand recognition are rarely discounted. Discounts are far more common at large supermarkets and specialty stores, but very infrequent at small general stores and almost nonexistent in convenience store chains.

Although there is no a priori reason to believe these measurement errors inherently generate systematic bias in the measured inflation rate, the recent macroeconomic setting and secular changes in the retail industry do give reasons to suspect that they create systematic upward bias. The share of retail sales in Japan has been shifting away from traditional small stores toward large supermarkets and discount stores in suburbs and toward inner-city convenience store chains. This may introduce systematic upward bias to the extent that current CPI procedures subsume some of the pure price differences across different types of stores as reflecting differences in service.

Biases created at lower levels can be quantitatively large precisely because they occur as a result of substitutions over very close substitutes: over time of the same brand, among different brands of the same good, and among neighborhood stores.

4.4.2   Services

After the 2000 revision, services comprise 48.4 percent of the CPI. There are no natural measures for the quantity of most services purchased, implying that expenditure data, such as FIES, are ill suited as the alternative data source for prices. Objective measurement of the quality of services is even more difficult. For these reasons, we have little to offer on biases from services.

Compared to commodity prices, there are reasons to believe raw price data are more accurate for some services in the CPI. For example, most utility rates and public transportation service prices are uniform and well documented. For these, there is little or none of the discounting so common for food and clothing. This applies also for price data on medical services. The bulk of payments are covered by public health insurance, and readily available and highly comprehensive price lists exist for individual treatments, various fees, and prescription drugs.

Setting aside quality issues, the biggest problem in service categories is underrepresentation of medical and health care in the CPI, as the weight is based on consumer out-of-pocket expenditure in the FIES and totally neglects payments for medical insurance. According to the *Survey on Medical Expenditure* (Ministry of Health, Labor, and Welfare, various years) in 1999, ¥30.9 trillion (8.1 percent of national income) was spent on medical care. Out-of-pocket expenses covered by FIES were only 14.6 percent of that. In the current CPI, the weight for medical care is 2.4 percent and for health care is 1.4 percent, a total of 3.8 percent.

The medical- and health-related items in the CPI are limited to those not covered by typical health insurance. Thus, nonprescription drugs, physical check-ups, and the basic hospitalization fee for normal delivery of a baby are included, but most other medical services are excluded. Not surprisingly, data indicate systematic differences in price indexes, depending on who directly pays the cost: the consumer, insurance, public institutions, and so forth (See Iwamoto 2000 for representative medical price indexes).

It also should be noted that the CPI contains several conceptual flaws in some other service prices. Especially noteworthy is imputed rent for home

owners. The actual rent data collected are those for rented dwellings; it is well known, however, that rented and owner-occupied homes differ greatly in capacity and quality. Measured rent is likely to include sizable upward bias to the extent that the recent improvements in the quality of owner-occupied homes are not properly incorporated. Bear in mind, however, that given the sheer magnitude of the diversity of dwellings across regions, types, and vintage, it is a formidable task even to estimate the size of the bias, let alone correct it.

4.4.3   Quality Change and New Products

Although quality changes and new goods are potentially the most important source of bias in the CPI, we do not investigate the problems in any depth here. Instead, we argue two points: First, in principle, the CPI would benefit enormously from careful and systematic improvements in incorporation of the effects of quality change and introduction of new products. Second, there is an important inconsistency between CPI and WPI regarding certain groups of items. We suspect the inconsistency stems at least partially from differences in quality adjustments in the two indexes. This is dealt with in a later section.

Some argue that, ultimately, measurement of quality should be aimed at measurement of contribution to the quality of life. For example, some say the measurement of medical services should be reformulated to measure the cost of cure, rather than the cost of treatment as is now the case (See Schultze and Mackie [forthcoming]). We do not engage in this debate here except to the extent that it is an aspect of the issue of the role of the CPI as a COLI, as we noted earlier.

In the current CPI, essentially nothing is done to address the effect on living costs from introduction of the new products. This is understandable, given that no established procedure to do so exists. On the other hand, the long delay in incorporating changes in the consumption basket by itself introduces large and rectifiable biases if price declines primarily occur soon after a product appears and before it is included in the CPI. That seems to be the regular pattern for many consumer durables, but it is conceivable that for other types of products, prices rise during the early stage.

It is only in the 2000 revision that the CPI included items such as personal computers and service charges for mobile telephones. The CPI still does not include fax machines, printers and other computer peripherals, or internet service provider charges!

As for quality change, in the current procedure, whenever a sample item or brand is considered different in quality from the previous item, an overlap method is used to take account of quality changes. In 2000, the CPI for the first time started using hedonic methods to estimate quality changes in personal computers, but, as of now, this is the only item utilizing the method.

Few empirical studies in Japan measure quality changes and assess the impact of changes on the CPI. Shiratuska (1997, 1999) are the only published results we are aware of that estimate the impact of quality change on CPI bias. He estimates that underestimates of quality changes result in an annual upward bias of 0.3 percent to 0.9 percent, with 0.7 percent the point estimate. However, he notes the estimate is based only on studies of a few consumer electronics and passenger cars.[6]

Most of Shiratuska's work uses data from the first half of the 1990s, so it is not clear if the same estimates apply to later periods. As will be shown, in the late 1990s, the consumer electronics component of the CPI registers a lower (actually, larger negative values) inflation rate than the comparable WPI rate.

For the U.S. CPI, Hausman (1999) estimates annual upward bias of 0.8 percent to 1.9 percent for telecom services as a result of not including cellular phone services in CPI until 1998. The potential bias can be substantially larger in Japan because the use of mobile phone increased so fast and the price declined so dramatically. In 2001, the number of cellular users surpassed the number of fixed telephone lines in Japan.

Sōmusho (2000) has conducted preliminary estimation of a hedonic price index for personal computers. They estimate a price decline from the 1995 average, set at 100, to 12.8 by mid-1999. This is a 36.7 percent annual decline. Thus, if the personal computer had been included in the CPI in 1995, that alone would have reduced the inflation rate by 0.2 percentage points each year during 1995–1999. (The personal computer weight in the current CPI is 0.54 percent). One can expect similar dramatic price decline for other items that now command sizable expenditure shares: fax machines (not included), printers (not included), mobile phones (0.74 percent), internet service providers (not included), and so forth.

More often than not, the same goods and services appear on lists related to both proper adjustments in quality and timely inclusion of new goods. This is because the most important quality changes typically take place when items are relatively new. In this sense, timing is crucial. If an item is included only after it has become a part of the standard consumption basket, much of the impact of quality change and consumer surplus associated with quality-adjusted price declines is missed.

4.5 Aggregation Biases

Aggregation procedures are a problem. The Japanese CPI is a fixed-weight Laspeyres index. The biases created by using fixed weights and tak-

6. Shiratsuka (1997) and his associates estimated hedonic price indexes for personal computers, camcorders, automobiles, and apparel. They found quality-adjusted personal computer prices declined 25 percent a year from 1990 to 1994, while unadjusted prices fell 3 percent. For camcorders, the annual quality-adjusted decline was 11 percent, but only 6 percent unadjusted. For automobiles, adjusted prices declined 0.4 percent, but increased 4 percent unadjusted.

ing arithmetic means are well known. Aggregation bias arises at every stage in the Japanese CPI.

At the bottom level, one representative brand of each item is chosen for data collection. This assumes away interbrand substitution and thus tends to create sizable upward bias. Fixed-weighting problems also appear in the selection of sample stores. As discussed later, this became serious in the 1990s as sales shifted away from small independent stores to larger chain-store discount outlets (see table 4.8).

The FIES has a significant sampling problem because it does not include single-person households. Given the large portion of the population living alone and the substantial deviation of consumption patterns of single-person households from others, the bias implicit in this procedure is potentially important. Starting in late 2002, FIES is being expanded to cover single-member households.

In an earlier step to improve data quality in October 2001, Sōmusho started a new consumption survey covering 20,000 households and focusing on items the basic FIES is ill suited to cover, such as high-priced products purchased infrequently and services. The new survey includes appliances, personal computers, other consumer electronics, mobile phones, and internet service providers, as well as some services already covered in FIES. The survey is conducted by a semiprivate research organization and includes single-member households. Zero or negative inflation in recent years probably has lessened the size of aggregation bias in comparison with economies with a mild but positive inflation rate.

4.5.1   Higher-Level Aggregation Bias

At higher-level aggregation, it is well known that the current fixed-weight Laspeyres index using arithmetic means tends to produce some upward bias in the CPI. This is the case because whenever relative price changes, people do tend to buy more of the goods and services whose relative price declined and buy less of those which have become more expensive. In short, people change the consumption shares with their response to changes in relative prices. The assumption of fixed weights neglect this substitution and hence tends to overstate/understate the impact of price increase/decrease. This problem of using fixed weights is not unique to the Japanese CPI. The procedure to measure the bias is simple and straightforward: Annual expenditure weights from FIES for the eighty-five lowest-level categories are used to compute chained Fischer and Tornqvist indexes that are compared to the CPI, which uses the same price data but with fixed 1995 weights. Table 4.4 summarizes Shiratsuka's (1997) calculations and extends them to 1995–2000.

The bias is not large for years since 1995, except for 1999. Relatively large bias in the CPI inflation rate for 1999 (i.e., the change in CPI from 1998 to 1999) probably reflects relatively large changes in consumption weights after the increase in consumption tax from 3 to 5 percent in April 1998.

Table 4.4   Aggregation Bias (annual percentage rates except as noted)

| | Fixed Weights | | | | Chained | | | |
| | Laspeyres | | Tornqvist | | Tornqvist | | Fischer | |
	CPI Index	Inflation	Inflation	Difference[a]	Inflation	Difference[a]	Inflation	Difference[a]
1996	100.180	0.180	0.154	0.026	0.154	0.026	0.154	0.026
1997	101.869	1.689	1.651	0.038	1.657	0.032	1.649	0.032
1998	102.613	0.744	0.713	0.031	0.716	0.028	0.703	0.028
1999	102.242	-0.371	-0.498	0.127	-0.440	0.069	-0.429	0.058
2000	101.415	-0.827	-0.877	0.050	-0.864	0.037	-0.870	0.043
1995–2000	n.a.	0.283	0.229	0.054	0.245	0.038	0.241	0.042
1970–1995	n.a.	4.438	n.a.	n.a.	4.313	0.125	4.216	0.222
1990–1995	n.a.	1.153	n.a.	n.a.	1.152	0.001	1.272	-0.119

Source: 1970–1995 and 1990–1995 are from Shiratsuka (1997).

Note: n.a. = not available

[a]Difference between the CPI inflation rate in column (2) and the inflation rate in column to the left. As discussed in the text, this is an indicator of upward bias in the CPI inflation rate.

Compared to chained Tornqvist or Fischer indices, the fixed-weight Laspeyres generates roughly 0.04 percent upward bias per year in the five years through 2000. There is larger bias in earlier periods—on the order of 0.1 percent.

Although the magnitude is not large, aggregation bias is serious because it always exists and accumulates forever. Thus, it can have a quantitatively large impact when tracing living standards for generations. Aggregation bias arises due to the underrepresentation of the scope of substitution whenever the relative prices of goods and services change over time. The results indicate that the bias is smaller in the more recent years primarily because of smaller variations in relative prices.

Notice that a low or negative inflation rate per se does not reduce aggregation bias. What matters is changes in relative prices. These results only confirm that relative price variability at higher-level aggregation is positively correlated with the inflation rate.

4.5.2   Discounts and Intertemporal Substitution

Biases created within each item, an aspect of lower-level aggregation, is now considered. There are two issues: selection of a particular brand of an item and how price observations are collected. In a sense, bias at this level is the easiest to deal with because, in principle, there is not much room for disagreement. The extent to which different brands of an item are substitutable is an empirical question that can be answered with reasonable accuracy if sufficient data are collected. Substitutions across brands within each item is addressed later.

Here the issue is substitution over time of the same brand—that is, the extent to which consumers can exploit periodic discounts. This appears to be quantitatively important, and how much substitution occurs depends primarily on consumer knowledge and the ability to hold inventory at home. Feenstra and Shapiro (2001) is an early attempt to incorporate home storage and shopping patterns into CPI measurements (also see Ariga, Matsui, and Watanabe 2000).

In principle, the upward bias due to the survey procedure described earlier applies only to the level, not necessarily to changes, in the index. The problem is essentially that the procedure systematically truncates the low price observations. This truncation may or may not generate upward bias in the inflation rate. Circumstantial evidence indicates, however, that it does indeed produce sizable upward bias in the measured inflation rate, as retailers reduce average sales price by further lowering the discounted price or increasing the frequency of discounts.

The easiest way to demonstrate the inflation bias created by intertemporal, intrabrand substitution is to compare the actual average purchase price to hypothetical price data, which the CPI would collect following the data collection procedure described earlier. For this exercise, we use point of

Table 4.5   Bias Due to CPI Data Collection Procedure (% per year)

	Mean Inflation			Standard Deviation[a]	
	Weighted Average	CPI Procedure	Upward Bias	Weighted Average	CPI Procedure
Mayonnaise	−1.36	−0.38	0.98	.0148	.0208
Ketchup	−3.12	−0.41	2.71	.0195	.0305
Soy sauce	−2.25	0.00	2.25	.0343	.0434
Liquid soup base	−2.94	−0.30	2.64	.0238	.0429
Laundry detergent	−2.73	−0.10	2.83	.0298	.0149
Instant coffee	−5.44	−1.45	3.99	.0378	.0957

[a]Annual log differences.

sale data prepared by the Distribution Economics Institute (POS-DEI). (See appendix A for details regarding the data sets).

Table 4.5 covers six selected items sold at sample large-scale retail stores during the twenty-four months starting April 1995. The results are consistent across all of the items: The current CPI procedure consistently overestimates the inflation rate because most special-sales prices are dropped from the survey. Notice that the results indicate that the decline in the average purchase price occurred primarily as a result of lowering the discount price or increasing the frequency of the discounts. Moreover, as Shiratsuka (1997) pointed out, the current procedure substantially increases noise, as it only sporadically picks up sales discounts. Table 4.5 shows that standard deviations in the inflation rate under the current survey procedure are substantially higher than those of average purchase prices for most items.

Unfortunately, there is no unambiguous way to estimate the extent to which the bias due to survey procedures applies to other items in the CPI. It is known that periodic price discounts (specials and sales) are quite widespread in most medium- to large-scale retail stores. Discounts typically apply to processed food, toiletries, cosmetics, household appliances, and some clothing. In other words, for most items sold at large-scale retail stores, one expects periodic discounts. Table 4.5 indicates that the current CPI creates systematic upward biases for these items mostly in the order of 3 percent per year.

4.5.3   Substitution Across Brands

The CPI chooses a single brand to represent the price movement of each item. In general, ignoring substitutions across brands results in an upward bias in the level of the cost of living, but it is not certain if it results in any bias in the inflation rate. If the relative price of different brands is stable over time, the bias may well be negligible in computing the CPI.

Figure 4.1 shows three price indexes compiled from point of sale data prepared by the Sezon Research Institute (POS-SRI) for liquid condiment,

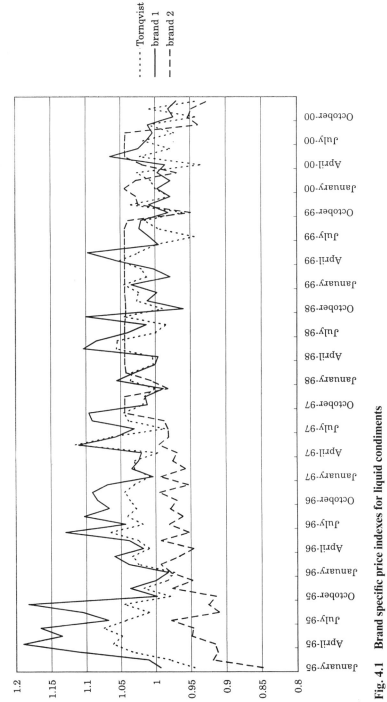

Fig. 4.1 Brand specific price indexes for liquid condiments

Table 4.6   Mean Inflation Rates and Within-Item Variances

	Mean Inflation Rate (%)	Variance[a]
Instant coffee	0.4477	.016
Facial tissue	0.1006	.0062
Mayonnaise	−0.2258	.0041
Yogurt	−0.1324	$.94 \cdot 10^{-5}$
Liquid condiments	0.0781	.0080
Fruit juice	0.2465	.092
Fresh milk	−1.4649	.019
Sugar	−11.8878	.038
Wheat flour	0.2117	.0061
Soy sauce	−0.1937	.0043
Cooking oil	0.2850	.0070
Sanitary napkins	0.9755	.052
Laundry detergent	−0.0627	.060
Kitchen detergent	−0.0738	.0078

[a]Monthly average for indexes of brand-specific inflation normalized to set the annual average for 2,000 equal to 1. The variance of mean inflation rate across different brands within each item is shown in the second column.

one of the fourteen items included in the 1997 *National Survey of Prices, Special Volume on Bargain Prices*. Along with the Tornqvist index for the item, the figure shows indexes for the brands that registered the lowest and the highest inflation rate from 1995 to 2000. Variations across brands are very large indeed.

Table 4.6 shows the intraitem sample variances for the fourteen items and the monthly inflation rate for the corresponding item-level Tornqvist index. A simple panel regression of monthly item-level price variances on inflation rate (ifr) for fourteen items yields

(1)
$$\mathrm{var}_t^i = \sum_{k=1}^{14} \mathrm{constant}^k - .0363 ifr_t^i (.023)$$

$$R^2 = .0874$$

The result (standard errors in the parenthesis) indicates that deflation (−*ifr*) coincides with increase in price variations across brands. These findings thus indicate that, at least for these fourteen items, consumers have ample opportunities to substitute among brands.

In Ariga, Matsui, and Watanabe (2000), we used daily POS data for two rival brands of curry paste sold at selected supermarket stores. Table 4.7 shows the impact of price discounts on sales volume.

If brand B also is at a discount price, average sales volume of brand A at a discount price is 57.4, which is 19 percent smaller than the average sales volume (70.7) at a discount price if brand B is sold at regular price. The impact of brand A's discounted sales on brand B at discount price is even

Table 4.7   **Substitution across Brands: Curry Pastes**

	Brand A's Price	
Sales Volume	Regular	Discounted
Brand A		
Brand B's price is regular	5.4	70.7
Brand B's price is discounted	5.0	57.4
Brand B		
Brand B's price is regular	3.1	2.9
Brand B's price is discounted	42.3	29.2

Note: Unit of measure is the average number of sales units per day.

larger, more than 30 percent (compare 29.2 against 42.4). On the other hand, pricing has a much smaller impact on volume at regular price, around 6 percent to 8 percent (5.0 versus 5.4 for brand A and 2.9 versus 3.1 for brand B).

Given the large impact of periodic price discount on sales, these figures suggest the presence of heterogenous consumers, as well as sizable inter-brand substitutions in response to changes in relative prices. Although these findings strongly indicate that price data of any particular brand can be a highly misleading indicator for overall changes in prices of different brands of each item, it is not possible to provide estimates of the magnitude of the inflation rate bias created by brand substitutions per se. Given the analysis on intertemporal substitution, it is probably not very productive to try to estimate the effects alone, as substitution in this aspect is closely related to intertemporal substitution and periodic price discounts.

There also are difficulties from the extremely high rate of new brand introductions and retirement of old brands, particularly among items in the food, household appliances, toiletry, and clothing groups. Shifts in sales shares from one brand to another not only are highly frequent but also unpredictable. This makes it practically impossible to obtain reliable estimates of substitution elasticities for the wide range of goods in the CPI. Again, these observations indicate the problem inherent in choosing a single specific brand to represent the spectrum of brands of each item. It is far more satisfactory and actually easier to use price averages across brands.

4.5.4 Substitution Across Stores

According to the current CPI procedure, the survey selects the most representative store within each survey precinct for each item. Nationwide, the survey has roughly 700 precincts. Usually the store with the largest sales volume is chosen for the item.

Table 4.8 shows the changes in shopping points in the *National Survey of Family Income and Expenditure*. As expected, regular stores lost shares

Table 4.8   Share of Expenditures on Selected Items, by Type of Retail Outlet, 1984–1994 (%)

	Regular Small-Scale	Supermarkets	Department Stores	Convenience Stores	Cooperatives	Discount[a]
Total						
1984	50.8	28.9	10.0	0.0	4.6	0.0
1994	40.5	30.3	9.3	1.1	6.3	4.0
1999	34.0	35.3	9.1	1.7	5.9	5.4
Food						
1984	40.6	44.9	3.5	0.0	7.0	0.0
1994	25.2	49.2	4.1	1.9	10.4	2.3
1999	16.7	57.5	4.5	2.6	9.8	2.7
Appliances						
1984	46.3	24.1	15.1	0.0	4.3	0.0
1994	37.1	22.7	10.8	3.1	5.8	12.5
1999	32.3	26.6	9.4	3.0	5.3	16.7
Clothing						
1984	36.9	18.1	37.6	0.0	1.8	0.0
1994	33.7	17.7	34.0	1.3	2.1	11.2
1999	28.7	20.5	36.5	1.4	2.3	10.6

Source: Sōmusho (various years).

Note: Row totals do not add to 100 percent because not all store types are included.

[a]Mass-marketing specialty discount stores.

across the board in the fifteen years from 1984 to 1999. The decline is especially large in food.

Sōmusho (2000) explains the selection procedure for precincts and sample stores. It is not entirely clear, however, to what extent the delay or failure in changing sample retail stores contributes to selection bias in the CPI. According to Sōmusho (2000a, 75), "the latest store selection is fairly close to the 1999 distribution," which is shown in table 4.8.

Shiratsuka points out that "the shift from department stores and small general stores to discount outlets has largely subsided," so that price differentials have "settled down to a level consistent with the difference in service quality" (1999, 90). However, table 4.8 suggests the shift is still very much an ongoing process.

The current CPI revises sample store selections in two ways. Every five years the most representative store is chosen for each commodity group in each precinct. This reflects changes in market shares across different types of retail shops in each precinct and commodity group. In principle, the CPI uses the overlap method to correct for underlying differences in retail services between sample stores before and after the changes. Sample stores also are replaced on an ad hoc basis. This is necessary when stores are closed or stop selling the sample product. In such cases, price data are directly connected and no adjustments are made in prices. In the case of services, the overlap method is used.

To sum up, the current procedure uses direct comparison methods only

Table 4.9   **Average Across-Store Price Differentials for Fourteen Items**

	Small Stores	Supermarkets	Mass Discount	Co-ops
Regular price	100	95.4	95.0	94.4
Discount price	78.7	64.9 (17.5%)	68.9 (12.5%)	68.7 (12.7%)
Case 1[a]	89.4	74.0 (16.7%)	76.8 (14.1%)	81.6 (8.7%)
Case 2[b]	95.7	74.0 (22.7%)	76.8 (19.8%)	89.3 (6.7%)

Source: Sōmusho (1998).

Note: Small-store regular price = 100. Percentages in parentheses are the discount from the small store's price for each of the cases.

[a]In determining the average price for Small Stores category, 50 percent of volume is assumed to be sold at a discount.

[b]In determining the average price for Small Stores category, 20 percent of volume is assumed to be sold at a discount.

for ad hoc sample-store replacements for commodities. One expects that in the case of an ad hoc replacement, the replacing store is selected in a way that retains the characteristics of the previous sample store. It is not clear to what extent overall the overlap and direct comparison methods are used. As a result, it is not known how much of the price differentials across stores are subsumed and assumed away using the overlap method. We suspect that whenever major changes in the characteristics of sample stores occur, the overlap method is used so that the CPI attributes the price differentials across old and new sample stores to differences in the quality of retail services. In short, even if the CPI has been correctly adjusting the sample store distribution to changing shopping patterns, most within-brand price differentials across different types of stores are assumed away.

In principle, we agree that some price differentials reflect differences in service quality. On the other hand, given the long history of restrictions on entry of large-scale retail stores and the fact that consumers do shift purchases from general small-scale stores to supermarkets and mass-marketing specialty stores whenever such stores are opened in the neighborhood, it seems clear that some of the price differentials are indeed pure price differentials, reflecting the local monopoly power element of retail pricing. Tables 4.9 and 4.10 offer some evidence, using cross-sectional data on retail prices of fourteen items at a variety of retail stores at many locations collected by the *1997 National Survey of Prices*.

Table 4.9 shows the difference in actual retail prices of the items across different types of stores. Ariga, Matsui, and Watanabe (2000) found that for two brands of curry pastes sold at sample supermarkets 31 percent of daily observations were of discounted price, but 72 percent of volume was sold at discount prices. More generally, for a sample of eighteen supermarkets, we found that share of sales at discount prices was 70 percent. Small general stores and co-ops offer price discounts much less frequently.

We used the survey data to run simple cross-sectional regressions on av-

Table 4.10   Impact of a Nearby Rival Store on Retail Prices

	log (Regular Price)	log (Discount Price)
Large Store	−.0401	−.0426
	(6.16)	(4.50)
Supermarkets	−.0579	−.243
	(2.84)	(8.18)
Mass-discount	−.170	−.315
	(4.24)	(5.42)
Co-op	−.116	−.180
	(2.63)	(2.79)
RS	−.082	−.155
	(4.48)	(5.82)
RS × supermarkets	.0659	.122
	(3.14)	(3.98)
RS × mass-discount	.0898	.139
	(2.17)	(2.31)
RS × co-op	.120	.123
	(2.62)	(1.86)
Adjusted R^2	.995	.978

Source: Sōmusho (1998).

Notes: Results of OLS cross-sectional regressions. Numbers in parentheses are t-statistics. RS = rival store.

erage regular and discount prices over a set of dummy variables, including one representing the presence of nearby rival stores, to indicate that some of these price differences reflect pure price differences. The results in table 4.10 show that both regular and discount prices are significantly lower among stores with nearby rival stores.

Specifically, among small-scale stores with nearby rivals (RS), the regular price is 8.2 percent lower than in comparable stores without a nearby rival. The impact of a nearby rival on the discounted price is 15.5 percent. In other words, the results suggest that a significant portion of price differences between large-scale and small-scale stores reflects the effect of local competition on pricing, rather than differences in service quality.

The same source shows that 26 percent of small-scale regular stores reported no nearby rival, whereas for large-scale supermarkets, only 3.7 percent reported no nearby rival. Notice also that the impact of a nearby rival on prices is far smaller in the case of supermarkets, mass-marketing specialty stores, and co-ops. Setting aside the difference in geographical sizes of markets for respective types of stores, the data strongly indicates the monopolistic power of many small-scale retailers. We conclude from these results that sizable price differences exist between small-scale general retailers and large stores, and that some of these differences reflect lack of local competition for some small-scale retailers.

As indicated in table 4.8, continuing shifts in sales share away from small-scale to large-scale stores should have generated sizable price declines for average consumers. For the sake of argument, suppose that a 10 percent pure price difference exists between the two types of retailers on average. This implies a roughly 0.1 percent upward bias in the CPI from not accounting for the pure price differences resulting from shifting shares. This is computed by multiplying the 6.5 percent decline in the share of small-scale stores by the 10 percent price differential over five years. In any case, unless we know the extent to which the overlap method is used for each type of sample store replacement, the effect on CPI bias cannot be estimated with any degree of accuracy.

The current store selection method poses other problems. The price differences in table 4.9 are likely to generate sizable variations in average purchase prices across households, depending on residence location, income, member composition, age, and other attributes. Choice of a single representative store in each precinct for each item inevitably masks these variations. Such considerations are important if the CPI is used as a COLI. More generally, the current CPI system is ill suited for incorporating cross-sectional and intertemporal variations in shopping behavior, and this has consequences on the COLI.

4.6   A Curious Discrepancy between CPI and WPI

This section compares CPI and WPI data for two groups of commodities to get some idea of the likely magnitude of the bias created by quality change.

Until the mid-1990s, with the exception of consumer electronics, the CPI inflation rate tended to be higher than the WPI rate for most items common to both indexes. Circumstantial evidence suggests significant upward bias in CPI, or downward bias in WPI, or both due to quality changes in the longer run, although at least since the mid-1990s this may not be the case. In the last ten years, the annual impact of all quality change on the WPI is estimated to be around 0.3–0.4 percent by the Bank of Japan (2001b).

The groups being compared are processed food and consumer electronics. The likely magnitude of quality improvement in processed food in the WPI is around 0.1 percent per year (Bank of Japan 2001b). Given the magnitude of the estimation error, we take the effect as essentially zero, and this is the primary reason the group is used in the analysis as the benchmark. For consumer electronics, the potential impact of quality change on CPI bias is one of the largest among items in the index.[7]

---

7. Automobiles have the largest effect (–3.1 percent per year) on its subindex. However, the WPI has indexes for three different types of passenger cars, while the CPI has only one. Hence we decided to use consumer electronics as an example.

Table 4.11   Comparison of CPI and WPI (annual percentage rates)

	1980–2000		1990–2000	
	CPI	WPI	CPI	WPI
Food	0.83	0.68	0.25	−0.35
Consumer electronics	−3.33	−1.49	−6.12	−3.32
Import price index	n.a.	n.a.	−5.76	−2.49

Note: CPI weights are used for both CPI and WPI. n.a. = not available.

Using CPI weights, the average inflation rates of the two indexes for the two groups using only items commonly found in both is shown in table 4.11. The result for consumer electronics implies retail prices declined relative to wholesale prices by as much as 25 percent during the 1990s. If the sample period is extended back to 1980, the average annual difference is 1.9 percentage points, which translates into a decline in relative retail price of as much as 66.4 percent. This is suspect because the distribution margin is at most around 30 percent of the retail price and available statistics suggest at most a modest decline in the retail margin during the period—perhaps a few percentages of the retail price. In other words, either CPI, or WPI, or both must contain sizable biases.

One possibility is that WPI severely underrepresents the price declines. In the 1990s, many consumer electronics firms relocated plants to Asian developing economies and the import of these goods quickly replaced domestic production. In the 1995 revision of WPI, the Bank of Japan started collecting import price indices of these products.

The bottom row of table 4.11 shows the weighted inflation rate of consumer electronics during 1995–2000, with WPI replaced by the corresponding import price index. The result is essentially the same. Although the coverage of imported price indexes is far from exhaustive, it seems unlikely that the deviation can be due solely to the rapid price decline of imports. Another possibility is that the large difference in price levels between domestic and imported products is the root cause. The rapid decline of retail prices could reflect rapid replacement of high-priced domestic items by cheaper imports, even if the imported goods' prices did not decline faster than the domestic ones.

It is conceivable that the Bank of Japan has severely underestimated the underlying quality changes of these products, more so than Sōmusho did for the CPI. We consider this highly unlikely, given the nature of the debate between Bank of Japan and Sōmusho on the possible upward bias of CPI. Another possibility is that CPI overestimates quality change, and so it underestimates the inflation rate for this group. There is reason to believe that this hypothesis has merit and thus needs further investigation.

There are differences in quality adjustment methods between the two indexes. According to Bank of Japan (2001b), the most popular method for dealing with quality change in the WPI is cost comparison. It is used for about 30 percent of WPI items. In contrast, Sōmusho states that the CPI uses either the overlap or the direct comparison method. Although Sōmusho does not reveal how many items are quality adjusted and by which methods, it says that "whenever a sample brand is replaced, unless there are reasons to believe that the new and old brands are essentially the same quality, the overlap method is used" (2000a, 114; author's translation). Hence, it is reasonable to say that virtually all substantive quality adjustment in CPI is done using the overlap method. Bank of Japan also uses the overlap method, but only on about 10 percent of WPI items.

Overlap methods can generate sizable overestimate of quality change if the retail price of the existing brand declines substantially in anticipation of a forthcoming future brand. Suppose the CPI survey collects prices for brand b until period t and then replaces it with b' at $t + 1$. Replacement typically occurs because of a decline in the brand's market share or its disappearance from the sample store. Overlap methods treat the price differential between the current and replacement brand b' as reflecting an underlying quality difference, so the price index for item i is computed as

$$(2) \qquad p_t^i = \frac{\mathrm{rp}_t^b}{\mathrm{rp}_0^b}$$

$$p_{t+1}^i = p_t^i \frac{\mathrm{rp}_{t+1}^{b'}}{\mathrm{rp}_t^b}$$

where rp^b is the survey price of a particular brand. Substantial overestimate of the quality change can occur if the relative price

$$\frac{\mathrm{rp}_{t+1}^{b'}}{\mathrm{rp}_{t+1}^b}$$

does not properly represent the quality difference. In particular, a disappearing brand might be heavily discounted around the time of replacement. In that case, quality improvement is overestimated, and the method introduces downward bias in the inflation rate.

Sōmusho (2000), using color televisions as an example, reports that a chained index using overlap methods generates a 46 percent decline in the index for the three-year period 1995–1998, which can be compared to a decline of 27 percent in the hedonic price index and 25 percent in the published CPI index. On the other hand, estimates by Shiratsuka (1997), discussed earlier, suggest significant upward bias in CPI due to underestimation of quality change during the first half of 1990s. Our previously shown results cast some doubt on the alleged upward bias in CPI for this reason.

All in all, for the late 1990s, we cannot make any definitive statement on even the direction of bias created by quality change. But, in any case, it is certain that there are important inconsistencies in quality adjustments between the CPI and WPI for at least some product groups.

4.7   Impact of Shopping Patterns on COLI

The current CPI almost totally ignores the impact on COLI of diverse shopping patterns by different types of consumers. This is also true of CPIs in most other countries. In Japan, there are supplementary CPI indexes incorporating differences in consumption patterns across different types of households. They do not incorporate the impact of shopping patterns on the respective COLI, however.

In appendix B we develop a simple model of cost minimization and demonstrate the impact of shopping and storage costs on shopping and purchase decisions. Two points emerge: First, pricing patterns of retail stores significantly influence consumer decisions on shopping timing and purchase. Second, large variations in shopping and storage costs, as well as average purchase price, result from variations in pricing policy across different types of stores. Moreover, variations in consumer shopping and storage costs influence which store is the optimal choice. These results suggest that the variation in COLI across regions and household types can be much larger than what the current CPI indicates.

4.8   Estimation of Commodity CPI Biases

Inevitably, estimation of bias involves many subjective judgments and is likely to contain sizable errors. The potential impact of each source of bias differs across categories, as does our ability to estimate its direction and magnitude. For this reason, our analysis on bias will be confined to the commodity CPI; services are not considered.

Commodity CPI comprises 51 percent of overall CPI. We provide two results: The first compares CPI with COLI using unit prices in FIES, the second is the COLI for fourteen selected items using POS-SRI. The two are consistent in suggesting sizable upward bias in commodity CPI.

Table 4.12 compares four COLI indexes for a variety of CPI categories. In the comparison, unit price indexes in FIES are used because CPI item selection is based on FIES, which collects unit prices for about 200 items.

The large deviation between the two indexes for clothing (2 percent per year) is consistent with consumers rapidly shifting from domestic to imported and from small-scale to mass-marketing specialty stores. This shift started with the rapid expansion of several chain stores specializing in men's suits and other formal clothing. The department stores, traditionally the most popular choice for such items, lost share. Beginning in the late 1990s, the shift has been concentrated in more casual clothing and under-

Table 4.12   COLI Average Annual Inflation in CPI and FIES (%)

	(C,C)[a]	(C,K)[b]	(K,C)[c]	(K,K)[d]	CPI-FIES[e]
		1980–2000			
Food	0.83	0.70	0.44	0.56	0.27
Clothing[f]	1.31	1.41	0.20	0.03	1.28
Consumer electronics	–8.62	–6.05	–4.80	–3.41	–5.21
Six items in *Survey of Prices*	0.11	0.45	–0.55	–0.69	0.80
CPI except CE	0.57	0.67	0.32	0.45	0.12
CPI except services and CE	0.63	0.75	0.32	0.59	0.14
Overall CPI versus overall FIES[g]	1.54	n.a.	n.a.	0.64	0.90
		1990–2000			
Food	0.25	0.20	–0.54	–0.35	0.60
Clothing	0.72	0.73	–1.19	–1.39	2.09
Consumer electronics	–6.12	–5.92	–2.89	–3.32	–2.80
Six items in *Survey of Prices*	0.03	0.38	–0.81	–1.43	1.46
CPI except CE	0.32	0.26	–0.46	–0.40	0.72
CPI except services and CE	0.11	0.20	–0.81	–0.51	0.62
Overall CPI versus overall FIES[g]	0.89	n.a.	n.a.	–0.46	1.35

Note: CE = consumer electronics. n.a. = not applicable.
[a]Original CPI fixed-weight Laspeyres index.
[b]The CPI price data and FIES monthly expenditure share used to compute a Tornqvist index.
[c]The CPI fixed weights and FIES unit prices used.
[d]Tornqvist index using unit prices and expenditure shares from FIES.
[e]Difference between CPI inflation rate and unit-price inflation rate in FIES.
[f]1987–2000.
[g]Baskets in two indexes differ.

wear. Among others, the UNIQLO chain registered explosive growth in sales and profits.

Table 4.13, comparing POS-SRI Data with the CPI shows an upward bias in the CPI on the order of 1.5 percent per year. For six of fourteen items selected in the *1997 National Survey of Prices*, FIES also reports unit prices. The difference from the CPI for these groups is again around 1.5 percent per year. These estimates are very close to the bias estimated in table 4.13. Although the two baskets differ, an index computed by aggregating all FIES items yields a 1.35 percent lower inflation rate than the overall CPI.

The conclusion is that, for at least food and clothing groups, the CPI since the mid-1990s has sizable upward bias, most likely in the range of 1.5 percent to 2 percent per year. We believe a bias of similar magnitude exists for other items commonly sold at mass retail stores (such as appliances and toiletry goods), so that roughly two-thirds of commodity CPI belongs to groups we believe are biased upward by 1.5–2.0 percent per year.

To be conservative, assume the bias arises only for purchases of these commodities at large retailers and that two-thirds of purchases are at mass

Table 4.13   Inflation Rates for Sixteen Selected Items (%)

	1995	1996	1997	1998	1999	2000	1995–2000 Average
POS-Laspeyres	−5.15	4.32	−7.66	0.72	−2.85	−6.47	−2.85
POS-Tornqvist	−5.05	3.17	−7.95	1.85	−2.80	−5.74	−2.75
CPI	−2.15	−2.07	−0.30	−1.00	−0.95	−2.28	−1.46

Notes: The numbers shown are annual inflation rates. The first two use POS-SRI data (see appendix A for the data source). The first row uses CPI weights and computes Laspeyres index, whereas the second is a chained Tornqvist using annual weights computed from the sales data in POS-SRI. The last row is computed using item level indexes and respective weights in CPI.

retailers. Applying the low end of the bias range, 1.5 percent per year, suggests a bias of 0.67 percent in the CPI. Using 2.0 percent, the impact on CPI is roughly 0.9 percent. Even assuming the CPI bias is zero for other commodities and also for samples taken at small-scale stores, the effect on overall commodity CPI must be 0.5 percent to 1.0 percent per year. The difference between unit price inflation in FIES and the CPI inflation rate among comparable items, other than consumer electronics and services, is about 0.6 percent per year (table 4.12), which is within the range just estimated.

We believe that 0.5 percent to 0.6 percent per year is a conservative estimate of the upward bias in the CPI as a measure of COLI because service prices, which comprise roughly 50 percent of the overall CPI, have not been covered in the analysis. Upward biases in many important items in this category is likely. On the other hand, the comparison of CPI with WPI indicates a potential downward bias in the CPI.

4.9   Some Suggested Ways to Improve CPI

Japan's CPI contains upward biases and has other problems. Some of the problems can be corrected or at least alleviated. The following sections make some suggestions for improving the CPI.

4.9.1   Upgrade Statistics Sections

The Statistics Bureau of Sōmusho, and most other statistics sections of Japan's central government, are seriously understaffed and suffer from meager budget allocations. There are fewer highly trained statisticians than is appropriate for the work, and there are no staff members with advanced economics degrees. Not only must more people be hired, but the new hires should be specifically skilled.

Staff and budget constraints severely limit the options available to improve CPI. For example, use of POS data is highly expensive because Sōmusho has to purchase them from the outside private sector. Needless to say, collecting POS data in itself is even costlier and practically impossible. Systematic attempts to estimate hedonic price indexes require large resources for data collection and estimation. In the United States, the Bureau of Labor Statistics (which prepares the U.S. CPI) quickly incorporated the recommendations of the Boskin Commission report on problems with the U.S. CPI (Schultz and Mackie [forthcoming]). Given the budget and staff size limitations, it seems very difficult for Sōmusho to carry out similar research with comparable speed.

4.9.2   Improve Data Collection

Many aspects of data collection methods need to be changed, most of them fundamentally. First, the revision of item selection and weights must be done more frequently. In principle, to the extent that the CPI uses FIES, this is a matter of automatic adjustments. FIES is monthly, but annual CPI revision is a more realistic goal. The need for continuity can easily be met by tracking CPI component indexes based on weights and item selections in the past. The additional tasks created by annual revision may not be large.

Utilizing other official data sources in compiling the CPI offers significant benefits. For example, the gain from coordinating data collection and compilation for CPI and WPI is obvious. Coordinating with other agencies also should be done, especially regarding service prices. In particular, there should be large gains in accuracy from utilizing other sources of data on medical and health care and housing expenses.

Seeking alternative data sources is a more fundamental change. Current collection relies exclusively on surveying sample retail firms. Given the time and resource constraint, the margin of improving data quality in commodity CPI may be fairly narrow to the extent that the current method is retained. However, we propose two alternative (complementary) data methods.

The first is to use POS data, which is available on a daily basis for essentially all the brands sold in sample retail stores. Moreover, POS data contain quantity data totally missing in the current survey. Such data are important for several reasons. Even if Sōmusho retains its current position that the CPI should be based on representative brands, POS data provide more accurate and timely information on which brand is the most popular. Being available on a daily basis makes allowing for sales and temporary price markdowns easy and straightforward. Sōmusho has used POS for collecting price information on one item—personal computers—since 2000.

The second complementary data source is to improve and modify FIES to make it usable as a source of CPI price information. The advantages of using consumer-side information are numerous. The consistency between the CPI basket and the actual consumption basket would be improved greatly. For the purpose of COLI, the actual mix of brands within each item and expenditure shares of items are the ideal set of information. To the extent that FIES accurately represents these choices, there should be no disagreement on how to best represent the consumption basket and relevant purchase prices. Improving the selection of sample retail outlets will not be necessary, as consumers themselves make the choice, which can be observed.

Adjustments to incorporate quality change are the most difficult and this paper has not covered the issue in any detail. We are sure there are important inconsistencies between CPI and other price data, especially WPI. The discrepancies are quantitatively large. Both CPI and WPI will benefit from proper coordination and joint work by Sōmusho and Bank of Japan.

4.9.3   Create an Independent Research and Appraisal Body

Resources should be used to establish an independent body to conduct research and systematic appraisal of major statistics. Such research is especially important for statistics compiled from many primary statistics, such as the National Accounts. Given the current state of information disclosure and the inevitable informational advantage of inside staff, such research must be conducted within the government rather than completely outsourced, although the research would benefit from using outside consultants.

The Statistics Council is a committee overseeing statistics collection and compilation activities of the central government. Although in the past the council made important policy recommendations to improve the official statistics, its current abilities are limited. Like other government councils, members are nongovernment officials and meet only a few times a year. Without a research staff working on a regular basis to monitor official statistics, its recommendations are necessarily abstract in nature and often too late. Given the autonomy of individual ministries, it is unclear to what extent the council has influence on changes in individual statistics produced in different ministries.

4.10   Conclusion

We have employed a variety of data and alternative aggregation evaluation methods to estimate biases in Japan's CPI. The results strongly suggest the presence of sizable upward bias in the commodity CPI. Our best estimate is at least 0.5 percent per year, excluding biases in services and from quality changes. The true bias is likely to be larger than this estimate, but far more extensive research is needed to obtain a more reliable figure.

After a journey into a maze of price data, we come back yet again to one of our first points: The Japanese government should allocate far more resources to collection, compilation, and timely disclosure of statistics. Although private data collection services have grown rapidly since the late 1980s, the need for official statistics is obvious and compelling. No private sector entity can realistically replace the statistics collection activities of the central government.

The potential benefit from improvement in indexes such as the CPI can be enormous, given that so much decision making is linked explicitly or implicitly to the CPI. Although many suggestions for improvements can be implemented within the current budget and staff allocations, the more fundamental, necessary changes require sizable increases in budget and staff.

We have pointed out several times the need for coordination within the government. This is straightforward. Statistics based on the same population of samples should use compatible data strata and the same method for coding, and the actual surveys should be merged to the maximum extent possible in order to minimize costs to respondents. Furthermore, there needs to be an independent body within the government conducting research and appraising the statistics.

Although we have focused on data collection and lower-level aggregation issues in CPI mismeasurement, we concur with the majority that the problems associated with quality adjustments and introduction of new goods are by far the most important and challenging. Moreover, shopping behavior and retail competition needs to be incorporated into CPI. These and other issues are left for future research. The central message of this paper is the need for fundamental changes in the way CPI is collected and compiled.

Appendix A
Comments on the Data

Four sets of data are used in the analysis of potential mismeasurements of CPI.

1. FIES (Somusho, various years)
The CPI uses this survey for the selection and weights of items. Aside from the expenditure records of the roughly 8,000 sample households, FIES also reports average unit purchase prices for 200 items. We use these unit price data as the benchmark for COLI estimates.

There are three major problems with using these unit prices as the COLI. First, the data cover only subsets of consumption expenditure and do not cover services. Second, they are averages of nominal purchase prices and do not incorporate any changes in quality. Third, there are large monthly fluctuations in the data, partially reflecting measurement errors.

There are several advantages, however, over the current CPI as the benchmark of COLI. The unit price data reflect the average of the actual choices by sample households of items, brands, quality, and different types of stores, thus incorporating substitutions by households across the same categories. To the extent that quality changes not reflected in prices are not quantitatively important, the unit price and expenditure data provide the most natural measure of COLI. Another notable advantage is that the survey can be used to estimate COLI across different types of households: Although the current CPI supplements include a CPI series for several different types of households, they incorporate only the differences in weights across households (using the common average prices taken from the *Survey of Prices*).

2. *1997 National Survey of Prices, Special Volume on Bargain Prices* (Sōmusho 1998)

This survey selected sixteen items and collected cross-sectional data on regular and discount prices across regions, types of stores, and variety of other attributes, such as location characteristics and store sizes. We use data for fourteen of these sixteen items. We deleted two items, eggs and beef, because of the potentially large quality differences across samples.

3. POS-SRI (SRI, various years)

The POS data are compiled by the SRI on sixteen items for the seventy-two month period January 1995 through December 2000 for twenty stores in metropolitan Tokyo belonging to a national chain of supermarkets. The report provides average monthly prices and sales separately for regular and discount sales. We use the same fourteen items selected above.

4. POS-DEI (DEI, various years)

The POS data compiled by the DEI includes six items among the fourteen selected items above. The data are daily price and sales records for roughly 320 brand-store combinations for twenty-four months between April 1995 and March 1997.

Appendix B
Shopping-Storage Model

Consider a household that consumes at constant rate c per day. Assume it visits a retailer each $1/s$ days. The price of the consumption good is randomly drawn from a known distribution $F(p)$. Normalize this price so the highest price is 1. Shopping costs are δ per visit, storage cost is ε per day per unit, and costs associated with stock-out (i.e., running out of stocks or inventory) are ignored. For simplicity, assume the same amount, q, is purchased on each visit if the price is below some threshold level, $\hat{p}$. Since the amount purchased per visit must on average equal consumption (c), then

(A1) $sqF(\hat{p}) = c.$

Thus the amount of purchase per visit is given by

(A2) $q = \dfrac{c}{sF(\hat{p})}.$

The average time needed to consume the stored good is q/c. On average, the amount in storage is half the amount purchased, so the average storage cost per unit of time is

(A3) $\dfrac{1}{2}\varepsilon q = \dfrac{c\varepsilon}{2sF(\hat{p})}.$

The household minimizes average total cost (per unit of time) by the choice of $\hat{p}$ and s, taking δ, ε, and F as given.

(A4) $\displaystyle\min_{(\hat{p},s)} \cdot \left[c \int^{\hat{p}} pdF(p) + s\delta + \dfrac{c\varepsilon}{2sF(\hat{p})} \right]$

The POS-DEI data set can be used to obtain an empirical price distribution for the simulation. The data include daily sales and price data for six items sold at fourteen sample stores. Each data item includes twenty to thirty different brands. The top five brands by unit sales are chosen from each store for the simulation. The data span the two-year period, 7 April 1995 to 7 April 1997. Daily price data are used to compute the kernel price density function for each brand, each item, and each store.[8]

The range of parameters we used in simulation are:

$c = 0.2$ (one unit of purchase is equal to 5 days' consumption)
$\varepsilon = 0.001 \sim 0.01$
$\delta = 0.05 \sim 0.14.$

All are measured in rates per day. For example, $\varepsilon = 0.001$ is equivalent to depreciation at 0.1 percent per day if the good is purchased at the regular (high) price. Using the minimum wage in Okinawa (the lowest) of around ¥600 per hour to set the low end and assuming about one to two hours for shopping, shopping cost per visit ranges from ¥500 to ¥1,400, which translates to 5 percent to 14 percent of ¥10,000 of groceries. The upper limit corresponds to the roughly two-hour minimum wage in the Tokyo metropolitan area (= ¥708 per hour).

Table 4B.1 shows that across-store variations in total shopping cost and average purchase price are large. For the top five brands, total shopping cost varies by over 8 percent between store eight, the lowest, and store two,

8. The pricing patterns are not uniform, and the optimal shopping behavior incorporating the periodic price discounts are highly complex. For simplicity, we assume a random drawing of prices from the empirical price distribution. See Ariga, Matsui, and Watanabe (2000) for the dynamics of pricing strategy and shopping behavior.

Table 4B.1   Variations in Total Cost and Average Purchase Price across Fourteen
                  Stores (%)

	Total Cost		Average Purchase Price	
Sample Store	Top 5 Brands	Cheapest	Top 5 Brands	Cheapest
1. Co-op 1	+3.42	+8.75	+2.46	+10.33
2. Co-op 2	+3.51	+8.17	+2.65	+7.83
3. National chain A1	−2.731	−0.33	−6.15	+1.51
4. National chain A2	−0.58	−3.03	−2.83	−2.56
5. Unknown	−2.02	+6.62	−6.55	+8.16
6. Unknown	+0.26	−1.10	−2.33	−0.85
7. Unknown	−0.71	+8.06	−2.66	+9.66
8. Unknown	−4.74	+0.92	−6.63	+1.36
9. National chain B1	−2.53	−3.38	−3.49	−1.11
10. National chain B2	+.00	+2.68	−1.68	+6.64
11. Regional chain C1	−4.02	+2.44	−6.60	+6.67
12. Regional chain C2	+0.19	+2.23	−1.10	+4.87
13. National chain D1	+0.23	+3.00	−0.61	+4.20

Note: Numbers shown are percentage differences from Store 14 (not shown), which is used as the benchmark.

the highest. For average purchase prices, the range is also more than 8 percent (between stores eight and two). If consumers choose to buy the cheapest product, variations are even larger: more than 12 percent in total costs (stores nine and one) and close to 13 percent in average purchase prices (stores four and one). Variations in total shopping costs are smaller than those for average purchase prices because volume shopping of discounted items increases inventory holding costs.

Notice that the two co-ops tend to be more expensive, especially for bargain hunters. This reflects the fact that periodic discounts are less common in those stores than in supermarket chains.

Across-store variations in pricing patterns alone can give rise to sizeable variations in shopping frequency and storage. The other side of this fact is that consumers with different shopping and storage costs choose different stores, even if all the stores are identical except for the pricing policy. This follows from the large variation in optimal shopping and storage costs across stores even after controlling for unit shopping and storage costs. For example, when $\delta = 0.05$ and $\varepsilon = 0.001$, the shopping cost for the top-selling brand of item one varies between 0.045 and 0.113 and storage cost varies between 0.023 and 0.057.

To demonstrate this, table 4B.2 shows the cost-minimizing choice of store as unit shopping and storage costs are varied for the top-selling brand of item one. In this specific case, store five minimizes the total shopping cost for those with lower shopping and storage costs. For those with some-

Table 4B.2 Optimal Store Choice for Item 1, the Top Brand

	δ									
ε	.001	.002	.003	.004	.005	.006	.007	.008	.009	.010
.05	5	5	5	5	5	5	5	5	5	5
.06	5	5	5	5	5	5	5	5	5	5
.07	5	5	5	5	5	5	5	5	5	5
.08	5	5	5	5	5	5	5	5	5	5
.09	5	5	5	5	5	5	5	2	2	9
.10	5	5	5	5	5	5	2	9	9	9
.11	5	5	5	5	5	2	9	9	9	9
.12	5	5	5	5	2	9	9	9	9	9
.13	5	5	5	2	9	9	9	9	9	9
.14	5	2	9	9	9	9	9	9	9	9

Note: The optimal choice of store under each configuration of ε and δ is shown in each cell.

what higher costs, store two becomes the best choice, reflecting the fact that the optimal shopping and storage policy for store five involves sizable purchase at occasional but deep discounts. At even higher shopping and storage costs, the optimal choice shifts to store nine.

This example is not exceptional. Among the 3,000 simulation cases, each of the fourteen stores is the cost-minimizing choice in at least one case, although store ten has only one such case. Store three is the overall winner, being the best choice in 509 cases.

References

Ando, Albert. 2002. Missing household saving and valuation of corporations: Inquiry into Japanese National Accounts. *Journal of the Japanese and International Economies* 16 (2): 147–76.

Ariga, Kenn, Kenji Matsui, and Makoto Watanabe. 2000. Hot and spicy: Ups and downs in price floor and ceiling of Japanese supermarkets. Kyoto University, Institute of Economic Research. Mimeograph.

Bank of Japan. 2001a. Oroshiuri bukka shisū ni okeru hedonic approach (Hedonic approaches in the wholesale price index. Bank of Japan Working Paper no. 01-24. Tokyo: Bank of Japan.

———. 2001b. Oroshiuri bukka shisū no hinshitsu chōsei wo megutte (On quality adjustments in wholesale price index). Paper presented at Conference on Price Indexes. May–June, Tokyo.

Boskin, Michael J., Ellen Dulberger, Robert J. Gordon, Zvi Griliches, and Dale W. Jorgenson. 1996. *Final report of the advisory commission to study consumer price index*. Washington, D.C.: GPO.

Caves, David W., Lawrence R. Christensen, and W. Erwin Diewart. 1982. The economic theory of index numbers and the measurement of input, output, and productivity. *Econometrica* 50 (11): 1393–1414.

Diewert, W. Erwin. 1976. Exact and superlative index numbers. *Journal of Econometrics* 4:115–44.

Distribution Economics Institute (DEI). Various years. POS-DEI data set. Tokyo: DEI.

Feenstra, Richard C., and Matthew D. Shapiro. 2001. High frequency substitutions and the measurements of price indexes. NBER Working Paper no. 8176. Cambridge, Mass.: National Bureau of Economic Research, March.

Hausman, Jerry A. 1999. Cellular telephone, new products, and the CPI. *Journal of Business and Economic Statistics* 17 (1): 188–94.

Iwamoto, Yasushi. 2000. Jinkō-kōreika to iryōhi (Aging Japanese population and medical expenditure) Kyoto University, Institute of Economic Research. Mimeograph.

Matsuda, Yoshiro, Keiro Hamasuna, and Hiromi Mori, eds. 2000. *Kōza micro tōkei bunseki* (Microscopic statistical analysis). 3 vols. Tōkyō: Nihon Hyōronsha.

Matsuoka, Mikihiro, and Brian Rose. 1994. *The DIR guide to Japanese economic statistics.* Cambridge: Oxford University Press.

Ministry of Health, Labor, and Welfare. Various years. *Annual official estimate of national medical expenditure.* http://www.mhlw.go.jp/toukei/saikin/hw/k-iryohi/00/.

Schultz, Charles, and Christopher Mackie, eds. Forthcoming. *At what price? Conceptualization and measuring cost-of-living and price indexes.* Washington, D.C.: National Academies Press.

Sezon Research Institute (SRI). 2000. Ōte ryōhan-ten no POS data wo riyō shita bukka shisū ni kakakwaru kenkyū (Price index using POS data of a large scale retailers). Tokyo: Sezon Research Institute.

———. Various years. POS-SRI data set. Tokyo: SRI.

Shapiro, Matthew, and David W. Wilcox. 1996. Mismeasurement in the consumer price index: An evaluation. *NBER Macroeconomics Annual 1996* ed. 93–154. Cambridge: MIT Press.

Shiratsuka, Shigenori. 1997. *Bukka no keizai bunseki* (Economic analysis of inflation measures). Tokyo: University of Tokyo Press.

———. 1999. Measurement errors in the Japanese consumer price index. *Monetary and Economic Studies* 17 (3): 69–102.

Sōmusho (Ministry of Public Management, Home Affairs, Posts, and Telecommunications). 1998. *1997 national survey of prices, special volume on bargain prices.* Tokyo: Sōmusho.

———. 1999. *Statistics standards annual 1999.* Tokyo: Japan Statistical Association. Available at http://www.jstat.or.jp/.

———. 2000a. *Shōhisha bukka shisū sankō shiryō #17* (Reference documents for CPI #17). Tokyo: Sōmusho.

———. 2000b. *Statistics standards annual 2000.* Tokyo: Japan Statistical Association. Available at http://www.jstat.or.jp/.

———. Various years. *National survey of family income and expenditure.* Tokyo: Japan Statistical Association. Available at http://www.jstat.or.jp/.

U.S. Executive Office of the President, Office of Management and Budget. 2002. *Statistical programs of the United States government.* http://www.whitehouse.gov/omb/inforeg/03statprog.pdf.

5

Regulation, Distribution Efficiency, and Retail Density

David Flath

Japan's distribution sector employs about one-sixth of the nation's labor force and accounts for around one-eighth of the gross domestic product (GDP), large enough to matter for any economy-wide assessment of barriers to growth and efficiency. Moreover, the phrase "inefficient distribution" has been repeated so many times in reference to Japan that one might suppose the evidence of gross distortion is overwhelming: It is not.

Certainly, regulatory limits on large stores have had an effect on the numbers of stores of differing formats, but the undeniable peculiarities of Japan's distribution sector can be explained by the fundamentals: car ownership, size of dwelling, and geography. Accounting for such fundamentals explains much of the variation in retail density between Japan and other countries, as well as across prefectures within Japan. Moreover, changes in these factors can be related to changes in the structure of retailing.[1]

This chapter does three things: First, it compiles facts on the state of Japan's distribution system and puts them in historical and international context. This includes an explanation of retail store density and its relation to wholesale channels. Second, the chapter describes the logical frame-

David Flath is professor of economics at North Carolina State University.

This research was supported by a grant from the Abe Fellowship Program of the Social Science Research Council and the American Council of Learned Societies with funds provided by the Japan Foundation Center for Global Partnership. I also thank Tatsuhiko Nariu for many useful discussions, Anil Kashyap for his very helpful suggestions, and Gary Saxonhouse and others for their comments on the paper at the March 2002 conference in Tokyo sponsored by the National Bureau of Economic Research (NBER).

1. Other investigators who argue that factors besides regulation are important in discussions of Japan's distribution system include Nariu (1994), Maruyama et al. (1991), and Miwa and Ramseyer (2002). For an overview of my work and that of some other scholars, see Flath (2000, chap. 14).

work behind the still widely held view that regulation, in particular the Large Store Law (repealed in 2000), is the key determinant of the structure of Japan's distribution system, and then derives some testable predictions about what this implies. Third, it provides new evidence on whether the testable predictions are true. This includes looking at differences among prefectures and over time in retail density and format.

5.1   Characteristics of Japan's Distribution Sector

The peculiarities of Japan's distribution sector include the myriad of small stores and lack of large stores, multiple wholesale steps, and ubiquity of vertical restraints. Some relevant data are in table 5.1.

In the late 1990s, Japan had eleven stores per thousand inhabitants, almost twice the United States and four times the United Kingdom levels. The typical U.S. supermarket in 2000 was almost five times the size of the Japanese equivalent, which was not quite the size of two basketball courts. Many stores in Japan are family enterprises with even smaller

Table 5.1   **Features of the Japanese Distribution System**

Indicator	United States	Japan
Small Stores		
Stores per 1,000 persons (U.S. 1996, Japan 1997)[a]	6.1	11.2
Workers per store (U.S. 1992, Japan 1997)	11.7	5.1
Number of typical supermarkets[c] (U.S. 2000, Japan 1999)[d]	31,830[b]	18,709
Average store's floor space in m^2 (U.S. 2000, Japan 1999)[d]	4,143[e]	832
Average store's annual sales in respective millions (U.S. 2000, Japan 1999)[d]	$12	¥895
Long and Complex Wholesale Marketing Channels		
Percentage of labor force employed in		
Wholesale (1990–1993)	4.1	8.0
Wholesale (Japan 1996–1997, U.S. 1997)	3.8	5.9
Retail (1993)	11.4	10.4
Retail (Japan 1996–1997, U.S. 1997)	10.9	11.2
Percentage of wholesale sales to other wholesalers:[f]		
1985–1986	25	42
1997	n.a.	35

Source: Data are from table 5.2, except as indicated.

Note: n.a. = not available.

[a]The United Kingdom had 3.4 in 1994.

[b]Stores with annual sales of $2 million or more.

[c]In Japan, called "food specialty stores."

[d]For Japan, MITI (various years), and for the United States, the U.S. Food Marketing Institute (available at http://www.fmi.org/facts_figs/keyfacts/).

[e]That is 44,600 square feet, which is slightly smaller than a U.S. football field.

[f]For Japan, MITI (various years), and for the United States, Ito and Maruyama (1991).

floor space. The average number of workers per store in Japan is half the U.S. figure.

Fragmentation of the retail sector in Japan is accompanied by long and complex wholesale marketing channels. This is evident in several statistics. Japan's distribution sector employment is disproportionately concentrated in wholesaling compared to the United States, and the fraction of wholesalers' revenue from sales to other wholesalers is much higher in Japan.

Finally, the ubiquity of manufacturer-imposed pricing rules, customer assignments, and stipulations of exclusivity can be judged from the large fraction of wholesalers reporting participation in manufacturer-initiated distribution *keiretsu*: The figure was 45 percent in 1992, although this is down from 70 percent in 1986 (Small and Medium Enterprise Agency 1994, 180, table 9). No direct comparison with the United States can be made, but such practices frequently run afoul of U.S. antitrust laws and thus undoubtedly are less widespread.

5.2 International Perspective

This section presents a comprehensive comparison of Japan's distribution sector with those of other nations. Table 5.2 depicts statistics for the Organization for Economic Co-operation and Development (OECD) member countries on density of retail stores, employment per store, and value-added and employment in wholesaling and retailing. The countries are listed in ascending order of stores per thousand inhabitants in the mid-1990s. Japan is in the bottom third of the list, having moved up since 1982 when it had 14.3 stores per thousand.

A simple index of the average productivity of labor employed in the distribution sector relative to the average productivity of labor in the overall economy can be obtained by dividing the share of distribution sector value-added in GDP by the share of distribution sector employment in the total labor force. Countries with higher standards of living (i.e., relatively high gross national product (GNP) per person in purchasing power parity (PPP units) tend to have wider discrepancies in average labor productivity between distribution and other sectors. (The United States is a regression outlier, but Japan is not). This has a simple interpretation: It reflects the generally slower pace of technical change in services compared to manufacturing something first noted by William Baumol.[2]

Japan's index stands at 0.69, which is below the 0.75 average for all the countries. This is expected, given the high standard of living. (The United

2. A simple ordinary least squares (OLS) regression of the natural logarithm of the labor productivity index (for 1996–1997) on the natural logarithm of GNP per person measured in purchasing power units (for 1998) is ln (Index) = $4.1 - 0.45$ ln (GNP per person in PPP units), where t-stat = -3.8 number of observations = 20, and R^2 = 0.44.

Table 5.2   International Comparison of Distribution Sectors

	Retail outlets[a]			Share of Distribution in Total Employment					Share of Retail in Total Employment	
				Value-Added to GDP						
	Year of Data	Number	Employment Per Outlet	1993[b]	1996–1997[e]	Retail Only	1996–1997[e]	1993–1997[e]	1990[b]	1996–1997[e]
Luxembourg	n.a.	n.a.	n.a.	13.5	10.2	3.4	15.9	21.1	9.7	10.0
United Kingdom	1993	3.3	15.4	12.8	10.7	n.a.	17.1	16.4	11.3	10.0
Austria	1996	3.7	8.4	12.8	11.9	4.3	14.4	13.4	7.5	6.6
Australia	1992	4.0	10.8	n.a.	10.8	n.a.	20.8	17.4	13.1	9.9
Germany	1996	4.9	6.7	7.8	10.0	4.1	11.3	15.5	8.3	8.2
Sweden	1993	4.9	6.5	8.3	9.5	n.a.	11.9	12.9	6.9	4.6
Turkey	1996	5.0	0.9	16.0	14.4	5.4	12.5	n.a.	4.8	4.3
United States	1992	6.1	11.7	15.7	13.6[d]	6.7[d]	15.5	14.7[d]	11.4	10.9[d]
Denmark	1995	6.3	5.8	10.7	11.5	3.8	10.8	15.9	7.8	6.9
France	1996	6.6	3.7	12.2	9.2	4.0	13.8	13.8	9.3	7.2
Czech Republic	1996	6.7	13.3	10.7	10.8	3.7	16.4	15.0	13.6	8.5
Iceland	1990	6.7	n.a.	8.9	n.a.	n.a.	11.9	13.6	6.4	7.0
Canada	1985	6.8	8.3	10.0	9.3	n.a.	16.4	18.7	10.4	12.7
Netherlands	1996	7.4	5.0	12.7	12.0	3.7	16.2	15.1	12.3	6.9
Finland	1997	7.6	2.5	8.4	9.4	3.1	12.5	11.9	6.7	6.0

Switzerland	1996	7.7	6.5	14.7	n.a.	n.a.	13.9	n.a.	10.6	9.4
European community	1996	7.8	5.3	n.a.	n.a.	n.a.	n.a.	n.a.	n.a.	n.a.
Norway	1996	9.3	4.6	9.7	9.8	n.a.	13.9	15.2	6.0	8.8
New Zealand	1990	9.5	4.4	15.2	n.a.	n.a.	12.4	15.3	10.0	6.8
Italy	1996	9.8	2.6	15.3	12.6	2.9	19.3	17.3	10.3	7.6
Japan	**1997**	**11.2**	**5.1**	**12.5**	**11.8**	**5.0**[e]	**18.4**	**17.1**	**10.4**	**11.2**
Hungary	1997	12.1	1.5	10.8	10.2	4.7	12.4	13.9	11.5	10.7
Mexico	1993	13.0	13.2	n.a.	15.1	n.a.	14.9	n.a.	n.a.	15.2
Belgium	1996	13.7	1.9	n.a.	10.9	n.a.	15.9	13.3	7.3	12.7
Spain	1992	14.2	2.7	14.2	13.3	n.a.	16.7	22.3	11.0	12.8
Ireland	1997	14.4	2.5	7.9	n.a.	n.a.	14.3	n.a.	11.8	9.6
Portugal	1996	15.2	2.4	8.9	13.3	4.4	16.4	17.2	5.2	8.4
Greece	1993	17.6	3.1	9.6	13.1	6.5	15.5	14.4	9.3	15.6
Korea	1997	18.5	2.2	11.7	n.a.	n.a.	22.0	n.a.	n.a.	9.2
Poland	1997	24.8	1.0	18.9	18.4	n.a.	16.4	13.2	5.2	7.4

Note: Value added to GDP by retail sector. n.a. = not available.

[a]OECD (2000), except as noted.

[b]Pilat (1997, 17, table 2.1).

[c]Boylaud and Nicoletti (2001, 256, table 1).

[d]Statistical Abstract of the United States (available at http://www.census.gov/prod/www/statistical-abstract-02.html).

[e]McKinsey Global Institute (2000, exchibit 1).

States does not fit the pattern; its index of 0.92 is above the international average.) The upshot is that the variation in the index across countries probably is more reflective of international differences in average productivity of manufacturing than of distribution. Countries with lower standards of living tend to have more stores per person and smaller average store size (measured as average employment per store). The association often made between Japan's ubiquity of small stores and economic backwardness is based on this pattern.

5.3   Explaining Retail Store Density

There are two broad types of economic models for explaining the overall density of retail stores: the social optimality approach, which presumes that the density of stores attains the economic optimum without explicitly modeling how prices are set, and the explicit pricing and free entry approach, which presumes that the density of stores is the maximum consistent with positive profits given some explicit model of pricing by firms. Flath (1990) and Matsui and Nariu (2001) adopt the social optimality approach; Heal (1980) and Gabszewicz and Thisse (1986) model pricing explicitly and presume free entry.

The comparative statics of store density are qualitatively the same for both types of models. A proliferation of stores shifts some costs of storing and transporting goods from households to the distribution sector. Thus, it is appropriate to base empirical analysis of international variation in retail density on factors associated with the costs of transporting and storing goods of both households and firms. This is exactly the approach taken by Flath and Nariu (1996) using data from the early 1980s. Here that exercise is repeated with more recent data.

Table 5.3 presents data on some variables associated with the costs and benefits of a proliferation of stores for various OECD nations, mostly from around 1996. The variables are proxies for things that affect the relative efficiency of households and firms at storing and transporting goods.

Crowded living space (CRWDNG) increases willingness to pay a premium to shop nearby. Car ownership (CARS) lowers household costs of shopping and thus lowers the premium. The more urbanized an economy (URBAN), then for any given expansion in the number of stores per person, the smaller the effect on the average distance between stores and residences, and so the smaller marginal benefit from proximity. If a nation is geographically compact (LENGTH) like Japan, rather than dispersed over half a continent like the United States, the added cost of restocking a multiplicity of stores is reduced. A proliferation of trucks (TRUCKS) and the infrastructure of roads that make it worthwhile to use trucks lower the added costs of restocking a multiplicity of stores as opposed to a smaller number of larger ones.

Table 5.3   Factors in Retail Density, 1998

Variable[a]	STORES[b]	CRWDG[c]	CARS[d]	URBAN[d]	LENGTH[f]	TRUCKS[g]	GNPPP[g]	GNP[h]
United Kingdom	0.5	3.4[i]	374.2	89	15.7	47.1	20,640	21,400
Austria	0.6[j]	3.7	479.9	65	9.2	38.3	22,740	26,850
Australia	n.a.	4.0	472.3	85	88.0	110.5	20,130	20,300
Germany	0.5	4.9	507.6	87	18.9	28.9	20,810	25,850
Sweden	0.6[j]	4.9	426.1	83	21.2	38.0	19,480	25,620
Turkey	1.3	5.1[i]	63.8	73	27.8	15.7	n.a.	3,160
United States	0.5	5.8[i]	480.6	77	96.8	280.9	29,340	29,340
Denmark	n.a.	6.3	354.2	86	6.6	56.2	23,830	33,260
France	0.7	6.6	455.8	75	23.5	92.1	22,320	24,940
Iceland	n.a.	6.7	510.9	92	10.1	62.0	22,830	28,010
Canada	0.5	6.8	440.8	77	99.9	121.2	24,050	20,020
Czech Republic	1.0	6.8[i]	358.0	66	8.9	41.1	n.a.	5,040
The Netherlands	0.7	7.4	566.3	89	6.4	100.6	21,620	24,760
Finland	0.7[j]	7.6	388.7	64	18.4	54.0	20,270	24,110
Switzerland	0.6	7.7	476.5	62	6.4	37.6	26,620	40,080
Norway	0.6	9.3	405.9	74	18.0	88.9	24,290	34,330
New Zealand	0.5	9.5	440.5	87	16.5	99.7	15,840	14,700
Italy	0.8[j]	9.8	538.2	67	17.3	50.7	20,200	20,250
Japan	**0.6[j]**	**11.2[j]**	**395.1**	**79**	**19.4**	**163.8**	**23,180**	**32,380**

(*continued*)

Table 5.3 (continued)

Variable[a]	STORES[b]	CRWDG[c]	CARS[d]	URBAN[d]	LENGTH[f]	TRUCKS[g]	GNPPP[g]	GNP[h]
Hungary	0.5	12.1	234.2	66	9.6	32.2	n.a.	4,510
Mexico	1.4	13.0	97.8	74	44.2	45.9	8,190	3,970
Belgium	0.5[j]	13.7	437.1	97	5.7	45.0	23,480	25,380
Spain	0.7[j]	14.2	389.2	77	22.5	81.6	16,060	14,080
Ireland	n.a.	14.4	266.8	58	8.4	31.1	18,340	18,340
Portugal	0.7	15.2	308.0	61	9.6	36.3	14,380	10,690
Greece	n.a.	17.6	254.9	60	11.5	93.2	13,010	11,650
Korea	1.1	18.5	163.4	84	10.0	46.1	12,270	7,970
Poland	2.0	24.8	229.7	65	18.0	40.8	6,740	3,900

Notes: Data are for 1998 or nearest year for which data are available. n.a. = not available.

[a]Name of variable in regression analysis.

[b]Store density; stores per 1,000 inhabitants (table 5.2, except as noted).

[c]Crowding; rooms per person (United Nations Statistics Division 2003, except as noted).

[d]Car density and truck density; such vehicles per 1,000 inhabitants (Statistics Bureau 2001, table 8-2).

[e]Urbanization; Urban population as percentage of total (World Bank 2001, 232, table 2).

[f]Square root of the country's area (1,000 square kilometers, World Bank 2001, 232, table 2).

[g]The GNP per capita adjusted to PPP in U.S. dollars.

[h]The GNP per capita in U.S. dollars.

[i]Using data from Boylaud and Nicoletti (2001, 256, table 1); Czech Republic, Japan, and Turkey are 1997 figures; United Kingdom is 1994 figures; United States is 1996 figures.

[j]Statistics Bureau (2001), rooms per dwelling (p. 296, table 13–6) divided by persons per household (p. 32, table 2-10).

Table 5.4   **OLS Regressions Explaining International Variation in Density of Stores**

Variable	With CRWDNG	With CRWDNG Japan Excluded	Without CRWDNG	Without CRWDNG Japan Excluded
Constant	3.4	3.5	5.6	5.6
	(1.9)	(1.8)	(5.2)	(5.1)
URBAN	−0.4	−0.4	−1.4	−1.4
	(−0.4)	(−0.4)	(−1.7)	(−1.7)
ln CARS	−0.3	−0.3	−0.6	−0.6
	(−1.0)	(−1.0)	(−2.9)	(−2.8)
ln TRUCKS	0.5	0.5	0.5	0.5
	(2.1)	(1.9)	(2.6)	(2.4)
ln LENGTH	−0.3	−0.03	−0.4	−0.4
	(−2.0)	(−1.9)	(−2.8)	(−2.8)
ln CRWDG	0.6	0.6	n.a.	n.a.
	(1.5)	(1.5)		
Number of observations	23	22	28	27
R^2	0.40	0.39	0.40	0.41
Predicted value of STORES for Japan,				
t-test statistic for difference from	n.a.	11.8	n.a.	11.7
actual value (11.3)	n.a.	(0.08)	n.a.	(0.13)

Note: Dependent variable = ln STORES. Coefficients, with t-statistics in parentheses. n.a. = not applicable.

Table 5.4 shows that all of these contribute to the cross-country variation in number of stores per person in the expected way. The estimates in the first two columns include the average number of persons per room as an explanatory variable and a proxy for the dearness of household storage space. This variable is available only for some of the countries. Excluding it, and thus enlarging the sample, narrows the standard errors of estimates of the other coefficients. This possibly reinforces confidence that the results are qualitatively valid.

Japan is not a regression outlier. Stores per thousand persons predicted by regressions excluding Japan are 11.8 with crowding and 11.7 without, statistically indistinguishable from the actual value of 11.3. These results very much resemble those obtained in Flath and Nariu (1996) for a slightly different set of countries using data from around 1980.

The conclusion remains that Japan's relatively high density of retail stores is due to its paucity of private cars, confined household living space, geographic centricity, and superabundance of trucks. All of this pointedly leaves regulation out of the picture. Partly this reflects the lack of a suitable proxy for regulation that can be included in the regression equation, but it also reflects a judgment that regulation is a corollary of economic variables like the ones already in the equation. I return to this point later.

5.4   Wholesale Channels

The focus so far has been on the density of stores. A related issue is the extent to which Japan's complex wholesale marketing channels are induced by its high retail store density, as opposed to reflecting some idiosyncrasy.

Proliferation of stores induces branching of logistical arteries to economize on transport costs. Such branching does not by itself imply a multiplicity of wholesale steps, but would seem to lower the costs of a profusion of wholesalers.

Evidence suggests Japan's high retail density and wholesale complexity are intertwined. Nariu and Flath (1993) construct estimates of the average number of steps in matched wholesale industries of Japan and the United States for the early 1980s. Besides confirming that Japanese wholesale channels have, on average, more steps (1.8) than U.S. ones (1.4), we also showed that the variation in number of steps across wholesale marketing channels is highly correlated between Japan and the United States, and for consumer products, it is also related to the relative density of stores.[3]

In other words, there are common influences operating on the length of wholesale channels in both countries. Also, the number of wholesale steps in Japan is greater for products (such as food) that have many retail stores compared to the United States. This suggests that Japan's elephantine wholesale sector is to some extent due to its proliferation of stores.

5.5   The Large Store Law

The regulation that bears most directly on the density of retail stores in Japan is the Large Store Law. It is the essential reason why Japan has far fewer department stores and general merchandise superstores per person than the United States, as McCraw and O'Brien (1986) were early to recognize.

Bureaucratic obstacles have been placed on establishment of large stores since the Department Store Act of 1937. Suspended in 1947, but reinstated in 1956, it required approval of the national government for the opening of the new department stores anywhere in Japan. In 1974, the Large Scale Retail Store Law replaced the Department Store Act. It made the extent of floor space, rather than the nature of the store, the criterion for necessitating approval. The cut-off was 3,000 square meters in the largest cities and 1,500 square meters everywhere else. At the time, almost all stores larger than the cut-offs were department stores. In 1978, the law was completely revamped to broaden coverage to include all new stores over 500 square meters, which meant it would apply to many grocery stores.

3. In Nariu and Flath (1993, 94, table 6-3) we present an OLS regression: 0.30 + 0.60 (number of steps in matching U.S. wholesale industry) + 0.09 (stores per household in Japan divided by stores per household in the United States for retail category corresponding to the wholesale industry), where t-stat = 4.1; t-stat = 3.3; number of observations = 24; and R^2 = 0.57.

The process of securing approval to open a large store was torturous, typically requiring two years or longer. The process, directed by the Ministry of International Trade and Industry (MITI), involved hearings before local panels that included owners of existing stores that would suffer if the proposal was approved. The panels tended either to recommend against approval or propose restrictions on the hours or days the store could operate. In many cases they proposed such onerous requirements as offering of classes in cultural activities, like calligraphy or floral arrangement, at prices that did not cover costs. The MITI tended to adopt these recommendations and proposals; Larke (1994) offers further detail on the process. Unsurprisingly, following adoption of the 1978 amendments, applications to open new stores dropped to a trickle: in 1984 there were fewer than 500.

In 1989, the U.S. government identified the Large Store Law as a structural impediment to the sale of U.S.-made consumer products in Japan, arguing in negotiations with Japan for repeal or relaxation of the law. Japan responded first by amending the law in 1992 to shorten the process for reviewing applications, then in 1994, by raising the cut-off to 1,000 square meters, which is about one-fourth the size of the typical U.S. grocery store.

As shown in table 5.5, the number of large stores in operation did increase after 1994. However the overall number remains low compared to the United States. In 1997, there were only around 24,000 stores larger than 1,000 square meters in all of Japan.

In May 1998, the Diet replaced the old law with a new one (actually with three new laws) that place details of the regulation of large stores under control of prefectural governments but mandates that they consider only environmental factors, such as noise and traffic, and not any economic

Table 5.5   **Number of Large Stores in Japan, 1985–1999**

	Large Stores						All Stores	
	Class 1[a]	%[c]	Class 2[b]	%[c]	Total	%[c]	Total	%[c]
1985	3,662	n.a.	9,624	n.a.	13,286	n.a.	1,628,644	n.a.
1988	4,027	3.2	10,605	3.3	14,632	3.3	1,619,752	−0.2
1991	4,429	3.2	11,082	1.5	15,511	2.0	1,591,223	−0.6
1994	3,351	−8.9	14,292	8.8	17,643	4.4	1,499,948	−1.9
1997	4,350	9.1	17,542	7.1	21,892	7.5	1,419,696	−1.8
1999	n.a.	n.a.	n.a.	n.a.	23,897	4.5	1,406,884	−0.5

Source: MITI (various years).

Note: n.a. = not applicable.

[a]Class 1 includes larger stores (over 3,000 square meters in most regions, 6,000 square meters in selected wards of Tokyo and other large cities).

[b]Class 2 covers remaining large stores. In the 1999 Census of Commerce the distinctions were abandoned.

[c]Annual average percentage change since prior census.

harm to incumbent owners of small stores. The line between environmental factors and economic ones is sufficiently fuzzy that some prefectures may actually enact more severe restraints than existed under the previous regime (although I consider this unlikely). Other prefectures may remove the restraints on large stores altogether.

5.6   Regulatory Distortions

Regulatory distortions definitely exist in Japan's distribution sector; table 5.6 summarizes them. The sparseness of large stores clearly is the result of regulations. Restricting the number of large stores may have had a secondary, distorting effect on Japan's foreign trade insofar as imported consumer products until the 1990s were generally more effectively distributed through large, upscale department stores, such as Mitsukoshi and Takashimaya.

The multiple wholesale steps and disproportionately large employment in wholesaling may in large part also be a secondary effect of the proliferation of small stores and thus an indirect result of regulatory protection of small stores. For example, Nariu and Flath (1993) offer a regression equation linking multiplicity of wholesale steps and proliferation of stores.

Regulations regarding inward foreign direct investment (FDI) may have

Table 5.6   Regulations Distorting Distribution Sector Resource Allocation

Regulation	Nature of Effect on Distribution Sector	Comment
Large Store Law 1974–2000	The law severely limited number of stores with large floor space, including department stores and general merchandise superstores and contributed to survival of small traditional stores.	The law was repealed in 1998, but in effect until April 2000 and administered by national government.
Large-Scale Retail Store Location Law 2000–Present	The law was enacted with repeal of the Large Store Law.	The law vests prefectures and municipalities with authority to limit large stores (1,000 square meters or greater). Supposedly, criteria is to be confined to environmental factors only, such as noise and traffic, but skepticism is warranted.
Automotive inspection (*shaken*)	The Road Vehicles Act (revised 1995) mandates comprehensive safety inspections of private passenger vehicles every two years beginning with the third year the car is in operation.	This usually entails purchase of numerous replacement parts. The cost inhibits car ownership and thus helps perpetuate the advantage of nearby small neighborhood stores over larger, more distant stores.

had a relatively large effect on distribution. A disproportionately large share of FDI in Japan (and elsewhere) is in wholesaling. Japan's vanishing small stock of inward FDI, in comparison with the United States and the European Union (EU), has been linked to Japanese government restrictions relaxed around 1980. The relative absence of foreign-affiliate wholesalers in Japan could inhibit competition and protect inefficient domestic incumbent producers and distributors. (For a close investigation of FDI in Japan's wholesale industry and its effects on import penetration, see Flath 2001.)

Enforcement also matters. Vertical restraints are often presumptively in violation of the antimonopoly law of Japan, but they nonetheless appear to be widespread. Penalties for violations are notoriously weak and the resources devoted to enforcement are quite parsimonious. See Flath (1989) for a discussion of vertical restraints in Japan.

Large stores do not necessarily compete only with small ones: they also complement them, perhaps offering agglomeration economies. In other words, there are possible negative effects on small stores from regulatory limits on large ones. Empirical analysis is needed here.

5.6.1   Evidence Regarding Regulatory Distortion

As a first pass at assessing whether the distorting effects of these regulations might be significant, consider some data from the McKinsey Global Institute (2000). The authors construct estimates of value-added per hour of labor across stores of different kinds in Japan and the United States in the mid-1990s. They conclude that traditional mom-and-pop stores in Japan have lower average labor productivity than do large stores in Japan and that they account for a disproportionately large share of total labor input, as compared to the United States (table 5.7).

Overall average labor productivity in Japan's retail sector is only about half that of the United States. Closing that gap would increase Japan's GDP measurably. How much? Here is a rough calculation. Suppose, for the sake of argument, that only regulatory barriers limit the number of general merchandise stores and supermarket groceries and that eliminating those barriers would double the labor hours that each group worked in 1997 (to roughly match the U.S. pattern), shifting workers from traditional stores. Also suppose that as this occurred, value-added in traditional stores fell in proportion to the withdrawal of labor, while value-added in other stores remained unchanged as wages displaced their profits. Each year this would eliminate a deadweight loss equal to about 0.25 percent of Japanese GDP.[4]

4. If labor hours in general merchandise stores and supermarkets doubled from the 1997 levels with no change in value-added (as wages displaced profits), the value-added per hour would fall by half in each. The deadweight loss thus eliminated equals the area of a Harberger triangle with right sides equal to the initial labor hours and half the initial value-added per labor hour. In other words, the recovery of deadweight losses amounts to about 25 percent of initial value-added: $0.25 \, (2.2 + 3) = ¥1.3$ trillion, which is around 0.25 percent of Japan's GDP.

Table 5.7   Comparison of Retail Stores in Japan and the United States

	Total Sector	GMS[a]	Supermarkets	Specialty Chains	Convenience Stores	Department Stores	Traditionals
Share of sales							
Japan 1988	n.a.	7	7	34	3	10	37
Japan 1997	n.a.	8	12	36	4	9	30
United States 1995	n.a.	15	24	35	3	7	17
Share of labor hours							
Japan 1997	n.a.	4	8	23	2	8	55
United States 1995	n.a.	14	21	35	3	8	19
Value-added							
Japan 1997[c]	25.5[b]	2.2	3.0	12.0	1.0	2.0	3.0
Per hour Japan 1997[d]	50	106	73	102	96	48	19
As percentage of the United States	50	93	60	84	88	70	33

Source: McKinsey Global Institute (2000, 27, exhibit 4 and 28, exhibit 5).

Note: Categories of stores do not correspond exactly to those of the Census of Commerce of Japan. Presumably, this is because of the need for correspondence between the types of stores in Japan and the United States. n.a. = not applicable.

[a]Discount and general merchandise stores.

[b]Five percent of GDP.

[c]In ¥ trillions.

[d]U.S. retail average = 100.

Furthermore, suppose that as a result of the changes in retailing, Japan's wholesale sector also evolved to more resemble U.S. wholesaling in terms of labor productivity. Employment would fall by 2 percent to 4 percent of the labor force, freeing millions of workers for employment elsewhere in the economy. If this reasoning holds any validity, the distortions afflicting Japan's distribution sector are enormous. But the calculation is highly suspect.

With the obvious difficulties in measuring labor hours and productivity in small, family-operated stores set aside, the calculation accepts that any differences between Japan and the United States in allocation of labor across store types and between the retail and wholesale sectors are wholly the result of distortions and could be eliminated by an act of government policy. If this were true, then large stores of Japan ought to be immensely profitable. They are not. The bankruptcies of the Sogo department store chain and MyCal supermarket chain are reminders of this fact.

5.6.2   Vehicle Inspections

Although the following analysis suggests that the distorting effects of the Large Store Law may have been less than is often supposed, it also indicates that regulations not specifically focused on that sector may have a distorting effect. Regulations that unnecessarily or wastefully increase the cost of owning and operating a private car indirectly favor small stores over large ones by enhancing household willingness to pay for proximity to stores.

Japan does indeed have such a regulation, the requirement that private car owners submit their vehicles to comprehensive inspections every two years beginning with the car's third year on the road. These vehicle inspections (*shaken*, in Japanese) are made unnecessarily expensive by the limited number of shops licensed to conduct them and by the onerous requirement that numerous working parts be replaced if an older car is to pass (Beck 1993). This is widely cited as the reason why the average vehicle age in Japan is 5.8 years compared to 8.3 years in the United States, and the average annual mileage per car in Japan is only about half that of the United States (Japan External Trade Organization [JETRO] 2002).

As recently as 1990, Japan had a mere 291 cars per thousand persons. As a first pass at assessing whether increasing car ownership may have run its course, consider a simple regression of cars per thousand persons on GNP per person in purchasing power units using 1998 data. The predicted value for Japan is 450.1, while the actual number is 395.1. The 12 percent difference is not statistically significant.[5]

---

5. The log linear OLS regression is ln (cars per thousand) $= -2.9 + 0.9$ ln (GNP in PPP units) $- 0.13$ (dummy equal to one for Japan), where t-stat $= 6.6$; t-stat $= 0.5$; number of observations $= 26$; and $R^2 = 0.65$.

My guess is that a further dramatic increase in car ownership in Japan is unlikely, but a lagged response of retail structure to the past increase in car ownership may still play out over the coming decade and beyond.

5.7   Retail Formats

Japanese statistics define eight store formats (table 5.8). Format is determined by whether or not a store is self-service and by the mix of merchandise it offers in three broad categories (clothing, food, and living [*jun-kanren*]). Large stores are primarily department stores, general merchandise superstores, and specialty superstores. Similarly, these formats tend to be large stores. The essential difference between general merchandise superstores and department stores is that the former are self-service stores while the latter are not.

Table 5.9 provides time series on the numbers and average scale of stores in each format. Note the 1997 changes in the definitions of specialty superstores and convenience stores. Before 1997, the specialty superstore category included stores larger than 500 square meters, which meant they were all subject to the Large Store Law. Then, stores as small as 250 square meters were reclassified from other superstores to specialty superstores if their product-mix concentration met the specialty requirement. This tripled stores in the category. Department stores and general merchandise superstores have decreased in number from 1997 to 1999, their travails documented in numerous news accounts.

Table 5.8   **Store Formats in Japan**

Category	Product Mix,[a] Other Requirements
	Self-Service[b]
General Merchandise superstores	At least 10%, but no more than 70%, of sales in each category
Specialty superstores	At least 70% of sales in a category[c]
Convenience stores	Includes food. Open at least 14 hours per day[d]
Other superstores	Self-service stores not in the other three categories
	Non-Self-Service
Department stores	At least 10%, but no more than 70%, of sales in each category
Specialty stores	At least 90% of sales in one category
Semispecialty stores	Between 50% and 90% of sales in one category
Other non-self-service stores	Non-self-service stores not in the other three categories

Note: as established by the Census of Commerce of Japan for 1997 and later years.

[a]Within three categories: clothing, food, and living (*jun-kanren*).

[b]A store is self-service if at least half the floor space is devoted to sale of merchandise in prepackaged or final form, at a price marked on the product, to customers who move freely about the store with a cart or handbasket, and who pay no fee to enter the store.

[c]Size is greater than 250 square meters. Before 1997, threshold was 500 square meters.

[d]Size range is 30–250 square meters. Before 1997, range was 50–250 square meters.

Table 5.9   Characteristics of Stores in Japan, 1985–1999

	1985	1988	1991	1994	1997	1999
			All Retail Stores			
Number	1,628,644	1,619,752	1,591,223	1,499,948	1,419,696	1,406,884
Employees[a]	3.9	4.2	4.4	4.9	5.2	5.7
Area (m²)	n.a.	n.a.	79	93	105	111
Sales[b]	62	71	88	96	104	102
			Department Stores			
Number	438	433	455	463	476	394
Employees[a]	431	446	456	444	392	427
Area (m²)	n.a.	n.a.	15,063	16,340	17,133	19,134
Sales[b]	17,762	20,930	25,086	22,981	22,416	24,633
			General Merchandise Superstores			
Number	1,389	1,478	1,549	1,804	1,888	1,670
Employees[a]	138	136	142	151	160	192
Area (m²)	n.a.	n.a.	5,659	6,316	7,166	8,020
Sales[b]	4,258	4,491	5,268	5,175	5,274	5,299
			Specialty Superstores			
Number	5,873	6,397	7,130	9,354	11,656	14,455
Number[c]	n.a.	n.a.	*20,827	*25,171	*32,209	*35,531
Clothing	520	571	618	849	*4,549	*4,780
Food	4,707	4,877	5,185	6,231	*17,623	*18,707
Living	646	949	1,327	2,274	*10,037	*12,044
Employees[a]	37	38	37	39	*24	*29
Area (m²)	n.a.	n.a.	n.a.	1,207	*731	*840
Sales[b]	983	1,000	1,122	1,115	*635	*668
			Convenience Stores			
Number	29,236	34,550	41,847	48,405	33,167	37,025
Number[c]	n.a.	n.a.	*23,837	*28,226	*36,631	*39,628
Employees[a]	7	9	8	10	*11	*14
Area (m²)	n.a.	n.a.	*94	*98	*99	*103
Sales[b]	116	145	167	172	*143	*155
			Other Superstores			
Number	59,643	53,834	67,473	80,036	103,273	67,476
Number[c]	n.a.	n.a.	*72,027	*84,878	*120,721	*86,367
Employees[a]	6	7	6	6	*4	*6
Area (m²)	n.a.	n.a.	n.a.	128	*89	*110
Sales[b]	124	144	143	132	*83	*98
			Specialty Stores			
Number	1,004,883	1,007,756	1,000,166	930,143	839,969	920,277
Clothing	149,246	151,370	154,656	147,478	126,383	134,329
Food	290,789	293,203	283,570	263,681	230,163	249,287
Living	564,848	563,183	561,940	518,984	483,423	536,661
Employees[a]	3	4	4	4	4	5
Area (m²)	n.a.	n.a.	53	61	63	63
Sales[b]	47	51	65	66	71	68

(*continued*)

Table 5.9   (continued)

	1985	1988	1991	1994	1997	1999
		Semispecialty Stores				
Number	524,885	513,338	470,289	429,108	385,748	319,685
Clothing	74,232	78,608	76,903	65,733	62,882	54,928
Food	271,593	253,352	224,756	185,509	154,736	131,465
Living	177,644	179,715	166,740	175,857	168,130	133,292
Employees[a]	3	3	4	4	4	4
Area (m²)	n.a.	n.a.	62	69	74	76
Sales[b]	47	54	67	76	82	75

Source: MITI (various years).

Note: Asterisks indicate data based on 1997 definitions rather than earlier ones. n.a. = not available.

[a]Average number per store.

[b]Average annual sales in ¥ millions.

[c]Using 1997 definitions, for which see text.

Table 5.10   **Composition of Total Sales Across Formats of Stores, 1985–1999 (%)**

	1985	1988	1991	1994	1997[a]	1999[a]
Department store	7.6	7.9	8.1	7.4	7.2	6.7
General merchandise superstore	5.8	5.8	5.8	6.5	6.7	6.2
Specialty superstore	5.7	5.6	5.7	7.3	*13.8*	*16.5*
Convenience	3.3	4.4	5.0	5.8	*3.5*	*4.3*
Other superstore	7.3	6.8	6.9	7.4	*6.8*	*5.9*
Specialty	46.0	45.2	45.9	42.6	40.4	43.5
Semispecialty	24.0	24.2	22.4	22.9	21.3	16.7
Other	0.2	0.1	0.2	0.0	0.2	0.3

Source: MITI (various years).

[a]Changes in definitions of specialty superstores, convenience stores, and other superstores in 1997 increases specialty superstores relative to the other two formats and makes the series for the three formats discontinuous. Data using the new definitions are in italics.

There is no category for small family-owned stores as such: Most are either specialty or semi-specialty stores. Two-thirds of them are sole proprietorships. Only 5 percent of specialty superstores and no large stores are sole proprietorships.

Between 5 percent and 10 percent of specialty and semispecialty stores are contained within the premises of large stores (i.e., boutiques within larger stores). The total number of such stores (not themselves large, but contained within the premises of ones that are large) has remained around 100,000 since 1991.

Table 5.10 shows the time series for composition of total sales across the types of store. These data reflect the same trends in numbers of stores.

Table 5.11   **Spread of Car Ownership, 1965–1998**

	Cars Per 1,000 Persons[a]	Change (%)[b]
1965	22	n.a.
1970	85	30.7
1975	154	12.7
1980	202	5.6
1985	230	2.6
1990	291	4.8
1995	360	4.4
1998	394	3.1

Source: Government of Japan (various years).
Note: n.a. = not applicable.
[a]Passenger cars.
[b]Average annual percentage change from previous entry.

5.7.1   Influences on the Number of Stores by Format

The Large Store Law has limited the number of stores with large floor space. Almost all of these are department stores, general merchandise superstores, or specialty superstores. The law also ought to have induced increased numbers of stores of other formats. These include small family-owned, non-self-service stores that are mostly classified as specialty stores or semispecialty stores. Our next task is to measure these effects.

In measuring the effect of regulatory change on the number of stores, it is necessary to control for changes in other factors influencing retail density. These include increasing ownership of passenger cars, increasing average space per person in dwellings, and declining population density in cities as the suburbs expand. Increasing car ownership favors evolution towards a retail sector with fewer, larger stores. Declining population density per se has the opposite effect on retail density, but is probably itself an inevitable accompaniment of the move toward car ownership and larger dwellings. All three trends can be placed under the heading "suburbanization." Tables 5.11, 5.12, and 5.13 document them.

More living space means that storage space is less constrained, enabling households to shop less frequently for daily necessities and to maintain larger stocks, eroding the value to households of proximity to stores selling nondurables. The effect of larger, less crowded dwellings on the numbers of stores selling durables is possibly the opposite, leading to more such stores. But stores selling nondurables, such as food and daily necessities, are more numerous than the ones selling durables, such as furniture.

As population density becomes less, the marginal benefit to households of a proliferation of stores becomes greater. This effect arises because, as households are more diffuse, any given number of stores per household en-

Table 5.12   Changes in Japanese Dwellings, 1965–1998

	Rooms Per Dwelling	Persons Per		Area (m²) Per		Change in Area Per Person[a]
		Dwelling	Room	Dwelling	Person	
1963	3.82	4.43	1.16	72.52	16.36	n.a.
1968	3.84	3.96	1.03	73.86	18.63	2.6
1973	4.15	3.63	0.87	77.14	21.26	2.7
1978	4.52	3.47	0.77	80.28	23.17	1.7
1983	4.73	3.35	0.71	85.92	25.69	2.1
1988	4.86	3.21	0.66	89.29	27.86	1.6
1993	4.85	3.02	0.62	91.92	30.46	1.8
1998	4.79	2.83	0.59	92.43	32.70	1.4

Source: Government of Japan (various years).

Note: n.a. = not applicable.

[a]Average annual percentage change between years shown.

Table 5.13   Measures of Population Density, 1965–1995

	District Density[a]		Overall Density	
	Population[b]	Area[c]	Average[d]	Change[e]
1965	48.1	1.23	10,263	n.a.
1970	53.5	1.71	8,678	−3.3
1975	57.0	2.19	7,712	−2.3
1980	59.7	2.65	6,983	−2.0
1985	60.6	2.80	6,938	−0.1
1990	63.2	3.11	6,661	−0.8
1995	64.7	3.24	6,630	−0.1

Source: Government of Japan (various years).

Note: n.a. = not applicable.

[a]Densely inhabited districts are contiguous census districts with high population density (in principle, 4,000 inhabitants or more per square kilometer) within the boundary of a city, ward, town, or village constituting an agglomeration of 5,000 or more inhabitants.

[b]Population of densely inhabited districts as a percentage of Japan's total population.

[c]Densely inhabited districts as a percentage of Japan's total area.

[d]Overall population density per square kilometer.

[e]Annual average percentage change in density since previous census.

tails a greater average distance from each household to the nearest store, and the reduction in that distance with each given increase in number of stores becomes correspondingly greater. (See Flath [1990] for an algebraic treatment of this phenomenon.) The point here is that the gradual decline in average population density that has accompanied the proliferation of cars and increased spaciousness of dwellings has possibly in and of itself slowed the push towards fewer, larger stores in Japan.

5.8   Results from Analyzing Prefectural Differences

Regulatory effects should vary among prefectures because, although a national statute, the Large Store Law was implemented through locally administered advisory panels in each municipal jurisdiction. To measure these regulatory effects, I ran a set of regressions (detailed in box 5.1); the results are in table 5.14.

An examination of the first column estimates in table 5.14 reveals that car ownership and urban population density have influenced the overall density of stores in the expected way. Disappointingly, size of dwelling has

---

Box 5.1   Prefectural Regressions

To explain the numbers of stores of different kinds per person, I ran OLS regressions using data for each of Japan's 47 prefectures from five consecutive Censuses of Commerce of Japan (1985, 1988, 1991, 1994, and 1997; MITI, various years). The dependent variable is the natural log of the number of stores per 1000 persons. There is a different equation for each different format of store and for all stores.

The independent variables are the same in each equation and, as in Matsui and Nariu (2001), include a dummy variable for each prefectures. I do not report the estimates of coefficients on these dummies.

The independent variables of interest include the natural logs of the three variables being discussed, observed for each prefecture: passenger cars per 1,000 persons, dwelling floor space per person, and 1,000 persons per square kilometer in densely inhabited districts. To further control for the diffusion of population, I included the fraction of each prefecture's population residing in densely inhabited districts. It was necessary to log linearly interpolate between, or extrapolate from, housing census years and population census years respectively. Annual data are available for passenger car registrations.

The natural logarithms of the number of class 1 large stores and of class 2 large stores are included to measure the severity of regulation of large stores. So, for example, after 1994, large stores with floor space between 500 square meters and 1,000 square meters were automatically approved by MITI, but in the Census of Commerce these were still classified as large stores.

Table 5.14   OLS Log Linear Regressions Explaining the Numbers of Stores of Different Kinds Per Person, with Fixed Effects for Each of Japan's Forty-Seven Prefectures

Independent Variables	All	Department	General Merchandise Superstore	Specialty Superstore[a]	Convenience[a]	Other Superstore[a]	Specialty	Semi-specialty
Passenger cars per 1,000 persons	-0.17	0.57	0.19	0.46	0.72	0.89	-0.23	-0.35
	(-7.99)	(1.99)	(1.06)	(3.24)	(4.66)	(4.21)	(-7.07)	(-8.64)
Dwelling floor space per person (m²)	-0.01	-2.92	3.05	-0.15	0.74	-0.83	0.45	-0.60
	(-0.09)	(-1.51)	(2.51)	(-0.15)	(0.65)	(-0.54)	(2.03)	(-2.16)
1,000 Persons per km² in dense areas[b]	-0.37	2.68	0.00	-0.29	0.73	0.32	-0.67	-0.62
	(-4.12)	(2.22)	(0.00)	(-0.44)	(1.02)	(0.33)	(-4.85)	(-3.58)
Fraction of population in dense areas[b]	-0.36	0.42	-2.21	2.27	2.11	-2.75	0.25	-0.45
	(-2.09)	(0.18)	(-1.52)	(1.74)	(1.47)	(-1.40)	(0.94)	(-1.37)
Class 1 Large Stores[c] per 1,000 Persons	0.01	0.23	-0.04	-0.16	0.06	-0.21	-0.01	-0.01
	(0.88)	(1.48)	(-0.41)	(-1.61)	(0.57)	(-1.39)	(-0.81)	(-0.62)
Class 2 Large Stores[c] per 1,000 Persons	-0.10	-0.18	0.39	0.42	0.02	-0.08	-0.19	-0.11
	(-6.57)	(-0.85)	(3.01)	(3.37)	(0.17)	(-0.43)	(-7.89)	(-3.84)
R^2	0.98	0.71	0.84	0.98	0.98	0.96	0.96	0.98

Note: Dependent variable is number of stores per 1,000 persons. Coefficient estimates and t-statistics in parentheses. Each column is a different store type. All variables are in natural logs except the fraction of population residing in densely inhabited districts. Number of observations (except for specialty superstores and convenience stores); 235 = 47 prefectures × 5 years of observations. Sample = 5 successive Census of Commerce reports (1985, 1988, 1991, 1994, and 1997) by prefecture, except as noted. Coefficients on prefecture dummies are not reported.

[a]No observations for 1997.

[b]Densely inhabited districts are contiguous census districts with high population density (in principle, 4,000 inhabitants or more per square kilometer) within the boundary of a city, ward, town, or village constituting an agglomeration of 5,000 or more inhabitants.

[c]Class 1 and class 2 large stores are defined in table 5.6.

not exerted a statistically significant effect on overall density of stores (nor a coherent effect on numbers of stores of particular formats).

The number of class 1 large stores (floor space of 3,000 square meters or more, except in the central parts of major cities where it is 6,000 square meters or more, and a proxy for regulation) has no measurable effect on the overall number of stores. However, the density of class 2 large stores (those that are not class 1, and another proxy for regulation) is inversely related to the overall number of stores, as expected. Possibly this reflects the much greater temporal variation in the number of class 2 stores than in class 1 stores (shown in table 5.5).

All of the variables, including the number of class 2 stores, have inelastic effects on the overall number of stores. Over the period 1985–1997, the number of class 2 stores grew about 5 percent per year, while the overall number of stores shrank about 1.1 percent. Given the estimated elasticity of overall number of stores with respect to number of class 2 stores of –0.10, expansion of these large stores by itself accounts for a little less than half of the constriction in overall number of stores.

Relaxed regulation is a contributing factor to reduction in number of stores, slightly less important than increasing car ownership. The inelasticity of overall number of stores with respect to number of class 2 large stores of –0.10 generally argues against regulatory limits on large stores as being in any way crucial in explaining the proliferation of small stores. For example, quadrupling or quintupling the number of class 1 and class 2 stores would roughly match the density of such stores per person in the United States, but based on these estimates would still not dramatically reduce the overall number of stores in Japan.

If regulation mattered greatly, one would expect that in prefectures where the large store law was more loosely applied, overall retail density would be dramatically smaller than elsewhere. This does not appear to have been the case. Fundamentals, including those embedded in the prefecture by fixed effects, account for far more of the variation in overall store density both across prefectures and over time than does the regulatory-determined number of large stores.

The influences of the regulation variables and car ownership on density of stores of each format instill more confidence in the economic model underlying the specification and the interpretation of results just offered. The positive influence of the regulation-determined number of class 1 large stores on the number of department stores is evident, as is the positive influence of the number of class 2 large stores on the number of general merchandise superstores and specialty superstores. This comports with the fact that most of the department stores have very great floor space and thus are in class 1.

Car ownership generally undercuts specialty stores and semispecialty stores and promotes convenience stores, department stores, and self-service stores (i.e., superstores) of all kinds. The very large, positive influence of increasing car ownership on the number of convenience stores may be an important reason for their recent very rapid growth.

The size of the effect of car ownership on overall number of stores shown in table 5.11 (elasticity = –0.17) is quite a bit less than in the cross-country regression of table 5.4 (elasticity = –0.3). (The larger coefficient estimate [–0.6] from table 5.4 is perhaps biased by exclusion of the variable CR-WDNG pertaining to size of dwelling.) There is a simple explanation for this: The regulatory limit on the number of large stores in Japan is dampening the response of number of stores to increasing car ownership.

If this is true, then it suggests a way of quantifying the likely ultimate effect of deregulation on the overall number of stores: It might be roughly equivalent to the effect of doubling the responsiveness of overall numbers of stores to increased car ownership from an elasticity of 0.17 to 0.30. That is, one might expect the overall number of stores in Japan ultimately to fall by about 15 percent from its 1997 level (11.3 per thousand persons) to around 9.6 per thousand.

The picture that emerges is one that matches the earlier analysis of international data: Regulatory distortions account for little in explaining Japan's high density of stores.

5.9   Conclusion

The Japanese distribution sector certainly exhibits peculiarities. It has vastly more stores per person than most other rich countries. It also has particularly complex wholesale marketing channels with multiple steps and ubiquitous vertical restraints. This chapter has explored the reasons and found them to relate more to economics than to regulation. It also has shown how the peculiarities are complementary.

Scarcity of living space and the inconvenience of owning and operating a car has enhanced Japanese households' willingness to pay for nearby shopping. Japan's geographic centricity has facilitated development of a transport system and complex logistical arteries that lower the costs of continually restocking the many retail outlets. These factors combine to make a proliferation of stores in Japan not only inevitable, but also efficient. Given this, regulations protecting small stores from competition by large ones (mostly in the form of the Large Store Law and its successor, the Large Store Location Law) imply only minor economic distortions and encounter little effective political resistance. But as car ownership has grown, the distorting effects of regulations limiting large stores have become greater and politically less tenable.

A proliferation of small stores increases the economic advantages of logistical arteries with many branches, which in turn lowers the costs of a multiplicity of wholesale steps. The implied ubiquity of retailers and wholesalers increases the horizontal externalities that arise in promoting and marketing goods and that are the target of vertical restraints, such as customer assignments and exclusive dealing stipulations. The distortions that are an unwanted consequence of these sorts of stipulations lead to further manufacturer- and wholesaler-initiated stipulations on pricing and shipment quantities, which are tolerated by lax enforcement of antimonopoly laws.

Some of the fundamental forces accounting for Japan's proliferation of small stores are changing. For example, car ownership increased dramatically during the 1990s, and the average size of dwelling also is steadily increasing. Probably as a result, in the 1990s, grocery supermarkets and general merchandise superstores increased in number in Japan even as the overall number of stores steadily declined. Changes in implementation of the Large Store Law introduced in 1994 and its ultimate repeal and replacement with the Large Scale Retail Store Location Law in 2000 also have contributed to changes in the number and composition of Japan's stores.

Government policies shape the economy, but the reverse also is true. Regulations emerge from a political process in which economic forces operate (Becker 1983). In Japan, as elsewhere, the economy has shaped regulations, and regulation has reinforced inherent tendencies rather than fundamentally altered them.

References

Beck, John C. 1993. Japanese consumers as battering rams: Can they break down the non-market entry barriers to Japan's auto aftermarket industry? In *The Japanese distribution system,* ed. Michael R. Czinkota and Masaaki Kotabe, 281–94. Chicago: Probus Publishing Company.

Becker, Gary. 1983. A theory of competition among pressure groups. *Quarterly Journal of Economics* 98:371–400.

Boylaud, Olivier, and Giuseppe Nicoletti. 2001. Regulatory reform in retail distribution. *OECD Economic Studies* no. 32 (June): 253–74.

Flath, David. 1989. Vertical restraints in Japan. *Japan and the World Economy* 1:187–203.

———. 1990. Why are there so many retail stores in Japan? *Japan and the World Economy* 2:365–86.

———. 2000. *The Japanese economy.* Oxford: Oxford University Press.

———. 2001. Japanese distribution *keiretsu*, FDI and import penetration. Columbia University, Center on Japanese Economy and Business. Working Paper no. 199, May.

Flath, David, and Tatsuhiko Nariu. 1996. Is Japan's retail sector truly distinctive? *Journal of Comparative Economics* 2:181–91.

Gabszewicz, Jean Jaskold, and Jacques-Francois Thisse. 1986. Spatial competition and the location of firms. In *Location theory,* ed. J. J. Gabszewicz, J. F. Thisse, M. Fujita, and U. Schweizer, 1–7. New York: Harwood Academic.

Government of Japan. Various years. *Japan statistical yearbook*. Tokyo: Government of Japan.

Heal, Geoffrey. 1980. Spatial structure in the retail trade: A study of product differentiation with increasing returns. *Bell Journal of Economics* 11:565–83.

Ito, Takatoshi, and Maruyama, Masayoshi. 1991. Is the Japanese distribution system really inefficient? In *Trade with Japan: Has the door opened wider?* ed. Paul Krugman, 149–74. Chicago: University of Chicago Press.

Japan External Trade Organization (JETRO). 2002. *Survey on actual conditions regarding access to Japan: Replacement auto parts*. http://www.jetro.go.jp/ipie/access/e_jidosha.pdf.

Larke, Roy. 1994. *Japanese retailing*. London: Routledge.

Maruyama, Masayoshi, Kyohei Sakai, Yoko Togawa, Nobuo Sakamoto, Michio Yamashita, Masaharu Arakawa, and Hiroyuki Ito. 1991. Nihon no ryuutsuu shisutemu: Riron to jissho (The distribution system of Japan: Theory and empirics). *Keizai Bunseki* 123 (May).

Matsui, Kenji, and Tatushiko Nariu. 2001. Panel data analysis of the density of retail stores in Japan. Kyoto University faculty of economics. Working Paper.

McKinsey Global Institute. 2000. Why the Japanese economy is not growing: Micro barriers to productivity growth. http://www.mckinsey.co.jp/pdf/tocj.pdf.

Ministry of International Trade and Industry (MITI), Minister's Secretariat, Research and Statistics Department. Various years. *Census of commerce*. Tokyo: Government of Japan.

Miwa, Yoshirou, and Mark Ramseyer. 2002. *The japanese distribution system*. Oxford: Oxford University Press.

Nariu, Tatsuhiko. 1994. *Ryuutsuu no keizai riron* (The economic theory of marketing). Nagoya, Japan: Nagoya shuppankai.

Nariu, Tatsuhiko, and David Flath. 1993. The complexity of wholesale distribution channels in Japan. In *The japanese distribution system*, ed. Michael R. Czinkota and Masaaki Kotabe, 83–98. Chicago: Probus Publishing Company.

Organization for Economic Cooperation and Development (OECD). 2000. *OECD international regulation database*. http://www1.oecd.org/subject/regdatabase/.

Pilat, Dirk. 1997. Regulation and performance in the distribution sector. OECD Economics Department Working Paper no. 180. Paris: OECD.

Small and Medium Enterprise Agency, Ministry of International Trade and Industry (MITI), Minister's Secretariat, Research and Statistics Department. 1994. *Variation and current state of Japanese retail and wholesale enterprises, through the most recent 20 years of the basic survey of retail and wholesale enterprises*. Tokyo: Tsuusan toukei kyoukai.

Statistics Bureau, Statistics Study Center, Ministry of Public Management, Home Affairs, Posts and Telecommunications. Government of Japan. *Statistics of the world 2001*. Tokyo: Nihon Toukei Kyoukai.

United Nations Statistics Division. 2003. *Social indicators homepage*. http://unstats.un.org./unsd/demographic/social/default.htm.

World Bank. 2001. *World development report 1999/2000*. Oxford: Oxford University Press.

6

Inefficiency of Corporate Investment and Distortion of Savings Behavior in Japan

Albert Ando, Dimitrios Christelis, and
Tsutomu Miyagawa

6.1 Introduction

Malaise and stagnation notwithstanding, Japan is a rich country, and the Japanese have substantial individual wealth. However, the data suggest that somehow the accumulated net worth of the household sector (excluding land) is smaller than its savings should have achieved. In an earlier paper, Ando (2002) examined this capital loss and attributed some three-fourths of it to losses in the household-sector holdings of corporate equity. In this paper we examine in much further detail the components of this loss and the features of the operations of Japanese corporations[1] that possibly led to it.

The Japanese National Accounts are the starting point for a quantitative analysis, but the nature of some key measures complicates this. Other measures simply are not provided. Still, we believe that the available data and compelling circumstantial evidence support our propositions.

The most important problem we encountered during our investigation

Albert Ando was professor of economics and finance at the University of Pennsylvania and a research associate of the National Bureau of Economic Research. He passed away in September 2002. Dimitrios Christelis is a Ph.D. candidate in economics at the University of Pennsylvania. Tsutomu Miyagawa is professor of economics at Gakushuin University.

The authors are grateful for careful and detailed comments from Fumio Hayashi, Charles Horioka, Anil Kashyap, and Larry Meissner. We also wish to thank Monica Arellano for research assistance. Finally, we are especially indebted to members of the National Account Division, the Economic and Social Research Institute, Cabinet Office, for their cooperation and support in resolving a number of complex and intricate data problems. Albert Ando was particularly grateful for the support provided by the Abe Fellowship Program in the preparation of this paper.

1. Please note that our discussion of corporations is in the framework of the National Accounts, so we are looking at a much larger universe than just those firms that have equity publicly traded on stock exchanges.

was the extremely high depreciation recorded in the Japanese National Accounts. Thus, we have constructed a series of capital stock and depreciation that conforms more closely to international practice.

After our data adjustments, we find that the rate of return on assets in the corporate sector (whether or not land is included) is very low. Another way of expressing this is that there has been excessively large investment by the corporate sector in physical assets that seem to have low productivity or earning capacity. This idea of "excessive" investment is also borne out by the fact that the market value of the equity of the corporate sector is lower than the liquidation (or replacement) value (i.e., the market sees that the investment is of low quality). Another way to see the same point is to look at average Tobin's q (which is below 1).

This low market valuation (and low quality investment) seems to arise because of the corporate governance structure that permits low dividend payments. Since the level of dividends is so small and the historical pattern of dividends does not give any basis to expect them to increase, even when operating surplus and corporate profits after tax increase over time, there is no reason for the market to increase its valuation of corporate equities. Thus, households find themselves with very little value in their ownership of corporations: They are not rewarded for their savings, and this results in the small value of their net worth excluding the value of their land. Faced with this situation, households continue to save a large fraction of their income in an attempt to increase their net worth to a satisfactory level.

In addition, these low dividend payments leave cash in the hands of firms, which are then able to continue to make more low-productivity investments. In other market systems we would expect this to have been corrected by takeovers, which are very rare in Japan, as is well known.

The paper is organized as follows: Section 6.2.1 discusses the accumulation of net worth of the household sector, while section 6.2.2 examines land as a determinant of consumption behavior. Section 6.3.1 discusses corporate saving and dividend payments, and the balance sheet and the capital loss of the corporate sector are discussed in Section 3.2, Corporate investment behavior and financing decisions are addressed in section 6.3.3. Section 6.4 concludes.

6.2   Accumulation of Net Worth by the Household Sector

6.2.1   Household Net Worth and Saving

This section will present the capital loss incurred by the households in more detail than shown in Ando (2002).[2] Table 6.1 summarizes the accu-

---

2. Our results here are slightly different than the ones reported in that paper due to small revisions in our calculations.

Table 6.1   Household Sector Saving and Net Worth in 1990 Prices, 1971–1998 (¥ trillions)

		1971–1979	1980–1990	1991–1998	Accumulated
A.1	Reproducible tangible assets[a]	129.0	66.0	23.2	218.2
A.2	Flow	131.3	94.1	46.0	271.4
A.3	Reconciliation[b]	−2.3	−28.1	−22.8	−53.3
B.1	Nonreproducible tangible assets[a]	227.5	982.3	−538.5	671.3
B.2	Flow	−50.8	−84.3	−24.1	−159.1
B.3	Reconciliation[b]	278.3	1,066.6	−514.4	830.4
C.1	Net financial assets (excluding equity shares)	112.9	259.1	235.3	607.3
C.2	Flow	216.6	339.2	273.9	829.6
C.3	Reconciliation excluding inflation loss[c]	−1.5	−5.9	1.7	−5.7
C.4	Inflation gain (loss)	−102.2	−74.2	−40.2	−216.6
D.1	Equity	21.5	109.8	−93.1	38.2
D.2	Flow	5.7	2.1	−9.1	−1.4
D.3	Reconciliation	15.9	107.7	−84.0	39.6
E.1	**Net worth = A.1 + B.1 + C.1 + D.1**	**490.9**	**1,417.2**	**−373.2**	**1,534.9**
E.2	Flow = A.2 + B.2 + C.2 + D.2 = F.1 + F.2 + F.3	302.8	351.0	286.7	940.5
E.3	Reconciliation excluding inflation loss on net financial assets = A.3 + B.3 + C.3 + D.3	290.2	1,140.3	−619.6	811.0
E.4	Inflation gain (loss) = C.4	−104.2	−74.2	−40.2	−216.6
F.1	Savings	322.9	360.6	301.6	985.1
F.2	Net capital transfers	−6.4	−15.9	−20.4	−42.7
F.3	Statistical discrepancy	−13.7	6.4	5.5	−1.9

(continued)

Table 6.1   (continued)

	1971–1979	1980–1990	1991–1998	Accumulated
Excluding Land				
E.1a Net worth = A.1 + C.1 + D.1	**263.4**	**434.9**	**165.4**	**863.7**
E.2a Flow = A.2 + C.2 + D.2 = F.1A + F.2 + F.3	353.6	435.3	310.8	1,099.7
E.3a Reconciliation excluding inflation loss on net financial assets = A.3 + C.3 + D.3	12.0	73.7	–105.2	–19.4
E.4a Inflation gain (loss) = C.4	–102.2	–74.2	–40.2	–216.6
F.1a Savings = F.1 – B.2	373.7	444.9	325.7	1,144.2

Source: EPA (2000a), 86–89, 326–31.

Notes: The household sector includes nonprofit institutions. The SNA68 and our estimate of reproducible tangible assets were used. Constant prices were obtained using the deflator for total private consumption expenditure. Also see box 6.1 for additional information on the data.

[a]Gross fixed capital formation has been reduced by the amount of investment in land improvement using data provided by Mr. Mitsuo Hosen of the Economic and Social Research Institute, Cabinet Office, the Japanese Government. Corresponding adjustments were made to the investment in land and the reconciliation accounts of reproducible fixed assets and land.

[b]Including inflation loss

[c]For net financial assets, losses to creditors are gains to debtors, so the effects of general inflation are reported explicitly rather than as part of reconciliation. (See discussion in the text.)

mulation of net worth by the Japanese household sector from 1971 to 1998. Details on the data are in box 6.1 and the table 6.1 notes.

The E sections bring together information for the flows and changes in stocks. For 1971–1998, the sector's net worth increased some ¥1,535 trillion in 1990 prices (row E.1), whereas savings adjusted for net capital transfers and statistical discrepancy was about ¥940 trillion (row E.2 = F.1 + F.2 + F.3). Thus, the household sector had a net capital gain of ¥595 trillion (row E.1 minus E.2, which also is E.3 + E.4).

Box 6.1   Savings and Net Worth Data in Tables 6.1 and 6.7

In each table, A through D relate changes in the value of stocks to flows for four broad components of net worth. Changes in net worth components are not computed directly. Instead, they are related to the flow-of-funds data through a reconciliation calculation. One element of the reconciliation is changes resulting from general inflation. For three categories—reproducible tangible assets (A), nonreproducible tangible assets (B), and equities (D)—this inflation loss is not shown separately because one sector's loss is not another sector's gain. Thus, the reconciliation is the result of the difference between the price index for the asset and the deflator for total consumption expenditures.

For financial assets (C), losses to creditors are gains to debtors, so the effects of general inflation are reported explicitly (line C.4) rather than as part of the reconciliation entry (line C.3). Specifically, we multiplied the initial stock by the rate of change of the consumption expenditure deflator and recorded the resulting amount as inflation gain (loss). What is left is recorded as reconciliation.

Flow is positive when assets increase more than liabilities, and is negative when liabilities increase more than assets. For nonreproducible tangible assets (B), the flow is primarily net purchase (sale) of land by that sector. These assets are mostly land, but also include timber, fisheries, and subsoil assets. The National Accounts Division assures us that these are at market value. We do not know exactly how the information is obtained, but we have no choice but to accept it.

The structure of the National Accounts requires that the sum of the net acquisition of all items on the balance sheet equals savings recorded in the flow portion of the accounts *plus* net capital transfers received *plus* statistical discrepancy.

The overall gain is due entirely to land. Excluding land, overall capital losses were some ¥236 trillion (row E.1a minus E.2a, which also is E.3a + E.4a). Most of this is the inflation loss suffered on net financial assets (row E.4a). (Savings excluding land is F.1 minus B.2.)

Throughout most of 1971–1998, the net financial liability of the government sector was very small. Most of the net financial asset position of the household sector was matched by the net financial liability position of non-financial and financial corporations. The inflation loss of the household sector, therefore, was largely matched by the inflation gain of the corporate sector.

Why did this inflation gain of corporations not appear as an increase in the value of corporate equity owned by the household sector? During most of this period, corporations retained substantial earnings, yet the household sector gained less than ¥40 trillion in the value of corporate equity, far smaller than the accumulated retained earnings and capital gains of corporations combined. We believe this is one of the most unusual features of the Japanese economy. It may provide a clue to one of the causes for the low level of consumption by the household sector. We will therefore look carefully at the corporate sector and how its savings and accumulation of assets are related to the value of corporate equity outstanding.

6.2.2   Land

The household balance sheet is shown in table 6.2, column (5) for 1998 (tables for years 1970, 1980, and 1990 are available online at http://www. nber.org/data-appendix/ando_et_al). It is immediately apparent how large a share the value of land is in household net worth. The way the extraordinarily high price of land affects the savings behavior of the household sector and why one might want to exclude it from the net worth of that sector is the topic of this section. We believe that it is more insightful to exclude the land component of net worth. This is based in part on the fact that the household sector has been a small net seller of land throughout the period studied, 1971–1998, and that the proceeds were used to acquire other assets.

Another reason is the way Japanese households view land. For a typical family, the land on which its residence stands is both a major asset and, by definition, makes the imputed consumption of housing services very high. Thus, it is probable that a family views a rise in the price of land as representing both an increase in its assets and a rise in the cost of living, with each offsetting the other. If families can routinely borrow using land as collateral, a higher price of land may facilitate additional consumption. However, consumer borrowing, including mortgages, appears to be very low in Japan, suggesting either that the market is not well developed or that consumers do not wish to borrow. We therefore believe that most families view net worth excluding land as what is available to them over time.

Table 6.2   Sectoral Balance Sheet, 1998 Year-End, SNA93 Data (¥ trillions)

	Nonfinancial (1)	Financial (2)	Total ([1] + [2]) (3)	Government (4)	Households (5)	Rest of the World (6)
a. Reproducible physical assets	721.0	23.0	744.0	325.9	344.8	n.a.
b. Nonreproducible physical assets	433.2	22.1	455.3	162.1	1,083.4	n.a.
c. Total physical assets (a) + (b)	1,154.3	45.0	1,199.3	487.9	1,428.1	n.a.
d. Gross financial assets excluding equity	576.0	2,854.9	3,430.9	300.8	1,284.0	191.6
e. Gross liabilities excluding equity	−977.9	−2,902.1	−3,879.9	−549.6	−415.1	−362.8
f. Net financial position (d) + (e)	−401.9	−47.2	−449.1	−248.8	868.9	−171.1
g. Balance excluding equity (c) + (f) (Accounting net worth) [net] for corporate sector	752.4	−2.2	750.2	239.1	2,297.0	n.a.
h. Gross equity outstanding (market value)	−329.9	−69.0	−399.0	−10.2	n.a.	n.a.
i. Gross equity owned (market value)	89.3	138.6	227.9	62.8	80.7	n.a.
j. Net equity position (i) + (h)	−240.6	69.6	−171.0	52.6	80.7	37.9
k. Market valuation discrepancy −[(g) + (j)]	−511.8	−67.4	−579.2	n.a.	n.a.	n.a.
l. Household and government accounting net worth including equity (g) + (i)	n.a.	n.a.	n.a.	291.7	2,377.7 (6.59)[a]	n.a.
ll. Net worth excluding value of land (households only)	n.a.	n.a.	n.a.	n.a.	1,294.3 (3.59)[a]	n.a.
m. Tobin's Average q [−(j) − (f)]/(c)	0.557	n.a.	0.517	n.a.	n.a.	n.a.
n. Disposable income (households only)	n.a.	n.a.	n.a.	n.a.	360.7	n.a.

(continued)

Table 6.2 (continued)

	Nonfinancial (1)	Financial (2)	Total ([1] + [2]) (3)	Government (4)	Households (5)	Rest of the World (6)
	Hypothetical Equilibrium Pattern[b]					
h'. Gross Equity outstanding (market value)	-1,176.6	-658.4	-1,895.1	-10.2	n.a.	n.a.
i'. Gross equity owned (market value)	424.2	658.5	1,082.7	62.8	474.8	n.a.
j'. Net equity position (=g)	-752.4	2.2	-750.2	52.6	474.8	222.8
l'. Household net worth (g) + (i')	n.a.	n.a.	n.a.	n.a.	2,771.8 (7.68)[b]	n.a.
ll'. Net worth excluding value of land (households only)	n.a.	n.a.	n.a.	n.a.	(1,688.4) (4.68)[b]	n.a.

Note: Stocks of reproducible physical assets are our own estimates and include stocks of computer software. Other figures are taken from ESRI (2001). n.a. = not applicable.

[a]Figures in parentheses are ratios to disposable income.

[b]Assumptions used for the hypothetical equilibrium pattern (see also appendix C):

$i' = i$, $h' = h$, and $j' = j$ for the government (column [4])

$j' = g$ for corporations (columns [1], [2], and [3]).

$i' = j \cdot (i/j)$ in column (3), thus $h' = j' - i'$ in column (3).

In column (1), $i'(1) = i'(3) \cdot \{i(1)/[i(1) + i(2)]\}$. In column (2), $i'(2) = i'(3) \cdot \{i(2)/[i(1) + i(2)]\}$. In addition, $h'(1) = j'(1) - i'(1)$ and $h'(2) = j'(2) - i'(2)$.

$j'(5) + j'(6) = j'(3) - j'(4)$. In column (5), $j'(5) = [j'(3) - j'(4)] \cdot \{j(5)/[j(5) + j(6)]\}$. In column (6), $j'(6) = [j'(3) - j'(4)] \cdot \{j(6)/[j(5) + j(6)]\}$.

That said, there are families who own more land than they need for their residences or farms. For them, excess land is like any other asset that can be sold to finance consumption as the need arises. Thus, the value of land is part of their life-cycle net worth, and an increase in the price of land must be viewed as an addition to their resources. At the other extreme, for families who do not own any land and aspire to acquire it, an increase in the price of land is a significant increase in the cost of living without a compensating increase in their income. Although there are significant allocative consequences within the household sector, for the sector as a whole, the responses of these two extreme groups to a change in price of land should largely offset each other.

We will now look at the literature on the effect of land on consumption. There are two studies we are aware of that offer evidence on the effect of an increase in the price of land on consumption. Ogawa et al. (1996) introduce into a consumption function three components of wealth held by households: liquid financial assets, net illiquid financial assets, and tangible wealth (an estimate of the value of land and residential structures). They find that the coefficient of tangible wealth is very close to zero and its standard error is larger than the estimated value of the coefficient. They conclude that consumption is not affected by tangible wealth held by households. Because they define tangible wealth as the sum of the value of land and an *imputed* value of residential structures, their result does not bear directly on the effect of the price of land on consumption. However, because more than two-thirds of the fluctuation of the variable is due to changes in the value of land, which is itself due almost entirely to price variations, we may view his result as generally indicating that consumption does not respond to land price variation.

More direct evidence is provided by Murata (1999). She estimates a time series consumption function in the error correction formulation. The log of the consumption-income ratio is a function of the ratio of wealth to income and the ratio of land price to consumption prices, among other things. She obtains a small but significant negative coefficient for the ratio of land price to consumption prices. This again suggests that an increase in the relative price of land is unlikely to increase the consumption-income ratio.

There are two other studies we have looked at that are not helpful for our purposes. Dekle (1994) is hard to interpret because he regresses the level of consumption on the price of land and the rate of growth of output by prefecture without controlling for the level of income or wealth. Thus, the price of land can easily be a proxy for a basic resource variable in his estimation.

Takayama (1992) runs a regression of consumption on different measures of wealth and finds that the coefficient of net real assets (which consist essentially of real estate holdings) has a small positive value but is also highly significant. However, this variable is nonzero only for homeowners. Thus, because he does not control for home ownership in his regression, its coefficient can represent the effect of home ownership rather than the effect of the value of real wealth.

Regarded alone, none of the considerations reviewed above definitely justify focusing attention on net worth excluding land as a critical factor in determining the saving-income ratio, but together with the reasons given in the text, they provide reasonable support to doing so.

6.3   Savings and Net Worth Accumulation by the Corporate Sector

6.3.1   Income Flows

This section examines the savings and dividend payments of Japanese firms. It shows that they are not only exceptionally small, but that they have also decreased over time, thus providing an explanation of the low valuation of the firms. We must begin however by examining a variety of data problems that are present in the Japanese National Accounts and that can seriously bias any analysis of the corporate sector behavior.

First, both the "nonfinancial corporate enterprises" and "financial institutions" components include not just private businesses, but also public enterprises. It is impossible to separate them completely for years before 1990. This is also true of the total business sector, which includes unincorporated enterprises. With the new National Accounts based on the *System of National Accounts* (SNA93; United Nations et al. 1993), this is not an ongoing problem, but it will remain for prior periods. Thus, it is impossible to study long-term patterns in the behavior of the private business sector.

Second, even using SNA93, the National Accounts report neither the compensation of employees nor the value added of output by sector. Thus, it is very difficult to assess how productively labor and capital inputs are utilized. Because the way total value added is distributed to the factors contributing to production is important to our analysis, we use the whole economy excluding agriculture, housing, and government.

The method of computing depreciation in the National Accounts is a third source of difficulties. Depreciation is the change in value of a productive asset "as a result of physical deterioration, normal obsolescence, or normal accidental damage" (SNA 1993, 147, chap. 6.179). This can be calculated in several ways. For example, U.S. firms typically use different methods to compute depreciation for tax purposes and for financial reporting purposes. In the U.S. national accounts, depreciation, or the capital consumption allowance, uses uniform service lives and empirically based depreciation patterns (compared to a wide range of methodologies allowed by GAAP [Generally Accepted Accounting Principles] and the tax code), as well as current cost rather than historic cost, which is used for financial and tax reporting. The difference between this number and depreciation reported for tax purposes is called the capital consumption adjustment (hereafter CCAdj).[3]

Unfortunately, Japanese national income data historically do not include such a CCAdj. Rather, under the 1968 *System of National Accounts* (SNA68; United Nations 1968), depreciation using the tax code's provisions for service lives and historic cost was reported. Under SNA93, beginning with 1990 data, an adjustment that reflects the difference between historic and current cost is computed, but tax-code lives are still used. Depreciation using the tax code is (intentionally) faster than actual values. Using historical cost leads to under-statement in periods of high inflation. Adjustments to a current-cost basis were included with other items in the revaluation account under SNA68, but cannot be separated out to adjust the reported depreciation series (see Economic Planning Agency [EPA] 1978). Thus, we have to adjust the reported depreciation with our own estimate of the CCAdj using a method similar to Hayashi (1986).

We can see the effect of depreciation in table 6.3, which shows the way value added is distributed to the factors contributing to production. Table 6.3 presents data for the United States and for Japan using both National Accounts and our capital stock and depreciation estimates. The estimates that are used make a substantial difference in the evaluation of the sector's performance.

As we have just observed, the Japanese National Accounts do not provide information on either a measure of output or the compensation of employees for the corporate sector. We will therefore work with the whole economy less agriculture, housing, and government.[4]

First, let us compare the United States (part A) to Japan using National Accounts estimates (part B). The figures for 1970 are radically dissimilar, presumably because the Japanese economy was still in the process of a rapid transformation. It may also be because the data for this period are of lower quality, as the National Accounts only begin with 1970.

Over the entire period, there are a number of differences. The ratio of employee compensation to gross domestic product (GDP; column [7]) declined steadily in the United States, whereas it was increasing steadily in Japan. The ratio of operating surplus to GDP (column [8]) was declining sharply and steadily in Japan, whereas there is no particular pattern for the United States.

---

3. See http://www.bea.gov, click on Methodologies, and under "National Programs" see "A Guide to the NIPAs," M10–12.

4. Information on estimates of output and its composition for the housing sector were kindly supplied to us by the National Account Division, Economic and Social Research Institute, Cabinet Office. The GDP for Japan reported here reflects our estimates of the distribution of the imputed banking services among sectors. The U.S. figures incorporate the distribution estimated by the Bureau of Economic Analysis (BEA).

Table 6.3   Distribution of GDP in the Nonfarm Private Business Sector, Excluding Housing, 1970–1998

	Absolute Amounts					Percentage of GDP				
Year	GDP[a] (1)	Depreciation[b] (2)	Compensation of Employees (3)	Operating Surplus (4)	Capital Stock[c] (5)	Depreciation (6)	Compensation of Employees (7)	Operating Surplus (8)	Capital Stock (9)	Depreciation As % of Capital Stock (10)
	A. United States ($ billions)									
1970	687.7	65.0	460.1	162.6	1,013.2	9.5	66.9	23.6	147.3	6.4
1980	1,926.7	226.1	1,257.8	442.8	3,202.6	11.7	65.3	23.0	166.2	7.1
1991	3,995.7	512.5	2,536.9	946.3	6,622.7	12.8	63.5	23.7	165.7	7.7
1995	5,019.2	630.2	3,117.1	1,271.9	7,731.5	12.6	62.1	25.3	154.0	8.2
1998	6,093.0	759.6	3,757.1	1,576.3	9,006.8	12.5	61.7	25.9	147.8	8.4
	B. Japan, with National Account Estimates[d] (¥ trillions)									
1971	60.4	7.6	31.2	21.6	50.2	12.6	51.6	35.8	83.1	15.1
1980	176.7	26.7	105.1	44.9	213.1	15.1	59.5	25.4	120.6	12.5
1990	314.7	52.0	190.1	72.6	419.9	16.5	60.4	23.1	133.4	12.4
1995	343.7	64.1	226.1	53.5	548.0	18.6	65.8	15.6	159.4	11.7
1998	341.9	69.4	231.2	41.3	596.4	20.3	67.6	12.1	174.4	11.6
	C. Japan, with Our Estimates[e] (¥ trillions)									
1971	60.4	4.9	31.2	24.3	61.7	8.1	51.6	40.3	102.1	7.9
1980	176.7	21.6	105.1	50.0	276.2	12.2	59.5	28.3	156.2	7.8
1990	314.7	43.1	190.1	81.4	523.3	13.7	60.4	25.9	166.3	8.2
1995	343.7	54.9	226.1	62.7	678.3	16.0	65.8	18.3	197.4	8.1
1998	341.9	58.2	231.2	52.6	703.8	17.0	67.6	15.4	205.8	8.3

Source: Statistics for the United States from BEA web site http://www.bea.doc.gov. Statistics for Japan, from EPA (2000a), 168–79, 390).

Note: The GDP for Japan reflects our estimates of the distribution of imputed banking services among sectors. Imputed banking services were calculated based on interest flows and operating surplus. The U.S. figures incorporate the distribution estimated by the BEA.

[a]GDP less indirect business taxes.

[b]For the United States, depreciation is with a CCAdj. For Japan, we calculated an adjustment to make the National Accounts series current cost, following a methodology similar to the work of Hayashi (1986). For C, our estimates of capital stock and depreciation are used. Data for the Japanese housing sector was provided by Mr. Mitsuo Hosen of the ESRI.

[c]Capital stock is as of the beginning of the year.

[d]National Accounts estimates of reproducible fixed assets are used.

[e]Our estimates of reproducible fixed assets used.

Although the share of depreciation (column [6]) was increasing during the 1970s and 1980s for both, it is much larger for Japan and continued to increase in the 1990s, whereas for the United States it stabilized. As for the capital-output ratio (column [9]), there was a steady increase for Japan, and no particular pattern for the United States. The ratio of depreciation to capital stock (column [10]) was increasing in the United States but falling in Japan.

It is hard to see how the difference in the depreciation rate (12 percent in Japan versus 8 percent in the United States, as shown in column [10]) can persist when the technologies available in both countries are approximately the same. It is possible that when the Japanese economy was still going through its rapid transformation—that is, until the early 1970s—depreciation did indeed proceed more rapidly in Japan than in the United States. It is furthermore conceivable that this higher depreciation rate became incorporated into Japan's accounting practices and tax code and thus has persisted even after the economy matured and "true" depreciation became roughly comparable to that for the United States. In such a case, rational managers presumably would not abandon capital stock before it was economical to do so. That would create a situation in which data for capital stock and depreciation are seriously biased relative to their true quantities.

To remedy this situation, we constructed a series for net capital stock and depreciation that uses current costs and empirically based depreciation patterns. Our series is based on depreciation rates suggested by Hulten and Wykoff (1981), as adapted to the Japanese case by Hayashi and Inoue (1991). We leave the National Accounts estimates for residential houses untouched. The details of our reconstruction are reported in appendix A (available online at http://www.nber.org/data-appendix/ando_et_al), and results are recorded in part C of table 6.3.

Our estimate of the net stock of capital stock in 1998 is 18 percent larger than the National Accounts estimate. Our depreciation estimate is 16 percent smaller than the National Accounts estimate, adjusted by us to reflect current costs. As a result, our overall depreciation rate for Japan during the 1990s is around 8 percent, which is about two-thirds of the (approximately) 12 percent implied by the adjusted national accounts data. A simple theoretical example of the consequences of assuming a depreciation rate much higher than the one that actually prevailed in the economy is in appendix B (available online at http://www.nber.org/data-appendix/ando_et_al).

If this accounting bias took place in the United States, where the financial markets are well developed and investors are constantly seeking arbitrage opportunities, sooner or later the market value of equities would adjust to correct it. If the market value persisted in reflecting the biased accounting records, in the United States, an attempt at a takeover of a firm would be likely to occur. In Japan, however, since corporations are seldom subjected to a takeover or merger challenge, such biased data may well be accepted in the equity market and persist for a long time. We believe that these accounting biases are some of the factors contributing to the creation of a large market valuation discrepancy in the Japanese corporate equity market that is to be discussed later.

Having adjusted depreciation, let us now proceed to a review of the dividends and retained earnings of Japanese nonfinancial corporations and financial institutions. Be reminded that these sectors include both private corporations and public enterprises and that we are looking at this mixture. Our impression is that the size of public enterprises is especially large in the case of the financial institutions sector.

In table 6.4, parts A and B, we present data for 1990 to 1998 using the revised National Accounts on the basis of the SNA93. We cannot use data based on the SNA68 since the definition of dividends paid by financial institutions contained a number of items, including a part of imputed property income due to holders of life insurance policies, that swamped dividends paid to equity holders (see EPA 2000b). The data based on the SNA93 give figures for dividends paid to equity holders separated from other payments, and the difference is very large. For 1998, gross dividends paid by financial institutions in the old accounts were ¥4.4 trillion, whereas they are only ¥0.7 trillion in the new accounts. For this reason, in this subsection in which the income of equity holders is one of the central issues, we have no choice but to confine our discussion to the period 1990–1998 because the data on an SNA93 basis are available beginning only in 1990.

Table 6.4   **Corporate Sector, Savings, and Net Dividends Paid, SNA93 Data (¥ trillions)**

	1990	1991	1992	1993	1994	1995	1996	1997	1998
			A. Nonfinancial Corporations						
1. Savings A[a]	7.41	4.42	2.15	3.18	3.25	5.53	10.27	14.69	10.15
2. Savings B[b]	n.a.	−4.40	−7.90	−7.95	−7.60	−9.11	2.19	5.39	0.72
3. Savings C[c]	10.33	6.15	2.88	2.61	2.96	6.25	14.63	18.11	12.39
4. Net dividends paid	2.78	2.74	2.61	2.62	2.39	2.88	2.50	2.56	2.25
			B. Financial Institutions						
5. Savings A[a]	6.17	6.89	6.05	5.67	4.69	6.58	8.63	9.64	10.32
6. Savings B[b]	n.a.	7.67	7.43	7.14	6.61	8.52	10.39	11.34	11.78
7. Savings C[c]	6.96	7.29	6.90	6.51	5.96	8.06	9.84	10.80	11.16
8. Net dividends paid	−0.33	−0.36	−0.34	−0.32	−0.26	−0.34	−0.41	−0.45	−0.41

Source: ESRI (2001, 94–97, 500–09).

Note: n.a. = not available

[a]Using National Accounts depreciation (thus, at historical cost).

[b]Using National Accounts depreciation and CCAdj.

[c]Using our estimates of depreciation (based on Hulten-Wykoff service lives and current cost).

Later in the paper, where it is essential to cover a longer period, we attempt to avoid dealing with dividends paid by financial institutions.

In addition, there are dramatic differences in the size of retained earnings of these two sectors between the old accounts and new accounts. These differences appear to be mostly due to changes in current transfers. We have not yet found specific references to this issue in the National Accounts Division's explanation of changes. We would, however, venture a guess that the Division changed the procedure for handling the write-off of bad debts and that this is the main reason why there has been such a large change in current transfers and, hence, retained earnings.

Under these circumstances, it is extremely difficult to make coherent sense of these partial income statements for corporations. The best we can do is to offer a few observations that may be useful for future investigation.

1. The net dividend payment by the nonfinancial corporate sector is steady at about ¥2.5 trillion per year (table 6.4, line 4). The payment of net dividends by financial institutions (line 8) is negative and around ¥–0.3 trillion. Thus, these two sectors together paid other sectors of the economy, primarily the household sector and the rest of the world sector, a total of 2.2 trillion yen in dividends per year during the period 1990 to 1998. This contrasts with dividend payments by American corporations (financial and nonfinancial combined) during the same period, starting at $144 billion in 1990 and steadily increasing to $309.2 billion in 1998.[5] At an exchange rate of ¥120 to a dollar, American corporations paid roughly ten times the amount of dividends that were paid by Japanese corporations.

2. If we accept the figures reported in the National Accounts for the nonfinancial and financial corporate sectors combined, corporate retained earnings, after tax (savings) adjusted for CCAdj, were close to zero for the period 1990 through 1995 as shown in table 6.4. For the years 1996, 1997, and 1998, the corporate retained earnings were over ¥10 trillion. For the entire period 1990–1998, their average was about ¥5 trillion per year. If we replace the national accounts estimate of depreciation with our own estimate, the retained earnings (savings with CCAdj) would be roughly ¥10 trillion greater per year, or around ¥15 trillion on average. This difference reflects the difference between depreciation with CCAdj given by the national accounts and our own estimates, shown in table 6.3, column (2). We can see the importance of making sure that the estimate of depreciation is reasonable and realistic. The retained earnings after tax with CCAdj and IVA (Inventory Valuation Adjustments) for U.S. corporations (nonfinancial and financial combined) fluctuate over time, but on average they are approximately $125 billion per year. The Japanese figure is roughly one-

5. As shown in Table 1.16 of the U.S. National Income and Product Accounts; available at http://www.bea.gov/bea/dn/nipaweb/TableViewFixed.asp?selectedTable=26&FirstYear=2001&last year=2002&Freq=Qtr.

third of the U.S. amount if we take the national accounts estimate of depreciation, whereas it is about equal to the U.S. amount if we take our own estimate of depreciation.

3. Even though we believe that Japanese corporations have retained more earnings and that their capital stock is probably larger than recorded, we suspect that the retained earnings of Japanese corporations have not contributed to the value of equities at all. One reason for our suspicion is shown in table 6.5, where the historical record of the amount of dividends paid by nonfinancial corporations is shown. We have to rely on the data on the SNA68 basis here, since we wish to have a long time series. Therefore, we cannot work with the dividend payments of financial institutions. Since we do not have information on the output of corporations, we report

Table 6.5   Dividends of Nonfinancial Incorporated Enterprises, SNA68 Data (¥ trillions)

Year	Dividends Paid	Dividends Received	Net Dividends Paid	Sector GDP[a]
1970	1.521	0.501	1.020	58.2
1971	1.622	0.529	1.092	63.7
1972	1.782	0.585	1.197	72.8
1973	2.233	0.770	1.463	89.2
1974	2.579	0.925	1.655	104.9
1975	2.424	0.858	1.566	113.3
1976	2.477	0.871	1.606	127.9
1977	2.334	0.871	1.464	141.5
1978	2.729	0.975	1.754	156.1
1979	2.914	1.027	1.887	170.2
1980	3.190	1.174	2.016	185.6
1981	3.502	1.289	2.213	199.8
1982	3.291	1.210	2.081	210.1
1983	3.378	1.216	2.161	218.4
1984	3.453	1.250	2.203	233.3
1985	3.698	1.604	2.095	249.2
1986	3.845	1.842	2.003	258.5
1987	4.177	2.991	1.186	270.6
1988	4.420	3.666	0.754	289.5
1989	6.465	5.412	1.054	311.6
1990	5.597	5.451	0.146	337.2
1991	5.744	5.647	0.097	361.7
1992	5.599	5.394	0.205	370.2
1993	5.668	5.117	0.550	369.1
1994	5.265	4.468	0.798	367.1
1995	5.709	4.325	1.384	370.7
1996	5.899	2.918	2.981	382.4
1997	5.855	3.240	2.615	386.7
1998	5.691	3.231	2.460	374.1

Sources: EPA (2000a, 72–73). See notes for table 6.3 for calculation of GDP.
[a]Private business GDP, excluding the agriculture, housing, and financial sectors.

private, nonfarm, nonfinancial business GDP as the scale indicator. The most amazing fact is that nominal net dividend payments have hardly increased since 1970. In addition, there is a strange rise of dividends received from 1987 through 1995, making net dividends paid during this period extremely erratic and close to zero.

Retained earnings increase the value of equity, because they presumably contribute to increased profits and, hence, to future increases in dividends. In the case of Japanese corporations, however, the retention of substantial amounts of earnings by corporations, have not contributed to an increase in dividends at all. Thus, from the point of view of equity holders, retained earnings are of little value. Given the historical pattern of dividend payments, the market value of equity even at the end of the 1990s may be considered remarkably high. The average dividend-price ratio for those corporations listed at the Tokyo Stock Exchange, first division, and paying dividends for 1998, 1999, and 2000 is reported to be 1.3 percent, 0.9 percent, and 1.1 percent respectively (Bank of Japan 2002).

We have noted that there are substantial differences in the pattern of dividend payments and retained earnings of nonfinancial corporations between national accounts data on the SNA68 basis and data on the SNA93 basis. In table 6.6, we report dividends paid and received according to the data on the SNA93 basis. The pattern is indeed different, especially in the period 1987–1995 when the data on the SNA68 basis showed strange increases in dividends received. The pattern shown by the data on the SNA93 basis is perfectly smooth throughout the 1990s. The basic feature of the time pattern of dividend payments is common in both versions of data: Dividend payments show no sign of growth to reflect the increasing scale of the economy over time.

Table 6.6   **Dividends Paid and Received by Corporations, SNA 93 Data (¥ trillions)**

Year	Nonfinancial		Financial		Total[a]
	Paid	Received	Paid	Received	
1990	4.971	2.193	0.918	1.251	2.445
1991	5.090	2.347	0.837	1.195	2.385
1992	4.918	2.311	0.794	1.139	2.262
1993	4.960	2.336	0.857	1.172	2.309
1994	4.536	2.149	0.768	1.031	2.123
1995	4.942	2.057	0.717	1.061	2.540
1996	5.040	2.539	0.700	1.115	2.087
1997	5.100	2.544	0.718	1.167	2.108
1998	4.958	2.706	0.666	1.081	1.837

Source: ESRI (2001, 94–97).

Note: Includes nonfinancial and financial corporations. Excludes withdrawals of income from quasi corporations.

[a]Net payments.

We now turn our attention to the balance sheet of corporations and the relationship between the pattern of income and the structure of the balance sheet.

6.3.2 Capital Accumulation by Corporations and the Valuation of Corporate Equity

The consolidated balance sheet of the corporate sector is shown in table 6.2, column (3). For those of us who normally operate outside Japan, there are some striking features. First, the value of land (see line [b]) is enormous, a substantial part of tangible assets. At the height of the asset bubble in 1987–1991, its value even exceeded that of reproducibles. If it is added to the denominator of the ratio of operating surplus to fixed capital, the rate of return becomes minuscule. From the point of view of valuing a firm, there is no justification for omitting the value of land. In practice, however, a firm that has held land for a long time may not be using its true economic cost. Indeed, regardless of when the land was acquired and what was paid for it, there is no reason to account for its cost properly if management does not feel the need to compensate the firm's equity holders properly.

Second, the net equity outstanding is a small fraction of the accounting net worth of corporations (defined in table 6.2, line [g]). When financial markets are functioning efficiently and expectations on the contribution of reproducible physical assets to earnings are realized, accounting net worth and the market value of net equity should be close, if not necessarily equal, to each other. However, in Japan they are not. Rather, there is a gap, which we term the market valuation discrepancy. This is calculated in table 6.2, line (k). When the market valuation discrepancy is zero, the reproduction cost of reproducible fixed assets and the market value of land are fully reflected in the "value of the firm" (defined as the value of net equity outstanding plus net financial liabilities). Another way of saying this is that Tobin's average q is 1. When the value of land is very large, however, the interpretation of this concept becomes somewhat ambiguous, but we believe that the only tenable generalization of the concept is the inclusion of the value of land in the denominator. The value of q so computed is reported in table 6.2, line (m). For the consolidated corporate sector, it ranges from a low of 0.32 in 1980 to a high of 0.52 in 1998.

When the average q is properly calculated, it is well known that its value can be reduced from unity, even in equilibrium, when the pattern of the depreciation allowance under the corporate profit tax system is accelerated relative to the pattern of economic depreciation (see, e.g., Gordon and Malkiel 1981). However, it can be shown that the quantitative effect of this mechanism is quite minor, less than 5 percent of the reproduction cost of capital. Therefore, this consideration alone cannot account for the deviation of q from unity reported in table 6.2.

The possible reasons why the estimated value of q deviates so substantially from unity must be the same as those listed above for the very large value of market valuation discrepancy.[6] When the market valuation discrepancy is negative and large, we are inclined to think of four possible reasons: (a) For whatever reason, the price paid for the reproducible fixed assets is no longer justified in terms of the anticipated income stream it will generate; (b) There is a dramatic change in the value of land; (c) There may be serious imperfections in the capital market; (d) There is a deliberate policy by management to maintain the pattern of a very small and stagnant payment pattern of dividends. We consider the fourth reason as the most likely.

Let us recall the observation with which we ended the preceding section, namely, that dividend payments by these corporations are not only very small, but also that they have not increased much at all. Here we face a serious data problem, because dividend payment information in the national accounts based on the SNA68 is not reliable, while the data based on the SNA93 is available only starting in 1990. We have no choice but to gain some sense of the pattern from these inconsistent data. Let us first look at the longer time series using the data based on the SNA68. Since net dividend payments by financial institutions are negligible, we can match net dividend payments of nonfinancial corporations reported in table 6.5 and the market value of their net equity outstanding in table 6.2. This dividend-price ratio averages approximately 2.6 percent for the period 1970–1998, declining during the period. Thus, in the 1970s it was 4.8 percent, in the 1980s it was 1.8 percent, and in the 1990s it was only 0.7 percent. This ratio is remarkably low, given that dividend payments did not grow at all, whereas the scale variable increased by seven times during the same period. For the 1990s, we can partially check this finding using the data based on the SNA93. Dividend payments on this basis are given in table 6.4, lines (4) and (8). The dividend-price ratio for 1999 is 1.9 percent (1.4 percent for 1991), confirming the pattern given by the data based on the SNA68. Therefore, we conclude that at least a partial reason why the market value of equity is so low is that dividend payments have been extremely small and did not grow over time. This is a puzzling pattern. If the accounting net worth is correctly estimated in the National Income Accounts (NIA) and the market value of equity is so depressed, in a well-functioning market, we would expect that someone would purchase the firm and liquidate its assets, realizing a major capital gain.

Table 6.7 traces development of the balance sheet for corporate capital

---

6. Others have estimated the Tobin's average q, and Hoshi and Kashyap (1990) summarize them conveniently. Basically, estimates of q using data from individual companies listed on the Tokyo Stock Exchange are close to unity, while those estimated using aggregate data are significantly less than unity. Both aggregate data and microdata require many adjustments and imputations for the purpose of estimating q, and a satisfactory resolution of this paradox will require a large-scale data analysis. It may be noted that the estimate of q using all firms appears to be considerably smaller than the one using only manufacturing firms.

Table 6.7   Corporate Sector Saving and Net Worth in 1990 Prices, 1971–1998, SNA68 (¥ trillions)

	1971–1979	1980–1990	1991–1998	Accumulated
A.1 Reproducible tangible assets[a]	167.3	193.9	91.7	452.9
A.2 Flow	212.6	278.2	211.7	702.6
A.3 Revaluation	-45.3	-84.3	-120.1	-249.7
B.1 Nonreproducible tangible assets[a]	86.2	519.4	-284.3	321.3
B.2 Flow	51.3	68.9	-1.4	118.8
B.3 Revaluation	34.9	450.5	-283.0	202.4
C.1 Net Financial Assets (excl. equity shares)	-52.6	-209.3	-40.5	-302.4
C.2 Flow	-158.1	-307.1	-75.6	-540.8
C.3 Reconciliation excl. inflation loss[b]	4.9	46.5	4.3	55.7
C.4 Inflation gain	100.6	51.3	30.8	182.6
D.1 Equity (accounting) = A.1 + B.1 + C.1[c]	200.8	504.0	-233.1	471.7
D.2 Flow = A.2 + B.2 + C.2 = E.1 + E.2 + E.3 + E.4	105.7	40.1	134.8	280.6
D.3 Reconciliation excl. inflation gain on net financial assets = A.3 + B.3 + C.3	-5.5	412.7	-398.7	8.4
D.4 Inflation gain = C.4	100.6	51.3	30.8	182.6
D.5 Equity (market)[c]	21.7	120.7	-72.7	69.7
D.6 Market valuation discrepancy[c]	179.1	383.3	-160.4	402.0
E.1 Savings	81.2	105.0	85.6	271.9
E.2 Net capital transfers	13.5	17.7	49.3	80.4
E.3 Statistical discrepancy	11.5	-13.2	-14.3	-16.0
E.4 Net equity transactions[d]	-0.4	-69.4	14.1	-55.6

Source: EPA (2000a, 80–83, 322–25).

Notes: The corporate sector can be decomposed into nonfinancial corporate enterprises as well as private corporations, and these are an especially large part of the financial institutions sector. It includes public enterprises and financial institutions. Our estimate of reproducible tangible assets is used. Constant prices were obtained using the deflator for total private consumption expenditure. Also see box 6.1 for additional information on the data.

[a] Gross fixed capital formation has been reduced by the amount of investment in land improvement using data provided by Mr. Mitsuo Hosen of the ESRI. Corresponding adjustments were made to the investment in land and the reconciliation accounts of reproducible fixed assets and land. Because our estimates are used, the accumulation of stock is considerably larger than the estimate presented by the National Accounts.

[b] For financial assets, losses to creditors are gains to debtors, so the effects of general inflation are reported explicitly rather than as part of reconciliation. (See box 6.1.)

[c] Accounting equity (D.1) differs from the market value of equity (D.5) by the market valuation discrepancy (D.6).

[d] This is new issues of equity minus acquisitions of equity. A minus sign indicates corporations were net purchasers of equity. During the most of the period, nonfinancial corporations were net sellers of equity but financial corporations were major purchasers.

stock in the same way table 6.1 does for the household sector (details on the data are also in box 6.1).

By definition, the sum flow of funds by use in table 6.7 (line D2) equals the total by source (line E). Unfortunately, the statistical discrepancy entry (E.3) is fairly large, but the most surprising item is net capital transfers received (E.2). For 1991–1998, these include the government bailout of firms in this sector, and it is nearly five times as large as accumulated retained earnings. It is also a sizable amount in the two earlier periods; we are not quite sure why.

Accounting equity (D.1) is divided between the market value of equity (D.5) and the market valuation discrepancy (D.6). In the Japanese National Accounts (and in SNA93) the discrepancy is designated as net worth. We believe that this designation is not only misleading but also gives users a wrong impression of the performance by corporations.

We find it surprising that the market value of these corporations increased by only ¥70 trillion between 1971 and 1998, whereas their accounting equity increased by ¥472 trillion, thereby increasing the market valuation discrepancy by ¥402 trillion. (Box 6.2 analyzes this gap.)

How does one explain the market valuation discrepancy? Part of the answer is that, in the corporate governance structure in Japan, management does not seem to feel any need to compensate equity owners. Thus, only token dividends are paid and scant attention is given to the market value of equity.

Management may have convinced itself that the token dividend payments define very low costs of internally generated funds, and thus investment in capital projects can be justified even when the expected rate of return is quite low. This is especially true if managers are encouraged to make their firms as large as possible, which is often said to be a goal of Japanese firms.

Beyond that, we believe that decision rules based on management's perception of the cost of internally generated funds contribute to other unusual features of the Japanese economy. These include a very high capital-labor ratio, a very low rate of return on capital for the corporate sector as a whole, and a dramatically small ratio of the market value of equity to the accounting value of firms. The puzzle is why new firms do not enter Japanese markets, follow the policy of efficient use of resources, and force older firms to reform. In any case, the apparent existing decision rules are an impediment to growth of the economy and the efficient allocation of resources.

This behavior may have historical roots. During the period immediately after World War II, most capital facilities were destroyed, obsolete, or both, so businesses needed to accumulate capital as quickly as possible to build plants and acquire new technologies. Thus, retaining as much of their revenue as possible for investment was a sensible policy, consistent with the

**Box 6.2   Decomposing the Market Valuation
             Discrepancy Increase**

Our starting point is the total of funds transferred from other
sectors of the economy to the corporate sector during 1971–1998.
This can be approximated using the data in table 6.7, column (4).

+	280.6	Accounting equity flow (D.2)
−	−16.0	Statistical discrepancy (E.3)
+	182.6	Inflation gain (C.4) (This is largely the counterpart of the ¥217 trillion inflation loss recorded in the household sector account, table 6.1, C.4.)
=	479.2	Total funds transferred to corporate sector.

If the sector is operating efficiently at all and the financial market
is functioning reasonably well, then the market value of the shares
of corporations in the sector should have increased at least by this
amount. It did not. The actual market value increased by only
¥69.7 trillion, creating a ¥409.5 trillion equity loss to owners.

The loss increases the market valuation discrepancy to the
extent individual items on the balance sheet of corporations did
not incur real capital gains and losses (data are from table 6.7).

+	409.5	Equity owners' loss	
+	8.4	Total capital gain of corporations, composed of:	
		−249.7	Loss on reproducible tangible assets (A.3)
		202.4	Gain on land (B.3)
		55.7	Gain on net financial assets (C.3)
+	−16.0	Statistical discrepancy (E.3)	
=	402.0	Increase in market valuation discrepancy (D.6)	

needs of very rapid economic development. We suspect that the pattern of
building as large a depreciation reserve as possible dates from this period.
If corporations do not have to pay dividends to shareholders, the cost of internally generated funds is essentially zero.

Such behavior can be maintained only if the demand for output is growing rapidly and if additional labor to match the rapid increases in capital is
available. This was the case in the high-growth era, as Japan could shift a
well-educated labor force from the agricultural sector to manufacturing
and high-technology industries on a large scale and its labor cost was lower

compared to the United States and Germany. It was therefore able to price its products sufficiently low to expand its share of the market.

As demand and labor-supply growth slacken, the gross rate of return on capital gradually declines, and presumably it becomes near the level of depreciation. At that point, firms must begin to reduce the level of investment and distribute excess funds to holders of equity.

Such a point was reached quite some time ago in Japan, but firms continued to operate as they had previously. In part this is because equity owners are in an exceptionally weak position to influence the policies of management. There are two related reasons for this. First, Japanese law encourages corporations to enforce strict majority rule in the election of board members, rather than permitting cumulative voting. This means minority shareholders have very little leverage with management. Second, the tradition of cross-shareholding arrangements among corporations makes it extremely difficult for outsiders to form a majority. Managers who detect the prospect of a hostile majority group forming can quickly arrange for friendly corporations to increase their ownership.[7]

6.3.3   Investment and Financing Decisions and the Rate of Return for Firms

We have singled out the dividend payment pattern as a noticeably unusual behavior of Japanese firms. We can also observe from table 6.3 that the operating surplus of the business sector in Japan appears to be a considerably smaller fraction of the value added less indirect taxes of the sector compared with the United States (15 percent versus 26 percent in 1998). Let us now consider if there is some connection between these two observations. In table 6.8, columns (1) and (2), we present the ratio of operating surplus to the value of reproducible and nonreproducible capital. The former is computed using our own estimate of depreciation, described in appendix A and adjusted for imputed banking services, while in the latter the value of reproducible capital is our own estimate. We are not sure that our estimates for the years 1971 through 1973 are reliable. There may be something unsatisfactory about the estimates of the capital stock reported in the *National Wealth Survey* (EPA 1970). Even starting from 1974, the rate of return on capital is quite low, and it declines steadily until it reaches a level of around 4 percent for nonfinancial corporations and 5 percent for the total business sector in the 1990s. Given that this rate is before the corporate profit tax, the rate of return is amazingly low.

This rate must be viewed as the measure of the marginal product of capital given the way it is computed. We are also interested in the rate of return

7. In chapter nine of this volume, Yafeh notes that minority shareholders have fairly good legal protection in Japan. This is true, and applies to different issues. His concern is with the way insider usually majority, shareholders treat other shareholders. Our concern is with the way management insiders treat *all* shareholders.

Table 6.8   Rate of Return on Corporations (Annual Percentage Rates)

	Return on Capital[b]		Market Rate of Return		
Period Average[a]	Nonfinancial Corporations (1)	Business Sector[c] (2)	Ordinary Income[d] (3)	Capital Gains[e] (4)	Total Return[f] (5)
1971–1980	7.36	11.69	8.05	−6.50	1.58
1981–1990	5.55	7.30	4.94	3.54	8.56
1991–1998	3.67	5.04	1.82	−2.87	−1.06
1971–1998	5.18	7.54	4.71	−1.88	2.91

Source: EPA (2000), 79–89, 248–249, 322–337, 390–391 and appendix 1.
[a]Geometric average.
[b]Operating surplus adjusted for rent, depreciation, and imputed banking services divided by the sum of the reproducible assets and land.
[c]Includes households, unincorporated enterprises, and corporations.
[d]Net interest and net dividends paid divided by the sum of net equity outstanding and net financial liabilities. That is, payments to owners and creditors as a percentage of the capital they provide to the firm.
[e]Nominal capital gains minus inflation loss divided by the sum of net equity outstanding and net financial liabilities.
[f]Geometric average. Due to the particular averaging procedure adopted, the sum of columns (3) and (4) is slightly different from column (5)

accruing to the investor in the firm. We consider the investor who owns the equity and debt of the firm in the same proportion as the outstanding quantities. In table 6.8, columns (3) through (5), we present the rate of return for such an investor. Column (3) is the ratio of dividends plus net interest payments to the sum of the value of equity and net financial liabilities. Column (4) records real capital gains and losses for the same base, and column (5) presents the total. This computation can be done only for the total corporate sector. The total rate of return is the amazingly low value of 2.91 percent. The rate reported in table 6.8, column (5) is for all corporations and is not strictly comparable with the one for nonfinancial corporations shown in column (1). Nevertheless, we should expect the one in column (5) to be smaller than the one on column (1), because the latter is the rate before corporate profit taxes, while the former is after corporate profit taxes.

In table 6.3, we have noted that the capital-output ratio for the total business sector of Japan is much larger than the corresponding ratio for the United States, certainly in the 1990s. For 1998, the Japanese ratio is 2.06, whereas it is 1.48 for the United States. We are not including land in these calculations, so that the price of land is not involved. This is consistent with the fact that the rate of return for Japan is very low, much lower than the typical rate obtained by using the U.S. data (see Ando, Hancock, and Sawchuck 1997).

When a business firm's perception of the cost of one factor is unrelated to the price charged in the market for that factor, as it appears to be the case for equity capital for Japanese firms, we should expect that many decisions of the firm deviate substantially from those expected in the standard optimizing firms. Let us speculate on the investment and financing decisions perceived by Japanese corporate managers in the simplest possible case in which the firm cannot borrow, it does not need land, and there is no corporate profit tax. Managers wish to finance their entire investment from internal funds every period and view their objective as increasing the size of their firms by a specific rate, g, indefinitely. This may not be a rational target, but any other arbitrary targets produce similar results. The managers also know that they have complete control of the internal funds (i.e., no dividends must be paid). They then must satisfy the accounting identity:

$$(1) \qquad\qquad \Delta K = \rho K,$$

where ρ is the net rate of return on capital and thus ρK is the net income from the production process accruing to capital. Dividing both sides of equation (1) by K, we have

$$(1a) \qquad\qquad g = \frac{\Delta K}{K} = \rho.$$

In equation (1a), we are assuming that the production function is homogeneous of first degree and that the productivity increase is labor augmenting. The rate of growth of output is then equal to the rate of growth of capital on the steady state growth path, and they are both equal to g. Let us suppose that the managers also believe that they must satisfy the efficiency condition in the use of labor and capital:

$$(2) \qquad\qquad \frac{\rho + d}{w} = f\left(\frac{E}{K}\right),$$

where d is the depreciation rate, and w is the wage rate, and E is the number of hours worked. The managers view the net return on capital, ρK, as available for their firms without cost, since their firms do not have to compensate equity owners. To satisfy equation (1a), then, they choose K/E so that the value of ρ on the left-hand side of equation (2) becomes g:

The important point illustrated by this simple example is that the required rate of return on K is not at all related to anything in the market. If g is very small, the required net return on capital would also be quite small, and the capital-labor ratio would be correspondingly very large. The manager attempts to achieve an efficient combination of labor and capital from his point of view, but since the cost of capital is not related to the price of funds demanded in the market, his decision cannot be genuinely optimal.

Let us now consider a slightly generalized problem in which the firm is allowed to borrow, but still has to satisfy the modified version of equation (1):

(3) $$\Delta K = \rho K + \Delta L - rL$$

or

(3a) $$g = \frac{\Delta K}{K} = \rho + l(g - r),$$

where L is the loan taken out by the firm, r is the rate of interest charged on L, and l is the ratio L/K. Since the firm is not optimizing, there is no natural way to determine l, and we take its value as given. Then the value of ρ is again determined by the identity in equation (3a), and the capital-labor ratio is determined to achieve this value of ρ through equation (2). This time, there is an additional complication that, if r is greater than g, there seems to be no sensible motivation to take out the loan. If a specific value of l is viewed as required, however, a solution corresponding to it is feasible with ρ being larger than g.

As we have noted earlier, this is not an interesting or believable model of the behavior of a business firm. It does illustrate, however, the point that once the perceived price of a factor is not related to its market price, it is difficult to write an optimizing model and a number of strange consequences can follow. For a firm whose behavior is characterized by equations (2) and (3a), it is perfectly conceivable that its target rate of return, ρ, is extremely low, and that the capital-labor ratio turns out to be very large. Its behavior is not efficient in the normal sense, and the true cost of its production must be higher than that of genuinely efficient firms. Nevertheless, so long as owners of equity capital do not have to be compensated, the firm can go on indefinitely without being forced to liquidate. To prevent the market value of equity becoming zero, the firm may pay very small, constant dividends, without changing the basic feature of the model discussed above. It may be possible to construct a much more realistic and plausible model of a Japanese firm in which competing interests of participants are described carefully. As long as the price attributed to the contribution of one or more factors by the management is significantly different from their market price, however, the distortion considered previously must be present, and the allocation of resources in the whole economy cannot be efficient.

6.4   Conclusion

In this chapter we have explored reasons why the market value of equity of corporations in Japan has not increased to reflect their accumulation of capital. One consequence of this situation is that the Japanese economy has been facing a condition of insufficient demand because households incur considerable capital losses in their corporate equity holdings and thus reduce their consumption. This condition does not seem to have any prospect of resolving itself unless a way can be found to transfer a substantial amount of resources from corporations to households via substantially increased dividend payments.

In the standard model of corporate finance, the present value of future dividend payments, allowing for the risk involved, determines the market value of equity. In equilibrium, that value is roughly equal to the value of accumulated capital, allowing for a variety of special conditions. This may be viewed as a consequence of nearly rational behavior on the part of management and the reasonably efficient functioning of markets for factors and output. Although real market conditions may never be in equilibrium, we expect that there will be general tendencies to move toward the equilibrium. Data covering a large number of corporations and a long period of time should point to where the equilibrium position is likely to be.

The data for Japan do not resemble such a picture. The historical pattern of net dividend payments is nearly constant in nominal terms over time and has nothing to do with the accumulation of capital by corporations. Typical market participants therefore can only assume that this pattern is likely to continue. Such an expectation can support only a very low level of the value of equity, and this distorts savings behavior.

During the high-growth era, Japanese firms had some justification for retaining and reinvesting earnings. By the early 1990s, however, readily available technologies enabling increased productivity had become limited, and Japan's labor cost had reached approximately the same level as, or perhaps even above, that of the United States. To maintain balance between aggregate demand and aggregate supply, therefore, the savings rate must become lower, and consumption demand must be expanded.

What can be done achieve this and thus remove a serious impediment to growth? Changes in corporate governance to give equity holders the capacity to deal with management on more equal terms must be considered. A complete reform of the accounting system also would be helpful. The government should consider changing the corporate profit tax system. The reformed tax system would encourage corporations to pay out funds when sufficiently profitable internal investment opportunities are not available.

We have estimated the "lost" wealth and the financial cost to Japan of the market valuation discrepancy. The household sector's lost wealth is presented in the bottom panel of table 6.2. Essentially, the calculation turns on estimating what the value of equity would be if Tobin's q were equal to 1 (a more detailed explanation is given in appendix C, also available at http://www.nber.org/data-appendix/ando_et_al).

At the end of 1998, the total value of net equity outstanding for all corporations (table 6.2, column [3]) would have been ¥750 trillion (instead of the actual ¥171 trillion), of which the household sector would have owned ¥475 trillion (rather than its actual ¥81 trillion). This is 395 trillion yen in lost wealth.

If the marginal propensity to consume out of net worth is 0.04, a reasonable value in terms of available estimates, consumption could have been larger by almost ¥16 trillion without any multiplier effect. With a very small multiplier of 1.5, additional consumption could have been more than ¥23 trillion. That would have been enough to put the Japanese economy back into full employment.

Appendix A
Determining Capital Stock in the Business Sector in Japan

There are several types of reproducible fixed assets reported by the Economic and Social Research Institute (ESRI) of the Japanese government in the National Accounts. However, as several authors have pointed out, Japan's depreciation rate is very much higher than the U.S. rate (for example Hayashi 1986).

Depreciation rates in the Japanese National Accounts are the same as those in the tax code, so it is possible that depreciation is overestimated. Thus, we decided to construct estimates of reproducible fixed assets, excluding housing, for the business sector (i.e., excluding general government but including public enterprises) by item and sector. In this appendix we describe the procedures followed. We decided to use National Accounts estimates of dwellings and their depreciation, given that housing in Japan has some characteristics (such as a substantial portion built with wood) that make unusually high depreciation rates not implausible.

We have constructed the stock of each type of reproducible fixed asset by first determining the benchmark stock, updating the stock each period using the perpetual inventory method, and then computing the stock and depreciation by sector.

Calculation of Benchmark Stock

The National Accounts do not report gross investment data by business sector and asset type, so we are not able to construct the capital stock of the business sector directly. Instead, we begin by constructing the aggregate capital stock. First, we calculate the benchmark stock using the National Wealth Survey of 1970 (EPA 1970), from which we get the net stock value for the business sector, defined as the sum of the whole private sector, public corporate sector, and nonprofit institutions.

We include all assets with the exception of the residential stock and the stock corresponding to investment in land improvement and divide it into five types: (a) buildings, (b) structures, (c) machines and tools, (d) transportation equipment, and (e) plants and animals. The *National Wealth Survey* (EPA 1970) is at 1970 prices. We convert it to 1990 prices using the stock deflator reported in National Accounts, table 6.4.1 ("Closing Stocks of Net Fixed Assets" EPA 2000a).

Accumulation of Capital Stock

To accumulate capital stock using the perpetual inventory method, we need the investment series and depreciation rate by asset. Investment data by asset in the National Accounts covers all sectors, including the general government sector. Using the ratio of government to aggregate investment, we can impute government investment by item, exclude it from the aggregate, and thus obtain investment by item for the business sector as a whole.

We adopt depreciation rates for fixed capital using those reported by Hayashi and Inoue (1991). Their data for machinery and transportation equipment includes information on early retirement of capital, whereas the National Accounts do not. Thus, following their suggestion, we augment their depreciation rates (based on Hulten and Wykoff 1981) by 40 percent to take account of this omission.

For buildings, we use the rate reported by Dean, Darrough, and Neef (1990). For remaining structures, we augment Dean, Darrough, and Neef's rates by 20 percent, as Hayashi and Inoue (1991) suggest. For plants and animals we apply the rate used in the United States by the Bureau of Economic Analysis, as reported in Fraumeni (1997).

Depreciation rates by asset type are as follows:

0.047 Buildings
0.056 Structures
0.157 Machinery, tools, and furnishings
0.245 Transportation equipment (including ships)
0.023 Plants and animals

Using these rates and the perpetual inventory method, we calculate the capital stock from 1970 to 1998. An adjustment is made for the 1995 Hanshin-Awaji (Kobe) earthquake by subtracting the estimated losses (provided by Mr. Mitsuo Hosen of the ESRI) from the capital stock at the end of 1995.

Assets lost in the 1995 Hanshin-Awaji earthquake (in ¥ billions) are as follows:

3,088   Buildings
1,895   Structures
   22   Machinery, tools, and furnishings
   88   Transportation equipment (including ships)

Calculation of Capital Stock by Sector

The *National Wealth Survey* of 1970 (EPA 1970) can be used to construct capital stock by type and sector. Gross investment by sector can be obtained from the National Accounts.

Because housing is excluded from our stock calculation, we have to subtract housing investment, which is recorded in the National Accounts only for the combined corporate sector and for the combined household and nonprofit institutions sector. We assume that only households and nonfinancial corporations invest in residential structures. This seems innocuous, as we combine households and nonprofit institutions in any event and financial institutions hold a negligible amount of residential structures (0.49 percent), as reported in the *National Wealth Survey* (EPA 1970).

We need the depreciation rate by sector to accumulate the stock. To obtain it, we calculate aggregate depreciation by item, the sum across items, and then divide by total stock. This provides an implied depreciation rate, which is used for each individual sector. This implied rate is, on average, a little above 8 percent, which is a considerably less than the rate obtained from the National Accounts (table 6.3).

Having obtained gross investment and depreciation, we can use the perpetual inventory method to obtain capital stock by sector. We allocate the total loss of assets due to the Hanshin-Awaji earthquake reported above to each sector according to the stock held at the end of 1994.

The results of our calculations are shown in tables 6A.1 and 6A.2. Table 6A.1 shows our calculation of capital stock and depreciation by item and compares the totals to the corresponding National Account magnitudes. Our estimate of aggregate stock shown (column [11]) is roughly 20 percent higher than the National Account's (column [13]).

The difference in depreciation is considerable, especially in the early years. This is to be expected, as in those years our estimate of the stock is not very different from theirs, whereas our depreciation rates are considerably smaller. In later years, the difference in stock becomes bigger, and thus the difference in depreciation becomes smaller, although still sizeable. Note that column (14) reports National Accounts depreciation at original cost (i.e., at 1990 prices) and thus has to be augmented by an estimate of the capital consumption adjustment (column [15]) to be comparable to our estimate of depreciation in column (12).

Table 6A.2 reports stocks and depreciation for nonfinancial corporations and financial institutions.

Table 6A.1   Capital Stock and Depreciation by Asset Type, 1970–1998: Our Estimates Compared to National Accounts (1990 ¥ billions)

| | Buildings | | Structures | | Machines and tools (including plants and animals) | | Transportation and machines[a] | | Business sector | | | | |
| | | | | | | | | | Our totals | | National accounts totals | | |
Year	Stock (1)	Depreciation (2)	Stock (3)	Depreciation (4)	Stock (5)	Depreciation (6)	Stock (7)	Depreciation (8)	Stock[b] (11)	Depreciation (12)	Stock (13)	Depreciation (14)	CCA[d] (15)
1970	50,961	n.a.	50,768	n.a.	31,640	n.a.	6,586	n.a.	139,956	n.a.	126,268	n.a.	n.a.
1971	57,527	2,395	59,680	2,863	36,383	4,824	8,100	1,614	161,691	11,696	145,760	24,124	-4,281
1972	64,382	2,704	68,863	3,366	40,296	5,600	9,547	1,985	183,088	13,654	165,265	24,134	-5,251
1973	71,782	3,026	78,650	3,884	45,876	6,276	10,842	2,339	207,151	15,525	186,975	26,911	-3,580
1974	77,927	3,374	87,709	4,436	50,054	7,146	11,048	2,656	226,738	17,612	204,093	29,564	417
1975	83,292	3,663	96,624	4,947	52,229	7,776	11,100	2,707	243,244	19,092	218,705	26,519	1,477
1976	88,313	3,915	104,902	5,450	54,794	8,154	11,092	2,719	259,102	20,237	232,141	23,264	2,682
1977	92,848	4,151	112,860	5,916	57,097	8,526	11,284	2,718	274,088	21,311	244,367	24,257	3,041
1978	97,529	4,364	121,048	6,365	59,700	8,825	11,843	2,765	290,120	22,319	257,429	25,022	3,294
1979	103,029	4,584	129,567	6,827	63,758	9,135	12,805	2,901	309,158	23,447	273,542	26,139	3,082
1980	109,718	4,842	137,275	7,308	68,439	9,623	13,742	3,137	329,174	24,910	290,400	28,417	3,722
1981	116,285	5,157	144,738	7,742	73,715	10,177	14,558	3,367	349,296	26,443	307,256	29,681	3,071
1982	122,295	5,465	151,491	8,163	79,392	10,822	14,883	3,567	368,062	28,017	322,451	31,119	3,545
1983	127,849	5,748	157,527	8,544	84,941	11,530	15,345	3,646	385,663	29,468	336,063	32,417	3,665
1984	133,663	6,009	163,671	8,885	93,213	12,222	15,787	3,760	406,334	30,875	351,952	33,857	4,203
1985	140,360	6,282	169,484	9,231	102,705	13,330	16,737	3,868	429,286	32,711	369,796	36,057	4,197
1986	147,540	6,597	175,495	9,559	111,212	14,612	17,740	4,101	451,988	34,868	387,562	38,304	3,743
1987	154,378	6,934	182,304	9,898	119,969	15,765	19,236	4,346	475,887	36,944	406,081	40,523	3,634
1988	162,359	7,256	190,437	10,282	132,201	16,948	20,798	4,713	505,796	39,199	429,843	43,050	3,759
1989	172,662	7,631	199,637	10,741	146,818	18,664	22,842	5,096	541,959	42,131	459,333	46,183	2,653
1990	184,509	8,115	210,208	11,260	163,228	20,744	24,999	5,596	582,944	45,715	493,368	51,413	3,511
1991	198,854	8,672	220,997	11,856	178,674	23,093	26,790	6,125	625,315	49,746	528,323	54,329	4,252
1992	212,736	9,346	230,645	12,464	189,166	25,308	27,490	6,563	660,037	53,681	555,609	57,621	5,238

(continued)

Table 6A.1   (continued)

	Buildings		Structures		Machines and tools (including plants and animals)		Transportation and machines[a]		Business sector				
									Our totals		National accounts totals		
Year	Stock (1)	Depreciation (2)	Stock (3)	Depreciation (4)	Stock (5)	Depreciation (6)	Stock (7)	Depreciation (8)	Stock[b] (11)	Depreciation (12)	Stock (13)	Depreciation (14)	CCA[d] (15)
1993	224,542	9,999	238,749	13,008	193,826	26,769	27,092	6,735	684,208	56,511	572,052	59,391	7,148
1994	234,409	10,553	245,905	13,465	196,356	27,349	26,457	6,638	703,127	58,005	582,980	58,795	7,328
1995	240,783	11,017	250,515	13,869	202,505	27,598	26,452	6,482	720,255	58,967	592,181	58,905	6,226
1996	248,763	11,317	257,171	14,129	217,158	28,401	26,707	6,481	749,798	60,328	608,917	60,240	7,179
1997	258,638	11,692	263,877	14,504	234,772	30,522	26,612	6,543	783,899	63,261	629,753	63,284	8,366
1998	266,726	12,156	268,879	14,883	246,108	33,063	25,473	6,520	807,186	66,621	641,504	65,776	9,285

Source: EPA (2000a, 79–89, 248–49, 322–37, 390–91; see appendix A).

Notes: Includes nonprofit institutions. Capital stock is reported on a year-end basis. n.a. = not available.

[a]Includes ships.

[b]Sum of stock of the four specific categories (columns [1], [3], [5], [7]).

[c]Sum of depreciation of the four specific categories (columns [2], [4], [6], [8]).

[d]Imputed capital consumption adjustment (CCA), excluding housing, from National Accounts. Calculated using data on real capital stock and flows. Note this CCA is not the same as the capital consumption adjustment (CCAdj) used by the United States—see discussion in the text under Depreciation.

Table 6A.2   **Estimates of Capital Stock and Depreciation of Nonfinancial and Financial Corporations**

Year	Reproducible Fixed Assets of Nonfinancial Corporations (excluding housing)	Depreciation of Reproducible Fixed Assets of Nonfinancial Corporations (excluding housing)	Reproducible Fixed Assets of Financial Institutions (excluding housing)	Depreciation of Reproducible Fixed Assets of Financial Institutions (excluding housing)
1970	107,433.5	n.a.	3,471.2	n.a.
1971	126,086.7	8,978.4	3,815.4	290.1
1972	144,164.8	10,647.5	4,117.7	322.2
1973	163,919.0	12,224.6	4,614.4	349.2
1974	179,876.5	13,936.3	5,006.4	392.3
1975	192,334.2	15,146.5	5,344.1	421.6
1976	203,661.9	16,001.7	5,601.3	444.6
1977	214,825.1	16,751.1	5,881.3	460.7
1978	226,630.4	17,493.2	6,123.0	478.9
1979	241,265.9	18,315.9	6,452.8	494.8
1980	257,061.1	19,440.0	6,852.4	519.9
1981	273,501.5	20,650.2	7,251.0	550.5
1982	289,390.9	21,937.7	7,562.7	581.6
1983	303,833.8	23,169.4	7,911.3	605.5
1984	321,308.6	24,324.4	8,349.6	633.4
1985	340,895.5	25,866.4	8,743.7	672.2
1986	360,335.0	27,688.6	9,227.0	710.2
1987	380,552.0	29,452.7	9,962.1	754.2
1988	405,534.9	31,346.0	11,156.9	820.6
1989	436,000.6	33,779.7	12,792.5	929.3
1990	471,103.9	36,777.2	14,760.0	1,079.1
1991	507,740.1	40,201.9	16,438.4	1,259.6
1992	537,485.5	43,587.9	17,679.9	1,411.2
1993	559,048.6	46,018.1	18,460.6	1,513.7
1994	576,722.5	47,394.7	19,105.6	1,565.0
1995	593,505.1	48,365.8	19,262.8	1,602.3
1996	621,008.5	49,711.4	20,180.7	1,613.4
1997	653,546.3	52,395.0	21,423.6	1,702.7
1998	676,024.1	55,542.8	22,568.1	1,820.7

Source: See appendix A.
Note: n.a. = not available.

Appendix B
Adjusting Depreciation and Capital Stock

In order to interpret the differences between parts B and C of table 6.3, let us consider the consequence of constructing the data for depreciation and the net capital stock assuming a depreciation rate much higher than the one that actually prevailed in the economy. We have the identity:

(A1) $$IG_t - D_t = K_t - K_{t-1},$$

where IG_t is gross investment, D_t is depreciation, and K_t is the stock of capital at the end of period t. Dividing equation (A1) by K_{t-1}, we have

$$\frac{IG_t}{Q_t} \times \frac{Q_t}{K_{t-1}} - \frac{D_t}{K_{t-1}} = \frac{K_t - K_{t-1}}{K_{t-1}},$$

where Q is the value added measure of output. On a steady growth path, the rate of growth of Q_t should be equal to the rate of growth of K_t. Denoting this growth rate by g and defining d_t as D_t/K_{t-1} and ig_t as IG_t/Q_t, we have, on the steady state growth path,

(A2) $$ig \times \frac{Q_t}{K_{t-1}} - d = g$$

$$\frac{K_{t-1}}{Q_t} = \frac{ig}{d+g}.$$

The Japanese economy has not been on a steady state growth path. Therefore, we cannot apply equation (A2) to the Japanese data directly. However, we can rely on the reasoning leading up to equation (A2) to formulate a hypothesis concerning the potential biases that are likely to be present in the Japanese data. For this purpose, let us note that the quantity ig is known, and there is no reason to suppose that information on this quantity is biased one way or another; the same is true of Q. The variable D is generated by multiplying K_{t-1} by an assumed value of d, and K_t is generated by the formula of equation (A1). Therefore, for a given g, if the assumed value of d is much larger than the true value of d, the recorded values of K and K/Q must be smaller than the true values of K and K/Q. For example, if ig is 0.2 and g is 0.02, and the true value of d is 0.08, then the true value of K/Q would be 2.0. If the value of d is incorrectly assumed to be 0.12, and the time series of K is generated by the perpetual inventory procedure, however, the resulting recorded value of K/Q approaches 1.5. That is, the estimate of capital stock under the assumption that d is 0.12 is roughly 75 percent of the correct value. Similarly, the estimate of depreciation, D, with the incorrectly large depreciation rate of 12 percent will be roughly 112.5 percent of the correct value.

Returning to table 6.3 and comparing the last values of columns (2) and (5) between parts B and C, we see that the estimates of the depreciation and capital stock with 12 percent depreciation rate are roughly 85 percent and 119 percent, respectively, of estimates with 8 percent depreciation rate. Given that the Japanese economy was by no means in a steady state equilibrium condition during the period leading up to 1998, we believe that our empirical results are within the reasonable range of our analytical predictions.

Appendix C

Computing Lost Household Wealth

To compute lost wealth we assume that there is no market value discrepancy for corporations—that is, the market value of net equity is equal to accounting equity, which is the same as saying that Tobin's average q is 1. We then made four additional assumptions, listed below, to create a hypothetical distribution of equities among sectors. This is used to calculate the household sector's adjusted net worth.

Assumptions Regarding Distribution

1. Government entries do not change, because virtually all its equity is in public corporations that are not traded and whose objectives are typically quite different from those of profit-seeking ones.

2. The ratio of equity owned to net equity for the corporate sector as a whole (table 6.2, column [3]) remains the same. That is, line $(i') = j' \cdot (i/j)$.

3. The ratio of nonfinancial equity owned to total corporate equity owned remains the same. That is, for line (i'), the ratio of column (1) to column (3) is the same as for line (i). The same is true for the ratio of column (2) to column (3).

4. The relative distribution of equities between households and the rest of the world remains the same. That is, for line (j'), the ratio of column (5) to (column [3] minus column [4]) is the same as for line (j).

References

Ando, A. 2002. Missing household saving and valuation of corporations: Inquiry into Japanese National Accounts I. *Journal of the Japanese and International Economies* 16 (2): 147–76.

Ando, A., J. Hancock, and G. Sawchuk. 1997. Cost of capital for the United States, Japan, and Canada: An attempt at measurement based on individual company records and aggregate national accounts data. In *Financing growth in Canada,* ed. P. J. N. Halpern, 71–134. Calgary, Canada: University of Calgary Press.

Bank of Japan. 2002. *Financial and economic statistics monthly* 41 (August). Tokyo: Government of Japan.

Dean, E., M. Darrough, and A. Neef. 1990. Alternative measures of capital inputs in Japanese manufacturing. In *Productivity growth in Japan and the United States,* ed. C. Hulten, 229–66. Chicago: University of Chicago Press.

Dekle, R. 1994. Market value estimates of Japanese saving and comparisons with the U.S.: Can the capital gains to land be included in "saving"? *Japan and the World Economy* 6:27–44.

Economic and Social Research Institute (ESRI), Cabinet Office, Government of Japan. 2001. *Annual report on National Accounts.* Tokyo: Government of Japan.

Economic Planning Agency, Government of Japan (EPA). 1970. *1970 national wealth survey of Japan.* Tokyo: Government of Japan.

———. 1978. *Shin kokumin keizai keisan no mikata, tsukaikata* (Guide for users of new National Accounts). Tokyo: Government of Japan.

———. 2000a. *Annual report on National Accounts.* Tokyo: Government of Japan.

———. 2000b. *Explanation of estimation procedure according to 1993 SNA,* prelim. ed. . Tokyo: Government of Japan.

Fraumeni, B. M. 1997. The measurement of depreciation in the U.S. national income and product accounts. *Survey of Current Business* 77 (July): 7–23.

Gordon, R., and B. Malkiel. 1981. Corporate finance. In *How taxes affect economic behavior,* ed. J. Pechman and H. Aaron, 131–92. Washington, D.C.: Brookings Institution.

Hayashi, F. 1986. Why is Japan's saving rate apparently so high? In *NBER macroeconomics annual 1986,* ed. Stanley Fisher, 147–210. Cambridge: MIT Press.

Hayashi, F., and T. Inoue. 1991. The relation between firm growth and Q with multiple goods: Theory and evidence from panel data on Japanese firms. *Econometrica* 59 (May): 731–53.

Hoshi, T., and A. Kashyap. 1990. Evidence on q and investment for Japanese firms. *Journal of Japanese and International Economies* 4:371–400.

Hulten, C., and F. Wykoff. 1981. The measurement of economic depreciation. In *Depreciation, inflation, and the taxation of income from capital,* ed. C. Hulten, 81–125. Washington, D.C.: Urban Institute.

Murata, K. 1999. *The consumption function in Japan.* Ph.D. diss. Oxford University, St. Anthony's College.

Ogawa, K., S. Kitasaka, H. Yamaoka, and Y. Iwata. 1996. An empirical reevaluation of the wealth effect in Japanese household behavior. *Japan and the World Economy* 8:423–42.

Takayama, N. 1992. *The graying of Japan: An economic perspective on public pensions.* Tokyo: Kinokuniya.

United Nations, Statistical Office, Department of Economic and Social Affairs. 1968. *A system of National Accounts.* Studies in Methods, series F, no. 2, rev. 3. New York: United Nations.

United Nations, Commission of the European Communities (EUROSTAT), International Monetary Fund (IMF), Organization for Economic Cooperation and Development (OECD), and World Bank. 1993. *System of National Accounts 1993.* New York: United Nations.

7

Is Japan's Innovative Capacity in Decline?

Lee Branstetter and Yoshiaki Nakamura

During the 1980s, a significant source of Japanese growth—and a major source of concern for Japan's trading partners—was the widely admired innovative capacity of Japanese firms. Over the course of the decade, Japanese firms entered and successfully competed in high-tech industries that had formerly been the preserve of U.S. and European multinationals. Japanese firms' expanding innovative capacity was clearly reflected in aggregate statistics on research and development (R&D) expenditures, patenting, and productivity, all of which showed a steady increase in R&D input and output. A mid-decade study by the National Academy of Engineering (1987) concluded that Japan was superior to the United States in twenty-five of thirty-four critical technologies.[1]

This situation changed quite dramatically over the course of the 1990s. Research and development spending by the private sector in Japan has stagnated during the Heisei recession. Measures of R&D *output* growth in

Lee Branstetter is associate professor of finance and economics at Columbia Business School, and a faculty research fellow of the National Bureau of Economic Research (NBER). Yoshiaki Nakamura is director of the general affairs division of the Kanto Bureau of Economy, Trade, and Industry in the Japanese Ministry of Economy, Trade, and Industry.

We thank the conference organizers, the conference participants, Masahiko Aoki, Ashish Arora, Amar Bhide, Hiroyuki Odagiri, David Weinstein, and Akira Goto for extremely helpful comments. We are also grateful to a number of Japanese corporate R&D managers and industry observers based in Japan and overseas for their candid responses to our questions on Japanese firm R&D activity. By prior agreement, their names must remain confidential. We are grateful to Takuji Saito (Hitotsubashi University), Masami Imai (University of California, Davis), and Yoshiaki Ogura (Columbia University) for excellent research assistance, and to the Research Institute of Economy, Trade, and Industry, the National Science Foundation, and the Columbia Center on Japanese Economy and Business for financial support. All errors remain our own responsibility.

1. See Okimoto and Saxonhouse (1987), Arison et al. (1992), and Mansfield (1988). A book-length treatment is Goto (1993).

Japan have declined relative to the United States and relative to Japanese historical trends. There is a widespread sense among Japanese R&D managers, industry observers, and government officials that the Japanese approach to technological innovation is no longer working effectively, and fundamental reform of the national innovation system must take place.[2]

It is important to note that technological factors have *not* been the primary drivers of the Heisei recession. Rather, the collapse of asset prices, the resulting crisis in the banking system, and the inappropriate macroeconomic policy responses of the Japanese government since the early 1990s have arguably been the primary cause.[3] However, the implications of the apparent decline in Japanese innovative capacity are quite serious for Japan's long-run economic prospects. When normal growth resumes, the maximum sustainable rate will depend in part on the ability of Japanese firms to develop and deploy new technology. If Japan's innovative capacity is growing at a slower rate than in past decades, this could limit Japan's future prospects.

This chapter examines Japan's R&D performance from the early 1980s using several complementary modes of analysis. First, we examine evidence from aggregate economic statistics concerning changes in Japanese R&D. Second, we analyze comprehensive data on R&D inputs and outputs for a panel of nearly 200 Japanese firms. Microeconometric analysis of this data set allows us to examine where any downturn in R&D activity is concentrated, what Japanese firms are themselves doing to rectify the downturn in performance, and what effects these steps have had to date. Third, we relate the results of ten interviews of corporate R&D managers and informed industry observers concerning their perceptions of changes in Japanese innovative capacity and the reasons for these changes.

The main empirical contribution of this essay is to document, at the microlevel and the aggregate level, a slowdown in the growth rate of Japanese research productivity. We find that after a decade of convergence with the United States in terms of R&D inputs and outputs in the 1980s, Japanese and U.S. innovation trends have diverged sharply in the 1990s. Measured in a common currency, real R&D outlays in Japan have grown much more slowly than in the United States. The gap in patent output that was closing rapidly in the 1980s began expanding again in the 1990s.

Firm-level data show evidence of a slowdown in the growth of R&D productivity in Japan in the 1990s, controlling for R&D spending and other firm attributes. This slowdown does not affect all firms equally. By and large, the research productivity of the electronics industry, broadly defined, has continued to grow in line with the trends of the 1980s and early 1990s.

2. For a recent English article which quotes pessimistic Japanese experts at length on this subject, see Normile (2002).
3. For research supporting this view, see Posen (1998).

On the other hand, firms outside the electronics industry have performed less well.

Why has Japanese R&D productivity grown more slowly in the 1990s? A full-fledged investigation of this question is beyond the scope of this paper. However, drawing on our interviews with Japanese R&D managers and evidence from other economic studies, we are able to present some possible explanations. As they have reached the technology frontier, Japanese firms have had to reorient their R&D efforts from the application and refinement of existing, relatively well-developed technology to the creation of more fundamental breakthroughs.[4]

The shortage of Ph.D.-level engineers and the relative weakness of Japanese academic science may have inhibited the effectiveness of more technologically ambitious R&D in Japan. Furthermore, attempts to create large, centralized corporate labs focused on more basic R&D have apparently run into the same problems that large-scale U.S. corporate R&D labs were criticized for in the 1980s, including a lack of focus on the needs of a rapidly evolving marketplace.[5] Finally, the absence of a venture capital industry and the types of institutions that support start-ups in the United States seem to have made it difficult for established Japanese firms to partner in product development with more entrepreneurial and efficient smaller firms.

Having noted the problems, Japanese R&D managers are trying to respond to them. Conversations with Japanese R&D managers reveal several steps firms are taking to restructure R&D operations and improve research productivity. This chapter presents evidence on the impact of one such step—the forging of technology alliances with U.S. firms. We find that this strategy leads to increased flows of technological information to Japanese firms. We also present evidence that is consistent with the view that these increased knowledge flows raise overall inventive productivity. This suggests that at least some of the responses of the private sector are having the desired impact.

In terms of public policy implications, we note that the Japanese government has undertaken a number of reforms to help Japanese firms make the leap from more applied to more basic R&D, including strengthening the Japanese patent system, increasing public expenditures on research, expanding graduate education in Japan, and removing some of the legal and regulatory barriers to the formation of venture-capital–backed start-up firms. However, in the context of a stagnating economy, many of Japan's firms have been forced to limit their R&D spending and shift R&D personnel into operational functions—and the longer the recession lasts, the more likely it is that these steps could have long-lasting negative effects on

---

4. For an insightful perspective on this shift, see Goto (1997).
5. See Rosenbloom and Spencer (1996).

research productivity. Perhaps the most important step the Japanese government can take in the short-run to revive Japan's innovative performance is to stimulate macroeconomic growth.

7.1 Comparative Perspective

After nearly a decade of stagnation in Japan, it is sometimes difficult to recall the unease, even fear, that Japan's seemingly unstoppable economic advance during the 1980s once generated among U.S. industrialists and policy makers. To set the stage for the analysis here, it is worth reviewing some of the evidence on Japan's expanding technological capability.

As the Japanese economy expanded in the 1980s, R&D spending steadily increased.[6] Moreover, the effectiveness with which Japanese firms applied this R&D expenditure to successful generation of useful inventions also seemed to be increasing. Researchers noted that Japanese firms produced more patent applications per R&D dollar than U.S. firms, and that this ratio was not declining, as it seemed to be in the rest of the industrialized world.[7]

Scholars familiar with the idiosyncratic features of the Japanese patent system prior to its substantial reform in 1988 were quick to point out that many more patent applications were required to protect the same amount of intellectual property in Japan, and that straightforward comparisons of Japanese and U.S. patent counts were likely to exaggerate Japan's technological prowess.

However, because of the importance of the U.S. market, Japanese firms were also quite aggressive about patenting in the United States. Over the course of the late 1970s and 1980s, Japanese firms rapidly increased their level of U.S. patenting in absolute numbers and relative to U.S. counterparts. Given that the two sets of firms were competing under the same patent system with the same set of rules and examiners, this seemed to buttress the case that the Japanese were closing the technological gap with their U.S. rivals.

Careful microstudies of Japanese innovation, such as Mansfield (1988), also suggested that Japan's R&D capability was formidable, particularly its applied R&D capability. Mansfield's statistical results suggested that applied R&D expenditure in Japan had a *much* stronger impact on firm-level total factor productivity (TFP) growth than it did in the United States. On the other hand, basic R&D spending seemed to be far less effective. Likewise, a comparative analysis of product development in the automobile industry in Japan, Europe, and the United States by Clark and Fujimoto (1991) carefully documented Japanese firms' enormous lead over rivals in terms of the resource cost of product development.

6. Time-series on Japanese real R&D spending appears in *Gijutsu Yōran* (2000).
7. See Okimoto and Saxonhouse (1987) for a discussion of these issues.

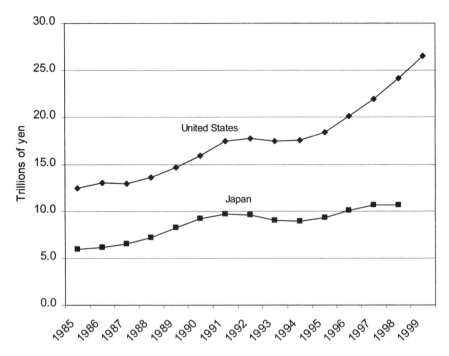

Fig. 7.1   Private sector R&D spending in the United States and Japan, 1985–1999

Source: Gijutsu Yōran (2000).

Note: The *y* axis is real private sector R&D spending converted into ¥ trillions using Organization for Economic Co-operation and Development (OECD) purchasing power parity exchange rates for each year.

The picture of expanding relative Japanese technological capability changed substantially in the 1990s, as figure 7.1 shows. The U.S. private sector R&D spending grew quite rapidly in real terms, reflecting robust macroeconomic growth and the especially rapid growth of high-tech industries. In striking contrast, the increase in Japan was modest, and spending actually declined in two years. Posen (2001), arguing that Japanese innovative capacity has been unaffected by the 1990s recession, stresses that the ratio of R&D expenditure to GNP has remained high in Japan—in fact, it is higher than in the United States. Unfortunately, this reflects the fact that the Japanese economy has scarcely grown over the 1990s.

The difference in trends in R&D inputs is reflected in the aggregate statistics on R&D outputs. For instance, the counts of patents taken out by Japanese firms in the United States grew much more slowly after 1990 than in the 1980s, whereas the reverse was true for the United States. Figure 7.2 illustrates this divergence, aggregating across all U.S. patent classes.

Figure 7.3 illustrates a similar pattern of convergence followed by divergence within the cluster of patent classes that are most closely connected to

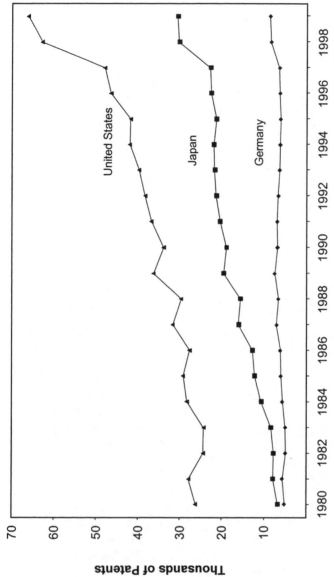

Fig. 7.2   Counts of patents granted by the U.S. Patent and Trademark Office, 1980–1999 (Units of the vertical axis are thousands of patents)

Source: Authors' calculations based on the National Bureau of Economic Research (NBER) Patent Database.

Note: The figure shows a dramatic jump in patenting after 1997. This may relate to a change in U.S. patent law regarding the length of patents, as pointed out by Hicks et al. (2001). The law included a clause allowing patents filed before 8 June 1995 to receive certain procedural advantages. The expiration of these patents could be set either seventeen years from the grant date or twenty years from the priority date, whichever was later. Patent attorneys evidently encouraged their clients to speed up their patent filing in order to meet this deadline. Because of the delays typical in the patent review procedure, an increase in patents granted would not be obvious in the data until two to three years after the deadline.

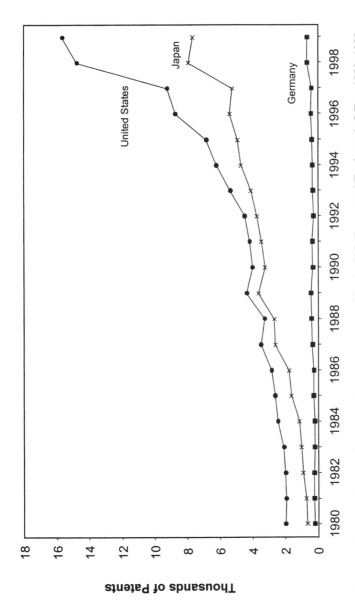

Fig. 7.3   Counts of information technology patents granted by the U.S. Patent and Trademark Office, 1980–1999 (Units of vertical axis are thousands of patents)

Source: Authors' calculations based on the NBER Patent Database.

Note: See note to figure 7.2.

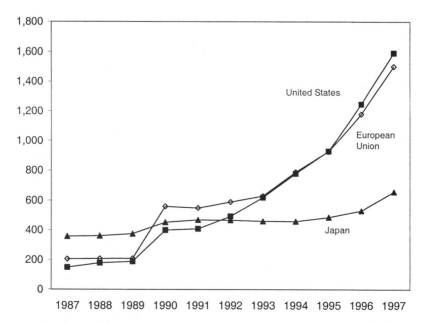

Fig. 7.4   Patent applications by nationality of inventor, 1987–1997 (Units of the vertical axis are thousands of patents)

Source: Gijutsu Yōran 2000.

Note: This measures patent applications generated by inventors in the indicated country and submitted worldwide.

computers and information technologies. Patenting levels converged up to 1988, but then, from 1993 on, U.S. firms' patenting in these fields exploded, greatly outstripping the growth in Japanese patents for the rest of the 1990s.[8] It is important to note that the relative decline in patents is seen not only in the U.S. patent system. Looking at worldwide patent applications, there have been striking increases in the quantity of applications from inventors based in the United States and Europe, but not in Japan. Figure 7.4 illustrates the trends.

This review of aggregate statistics suggests that there is something real behind the more steadily insistent concerns being raised in Japan about the Japanese national innovation system and its comparative performance.[9] However, it also raises an important question. Is the relative decline in Japanese innovative output simply a function of relative declines in R&D

8. Posen (2001) stresses that many of the top ten patenting firms in the United States are Japanese multinationals. Unfortunately, the strong performance of these firms is evidently not representative of the innovative performance of their industries.

9. For a forceful presentation of the view that Japan's relative innovative performance has not changed since the 1980s, see Posen (2001). While we strongly agree with Posen's main point—that Japan's poor macroeconomic performance in the 1990s has little direct connection with the efficiency of its R&D activity—we believe that his rather optimistic view of the Japanese innovation system is not consistent with some of the evidence presented in this paper.

spending, or has there been a slowdown in the growth of Japanese firms' innovative capacity, even after controlling for changes in R&D spending? This question is addressed in the next section.

7.2   A Microanalysis of R&D Productivity

In this section, we utilize data collected on R&D inputs and outputs at the level of the firm to estimate a simple knowledge production function.[10] Let innovation for the ith firm be a function of its R&D input, such that

(1) $$N_{it} = R_{it}^{\beta}\Phi_{it},$$

where

(2) $$\Phi_{it} = e^{\sum_c \delta_c D_{ic}} e^{\sum_t \gamma_t T_t} e^{u_{it}}$$

The δs can be thought of as exogenous differences in the technological opportunity across c different technological fields that are stable across time, Ds are dummy variables to control for differences in the propensity to generate new knowledge across technological fields (indicated by the subscript c), Ts are year dummies.

The γs can be thought of as changes in the overall effectiveness of the R&D process, common to all fields, over time. These latter coefficients will be crucial to our analysis. We want to observe whether, conditional on R&D spending, the overall effectiveness of private sector innovative activity is increasing, decreasing, or unchanging over time. Our inference concerning this will be based on the pattern revealed by the γ coefficients.

Taking the logs of both sides of equation (2) yields the following log-linear equation.

(3) $$n_{it} = \beta r_{it} + \sum_t \gamma_t T_t + \sum_c \delta_c D_{ic} + \varepsilon_{it}$$

In equation (3), n_{it} is innovation, r_{it} is the firm's own R&D investment, and ε is an error term.

7.2.1   Measuring Innovation

There are no direct measures of innovation, but if some fraction of new knowledge is patented, such that the number of new patents generated by the ith firm is an exponential function of its new knowledge,

(4) $$P_{it} = e^{\sum_c \alpha_c D_{ic}} e^{\xi_i N_{it}},$$

then the production of new knowledge can be proxied by examining the generation of new patents. Taking the logs of both sides of equation (4) and substituting into equation (3) yields

---

10. The empirical methodology here borrows heavily from Branstetter and Sakakibara (1998) and Branstetter (2001a), which in turn are strongly influenced by Jaffe (1986). The exposition follows those earlier papers quite closely.

(5)
$$p_{it} = \beta r_{it} + \sum_t \gamma_t T_t + \sum_c \delta_c D_{ic} + \mu_{it},$$

where p_{it} is the log of the number of new patents and the other variables are as before, except for the error term. We allow the new error term to contain firm fixed effects, such that there can be time-invariant differences in the propensity to patent among firms within industries. Because firms in our sample do not change their primary industry affiliation over time, the industry effect would fall out with the firm fixed effect in a standard fixed effects regression.

As written, equation (5) suggests that the log of patent counts should be our dependent variable. Some firms in our sample are observed to take out zero patents in a given year, which creates an obvious problem because one cannot take the log of zero. In the earlier micro-R&D patents literature, it was customary to take the log of the count of patents plus 1 to get around this. However, this somewhat arbitrary transformation of the dependent variable could bias the results.

Instead, we have used count data statistical models to conduct our analysis. In particular, we use the fixed effects, negative binomial estimator developed by Hausman, Hall, and Griliches (1984) to estimate a version of equation (5) in which a 0 realization of the dependent variable does not pose any kind of mathematical problem.

7.2.2   Data Gathering

To implement this approach, we collected data on the patents granted to Japanese firms in the United States (dated by year of patent application), patents applied for by Japanese firms in Japan, R&D spending, and industry affiliation. Further information on data sources and construction is provided in the appendix.

Is our sample reasonably representative of Japanese industrial R&D activity, and does this degree of representativeness change over time? In Japan, R&D spending and patenting have historically been highly concentrated in the larger industrial firms. A panel of large industrial firms in the United States would become steadily less representative of U.S. patenting over the 1990s because of the rising role of universities and high-tech start-up firms in U.S. inventive activity.[11] In Japan, there is no evidence of a similar shift.[12] Because our sample includes most of the leading R&D-performing firms in Japan, we believe it is representative of industrial R&D activity.

For our purposes, the use of U.S. patents is actually the preferred metric of innovative output. A major patent reform in Japan in 1988 allowed Japanese firms to change the number of claims per patent, making it at

---

11. See Hicks et al. (2001) for documentation of the increased role of smaller firms and universities in U.S. patenting.
12. Goto (1997) affirms this and comments on its implications for the future of industrial innovation in Japan.

least theoretically possible for Japanese firms to protect the same amount of intellectual property with a smaller number of patents. It is thus difficult to draw long-term inferences about changes in research productivity using Japanese patent application counts because the relationship between innovations and patents has shifted over time.[13] There was no such change in the U.S. patent system over our sample period.

Furthermore, Japanese firms tended to submit patent applications to the U.S. Patent and Trademark Office for the ideas they perceive, at least *ex ante,* to have the most promise, so that a U.S. patent count series represents a quality-adjusted measure of innovative output. Finally, thanks to the availability of U.S. patent data in electronic form, it is possible to conduct an additional quality adjustment by measuring the number of citations received by a patent from subsequently granted patents over some fixed time period—in our case, four years.

7.2.3   Drawing Inferences from the Data

The first column of table 7.1 presents results of a fixed effects negative binomial regression of U.S. patent counts on firm R&D spending and our year dummy variables. Controlling for R&D spending at the firm level, the coefficients on the time dummies trace out changes in the level of R&D output that are common to all firms. In other words, it gives us a sense of how innovative output is changing, on average, after we have controlled for inputs.

Figure 7.5 graphs the pattern traced out by the time dummies, along with the 95 percent confidence bounds. The picture that emerges is fairly striking. From the mid- to late 1980s, one sees a sharp increase in average innovative output. This growth largely ceases in the early 1990s, suggesting that R&D productivity reached a plateau around 1990 and grew little thereafter.[14]

Is this cessation of R&D productivity growth real or an artifact of the data? The substitution of observable patents for unobservable innovation creates some problems for our statistical inference. The γ coefficients measure not just changes in the productivity of R&D activity over time, but also changes in the propensity to patent in the United States over time. It could be, for instance, that Japanese firms are generating larger numbers of innovations over time but, in order to economize on the costs of protecting their intellectual property rights, they are being more selective about which patents they take out in the United States. In other words, a count-based output measure would show a flattening of innovative productivity where there was none.[15]

---

13. For an empirical study of the effects of this patent reform on Japanese innovation, see Sakakibara and Branstetter (2001).
14. Including deflated sales as an additional regressor yields results qualitatively similar to those presented here.
15. We thank Hiroyuki Odagiri for stressing this point.

Table 7.1   Japanese R&D Productivity Trends

Note: Fixed effects negative binomial regression models, and observations = 2,726. Standard deviations are in parentheses.

Variable	Patent Counts	Citation-Adjusted Patent Counts
Log (real R&D)	0.294	0.385
	(0.0206)	(0.0190)
1982	–0.0501	–0.0706
	(0.100)	(0.109)
1983	–0.0776	–0.0714
	(0.0940)	(0.101)
1984	0.0751	0.146
	(0.0907)	(0.0972)
1985	0.131	0.167
	(0.0894)	(0.0962)
1986	0.208	0.259
	(0.0873)	(0.0936)
1987	0.261	0.328
	(0.0863)	(0.0923)
1988	0.403	0.431
	(0.0844)	(0.0907)
1989	0.553	0.586
	(0.0830)	(0.0891)
1990	0.541	0.552
	(0.0832)	(0.0894)
1991	0.552	0.535
	(0.0830)	(0.0890)
1992	0.486	0.473
	(0.0836)	(0.0896)
1993	0.513	0.516
	(0.0840)	(0.0889)
1994	0.559	0.552
	(0.0827)	(0.0889)
1995	0.609	0.396
	(0.0827)	(0.0908)
1996	0.571	0.0720
	(0.0841)	(0.0958)
1997	0.463	–0.193
	(0.0849)	(0.0988)
Constant	–0.515	–1.32
	(0.115)	(0.109)
Log likelihood	–8,173.9	–10,179.2

To try to get around this possibility, we constructed a measure of patent output in which we adjusted for the number of citations received by each patent up to four years after it was granted. If the number of patents taken out in the United States is going down because only the upper tail of the quality distribution of innovations is actually being patented, then an out-

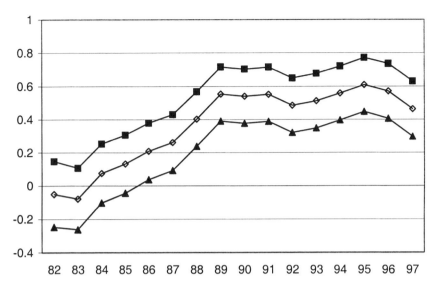

Fig. 7.5   Trends in Japanese R&D productivity, 1982–1997: Regression results from table 7.1, column (1)

Note: Year dummy coefficients from table 7.1, with associated 95 percent confidence bounds.

comes measure that controls for innovation quality would be less likely to generate a spurious result of flat productivity growth.

The second column of table 7.1 presents results from such a regression; Figure 7.6 graphs the coefficients along with their 95 percent confidence bounds. The picture that emerges is similar to that in figure 7.5.

The next set of regression results segments our sample into industry groups to see how research productivity trends differed among industries. Figure 7.7 indicates that the research productivity of the electronics industry, broadly defined, has continued to grow through the mid-1990s more or less in line with the trends of the 1980s. In contrast, there is a *decline* in research productivity for manufacturing firms outside the electronics industry. That is, controlling for innovative inputs, these firms are generating less innovative output, on average, then they were in the late 1980s. Regression results based on citation-adjusted patent output measures indicate a similar pattern.

Table 7.2 presents results based on Japanese patent applications. If one pools data across all firms, these data suggest a continuing rise in innovative productivity through the mid-1990s, but a slowdown in growth relative to the trends of the 1980s. Splitting the sample along industry lines indicates electronics firms outperformed firms in other industries. In both cases, a slowdown in productivity growth is evident, occurring sooner among firms outside of electronics. While there were substantial increases

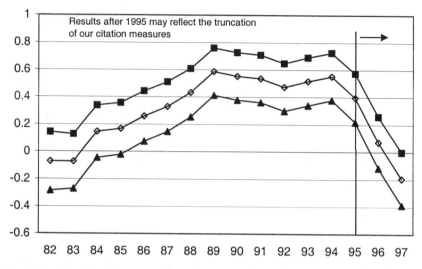

Fig. 7.6   **Trends in Japanese R&D productivity, 1982–1997: Regression results from table 7.1, column (2)**

Note: Year dummy coefficients from table 7.1, with associated 95 percent confidence bounds. The sharp decline in measured productivity in the last years of our sample is an artifact of our data. Detailed studies of patent citations show that it takes several years for citations to a particular invention to peak (see Jaffe and Trajtenberg 1996). A patent applied for in 1996 would not be granted, on average, until 1997 or 1998—possibly even later. Thus, we are picking up less than four years' of citations. For this reason, coefficients on year dummies for years later than 1995 should be viewed with caution. Nevertheless, we see this graph as providing confirming evidence of a stagnation of R&D productivity growth in the 1990s.

in R&D productivity in the early 1990s for electronics firms, the increase is much less impressive outside that sector.

If the number of claims is rising fast enough to offset the slowdown in the growth of patent applications, then one can argue that the data are consistent with increased innovation in both categories. This possibility indicates the need for caution in interpreting results based on Japanese patent data. For a study of Japanese innovation trends in the immediate aftermath of the 1988 patent reform, see Sakakibara and Branstetter (2001).

A breakdown of R&D productivity trends by firm size suggests that, outside the electronics sector, relatively smaller firms are more likely to show progress in research productivity than larger firms. These findings are not reported here due to space constraints, but they were confirmed using U.S. patent output data as well.

What can we conclude from our preliminary exploration of the firm-level data? Our results suggest that changes in Japan's absolute and relative performance are not simply or solely the result of a decline in firms' R&D spending. Although we find some evidence of an actual *decline* in research productivity in some sectors, the more robust result is that the broad-based

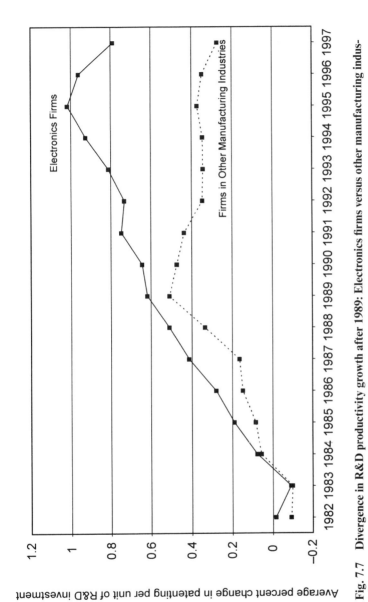

Fig. 7.7 Divergence in R&D productivity growth after 1989: Electronics firms versus other manufacturing industries

Source: Authors' regression results

Note: The measured decline after 1995 could reflect, in part, the truncation problem in our data referred to in figure 7.6. Not all patents applied for in 1996 and 1997 were granted by 1999.

Table 7.2   **Japanese R&D Productivity Trends**

Note: Fixed effects negative binomial regression models using Japanese patent application data. Standard deviations are in parentheses.

Variable	Patent Counts	Patent Counts (electronics)	Patent Counts (other manufacturing)
Log (Real R&D)	0.119	0.0470	0.186
	(0.0147)	(0.0236)	(0.0212)
1982	0.140	0.216	0.109
	(0.0677)	(0.137)	(0.0748)
1983	0.201	0.214	0.210
	(0.0615)	(0.124)	(0.0682)
1984	0.264	0.230	0.288
	(0.0605)	(0.122)	(0.0669)
1985	0.349	0.316	0.362
	(0.0597)	(0.121)	(0.0659)
1986	0.455	0.508	0.424
	(0.0584)	(0.117)	(0.0648)
1987	0.501	0.552	0.466
	(0.0581)	(0.116)	(0.0646)
1988	0.533	0.638	0.479
	(0.0573)	(0.112)	(0.0644)
1989	0.557	0.694	0.486
	(0.0573)	(0.112)	(0.0645)
1990	0.511	0.638	0.441
	(0.0579)	(0.113)	(0.0651)
1991	0.489	0.642	0.404
	(0.0583)	(0.114)	(0.0659)
1992	0.675	0.847	0.576
	(0.0571)	(0.112)	(0.0645)
1993	0.651	0.836	0.555
	(0.0577)	(0.113)	(0.0648)
1994	0.698	0.871	0.622
	(0.0573)	(0.113)	(0.0641)
1995	0.679	0.858	0.600
	(0.0578)	(0.114)	(0.0645)
1996	0.720	0.937	0.621
	(0.0587)	(0.116)	(0.0655)
1997	0.706	0.895	0.625
	(0.0587)	(0.118)	(0.0652)
Constant	0.763	0.671	0.734
	(0.0771)	(0.130)	(0.104)
Log Likelihood	−15,768.6	−5.772.1	−9,941.7
Observations	2,988	1,071	1,917

increase in Japanese research productivity that was so striking in the 1980s largely faded in the 1990s. The exception to this general trend is the electronics sector, which has continued to increase its innovative output, controlling for input. However, continued progress in R&D productivity in this sector has not prevented Japanese firms from falling well behind their U.S. rivals in such key patent categories as information technology. This may reflect Japanese firms' inability to match their rivals' expanding investments in R&D.

7.3   Factors Affecting R&D Productivity Growth

The stereotype of Japanese firms as effective imitators and implementers rather than innovators may have been accurate in the late 1970s and even the early 1980s, but by the late 1980s many Japanese firms had reached the technological frontier and their continued success increasingly has depended on their ability to advance that frontier. This is captured in our interviews with Japanese R&D managers and industry observers conducted in the United States and Japan in 2000 and 2001.

7.3.1   The Focus and Structure of R&D Activity

Since at least the early 1980s, each interviewed company has made a substantial commitment to R&D at the technological frontier within its industry. A large, central R&D operation was built up with the aim of creating important technical breakthroughs that could be incorporated into future products. Although our interviewees tended to be corporations recognized as technological leaders within their fields, this change in focus from applied to more basic R&D also is broadly reflected in larger, more representative surveys.[16] A change in the focus of R&D was inevitable—at one time, Japanese firms were the global low-cost suppliers of standardized products, but manufacturers in South Korea, Taiwan, and China are increasingly able to undercut Japanese firms. This means that Japanese firms have to compete on the basis of innovative products.[17] The R&D managers interviewed are universally dissatisfied with the results of their investment in frontier research. The view within firms seems to be that the central R&D laboratories have become bureaucratic, insular, and unresponsive to the needs of the firm. Research and development management has been unable to effectively translate the basic and frontier research into effective new products.[18] The critiques of central R&D operations echo those by

16. See Goto and Nagata (1997), Cohen et al. (1998), and the *Gijutsu Yōran* (2000) for evidence that the distribution of R&D effort across the categories of basic versus applied R&D (and process innovation versus product innovation) in the United States and Japan had essentially converged by the mid-1990s.
17. Goto (1997) offers some useful observations regarding this point.
18. An early evaluation of the effectiveness of the build-up in R&D spending, based on an econometric study of product introductions, is Wakasugi and Koyata (1997).

U.S. firms in the 1980s regarding their own central R&D operations—they were often seen as being unable to translate research advances effectively into new products.[19] In other words, a managerial perception that relative R&D performance has declined confirms the findings of our statistical analysis.

Our interviewees spoke admiringly of the way their U.S. counterparts restructured their R&D operations during the 1990s, and most of the interviewed firms were trying to restructure along the lines of the new U.S. model. The characteristics of the new structure of R&D are still emerging, but conversations with Japanese corporate R&D managers suggest that it includes five main features.

1. Greater reliance on R&D partnerships *outside* the traditional vertical *keiretsu* networks within Japan.
2. Greater reliance on foreign (especially U.S.) R&D partnerships and acquisitions of high-tech firms.
3. Greater emphasis on cooperation with universities, domestic and foreign.
4. A de-emphasis on centralized in-house R&D and a gradual downsizing of resources invested in central R&D facilities.
5. Increased interest and investment in corporate venturing programs.

Japanese firms, in conscious imitation of their U.S. counterparts, are placing increased emphasis on resourcing useful technologies from outside the firm. These can then be combined with the firm's own technical strengths to generate important new products. This increased R&D outsourcing is probably the overriding theme guiding departures from the traditional model of research. As part of this, because Japan still has relatively few high-tech start-ups and because the quality and level of academic research in Japan typically lags that of the United States, Japanese firms have moved aggressively to expand their efforts to tap U.S. technology networks.

7.3.2   Reasons for a Slowdown in R&D Productivity

A full-fledged investigation of the reasons why the innovation trends in the United States and Japan have diverged so sharply is beyond the scope of this chapter, but our exchange with R&D managers and a review of the related literature suggests some possible explanations.

The nature of Japanese industrial R&D has clearly changed in terms of its technological focus and its organization. First, Japanese firms have moved from a focus on largely applied R&D to an effort to generate more fundamental R&D breakthroughs, bringing them more in line with the U.S. allocation of industrial R&D effort. Second, in pursuit of this change

19. See Rosenbloom and Spencer (1996).

in focus, Japanese firms have concentrated engineering talent in upgraded central R&D labs.

Prior research and comments from our interviewees suggest that the shift in R&D focus may have placed Japanese firms at a relative disadvantage. As Saxonhouse has pointed out for decades, the Japanese higher education system produces far fewer Ph.D.s in the sciences and engineering than does the U.S. educational system.[20] Japan has produced many more engineering graduates at the bachelor's degree level per capita, and this may have been sufficient to propel Japan's technical advance while it was still behind the technology frontier. However, it is reasonable to think that, as Japanese firms have reached the frontier, it has become more important to have technical personnel with highly specialized training.

In some fields, such as software engineering, the shortage of engineers with advanced degrees is so acute that there have been references to a "soft crisis" since the late 1980s.[21] Even in the United States, demand for software engineers dramatically outstripped supply in the 1990s—but U.S. immigration law allowed the import of hundreds of thousands of foreign engineers to bridge the gap.[22]

Furthermore, evidence from U.S. industrial patents suggests that, at least in some fields, U.S. firms are increasingly building on academic science in their R&D efforts.[23] This also places Japanese firms at a relative disadvantage, since U.S. high-tech firms are able to work with and build on the research of the world's most celebrated research universities and institutions. Despite important advances over the postwar period, the quantity and quality of publicly funded research in Japanese universities and research institutes typically lags behind that conducted in the United States. Although the results of this kind of public science are generally published in easily accessible scientific journals, understanding and applying the most recent developments may require a degree of familiarity with and connection to it that is harder to come by in Japan than in the United States.[24]

The centralization of R&D effort in Japan runs counter to the trends in the United States. Over the course of the 1990s, U.S. firms downsized their central R&D labs and increased emphasis on collaboration with other firms in R&D and product development.[25]

Some of this collaboration is with high-tech start-up firms, often backed

20. See, for example, Okimoto and Saxonhouse (1987).
21. See Finan and Williams (1992).
22. We thank Amar Bhide and Ashish Aurora for discussions on the role of immigration in propelling the U.S. high-tech boom of the 1990s.
23. See Narin, Hamilton, and Olivastro (1997).
24. There is a large literature on the historical role of U.S. universities in fostering technological progress. See, for example, Rosenberg and Nelson (1994).
25. Several papers in Rosenbloom and Spencer (1996) comment on these trends, including the contribution by Mowery and Teece.

by venture capital, and successful collaboration can lead to acquisition of the start-up by its established partners. For a variety of reasons, there has not been the same kind of venture capital activity in Japan. This means that the domestic set of potential partners is less diverse and, possibly, less technologically dynamic than it is in the United States. The larger Japanese corporate labs seem to have run into the same problems that beset their U.S. counterparts—bureaucracy, insularity, and a lack of connection with developments in the market. As we saw in our review of the aggregate statistics, total private sector R&D spending in the United States has continued to grow at a robust rate, but the allocation of that spending across organizational boundaries has changed in a way that has no parallel in Japan—which may help explain the differences in R&D productivity.

To its credit, the Japanese government has instituted a number of significant reforms over the course of the 1990s to address some of the perceived problems in the Japanese innovation system and help Japanese firms make the leap from more applied to more basic R&D. A series of patent reforms, begun in 1988 and culminating in the adoption by the Japanese Supreme Court of the doctrine of equivalents in 1998, have dramatically increased the intellectual property rights protections available to inventors under the Japanese patent system (Sakakibara and Branstetter 2001). The government has removed a number of legal restrictions that inhibited the operation of high-tech start-ups. Legal restrictions on the business activities of university professors have been lifted, in an attempt to foster the development of university-linked start-ups. Finally, there has been a substantial increase in Japanese public funding for R&D and for graduate education.[26] Unfortunately, to date these positive policy changes have had little visible impact on research outcomes.

The positive impact of these policy changes has probably been limited by Japan's poor macroeconomic performance, and this brings us to another potential explanation for the slowdown in R&D productivity—the long-run impact of Japan's lengthy recession. Because R&D at the technological frontier can be a very expensive investment with a highly uncertain payoff, firms under severe financial pressure are often forced to limit their R&D spending and transfer personnel out of R&D groups and into operational functions. If Japanese firms are forced to restrain their R&D investments and pare back the ranks of R&D personnel year after year, then they inevitably fall behind their international competitors and the further they fall behind, the harder it may be to catch up. While the nation's most successful firms have been able to maintain large R&D operations even in the face of Japan's unprecedented recession, the long recession may have left the research operations of others permanently impaired. Similarly, the viability of start-up enterprises is limited in an environment where the over-

26. See Normile (2002) for a summary of these and other recent changes.

all economy is shrinking or stagnating and equity markets are severely depressed.[27]

A full exploration of the increase in innovative activity in the United States is beyond the scope of this paper, but recent research suggests several potentially important casual factors. Clearly the robust economy of the 1990s provided firms with profits to reinvest in R&D. However, at the same time that R&D spending has been increasing, R&D productivity as measured by patents per R&D dollar has also been rising, so one cannot explain the difference in outcomes by focusing solely on the increase in inputs.

The increase has probably been driven in part by changes in scientific and technological opportunity. Important fundamental scientific breakthroughs in molecular biology, genetics, and genomics have helped fuel a sharp increase in the number of patents granted in fields associated with biotechnology. Likewise, there has been a substantial increase in software patenting.[28]

Corporate patents are increasingly citing scientific papers, suggesting that the link between science and innovation is tighter than in the past.[29] It is uncertain whether these breakthroughs will continue to generate opportunities for industrial application, but it seems reasonable that the ability of U.S. universities to play a leading role in these scientific breakthroughs has conferred some technological advantage on relatively proximate and better-connected U.S. firms.

However, as Kortum and Lerner (1999, 2000) point out, the increase in patenting is not confined to those clusters of technologies that have seen recent fundamental breakthroughs in academic science. Thus, one cannot argue that the increase in U.S. research productivity has been driven entirely by exogenous shifts in technological opportunity. In other words, it is not simply that Japan missed out on the U.S. surge in innovation because it lacked a strong presence in the software industry and the biotech industry, where the positive technological shocks of the 1990s were concentrated. Even in areas of traditional Japanese strength, U.S. firms have been relatively more successful. This point is driven home strongly in figure 7.3, which tracks innovation in information technology–(IT-) related patent classes.

Instead, Kortum and Lerner argue that the management of R&D has

27. There is an interesting contrast here with South Korean firms. Under the impact of the Korean economic crisis of 1997–1998, the R&D divisions of several Korean firms were spun off as high-tech start-ups. This arrangement kept South Korea's best corporate R&D personnel employed in research, albeit in a different organizational form. The fraying but still extant Japanese corporate commitment to lifetime employment has kept many researchers employed in their original companies, but not always in a research function.

28. For recent studies touching on these issues, see Cockburn and Henderson (2000) and Hicks et al. (2001).

29. See Narin, Hamilton, and Olivastro (1997) and Branstetter (2001b).

undergone an institutional change. Specifically, they assert that a system of small start-up firms financed by venture capital partnerships is more productive than the traditional big corporate R&D system, and they present evidence that the increase in innovation has been highest where venture capital investment is most concentrated.

Evidence on U.S. patents suggests that, as the large corporate R&D labs have downsized, knowledge generation by smaller firms and universities have more than compensated.[30] The early 2000s downturn in the IT sector and large-scale bankruptcies of venture-backed high-tech firms suggest that the ultimate power of this institutional innovation to propel increased innovation in the long run may have been overstated, but it is almost certain to have played an important role over the course of the 1990s.

Although the failure of R&D-intensive Japanese firms to keep pace with their U.S. counterparts is clearly a cause of concern for the firms themselves, one might question the implications of this for the Japanese economy as a whole. The macroeconomic impact of research success should be evident in measures of TFP. While estimates of Japanese TFP growth vary widely depending on the methodology and the level of aggregation at which the analysis was conducted, at least some studies suggest that the contribution of TFP growth to overall Japanese economic growth has been fairly modest in recent decades, even in the 1980s when research productivity was growing rapidly. Does this limit the economic relevance of our study? We would argue that Japan is unlikely to sustain rapid economic growth solely through increases in factor inputs in the medium-to-long run future. Barring radical changes in Japanese immigration policy, Japan's population will age rapidly and actually begin to shrink in coming decades, sharply limiting the growth in labor inputs. Likewise, if anything, Japan overinvested in physical capital in recent years—a point addressed elsewhere in this volume. The prospects of investment-led growth are therefore also limited. The sustainability of a reasonably high rate of macroeconomic growth would thus seem to require growth in TFP.[31]

Of course, one could also question the linkage between TFP growth and domestic R&D. Certainly, there are sources of TFP growth that are not directly linked to formal research and development activity. Furthermore, the economic impact of slower growth in research productivity at home can be cushioned by importing foreign-invented high-tech products. In addition, Japanese investors could realize some of the returns from foreign innovation by investing overseas. However, it is still likely to be the case that both Japan and the world as a whole will grow more slowly if Japanese R&D productivity continues to stagnate. Furthermore, modern growth theory has suggested a range of conditions under which foreign innovation

---

30. See Hicks et al. (2001) and Henderson, Jaffe, and Trajtenberg (1998).
31. We thank Jenny Corbett for discussions on these issues.

can be an imperfect substitute for domestic innovation.[32] If these conditions hold, the implications of Japan's R&D productivity slowdown for domestic economic growth could be even more severe.[33]

7.4   Tapping U.S. Technology

In the face of a perceived relative decline in R&D productivity, Japanese R&D managers have not stood still. While we eventually hope to explore all of the aspects of the Japanese industrial R&D restructuring outlined in the previous section as part of a long-term research project, here we focus on the international dimension of Japanese firms' R&D restructuring. In doing so, we endeavor to answer two questions. First, how and to what extent are Japanese firms seeking to obtain useful technological information from U.S. sources? Second, is this strategy working? In other words, have Japanese firms that have made the effort to tap U.S. technology networks benefited in terms of raising their R&D productivity? Drawing on recent research by one of the authors, we seek to shed light on these questions in this section.

As much prior research has documented, Japanese firms have historically been enthusiastic licensees of U.S. technology. However, the concept of tapping into U.S. technology networks that we attempt to measure here is more than passive implementation of technology developed by another firm. Rather, it is the incorporation of ideas developed outside the firm into the firm's own R&D operation. It is much more pro-active than simple licensing, and an important method by which this happens is the formation of technology alliances with U.S. firms. Japanese firms' overseas R&D facilities obviously also play an important role in these firms' efforts to learn from U.S. technological developments, but in this section, we focus on the impact of technology alliances.[34]

7.4.1   Research Alliances

Japanese firms have been aggressive about forming technology-sharing and technology-development alliances with U.S. firms. Several data sources track these over time, identifying the Japanese and U.S. partners.

32. See Grossman and Helpman (1991) and Feenstra (1996).
33. We acknowledge that our study focuses on a relatively narrow range of firms and industries that collectively constitute a relatively small part of the Japanese economy. However, these are precisely the firms and industries where formal R&D activity is most highly concentrated. Given that our objective is really to assess the changing productivity of formal R&D activity—rather than explain overall performance of the macroeconomy—we believe this focus is appropriate.
34. For evidence on the effectiveness with which Japanese firms have used their foreign direct investment (FDI) in the U.S. including their U.S. R&D facilities, to tap into technology networks, see Branstetter (2000). For more general studies on the scale of overseas R&D by Japanese firms, see Belderbos (2001) and Odagiri and Yasuda (1997).

The source used here, the Securities Data Corporation (SDC) alliance database, uses contemporary press accounts to track corporate alliances, including the technology alliances that are the focus of this section as a subset.[35]

7.4.2 Promoting Knowledge Flows

Do alliances with U.S. firms and universities promote flows of knowledge to Japanese firms? We assess this using data on the citations to prior U.S. inventions found in the U.S. patents of Japanese firms. We are careful to exclude all Japanese-invented U.S. patents from this set of "American" inventions. Using an empirical methodology developed in Branstetter (2000), we presume that the flow of patent citations is proportional to the flow of knowledge.[36]

Let C_{Jit} be the number of citations made by the patent applications Japanese firm i filed in year t to the cumulated stock of indigenous U.S.-invented patents granted as of year t. Note that the U.S. Patent and Trademark Office makes available data only on patent applications that are eventually *granted*. In this paper, patents are dated by year of application rather than year of grant, because it takes on average two years—sometimes much longer—to grant a patent.

We can write the expectation of C_{Jit} as a function of several other observables.

$$(6) \qquad E(C_{Jit}) = (N_{Jit})^{\beta_1}(N_{At})^{\beta_2}(e^{\beta_3 \text{Alliance}_{it}})(e^{\beta_4 \text{PROX}_i})R_{it}^{\beta_6}\alpha_i\alpha_t$$

Let E be the expectations operator. Here $E[C_{Jit}]$ is a function of the number of patents Japanese firm i has taken out in the U.S. in year t (N_{Jit}), the number of potentially cited indigenous U.S. patents that exist as of year t (N_{At}), the level of firm i's alliance activity with U.S. firms in year t (Alliance$_{it}$), and the extent to which firm i is at a point in the technology space which is densely populated by other indigenous U.S. patents (PROX$_i$).

Some Japanese firms might cite U.S. patents more frequently simply because they happen to be working on technologies in which a large number of indigenous U.S. inventors are active. If one wishes to control for this technological proximity, one could obtain a measure of a firm's location in technology space by measuring the distribution of its R&D effort across various technological fields. Let firm i's R&D program be described by the vector **F**, where

---

35. The authors subsequently began using an even more comprehensive database, the Cooperative Agreements and Technology Indicators Information System (CATI) database developed by John Hagedoorn at the University of Maastricht, to explore the impact of alliances more thoroughly.

36. This framework builds on the methodology of Jaffe and Trajtenberg (1996) and uses the citations data described in Hall, Jaffe, and Trajtenberg (2001). The exposition of the empirical framework follows Branstetter (2000) quite closely.

(7) $$\mathbf{F}_i = (f_1, \ldots, f_k)$$

and each of the k elements of $\mathbf{F}$ represent the firm's research resources and expertise in the kth technological category. These are constructed by aggregating the hundreds of patent classes in the U.S. Patent and Trademark Office system into fifty distinct areas. We then count the number of patents taken out by firm i in each of the categories over the full length of the sample period.

From the number of patents taken out in different categories, we can infer what the distribution of R&D investment and technological expertise across different technical fields has been. In the same way, we can also compute a vector of location in technology space for the aggregate of all U.S. inventors, treating them as though they belonged to a single giant enterprise, and denoting that as $\mathbf{F}_{US}$. This suggests that $PROX_i$ might be measured as

(8) $$PROX_i = \frac{\mathbf{F}_i \mathbf{F}'_{US}}{[(\mathbf{F}_i \mathbf{F}_i)(\mathbf{F}_{US} \mathbf{F}_{US})]^{1/2}}.$$

This is a technological proximity coefficient in the spirit of Jaffe (1986).

One may also wish to allow citations to be influenced by the firms' R&D spending (R_{it}) and by vectors of multiplicative fixed effects associated with the citing firm (α_i) and the (application) year in which the citation takes place (α_t). Including these fixed effects actually simplifies the equation, provided one is willing to make some assumptions. The stock of cumulated potentially citable indigenous U.S. patents will be the same for all Japanese citing firms in each year, so that the N_{At} terms are effectively absorbed into the time dummies. One may also want to assume that a firm's location in technology space relative to aggregate U.S. inventive activity is relatively fixed over time. In that case, the effect of the PROX measure is absorbed into the firm fixed effects in a standard fixed effects regression. Industry effects also will be absorbed into the firm effects, because firms in the sample do not change their primary industry affiliation over time.

The assumption that the technological proximity of a Japanese firm to U.S. inventive activity stays fixed over a long period is a strong one. The data permit us to allow this proximity measure to vary within firms over time, although we lack sufficiently rich patent data to do this for all firms or all years. The specification suggested by this line of thinking is

(9) $c_{Jit} = \beta_0 + \beta_1 p_{it} + \beta_2 r_{it} + \beta_3 \text{Alliance}_{it} + \beta_4 PROX_{it} + \sum_t \alpha_t T_t + \alpha_i + \varepsilon_{it}$

The focus of interest is on β_3. Do firms that engage in more frequent technology alliances and R&D joint ventures with the United States experience an increased tendency to cite U.S. patents? A positive, significant coefficient would suggest the answer is yes.

Table 7.3   Measuring Spillovers to Japanese Firms

Note: Negative binomial regressions, dependent variable is Citations, and Observations = 1.857. Variables of interest are in boldface. Standard deviations are in parentheses.

	Fixed Effects
Log R&D	−0.20
	(.014)
Log U.S. patents	.847
	(.016)
Proximity	.579
	(.085)
U.S. alliances	**.004**
	(.002)
Time dummies	Yes
Log likelihood	−6440.500

Source: Branstetter (2001c). In tables 7.3 and 7.4, one-period logged patents are used as a proxy for contemporaneous patents, for reasons given in Branstetter (2001c).

There is a data problem in that the dependent variable for a nontrivial number of observations is 0. We deal with this by estimating a fixed effects negative binomial version of equation (9). Results are given in table 7.3.

We see clearly that alliances have a positive, statistically significant impact on the measured flow of technological knowledge from the United States to Japanese firms when they are entered separately into the regression. Although the coefficient is small in magnitude, one must recall that it gives the increase in knowledge flows associated with the establishment of an additional alliance. Because some firms in our data set went from zero alliances to several dozen, the cumulative effect implied by the regression coefficients is quite substantial.

Our conversations with Japanese R&D managers suggest an important complementarity between overseas R&D facilities and R&D alliances. Often, overseas R&D centers are used as a base from which to search out alliance partners and, in many cases, the site of R&D centers is selected with current or potential alliance partners in mind. In future work, we hope to explore this apparent complementarity further.

7.4.3   Putting Knowledge Flows to Work

The finding that the establishment of research alliances enhances knowledge flows is of limited interest unless firms that receive greater knowledge flows from the United States are able to translate these flows into greater innovative productivity. Firmly establishing such a causal linkage is difficult, but in table 7.4 we present evidence that is at least consistent with such a linkage.

The first column reports the results of a fixed effects negative binomial regression. In this case, the dependent variable is our citation-adjusted

Table 7.4   Do Increased Knowledge Flows Raise Innovative Productivity?

Note: Negative binomial regressions, and the dependent variable is citation-adjusted patent output. Variables of interest are in boldface. Standard deviations are in parentheses.

	Fixed Effects (1)	Random Effects (2)
Log R&D	.031	0.023
	(.021)	(.027)
Log real sales	.011	.101
	(.034)	(.036)
Log U.S. patents	.956	.822
	(.016)	(.021)
Log citations to U.S. patents	**.0001**	
	(.00002)	
Dummy for citation greater than median		**.899**
		(.096)
Time dummies	Yes	Yes
Log likelihood	−6,119.5	−7,884.8
Observations	2,066	2,160

Source: Branstetter (2001c).

measure of U.S. patent output. We regress this on firm-level R&D spending and a firm-specific time-varying measure of knowledge flows from the United States.

This measure is the count of citations to U.S. patents—the dependent variable from our previous set of regression results. We see clearly that U.S. knowledge flows are positively associated with higher quality patent output, and that this association is robust to the inclusion of a control for patent counts.[37] The coefficient is very small, but the statistical interpretation of this coefficient is the increase in patent quality associated with an additional citation. Because some firms make hundreds of such citations in a single year's cohort of patent applications, the cumulative effects of a substantial increase in such citations could be quite substantial.

This point is demonstrated by the results in the second column. The measure of knowledge flow used in this column is a simple dummy variable equal to one if the firm in question receives higher than the median level of citations over the sample period. A random effects negative binomial regression shows that this variable is highly significant and large in magnitude, suggesting that there is a strong correlation in the cross section between high levels of knowledge flow and high levels of quality-adjusted patent output. Frequently-citing firms generate patents that are

37. The obvious relationship between counts of citations to prior U.S. patents and the number of successful Japanese patent applications requires the use of this control. This implies that our innovative output measure is, in effect, measuring the average quality of patents in a given cohort.

nearly 90 percent better, as measured by their ex post citations. We cannot interpret this as strong *causal* evidence of a linkage between knowledge flows from the United States and invention quality because there are likely to be important unmeasured differences in the research quality of firms which may be correlated with the frequency with which they cite U.S. patents. Nevertheless, these results offer large-sample statistical evidence consistent with the view expressed by our interviewees that tapping U.S. technology networks can be a useful component of an R&D reform strategy.

7.5 Conclusion

As the 1980s ended, Japanese firms were held up as exemplars of strength in technological innovation. As the twenty-first century begins, leaders in government and industry are calling for a reform of the national innovation system in order to raise the long-run sustainable growth rate of the Japanese economy. This chapter has demonstrated that there are reasonable grounds for concern about the relative performance of Japanese manufacturing firms in technology-intensive industries.

To answer the question posed by our title, we do not find strong evidence that Japanese innovative capacity has actually declined. However, that capacity has failed to grow at the rate of the 1980s. As a result, U.S. and worldwide patent statistics suggest that Japanese firms have fallen behind their U.S. counterparts in a number of sectors, even in areas where Japanese firms were formerly relatively quite strong and rapidly converging on U.S. levels of inventive output.

Microeconometric analysis suggests that this decline in relative performance cannot be entirely ascribed to a relative reduction in R&D inputs, though such a relative reduction has occurred. We find evidence consistent with the view that, outside the electronics sector, R&D productivity growth has stagnated in the 1990s and perhaps even declined. This view is strongly reflected in the U.S. patent data, and the results are robust to an adjustment for the quality of individual U.S. patents.

Anecdotal evidence from R&D manager interviews is strongly consistent with a slowdown or decline in Japanese R&D productivity relative to the firms' U.S. competitors and relative to their own experience in the 1980s. These interviews suggest that the structural shift in Japanese R&D over the course of the late 1980s and 1990s may have contributed to the observed stagnation in R&D productivity growth. Japanese firms are not well equipped for more fundamental research due to the educational backgrounds of their engineers, the weakness of Japanese academic science, and the lack of a robust domestic venture capital industry.

Firms are taking steps to increase the efficiency of their R&D operations, and one key strategy adopted to varying degrees by all interviewed firms includes an increased emphasis on tapping U.S. technology networks. In the absence of strong domestic institutions, Japanese firms are creating ties to U.S. universities, start-ups, and established firms. Our microeconometric assessment of the impact of one of the steps taken to accomplish this strategic goal finds that the formation of technology-sharing alliances with U.S. firms has a positive impact on knowledge flow from the United States to Japanese firms. Finally, we show that increased international knowledge flows are strongly correlated with higher levels of innovative performance, at least in the firm cross section. Therefore, Japanese firms that have most successfully tapped into U.S. technology networks enjoy a relatively higher level of R&D productivity.

In terms of public policy implications, as we have already noted, the government has taken a number of steps to improve Japan's academic science base and enhance the business environment for start-ups. However, these policy changes are unlikely to have substantial positive impact until Japan's overall macroeconomic situation improves. While the downturn in innovative activity is not to blame for Japan's poor macroeconomic performance, continued stagnation of the Japanese economy could have long-lasting negative effects on the research operations of Japanese firms. Thus, the most effective step the government could take in the short run to enhance Japan's innovative performance is to revive economic growth. A discussion of macroeconomic policies to accomplish that is beyond the scope of this paper, but we strongly concur with those who advocate the adoption of a positive inflation target by the Bank of Japan, tax cuts to stimulate growth, and a careful recapitalization of the banking system.

Like most empirical research projects, this essay leaves us with a number of unanswered (or only partially answered) questions which we hope to pursue in further work. First, do our tentative explanations for the observed decline in the growth of Japanese R&D productivity stand up to more rigorous empirical testing? Our current hypothesis suggests a negative relationship between a shift to more basic research and research productivity that could be explored more thoroughly. Second, have the other dimensions of R&D reform mentioned in the third section been enhancing research productivity? Our next examination of R&D restructuring by Japanese firms will consider all aspects of the process. We believe that this more comprehensive study could shed useful light on the extent of the restructuring, the degree to which different components have had positive effects on research productivity, and the role that public policy could play in enhancing the evolution of the Japanese innovation system.

Our interviews strongly suggested that the move toward partial outsourcing of R&D is a conscious imitation of a shift that is already well underway in the United States. A Japanese perspective on the global process of vertical disintegration of R&D may offer useful lessons on this process for the rest of the world.

Appendix

Data Sources

Japanese Patent Data

Japanese patent data are from Patent Online System (PATOLIS), a database maintained by the Japan Patent Information Organization (JAPIO). The data are counts of patent applications by firm and year.

U.S. Patent Data

The data on patents taken out in the United States by Japanese firms are from the NBER Patent Database, described in Hall, Jaffe, and Trajtenberg (2001). The data include counts of patent grants by firm and year. In our work, the patents are dated by the year of application rather than the year of grant. We also include a firm-specific measure of patent output that is quality-adjusted by counting subsequent citations received by these patents, as described in the text.

R&D Data

The overall R&D spending of individual Japanese firms is taken from several consecutive issues of the *Kaisha Shikiho* (Tokyo, 1980–1999), published by Toyo Keizai Shimpo Sha, and the *Nikkei Kaisha Jōho* (Tokyo, 1980–1984), published by the Nihon Keizai Shimbun sha. All R&D expenditure data is deflated by the R&D price index constructed by the Japanese Science and Technology Agency and reported in *Gijutsu Yōran* (2001).

Other Firm Variables

Data on firm sales and industry affiliation are taken from various issues of the Japan Development Bank Corporate Finance Database. Data on R&D alliances with U.S. firms are taken from the Securities Data Corporation (SDC) joint ventures database.

Sample Selection Issues

Firms were selected on the basis of availability of a sufficient quantity of R&D data and patent data in both Japan and the United States. We furthermore required that there be no major jumps in such series as capital stock over the course of the 1980s, thereby screening out firms involved in major domestic mergers or acquisitions. This means a handful of large R&D performers are omitted due to data irregularities. The screening tends to oversample R&D intensive firms relative to the population as a whole. A complete list of the firms in our sample and additional information on the sample are available from the authors on request.

References

Arison, Thomas, C. Fred Bergsten, Edward Graham, and Martha C. Harris, eds. 1992. *Japan's growing technological capability: Implications for the U.S. economy.* Washington DC: National Academy Press.
Belderbos, Rene. 2001. Overseas innovations by Japanese firms: An analysis of patent and subsidiary data. *Research Policy* 30:313–32.
Branstetter, Lee. 2000. Is foreign direct investment a channel of knowledge spillovers? Evidence from Japan's FDI in the United States. NBER Working Paper no. 8015. Cambridge, Mass.: National Bureau of Economic Research, November.
———. 2001a. Are knowledge spillovers international or intranational in scope? Microeconometric evidence from the U.S. and Japan. *Journal of International Economics* 53:53–79.
———. 2001b. Measuring the link between academic science and industrial innovation—The case of California's research universities. Columbia Business School, Economics and Finance Division. Working Paper.
———. 2001c. The roles of FDI and interfirm R&D alliances in international knowledge spillovers: Evidence from Japanese multinational firms. Columbia Business School, Economics and Finance Division. Working Paper.
Branstetter, Lee, and Mariko Sakakibara. 1998. Japanese research consortia: A microeconometric analysis of industrial policy. *Journal of Industrial Economics* 46 (2): 207–33.
Clark, Kim, and Takahiro Fujimoto. 1991. *Product Development Performance.* Boston: Harvard Business School Press.
Cockburn, Iain, and Rebecca Henderson. 2000. Publicly funded science and the productivity of the pharmaceutical industry. In *Innovation policy and the economy.* Vol. 1 ed. Adam Jaffe, Joshua Lerner, and Scott Stern, 1–34. Cambridge, Mass.: MIT Press.
Cohen, Wesley, Akira Goto, Akiya Nagata, Richard Nelson, and John Walsh. 1998. R&D spillovers, patents, and the incentives to innovate in Japan and the United States. Carnegie Mellon University, Heinz School of Administration. Working Paper.
Feenstra, Robert. 1996. Trade and uneven growth. *Journal of Development Economics* 49:229–56.
Finan, William, and Carl Williams. 1992. Implications of Japan's "soft crisis": Forcing new directions for Japanese electronics companies. In *Japan's growing technological capability: Implications for the U.S. economy,* ed. Thomas Arison, C. Fred Bergsten, Edward Graham, and Martha C. Harris, 136–146. Washington DC: National Academy Press.
Gijutsu Yōran (Indicators of Science and Technology). 2000. Tokyo: Science and Technology Policy Bureau of the Science and Technology Agency, Government of Japan.
Goto, Akira. 1993. *Nihon no gijutsu kakushin to sangyō soshiki* (Japan's technical progress and industrial organization). Tokyo: University of Tokyo Press.
———. 1997. Introduction to *Innovation in Japan,* ed. Akira Goto and Hiroyuki Odagiri. Oxford: Clarendon Press.
Goto, Akira, and Akiya Nagata. 1997. Technological opportunities and appropriating the returns from innovation: Comparison of survey results from Japan and the U.S. National Institute of Science and Technology Policy (NISTEP) Report no. 48. Tokyo: Science and Technology Institute.

Grossman, Gene, and Elhanan Helpman. 1991. *Innovation and growth in the global economy.* Cambridge: MIT Press.

Hall, Bronwyn, Adam Jaffe, and Manuel Trajtenberg. 2001. The NBER patent citation data file: Lessons, insights, and methodological tools. NBER Working Paper no. 8498. Cambridge, Mass.: National Bureau of Economic Research, October.

Hausman, Jerry, Bronwyn Hall, and Zvi Griliches. 1984. Econometric models for count data with an application to the patents—R&D relationship. *Econometrica* 52 (4): 909–38.

Henderson, Rebecca, Adam Jaffe, and Manuel Trajtenberg. 1998. Universities as a source of commercial technology: A detailed analysis of university patenting, 1965–1988. *Review of Economics and Statistics* 80 (1): 119–27.

Hicks, Diana, Tony Breitzman, Dominic Olivastro, and Kimberly Hamilton. 2001. The changing composition of innovative activity in the U.S.—A portrait based on patent analysis. *Research Policy* 30:681–703.

Jaffe, Adam. 1986. Technological opportunity and the spillover of R&D: Evidence from firms' patents, profits, and market value. *American Economic Review* 76:984–1001.

Jaffe, Adam, and Manuel Trajtenberg. 1996. Flows of knowledge from universities and federal labs: Modeling the flow of patent citations across institutional and geographic boundaries. NBER Working Paper no. 5712. Cambridge, Mass.: National Bureau for Economic Research, August.

Kortum, Samuel, and Joshua Lerner. 1999. What is behind the recent surge in patenting? *Research Policy* 28:1–22.

———. 2000. Assessing the contribution of venture capital to innovation. *RAND Journal of Economics* 31:674–92.

Mansfield, Edwin. 1988. Industrial R&D in Japan and the United States: A comparative study. *American Economic Review Papers and Proceedings* 78 (2): 223–28.

Narin, Fran, Kimberly Hamilton, and Dominic Olivastro. 1997. The increasing linkage between U.S. technology and public science. *Research Policy* 26:317–30.

National Academy of Engineering. 1987. *Strengthening U.S. engineering through international cooperation: Some recommendations for action.* Washington DC: National Academy Press.

Normile, Dennis. 2002. Japan asks why more yen don't yield more products. *Science* 296:1230–31.

Odagiri, Hiroyuki, and Hideto Yasuda. 1997. Overseas R&D activities of Japanese firms. In *Innovation in Japan,* ed. Akira Goto and Hiroyuki Odagiri, 204–228. Oxford: Clarendon Press.

Okimoto, Daniel, and Gary Saxonhouse. 1987. Technology and the future of the economy. In *The political economy of Japan.* Vol. 1, *The domestic transformation,* ed. Kozo Yamamura and Yasukichi Yasuba, 385–419. Stanford, Cal.: Stanford University Press.

Posen, Adam. 1998. *Restoring Japan's economic growth.* Washington, DC: Institute for International Economics.

———. 2001. Unchanging innovation and changing economic performance in Japan. In *Technological innovation and national economic performance,* ed. Richard Nelson, Benn Steil, and David Victor, Princeton, N.J.: Princeton University Press.

Rosenberg, Nathan, and Richard Nelson. 1994. American universities and technical advance in industry. *Research Policy* 23:323–48.

Rosenbloom, Richard, and William Spencer. 1996. *Engines of innovation: U.S. industrial research at the end of an era.* Boston: Harvard Business School Press.

Sakakibara, Mariko, and Lee Branstetter. 2001. Do stronger patents induce more innovation? Evidence from the Japanese 1988 patent reforms. *RAND Journal of Economics* 32 (1): 77–100.

Wakasugi, Ryuhei, and Fumihiko Koyata. 1997. R&D, firm size and innovation outputs: Are Japanese firms efficient in product development? *Journal of Product Innovation Management* 14:383–92.

8

Constraints on the Level and Efficient Use of Labor

Hiroshi Ono and Marcus E. Rebick

Japanese labor market institutions have been given substantial credit for Japan's enviable growth performance after World War II. The personnel management system—with its strong job protection, enterprise-based unionism, and intensive on-the-job training—is especially seen as a factor that allowed Japan to utilize imported technology so rapidly and success-fully. High levels of training, along with group-oriented activities, have also been linked to the high quality of the Japanese goods that reached export markets in the 1970s and 1980s. Indeed, many Japanese workplace prac-tices, such as quality-control circles, have been adopted to good effect in the United States and Europe. On the macroeconomic side, the coordi-nated but decentralized bargaining system is seen as providing for the wage flexibility that allowed Japan to adjust to supply shocks, such as the two oil crises, more rapidly than most other Organization for Economic Cooper-ation & Development (OECD) economies. Finally, the egalitarian nature of the compensation system has been credited with providing the wide-spread prosperity that underlies domestic demand.

The prolonged slowdown of the 1990s has led many to question whether the institutions that were appropriate for the past are as wholesome for the health of the contemporary and future economy. In particular, the rise in

Hiroshi Ono is assistant professor at the European Institute of Japanese Studies, Stock-holm School of Economics. Marcus E. Rebick is university lecturer and fellow of St. Antony's College and a member of the Nissan Institute of Japanese Studies, Oxford University.

The authors wish to thank Masayuki Kakuho and Hiromi Murata of Recruit Works Insti-tute, Minoru Ito of the Japan Institute of Labor, Koichiro Masuda, Fumio Ohtake, Kazumi Ota, Yasuo Takahashi, and participants in the March 2002 National Bureau of Economic Re-search (NBER), Center for Economic Policy and Research (CEPR), and European Institute for Japanese Studies (EIJS) conference and the Oxford Labor Economics Seminar. All omis-sions and errors are of course our own.

the unemployment rate since 1998 from around 3 percent to almost 6 percent has changed views about the macroeconomic role played by the labor market.

This disillusionment can be quickly summarized. Strong job protection makes it difficult for companies to effectively restructure their activities in response to the changing external environment. This means companies are less likely to improve their balance sheets. A poorly developed external labor market impedes movement of experienced and knowledgeable employees to companies where they might be more valuable. The government, lacking confidence in the external labor market's ability to absorb the unemployed, may have been reluctant to push for a more drastic resolution of the bad debt problem that hampers the financial system. Under conditions of weak demand, the coordinated bargaining system makes it difficult for employees to increase their incomes and thereby may reduce domestic demand. Wage restraint is contributing to the deflation that currently is making difficulties for the effective use of monetary policy to revive economic growth. The aging of the work force makes it difficult to maintain a system where rewards are delayed and provided through promotion.

In this chapter, we address impediments to growth of the labor supply that are affecting the economy. Broadly speaking these are barriers to interfirm mobility for career employees, especially older men, and the difficulty women face in developing meaningful careers after taking time off to raise children. The latter depresses the labor force participation of women, especially the middle aged who have high educational attainment. Both of these issues are closely tied to the Japanese personnel management system and the legal framework that supports it.

A third impediment to growth on the labor supply side is the reluctance to accept large numbers of immigrants into Japan. The outlook is that Japan will continue with its existing policies in the short- to medium-run, and we do not consider the issue. We also do not address the way in which the unemployment benefit system may induce individuals to remain unemployed or how retirement benefits may encourage earlier retirement. With respect to the unemployment rate and participation rate of those over sixty, Japan is doing as well, if not better, at using potential labor resources than other OECD countries. It should be noted that the institutional features of the economy that we view as impediments would be significantly less problematic if the economy was growing at the rates seen through the 1980s. If growth could be restored to 1980s' levels through a surge in consumer and investment demand, much of the estimated losses to labor input might well be eliminated. However, that is unlikely to happen.

In the next section we provide an outline of the state of Japanese labor in 2001, focusing on the extent to which institutions long seen as characteristic of the Japanese labor market have stayed the same or have been changing. Next, labor law and its consequences are discussed. We then look at impediments to the mobility of career employees (primarily men) that may be affecting growth; reasons why female labor force participation may be lower than levels seen in the United States are then examined. A quantitative perspective of the barriers is presented, including their overall implications for economic growth, the role of government policy in removing barriers is taken up, and we outline some areas in need of further research.

8.1 The Employment System

Although Japanese labor markets and institutions have been affected by the slump in growth that began in the 1990s, many of the main features remain largely intact. Widely noted aspects of the "Japanese model," such as enterprise-based unionism, low interfirm mobility, low unemployment, compensation within gender groups that is highly determined by age and seniority, large gender gaps in pay and promotions, and widespread use of mandatory retirement systems, have not dissolved in the face of the slowdown, despite press reports.

Evidence that the system has seen only minor change includes the following seven points:

1. Unions remain enterprise based, although union density has fallen steadily from around 35 percent at the time of the first oil shock (1973) to 21 percent in 2000.

2. Job tenure for full-time regular employees remains high (Chuma 1997) and may even be increasing for some age groups.

3. Interfirm mobility rates remain virtually unchanged (Rebick 2001), although the number of employees forced to move because of bankruptcies has risen since the Asian economic crisis of 1998.

4. The 5.4 percent unemployment rate in May 2002, although high by Japanese standards, remains lower than the OECD average of 6.9 percent (OECD standardized rates).

5. Although performance- and results-related pay are becoming more important components of compensation arrangements, there is still a close relationship between age (and, to a lesser extent, seniority) and pay. Japanese age-wage profiles are steep mainly because blue-collar workers, as well as white-collar workers, see large increases in pay with age and seniority. With the exception of the managerial class of employees, the variance of pay within age groups remains stable (Genda and Rebick 2000). All of this is testimony to the continuing presence of enterprise unions and the influence of large, unionized firms on wage-setting practices outside the organized sector.

6. The gender pay gap has narrowed for full-time employees (especially the young), but the gap in hourly pay between female part-time workers and male full-time employees remains large. Because some 40 percent of women work part-time, the overall gender gap remains large. Among eight OECD countries including Korea, only in Japan is gender—rather than

occupation, age, or industry—the most important determinant of wages (Tachibanaki 1998).

7. Japan has relatively few women in senior management or director positions compared with the United States or United Kingdom.

In spite of these observations, the Japanese model is evolving. Furthermore, most of the changes appear to be permanent, rather than temporary accommodations to economic conditions or the need for restructuring.

1. The proportion of individuals who are part-time or contract workers is increasing. In particular the percentage of employees working part-time has been rising steadily since the 1960s, reaching as high as 39 percent of women and 13 percent of men in 1999 (OECD 2001). The number of temporary agency workers remains low at about 1 percent of the work force, but has been increasing rapidly with liberalization of the laws regulating agency work.

2. There has been a decline in the family-based enterprise sector. Some women who would have been family workers and men who would have become self-employed after mandatory retirement are now in the part-time employee labor force. Although some of this trend may be due to small businesses suffering during the 1990s, much of it is due to other aspects of the fundamental restructuring of the economy that is taking place.

3. Managerial compensation is becoming much more sensitive to various measures of performance. This is shown not only by surveys across companies, but also by the fact that the variance of pay of middle-aged men with higher education degrees has been increasing since the mid-1980s (Genda and Rebick 2000).

4. Attitudes are changing, especially among young people. Although the rates of separation for young workers have not increased much, most young employees say that they expect to change jobs before mandatory retirement. Young workers are quitting jobs at an increasing rate despite the poor state of the economy. In 1999, 32 percent of university graduates and 47 percent of high school graduates quit their first jobs within three years, both rates increasing since 1996 (Ministry of Labor [MOL] 2000a).

5. There is an increasing level of part-time work among the young. Often referred to as "freeters," they may be finding it difficult to find desirable full-time jobs in the current economic climate (Genda 2001). On the other hand, because of greater affluence, they may feel less pressured into taking jobs they don't really want.

8.2   Worker Protection

The most obvious problem facing companies burdened with redundant workers is the difficulty in shedding workers. There is long-standing agreement between management and labor in Japan that allows management to move workers around in the company (or even to loan workers to other companies) in return for a guarantee of employment until mandatory retirement age (Gordon 1985, 1998). Since the late 1970s this has been altered somewhat: Employees might be sent to other companies prior to mandatory retirement provided that the guarantee of employment still holds. In most cases, the original company ensures there are no financial losses to those transferred, making supplemental payments to workers if necessary. Although this is seen as a commitment by management to labor, which might be upheld in order to maintain the reputation of the employer (and industrial peace), it is reinforced by Japanese case law. (The remainder of this section relies heavily on Chuma 1998.)

Japanese labor law does not, by statute, provide guarantees of continued employment to employees, except that employers must give thirty days notice of dismissals. The Japanese constitution, however, enshrines the individual's right to work (Article 27) and the right to a minimum standard of "wholesome and cultured living" (Article 25). On this basis, Japanese courts have interpreted the law to impose four main standards on employers wishing to dismiss workers. The employer must show that:

1. It is under severe duress, such as facing possible bankruptcy, and existing redundancies are unavoidable.
2. It has made efforts to avoid redundancies by taking measures such as cutting overtime, hiring freezes, transfers, seconding workers to other companies, or seeking voluntary retirements.
3. It has consulted with its labor unions and employees.
4. It has a rational procedure for selecting those to be dismissed.

This case law developed in the 1950s in reaction to the widespread dismissals that followed implementation of the disinflationary Dodge Line of 1949–50 and the numerous industrial disputes that followed. The courts were concerned about dismissals being used as a way of undermining labor union strength, and the four conditions were aimed primarily at establishing what constituted unfair labor practice under postwar labor laws. The courts also established that redress for violation of these principles is not only compensation paid to the fired worker, but also reinstatement with back pay. Again, this was to act as a deterrent to labor practices deemed unfair.

The rulings had an effect: In 1975, at the peak of post-oil shock dismissals, the proportion of separations that were "at the employer's will" stood at only 10 percent, compared to 21 percent in 1954, and through the late 1970s firms in general took every action to avoid dismissals (Chuma 1998). The case law was further strengthened through rulings in the late 1970s, at a time when a number of court cases examined dismissals for the purpose of labor adjustment during the downturn of the mid-1970s. In the 1970s and afterward, protection of workers from dismissals was extended to temporary and fixed-contract workers who had been repeatedly rehired after their contract expired and even to workers in the first, probationary year of employment.

Until 1998, the Labor Standards Law limited fixed-term contracts to one year or less. This was intended to force employers to offer indefinite-period contracts to employees. After the 1998 revision, the law allows contracts of up to three years, but only in the case where the employee is either over sixty, in a specialized occupation, or under other restricted circumstances determined by the Ministry of Health, Labor, and Welfare (MHLW). Furthermore, such a contract is renewable for only one year (Yamakawa 1998). This is a considerable restriction and has been heavily criticized (Ohtake 2001, Yashiro 1999). Since 1999, there have been a number of court rulings that have relaxed and, in at least one case, even dispensed with the framework of the four conditions, but it is still too early to know what overall effect these rulings will have (Yamakawa and Araki 2001).

8.2.1   Consequences

One problem with the level of job protection provided by dismissal case law has been the reluctance of employers to hire employees that they are not sure they wish to keep indefinitely. There also are negative externalities (Yashiro 1999). We later deal with one of the more serious of these: the lack of a well-developed external labor market and the information problems that result.

Another effect of current law is that it encourages companies to seek government help in the form of subsidies, protection from competition, and protection from creditors. Although labor case law was not responsible for this action, it is part of a general approach that provides economic security through employers rather than directly from the state or private insurance provision (Noguchi 1995). This may come at the expense of growth in total factor productivity (TFP). For example, Hayashi and Prescott (2002) note that TFP growth was exceptionally low at 0.8 percent per annum during 1978 to 1983, when the government took action to subsidize and otherwise support industries that were in need of restructuring and firms endeavored to avoid dismissals.

Although arguments can be made for worker protection from the viewpoint of economic efficiency, there is little rationale for imposing a penalty whereby workers must be reinstated with back pay. Chuma (1998) argues that it would be better to simply impose a cash penalty that employers should pay workers who have been dismissed in violation of the conditions. He also suggests that courts may not be in the best position to evaluate the financial concerns of the company and that if the "severe duress" condition is imposed too stringently it may compromise the survival of the firm over the long run.

If a firm can no longer produce competitively, its human capital may have lost value regardless of what the firm is paying the employee. The benefits of worker protection may be quickly outweighed by the costs when there is a widespread drop in the value of some kinds of firm-specific human capital.

8.3   Barriers to Mobility Between Firms

There are many barriers to mobility in the Japanese labor market. Table 8.1 gives us some indication of the problems from the point of view of employees, based on a survey by Recruit, an employment service, in which individuals who wanted to change jobs were asked why they found it difficult to do so. Of course, there also are corresponding issues on the employer side of the labor market. We analyze all of these beginning with information problems, skill mismatch, and lack of pension portability. Seniority pay and age-based discrimination are then taken up, followed by differentials in pay by firm size and egalitarian pay norms. Job protection, the result of both law and firms' employment practices, is analyzed as a cause of both excess workers within firms and skill mismatch.

8.3.1   Information Problems

A long-standing problem in the Japanese labor market concerns the lack of available employment information. Commonly, workers do not know exactly (in terms of quality or quantity) what skills they have, and employers are unclear about the skills they need. That is, there has been a symmetric *lack* of information, and this is almost certainly due to the poor development of the external labor market in an economy with overall low mobility. "Better information for job seekers" has been a recurrent slogan in a situation where job postings tend to be ambiguous and crucial information, such as job description and required skills, is lacking (Japan Institute of Labor [JIL] 1998).

Employment information can be categorized into extensive information, which consists of information available to all job-seekers, such as firm

Table 8.1   **Reasons Changing Jobs is Difficult: The Worker View**

Reason	Percentage Giving Reason
I exceed the age limit of the job postings	40.8
My work experience is not transferable to the general society	23.4
Returns to seniority will be lost and I will suffer wage loss	21.8
I do not know how to look for jobs	19.1
I will lose personal contacts established through my work	14.1
I will suffer a loss in my pension	13.5

Source: Recruit Works Institute (2001b).

size and wages, and intensive information, which is more likely to be of an inside nature, such as work norms and work atmosphere of the employer (Rees 1966). Access to intensive information is a benefit insofar as it improves the quality of the job match and subsequently leads to higher rewards and better job satisfaction (Granovetter 1974). Watanabe (1992) explains that workers are more likely to obtain intensive information through acquaintances or former employers. According to Recruit's (2001b) survey, 41 percent of job seekers gathered employment information through contacts with friends, family, and former employers, and 72 percent of those (30 percent of all those who found jobs) found jobs through this channel.[1]

A labor market that favors informal job-search methods disadvantages job seekers who are not endowed with network ties or otherwise must seek re-employment through formal means. Workers seeking employment by means of application through employment agencies experience considerable hardship. This includes longer duration of job search and a poor quality of match (JIL 1998). This is not a problem peculiar to Japan.

In a society where a market for job changers is only just evolving and one-fifth of workers surveyed said that they do not know how to look for jobs, it is not surprising that firms specializing in headhunting and re-employment services are growing rapidly. Human resource firms are focusing on the information mismatch between buyers and sellers of labor. Their services include helping employers grasp which skills are needed and helping job seekers identify what types of skills they have and the options available to them. The government is gradually deregulating the market for private employment services, including temporary employment agencies, through revision of the Dispatched Employees Law. All this may lead to improvement.

Access to privileged information from social networks may not be limited to employment information. The quantity and quality of social resources are determined not only by an individual's network of acquaintances, but also by virtue of belonging to a particular organization. Establishing important connections with business partners and gaining trust and reputation within the firm are important social resources that workers acquire through their jobs. However, in most cases, such resources are lost if a worker relocates to a different establishment. Social resources acquired through business can be a benefit that facilitates workers' upward mobility within firms, but it can also be an impediment to interfirm mobility as workers fear that they will lose the personal contacts established through work.

1. In Granovetter's 1974 study of male white-collar workers in Boston, 56 percent used contacts.

8.3.2 Skill Mismatch

Skill mismatch is a problem related to information availability, and it is of increasing concern in Japan. A survey of OECD economies reports that the Beveridge curve (which graphs unemployment rates against vacancies) has been shifting outward in Japan since the 1970s (Nickell et al. 2001) and has clearly accelerated in the late 1990s (Genda and Rebick 2000). This implies more jobs are available for any given unemployment rate, and that suggests there may be an increasing mismatch of skills. A survey of businesses and job seekers found that the level of vacancies (690,000) and applicants (740,000) across sixty occupational categories were fairly close, but within categories the ratio of vacancies to applicants ranged from 9.95 to 0.05 (METI-Recruit 2001).

A lack of necessary qualifications of job applicants, especially in some of the more specialized occupations, such as information technology (IT)-related work, also is highlighted in the METI-Recruit study. It is clear that information flows must be improved in several ways: Firms need to convey to training providers just what skills are needed, and that information must also reach those who seek training or need it as a result of being laid-off. Outplacement departments could do a better job in regard to the latter. Public funds for retraining are offered to both companies and individuals, and there are proposals to increase the level of funding.

8.3.3 Lack of Pension Portability

Closely related to the problem of seniority-based pay (taken up later) is the lack of portability of private, firm-based pensions. Japan implemented a policy equivalent to the U.S. 401(k) defined-contribution plan in October 2001. Prior to this, there were no tax advantages to saving outside of the defined-benefit plans offered by firms.

Firm-based pensions take a number of different forms and can make lump-sum payments or provide annuities after retirement, but they share the characteristic of offering benefits based on years of service and final base salary. A recipient with thirty-five years tenure typically gets two to four years of base pay (that is, not including semi-annual bonuses), with the higher rates going to the better-educated employees of large firms (MOL 2000b). Portability problems arise because payouts often are reduced more than proportionately if an employee leaves before mandatory retirement. At the same time, an individual with low tenure at mandatory retirement (due to switching firms) may suffer a more than proportional reduction in benefits. In other words, the likely losses in earnings from a move extend to losses in pensions.

Ichinose (2001) uses pension tables to compute the pension losses that would be experienced by individuals who leave a large firm (more than

1,000 employees) and move to a smaller firm at lower pay, which is the most common pattern. The losses are computed assuming that an individual is paid the average for the firm size and according to tenure. Pension losses can amount to ¥10 million to ¥20 million from an average pension of ¥35 million, depending on age at separation. The younger the age, the greater the loss. For this reason, firms, especially large firms, offer additional lump-sum payments to individuals who leave under early retirement plans. The additional payments—typically between ¥5 million and ¥10 million—cover some, but not all of the losses in pension value. In comparison to the overall losses of up to ¥100 million that may be realized by workers who lose their jobs at large firms at age forty, these are not large quantities but, as suggested by the responses in table 6.1, have some influence on behavior.

8.4   Seniority and Pay Structure

There are significant tenure effects on earnings from seniority in the Japanese workplace. The work of Koike (1988), Hashimoto and Raisian (1985), and Mincer and Higuchi (1988) drew attention to the importance of on-the-job training and the development of firm-specific human capital for Japanese men. Along with the case studies and direct surveys of Koike, the latter two papers highlighted the apparently large increase in earnings with tenure (seniority) in Japan compared to the United States.

Work by Ohtake (1998) and others using cross-sectional microdata has, however, modified this view substantially. First, Ohtake finds that the return to tenure was smaller than had earlier been reported, even in the past. Second, he shows that the returns to tenure fell between 1980 and 1992, while rising in the United States. The cross-sectional data suggest that the increase in earnings attributable to tenure is 1 percent to 2 percent per year in Japan, still somewhat higher than in the United States. This is mainly, but not entirely, due to the fact that seniority has a much larger effect on the earnings of Japanese blue-collar workers than their U.S. counterparts.

Although there may well be an explanation in terms of firm-specific human capital to support the high returns to tenure in Japan, there are other views of this pattern that suggest that it may be a compensation policy developed in the 1920s and strengthened in the immediate postwar period to motivate workers and to provide for basic needs. In this view, the returns to seniority can be reduced through managerial reform without having any adverse effect on productivity, if pay-for-performance systems are introduced. This seems to be what is taking place, albeit at a slow pace (Rebick 2001). If the returns to seniority were further reduced, this should naturally raise the rate of mobility and also lessen the motivation of the courts to maintain such high standards of legal protection. Some of the arguments used by the courts have made reference to the need for worker protection given the nature of the Japanese employment system, including the pay accorded to seniority (Chuma 1998).

The tenure effect is so important for Japan because the average tenure is higher in Japan than in most other OECD countries for all age categories, Italy being a notable exception. As a result, middle-aged Japanese employees stand to lose more by leaving their firm than their counterparts in most other countries. This is particularly important for the higher-paid employees of large Japanese firms who receive almost double the median tenure of those in smaller firms (Ohtake 1998, table 4.7). The losses in earnings experienced by workers who leave firms after many years have an effect on mobility because they will increase resistance to the employer by unions or workers who know they have the support of the legal system.

8.4.1 Age-Based Discrimination

A consequence of the long-term employment and seniority systems is that Japanese firms impose age limits when recruiting and hiring. Workers exceeding the age limit of the jobs posted continues to be the most common reason for workers not changing jobs (Recruit 2001a, JIL 2001a). For this reason, here we pay special attention to the overt age-based discrimination in Japan's labor market.

Over 90 percent of Japanese firms impose age restrictions, generally thirty-five to forty, on their job openings. There is little variation across industry, firm size, and city size (JIL 2001b). There are many reasons why firms impose age limits, but the primary concern is that older workers do not fit into the firm's current employment system (table 8.2). These reasons make sense in light of the previous discussion. Because of the prevailing

Table 8.2   Reasons Firms Give for Age Restrictions in Recruitment

Reason	Percentage Giving Reason
Older workers lack physical endurance	33.8
Older workers require higher wages	26.9
Occupational skills do not match firm's expectations	24.9
Desire to maintain a young workforce	23.8
To restrict number of job applicants	20.2
Older workers do not mix well with younger workers	14.9
Older workers are hard to handle	12.9
Older workers do not adapt well to corporate culture	9.9
To avoid exceeding the age structure of previous hires	8.8
Older workers lack motivation	6.7
Relative ease of hiring young workers	5.7
No posts for older workers and cannot accommodate them	4.8
Because other firms impose age limits	3.0

Source: JIL (2001b).

norm of long-term employment, there is still a stigma attached to older or mid-career job seekers and firms often view them as hard to handle or as unable to adapt well to the corporate culture. It is also likely that many individuals who have lost jobs in other companies are simply not as capable, so a potential employers' view that they do not adapt well applied in their former company. The hesitancy to hire mid-career workers is partly rooted in the notion of equity. Indeed, from table 8.2 we can infer that the reason for age restrictions is less because of the relative ease of hiring young workers and more because "older workers do not mix well with younger workers" to avoid exceeding the age structure of previous hires.

Under pressure for reform, guidelines to abolish age limits in recruiting and hiring were introduced in October 2001 as part of the revised Employment Measures Law. However, the guidelines specify ten cases of exception where limits are acceptable. One exception is phrased almost specifically to prevent disruptions in the seniority system: "Cases where recruiting or hiring is intended for workers under a certain age in situations where, in order to make wage payments regardless of age to new employees, companies will be required to revise present regulations determining wages mainly in accordance with age" (JIL 2001a).

As it stands, the guidelines are viewed mainly as a cosmetic gesture; it simply states that employers *should* make efforts to abolish age limits. Unlike some countries, the Japanese guidelines do not impose any penalty for violations. A cursory glance at job postings after the guidelines went into effect confirms that the vast majority continue to have age limits. (See, e.g., http://www.employment.yahoo.co.jp/.) It is thus questionable whether they will have any effective results in the foreseeable future. The example of other countries' experience suggests that the problem will not go away even if the law is imposed with greater force. The high levels of tenure held by Japanese workers, especially in large companies, mean that their losses of both earnings and specific capital are likely to present them with even greater problems than their counterparts elsewhere.

8.5   Firm-Size Differentials and Egalitarian Pay Norms

An important stylized fact about mobility in Japan is that employees tend to move to smaller firms. In 1997 there were 1,670,000 employees who switched firms, and, by definition, separations equaled accessions (MOL 1998, table 10). If we restrict attention to firms with more than 1,000 employees, there were 192,000 separations involving interfirm moves, but only 172,000 accessions. The main source of this mobility deficit for large firms is found in the fifty and over age group. One reason for this distorted mobility pattern may be found in the egalitarian pay norms (described in the next section) and the presence of firm-size pay differentials.

Smaller firms pay substantially lower wages than larger ones, even after differences in worker attributes are taken into account (Tachibanaki and Ohta 1994; Rebick 1992). The reasons small firms pay less are not completely understood. Whatever they are, it is unlikely that the underlying causes, many of which are rooted in Japan's industrial organization, will change over the short- or medium-term. As we explain in the next section, the lower average pay levels found in smaller firms make them more likely to hire older employees.

8.5.1   Maintaining Fairness

Baron (1988) emphasizes the role of peer groups and normative comparisons in shaping worker assessments of fairness and explains that worker perceptions of fairness concerning output and rewards are governed more by social comparison when there is greater homogeneity among workers. He explains that work force homogeneity "facilitates identification with peers and co-workers, and that such homogeneity (is noted to be) greater in Japanese than U.S. facilities" (Baron 1988, 516). Under a system where wages and promotion are determined primarily by age and seniority, careful measures are taken to ensure that workers are promoted in accordance with seniority and that deviations from the main career track are minimized. Promotion rates among Japanese establishments vary across time, firm-size, industry sector, and sectoral output growth (Ariga, Brunello, and Ohkusa 2000). However, comparisons between Japan and the United States have consistently shown that the variance in wages among Japanese organizations are smaller than their U.S. counterparts (see, e.g., Ohta 2000 and Shirahase 2002).

Bringing older workers into the work force disrupts the seniority structure and hence the wage structure, because the employment system presumes entry from below. This is a reason why the introduction of pay-for-performance systems that actually deliver high variance in outcomes has been so slow. The preference for egalitarian pay in the presence of pay systems that have a strong age consciousness means that firms often feel that it is necessary to pay mid-career hires as if they had similar seniority to those of the same age in the firm. For example, a survey of 13,000 establishments (MOL 2000c) indicates that in the majority of firms surveyed, new employees are *in principle* paid approximately the same as existing employees of the same age and occupation. Only 15 percent indicated that they would pay the new hires less than their age cohort, presumably because they lacked firm-specific experience. Since much of the value of older employees may be firm specific, they are much less valuable after changing firms. It is easier for smaller firms, with lower average pay levels to fit these employees into their pay structure in a way that does not violate the egalitarian norms of the firm. This is one of the reasons why we see a marked tendency for older employees to move to smaller firms. Exceptionally able or skilled employees may stay in the large firm sector or move up to larger

Table 8.3   Female Labor Force Participation and Part-Time Employment Selected
                   OECD Countries, 2000

	Participation[a]	Parttime[b]
Japan	59.6	39.4
Sweden	76.4	21.4
United States	70.8	18.2
United Kingdom	68.9	40.8
Germany	63.2	33.9
France	61.7	24.3
Italy	46.2	23.4

Source: OECD (2001).
[a]Percentage of females ages 15–64 in the labor force.
[b]Part-time female workers as a percentage of all female workers. Part-time is defined as less
than thirty hours per week, except Japan where it is less than thirty-five hours per week.

firms but, on average, employees tend to move down the firm-size hier-
archy.

We wish to emphasize that the combination of seniority- and age-related
pay, the preference for egalitarian pay for similar age groups, and the firm-
size differential distort the pattern of interfirm mobility in Japan. In particular, this means that the kinds of jobs available to older men in Japan will
be severely restricted, which in turn makes it more difficult for larger firms
to dismiss their employees.

8.6   Female Labor Force Participation

This section provides an overview of women's involvement in the Japanese labor force. Following sections analyze the specific barriers that have
made that involvement less than it might be: exclusion from firms' internal
labor markets and various aspects of the pension and benefit systems. Ini-
tiatives to reconcile work and family life are also taken up.

Table 8.3 shows female labor force participation rates and the rates of
part-time work for women in Japan and elsewhere in OECD countries. Although Japanese women do not have the lowest rate of overall participation, it is clear that they are far from having the highest. There is therefore
room for Japan to increase its labor inputs from this source. Furthermore,
Japanese women are more likely to work part-time (defined as less than
thirty-five hours per week) than most of their counterparts elsewhere.
There are a number of reasons why these situations exist.

Women are more likely to exit the labor force for child rearing or other
family responsibilities and later return to the labor force. This exit and re-
entry results in the M-curve pattern of labor force participation rates. The
M-curve has flattened since the early 1990s but as figure 8.1 shows, the mass

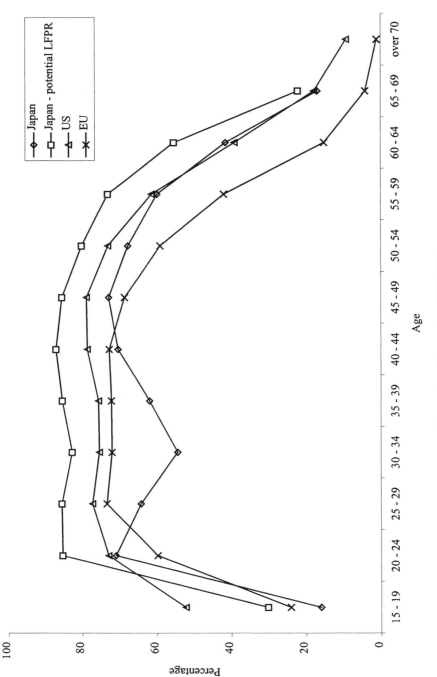

Fig. 8.1   Labor force participation rates by age cohort, selected countries, 1997–1999

Source: Japan, Statistics Bureau (1999); the United States and the European Union, International Labour Organization (2000).

exit of women in their thirties continues to be a pronounced pattern in international comparisons.

However, the proportion of women who want to work but cannot also is highest among the thirties age group. When this proportion is included in the actual participation rates, we obtain a curve that resembles Western counterparts. This curve, known as the potential participation rate curve, has received considerable attention in policy circles concerned with Japanese women's requirements for reconciling work and family life. The potential participation rates provide an upper bound of the number of women who could be employed under conditions where various institutional barriers have been removed. For example, Osawa (1998), citing results from the 1992 *National Survey on Lifestyle Preferences,* reports that actual participation will resemble potential participation if the proportion of women who would work under conditions of reliable child care facilities are included.

Another feature concerns the growth in part-time employment. As figure 8.2 shows, the proportion of women in regular employment has changed little since 1965. However, there has been a remarkable transition from the informal sector (self-employed and family workers) to part-time employment. This is attributable mainly to changes in industrial structure—a decline in agricultural employment and family-run work, a rise in work opportunities in firms (Nagase 1997), and a relative improvement of female wages (Shimada and Higuchi 1985).

Women's working patterns are better understood by first accounting for their nonmarket activities. Although expectations and attitudes concerning traditional gender division of labor are declining, Japanese women still face pressure to remain full-time mothers for children under school age and must maintain flexible work patterns to accommodate their nonmarket responsibilities. The Japanese government is attempting to change this situation through measures such as the New Angel Plan, which includes expansion of child care arrangements (MHLW 2001, 248–51).

Compounding these supply-side problems are demand-side impediments, such as the difficulty women face in being hired into the internal labor market and disincentives stemming from the unintended consequences in the tax and benefit system.

8.7   Exclusion from Internal Labor Market

Both men and women face problems if they change firms or leave the labor market for a time. Women are far more likely to temporarily leave the labor force. Japanese firms, especially the more desirable employers, typically create an internal labor market. This involves extensive training within the firm that presumes a long-term relationship between workers and employers. Employers thus seek workers who plan to remain with the

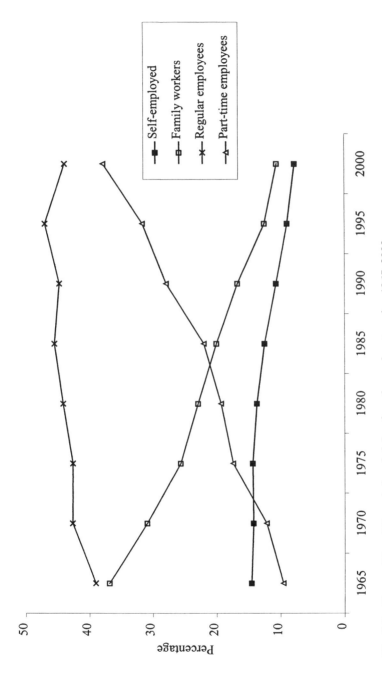

Fig. 8.2   Composition of Japan's female labor force by work categories, 1965–2000

Note: Part-time employees are those working less than thirty-five hours per week.

firm over a long period, so that the costs of their investments will not be lost. Because women are more likely to exit for reasons of marriage or child rearing, they face statistical discrimination (Brinton 1989). High-status positions in the seniority system are awarded to workers with long-standing tenure, so few women reach the upper echelons. Moreover, although Japanese women may enter large firms in equal proportions to men, only a very small proportion of the women even enter career-track positions. It is not that there has been a glass ceiling in Japan, it is that there has not even been a ladder.

The common route for women is to re-enter the labor force as part-time workers. Women who re-enter the market tend to find employment in smaller firms. In fact, Saso (1990) explains that older Japanese women are much more concentrated than young women in small firms and unskilled blue-collar occupations. Better educated married women with children are more likely to remain nonparticipants, other things being equal. This may be because the available jobs are not interesting or otherwise attractive to such women, who may prefer to develop nonmarket (leisure) activities.

Using census data for Japan and the United States, Brinton and Ngo (1993) estimate the index of gender segregation for the two countries in two occupational categories—managers/administrators and unskilled blue-collars. They find that segregation is greater in Japan among managers/administrators, and the segregation is greater among older age groups in Japan, while it remains stable across all age groups in the United States. Among unskilled blue-collar occupations, segregation is greater in the United States, and while it decreases with age in Japan, it increases with age in the United States.

These findings are consistent with the M-curve pattern of labor force participation among Japanese women. The likelihood of their placement into the internal labor market at the port of entry is lower than men's, but their attrition rate is even greater, as large numbers of women exit the labor force for family duties. When they re-enter, they do so into unskilled occupations. This pattern of labor mobility results in higher gender segregation among management occupations and lower gender segregation among unskilled occupations for older workers.

8.8   Tax and Benefit Systems

The structure of tax and benefit schemes distorts the labor supply behavior of married women in part-time employment. For example, the second earned income is treated in such a way that the after-tax income of some households may actually decline if the second income exceeds the limit (usually around ¥1 million per year). (Tax exempt status and pension benefits for spouses are not gender specific in Japan but we refer only to women, as we are analyzing their impact on married women in general and secondary wage earners in particular.)

In general, the schemes originally were introduced to protect married women from declines in household income when they moved from market work to household work. However, because they rest on the implicit assumption that married women should remain as full-time housewives, the unintended consequences of such "policies to protect full-time housewives" (Higuchi 1995) have come under severe scrutiny amidst increasingly diversifying patterns of women's employment. There is strong evidence that women in Japan adjust employment hours and annual income so as not to exceed the critical exemption levels (Horioka 1999).

As a good basis for discussion, table 8.4 presents 1990 and 2001 surveys that examine how employment patterns of married women in part-time positions are affected by taxes and benefits. An increasing number of respondents—36 percent in 1990 and 49 percent in 2001—adjusted their employment level in response to these policies. Moreover, 70 percent of the wives of salaried workers responded that they would increase their work hours if these policies were removed. (*National Survey on Lifestyle Preferences,* as cited in Nagase 2001). Clearly, the proportion of women who withhold labor as a consequence of such policies is not negligible.

The following discussion focuses on three factors—the tax exempt status of spouses, social security programs, and fringe benefits provided by employers—and examines how they may constitute disincentives to married women's employment. A noteworthy pattern observed across the three factors is that the adjustments in labor supply are more pronounced among educated women (Abe and Ohtake 1997; Higuchi 1995). There are three principal explanations for this. First, education is positively correlated with wages, so highly educated women reach the critical level of earnings

Table 8.4   Reasons Married Women in Part-Time Positions Gave for Adjusting Income

Reason for adjusting annual income	1990[a]	2001[b]
Any reason	35.7	49.1
To avoid paying income tax[c]	30.0	27.8
To avoid exceeding tax exempt and special tax exempt status for spouses	23.5	32.6
To receive fringe benefits from spouse's employer	12.0	15.7
So health insurance and pension covered by spouse	11.5	30.5
So spouse's employer will not find out that I am working	0.8	1.4
To avoid paying unemployment insurance	2.0	7.5

Note: Multiple answers were allowed

[a]*General Survey on Part-time Workers Condition* conducted by the MOL, as cited in Higuchi (1995).

[b]Recruit Works Institute (2001a).

[c]The *General Survey* also asked this question in two other forms: "I plan in advance so that my annual income will not exceed ¥1 million" (which is the usual tax-exemption) was checked by 16.2 percent of respondents and "I adjust my work patterns throughout the year so that my annual income will not exceed ¥1 million" by 13.8 percent.

more quickly than less educated women. Second, highly educated women have better knowledge of the lower and upper bounds of various exemptions and respond more sensitively. Third, wives' education is positively correlated with husbands' education (hence higher husbands' earnings), so they may have less incentive to work. Whatever the reasons, such an incentive structure depresses the rate of return to education for women, and discourages the younger generation of women from pursuing higher education.

8.8.1   Tax Code

The income tax code in Japan has undergone several revisions in the postwar period. The 1950 revision introduced a system that placed the tax burden on individual income instead of household income. However, because the per capita disposable income of a household declines as the number of dependents increases, the system also introduced exemptions for part of spousal income. In the latest version, introduced in 1988, spouse's income was tax exempt up to ¥700,000 annually, after which for each ¥50,000 incremental increase in income, the exemption decreased ¥50,000, so the exemption became zero at ¥1.4 million. This was an improvement compared to its predecessor because it eliminates kinks or discontinuities in (after-tax) household budgets. Still, even with the revisions, the marginal tax rate for households is higher when the spouse's income is between ¥1 million and ¥1.35 million, than when it is over ¥1.35 million.

Using the *General Survey on Part-Time Workers Conditions,* Abe and Ohtake (1997) examine the labor force participation rates of married women in part-time positions as a function of their annual earnings and show that the distribution is concentrated around the ¥1 million mark, with a significant drop in participation for earnings over that. Nagase (2001) shows similar results using monthly (not annual) income. Abe and Ohtake furthermore show that the distribution of work-hours becomes a bimodal distribution when adjusted for hourly wages, with spikes concentrated around the hours where the budget constraints are discontinuous. An increase in wages implies that workers reach the ceiling more quickly, so the consequence is that workers work less hours. In other words, there is no incentive for married women to increase their supply of labor under the current system.

There also is ample evidence that nonconvexities in the household budget distort the labor supply of women. Higuchi (1995) and Osawa (1993) present theoretical discussion of the impact of tax exemption schemes on women's labor supply before and after the revision of 1988.

8.8.2   Benefits and Pensions

Features of the social security system have been criticized for causing distortions in the labor supply of women. Under the current system, contributions to health insurance and public pensions are exempt for spouses provided that employment hours do not exceed 75 percent of hours worked by regular full-time workers and annual income does not exceed ¥1.3 million. (The physically challenged and workers over sixty can earn ¥1.8 million.) In addition, contributions to unemployment insurance are not required of a spouse with an annual income less than ¥900,000 who works less than twenty hours per week. Hatta and Kimura (1993) argue that the current pension system clearly favors households with full-time housewives, and that the removal of such "artificial barriers" to women's employment will encourage more women to seek full-time employment. The rise in regular employment will increase the base of pension payments and subsequently alleviate the current imbalance between payments and receipts in the pension system.

The labor supply of married women is furthermore constrained by the fringe benefits provided by their husband's companies. Abe and Ohtake (1997) suggest this is the most important barrier to married women earning more than ¥1 million per year. Higuchi (1995) reports that over 80 percent of Japanese companies provide fringe benefits for employee dependents (such as special benefits for families and children) averaging ¥9,300 per month in 1992, but 60 percent of the companies will terminate benefits if spousal income exceeds a certain level, usually around ¥1 million. The value of the benefit may not be substantial sum, but it affects the employment of 12 percent to 16 percent of married women (table 8.4).

8.9   Initiatives to Reconcile Work and Family Life

Under the Child Care Leave and Family Care Leave Law, child care leave became mandatory for enterprises with more than thirty employees, and family care leave became mandatory for all enterprises. Employees receive 25 percent of their wages while on leave. Despite this, a mere 0.6 percent of male workers took child care leave following the birth of a child in 2002, and this ratio has remained unchanged since 1997 (MHLW as cited in "Dansei no ikkyuu susumanu shocho" [No advances in child care leave among men in the ministries], *Nihon Keizai Shimbun* [Tokyo], 18 November 2002). The vast majority who take leave are women. Some 70 percent of women quit instead of taking maternity leave, citing reasons such as "it was not the right climate at work" (from the 1996 *National Survey on Family Planning,* cited in Breslin 1997, 292).

Companies that have re-employment schemes in which former employees are hired back receive subsidies to facilitate re-employment of women. The system is beneficial to both workers and employers insofar as it allows recovery of previous investment in employer-specific skills (Imada 1998). However, the proportion of companies that have the system stood at just 21 percent in 1996. Moreover, the system is subject to numerous terms and conditions. For example, only 14 percent of these firms will re-employ their returnees as regular employees. In short, the current system does not offer particularly promising prospects for women who seek re-employment.

The presence of small children dramatically reduces Japanese women's labor supply (Hill 1989; Nagase 1997; Ogawa and Ermisch 1996), to a degree beyond that witnessed in Western societies. For example, Tsuya, Bumpass, and Choe (2000) show that the percentage of wives employed among households with preschool age children is 37 percent in Japan and 58 percent in the United States. Studies have shown that maternity leave policies and access to child care facilities increase women's job continuity (with the same employer) or re-entry into the labor force (Nakamura and Ueda 1999). In particular, Higuchi, Abe, and Waldfogel (1997) show that child care leave had a positive and significant effect on married-woman job continuity in Japan, the United States, and United Kingdom, but the marginal effect was found to be largest in Japan. Although the number of women who take advantage of child care leave may be small, the authors argue that their findings are encouraging. They conclude that what is required is not only for companies to install child care policies, but to ensure an environment that allows workers to take advantage of such policies.

In response to growing worker demands, some Japanese companies have introduced family-friendly policies or measures that help employees reconcile the claims of work and family life (Sato 2000). Flexible working schedules, subsidies for the costs of family care, and provision of child care facilities in the workplace are common forms of these policies. The policies are a private initiative, but the MHLW has set up a system of awards for family-friendly firms to encourage their spread. The need for such policies is a high-priority issue in light of the changing values among Japanese workers. Survey results show that the proportion of men and women who support the traditional gender division of labor is rapidly decreasing, while the proportion of men and women who desire a balance between family and work is increasing. (Consider, e.g., the 1999 Nippon Hōsō Kyōkai (NHK) survey cited in Sato 2000.)

However, the implementation of family-friendly policies in Japanese firms remains limited. A MOL survey in 1997 (as cited in Sato 2000) found that 51 percent of Japanese firms had no family-friendly policies apart from the legal requirements. The survey also found great variation over firm size and industry, with large firms not surprisingly doing the most.[2]

2. The Ministry of Labor survey used a point scheme to tabulate the total number of points out of 24 family-friendly schemes installed by the employer. Close to 100 percent of establishments greater than 500 employees had installed some form of family-friendly policy averaging 11.7 points versus 44 percent and 3 points respectively among establishments with less than 30 employees, and over 95 percent of firms in finance and insurance had installed family-friendly policies averaging 7.8 points versus 40 percent and 1.5 points respectively in the construction industry (from the 1996 Survey on Women Workers' Employment Management, Women's Bureau, the Ministry of Labour, as cited in Sato 2000).

A common way for Japanese families to reconcile work and family life is to depend on extended family—that is, their children's grandparents (Morgan and Hirosima 1983). Empirical studies have found that coresidence with grandparents greatly increases the probability of women's entry into regular employment (Nagase 1997), and increases employment hours (Tsuya, Bumpass, and Choe 2000). However, it should be noted that the proportion of elderly in need of care is increasing, and the burden of care will likely fall on women (Ogawa and Ermisch 1996; Osawa 1990). Hence, reliance on grandparents to support women's work lives cannot be a long-term solution.

8.10   Quantifying the Barriers

Our approach to understanding the extent to which problems in the labor market are affecting economic growth is based on simple growth accounting and looks at the medium term. We look for unutilized (or underutilized) labor assets and assume that they can be moved into production evenly over a given period. This lets us know how much the *potential* growth of the labor input could be altered if the impediments to the supply of this labor were removed. The resulting figure can then be multiplied by labor's share of national output (roughly 70 percent in the Japanese case) to yield a potential increase in output to the economy. This contribution is a one-time increase but, for a fixed period, represents an increase in the potential growth rate. The calculation is necessarily crude and depends a lot on the assumptions behind the estimates of the amount of labor that is not being utilized. Still, this is a useful exercise to gain some idea of the scale of the losses experienced by the economy from labor market supply problems.

We divide losses into four categories. One is excess labor being carried by firms that are avoiding firing workers. We include in this category the extent to which employers are unable to dismiss workers whose productivity is low due to mismatch, although we do not treat them separately. The second is losses from factors that may be increasing the extent of mismatch in the economy and thereby raising the natural rate of unemployment. The third relates to women working part-time and the fourth to women not working at all.

8.10.1   Excess Labor

It is difficult to know the extent to which firms are carrying excess labor. The MHLW in its quarterly *Rōdō Keizai Dōkō Chōsa* (*Survey of Labor Economy*) reports the percentage of establishments surveyed that have surplus workers, as well as the percentage with labor shortages, for different industries and occupations. These are useful for understanding cyclical conditions and how they differentially affect different parts of the labor market, but they give no real sense of the size of the problem.

Japanese firms carry some employees on their payrolls who are sent home for spells, often on a rotating basis, during downturns. There are government subsidies in some cases to encourage firms to do this rather than dismiss the workers (Dore 1986). These individuals are addressed in the Labor Force Survey under a special category (*kyūgyōsha*) that includes all workers who are not at work on the survey day, including for illness or absenteeism. Hashimoto (1993) notes that the number of *kyūgyōsha* moves counter-cyclically and that adjustment in their number is generally less important than adjustment in hours and inventory as aspects of company reactions to the business cycle. The number of *kyūgyōsha* rose some 20 percent from 1989 to 2000, nowhere near the doubling of the unemployed. The increase represents some 200,000 employees, equal to 0.3 percent of total employment. This is a reasonable lower bound for the number of surplus workers in Japanese firms.

An approach for setting an upper bound is to look at figures for TFP growth and argue that slower TFP growth is due to labor hoarding during downturns. The 1990s were undoubtedly a period of slower TFP growth, as was the mid-1970s following the first oil shock. Hayashi and Prescott (2002) calculate, after taking account of working hours, that TFP grew at 3.7 percent between 1983 and 1991 and then at only 0.5 percent between 1991 and 2000. They calculate that capital deepening increased during the 1990s from the 1980s, so it is unlikely that any drop in TFP growth could be attributed to a drop in the rate of investment. If all of the drop is attributed to excess labor being held in firms, we see a loss of 3.2 percent in the potential growth rate, assuming that this surplus labor could have been reemployed productively elsewhere. This is unlikely, as it would imply that almost a quarter of the labor force was surplus to firms' needs by the end of the decade.

Still, if we assume that if firms were able to dismiss workers more easily, the economy could reach the OECD average for TFP growth per annum during 1979–1997 of 1.1 percent, then surplus labor kept in firms lowers TFP growth by up to 0.6 percent per year. (In practice, the effect would be smaller because the reallocated labor would lose much of its job-specific human capital.) This implies that the quantity of surplus labor currently is around 5 percent of the employed, about the same as the number of unemployed. This number often is quoted in press accounts, although it is unclear where reporters get their figures. We take it as the upper bound for the number of redundant workers in Japanese firms.

8.10.2   Skill Mismatch

The problem of skill mismatch and the outward shift of the Beveridge curve was discussed earlier. The 2000 Labor White Paper uses time series of the unemployment rate and the vacancy rate to estimate that the natural rate of unemployment has risen from just over 2.0 percent to 3.5

percent since 1993 (MOL 2000a). This is attributed mainly to structural change, particularly the decline in manufacturing, although aging of the work force is undoubtedly also part of the explanation. Using the result of the MOL, we attribute a loss of 1.5 percent in overall labor input to the mismatch problem in the labor market.

8.10.3 Female Labor Supply

We measure losses from barriers to the supply of women's labor as being losses from women working part-time and from women not participating in the labor force at all. We use the United States as a benchmark to estimate the extent to which labor market institutions reduce labor force participation. If Japan raised the participation rate of women from its level of 67 percent to the U.S. level of 77 percent, there would be an increase of about 15 percent in the female labor force input.

Japanese women put in around one hundred thirty-six hours per month, which is 82 percent of the one hundred sixty-five hours averaged by men. If employed Japanese women all worked as many hours as the men, they would increase their labor input by 21 percent. This is grossly unrealistic because some of these women are young and attending school; many would prefer to stay home with small children, even if child care is available; and many have household duties, including caring for elderly relatives, that take up much of their available time. However, it does serve as an upper bound for the effects of impediments that restrict hours of work. A plausible lower bound for the effect of disincentives to working full-time comes from Higuchi (1995). He estimates that married women who deliberately constrain their hours because of the tax and benefits system lower the overall labor input of women by 1.4 percent.

For our estimate of the contribution of impediments that encourage part-time work, we look at what would happen if the rate at which women twenty-five to sixty-four in Japan worked part-time was at the U.S. level (20 percent) rather than its actual 42 percent. (Women younger than twenty-five are excluded because many are still in school. Women over sixty-four are more likely to wish to work part-time regardless of impediments to working full-time.) Japanese women twenty-five to sixty-four work about half as many hours as their full-time counterparts. If 50 percent of them worked full-time, this would increase the female labor input by roughly 10 percent.[3]

Adding the two effects (and compounding), gives a total increase in the labor input of women of 26.5 percent. In terms of the overall labor force, this is an increase of around 11 percent. This figure is slightly smaller if ad-

---

3. Computed as the share of women working part-time multiplied by the share of hours of full-time women worked by part-time women multiplied by the share of women switching from part- to full-time work: $0.4 \cdot 0.5 \cdot 0.5 = 0.1$.

justed for quality. (Experience is an important component of quality and, on average, female workers have less of it than male workers.)

8.10.4   Overall Implications for Economic Growth

Table 8.5 summarizes the calculations. The results are intended to give some idea of how much of an impediment to economic growth the factors mentioned might be. Output might be increased by between 9 percent and 12 percent. This is approximately equal to a 1 percent increase in the potential growth rate of the economy over a ten-year period. This is, of course, only a one-time benefit that the Japanese economy could exploit, but it is hardly a negligible one.

One question that naturally arises is why the impediments to the mobility of male employees that we examined have not been a problem in the past. In fact, many of the institutions, including the strong protection of regular employees and the personnel management system, have previously been analyzed by many observers as great strengths (Koike 1988). Our argument is that these institutions have been successful under the strong demand conditions that characterized the macroeconomy in Japan up to the 1990s, but they have not been successful under stagnant demand thereafter.

Aging of the work force also means that Japanese personnel practices are in need of reform, but change has been slow so far (Ariga, Brunello, and Ohkusa 2000). Under these conditions, institutions which were well suited to a high-demand, moderate-to-rapid growth environment may become problematic. This is one area where better theoretical understanding of institutions under different growth environments is needed.

Table 8.5	Effect on Labor Input and Economic Output from Changes in the Labor Market (%)	
Factor	Labor Input	Economic Output[a]
Reduce excess labor held by firms	0.3–5.0	0.2–3.5
Reduce skill mismatch	1.5	1.1
Increase women's hours[b]	4.1	2.9
Increase women's participation[b]	6.2	4.3
Total[c]	12.8–17.5	9.0–12.2

Note: As explained in the text these are one-time effects that would be spread out over several years.

[a]Computed as the increase in labor input (stub column) times labor's share of output (70 percent).

[b]Computed by multiplying the figures in the text by the proportion of women in the labor force (41 percent).

[c]The effect of the two contributions concerned with women are compounded in calculating the total.

8.11   Role of Government Policy

Given that impediments to potential growth exist, how can government policy address them? We are unable to quantify the extent to which government actions may be able to address the issues raised here, but we can distinguish those areas where appropriate government policy should be able to increase effective labor inputs into the economy.

Table 8.6 provides a summary look at the role that government policy could play. Many of these policies are already being introduced or are under discussion in government deliberative councils. Looking at the mobility of male employees, it is clear that government legislation can change the nature of employment protection given employees. If the costs of dismissal can be reduced for employers, then this should release labor for more productive use. As suggested by Ohtake (2001), revision of the laws governing fixed-term employment should make it easier for employers to hire workers without making indefinite commitments to them. Both of these actions will undermine some of the loyalty of employees toward the firm, but this must be weighed against the demoralization felt by many employees who are not contributing much to the output of their firm.

There is probably not much that government policy can do to change the nature of personnel management in the Japanese firm, although it can continue to promote the development of defined-contribution pension schemes. In this area, government policy is moving in the right direction.

Barriers to midcareer hires are unlikely to be removed by government action. The prohibition of age limits in job advertisements is unlikely to have much effect on age discrimination, at least in the short run. Subsidies

Table 8.6   Government Policies to Reduce Labor Market Impediments to Growth

Labor market problem	Government Policy Measures
Employment protection	Legislation to reduce the cost of dismissals
Seniority pay structures and egalitarian pay norms	No measures
Pension portability	Encourage defined-contribution plans
Information problems in the job market	Further deregulation of the employment placement industry
Barriers to midcareer hires	Lead by example in the public sector
Government tax and benefit policies that discourage female labor supply	Abolish the exemption for dependent spouses and reform the benefit system to encourage greater participation of women
Female career interruptions during childbearing years	Encourage family-friendly workplaces with day care provision and re-employment for women who take short career breaks

to encourage midcareer employment have been tried in the past and are too blunt a tool: They may well be taken up by firms that plan to hire middle-aged and older workers anyway. The development of new career paths that can be entered by middle-aged men and women is something that firms will need to develop though their own action. The government may be able to play a useful role, however, by leading through example in its own employment policies.

The government is working at improving information provision in the labor market, but continued deregulation of the employment placement industry should help to change the environment. The government can play a leading role in the development of a more open environment for information through example, by making its own activities more transparent.

Much is already being done by the government to promote family-friendly policies at firms and to develop day care provisions so that women can remain at work. The government is contemplating major reform of the income tax system that will abolish many of the features that discourage women from participating or working longer hours ("Haigusha Kujowa Shukushō mata wa Haishi wo Fukuda Kanbō Chōkan" [General Secretary Fukuda Says That the Tax Exemption for Spouses Should Be Reduced or Abolished] *Asahi Shimbun*, 16 May 2002; available at http://www.asahi.com/politics/reform/security/K200205160307071.html.

8.12 Conclusion

This chapter has examined a number of personnel practices, laws, and regulations that lower the supply of labor in Japan. Broadly speaking, there are two kinds of impediments: those that restrict the movement of labor between firms and those that discourage women from participating to a greater extent. There has been a symmetric *lack* of information between employers and job seekers, and this is almost certainly due to the poor development of the external labor market in an economy with overall low mobility. It has been quite difficult for a worker over thirty to find attractive job opportunities. This is especially true for women re-entering the labor force. For married women, barriers also include disincentives in the tax system and the dearth of meaningful work, especially for women re-entering the labor force after rearing children. Despite changes, further modifications in the legal structure and practices of Japan's employment system are necessary to facilitate the diversifying patterns of employment and work attitudes of both men and women. Using other OECD countries and especially the United States as a benchmark, we estimate that removal of these barriers would increase the productive labor supply in Japan by 13 percent to 18 percent and thus could raise the potential growth rate of the Japanese economy by roughly 1 percent a year over a ten-year period.

There are a number of empirical and theoretical areas where further work is needed. First, we need to know more about the real extent of surplus labor within firms. This requires more detailed surveys of individual firms than have been carried out. Second, regarding midcareer hires and their pay, research is needed beyond the qualitative studies done by the government, especially concerning actual pay levels. Longitudinal data on individuals are needed to see who manages to make a midcareer move successfully. Third, further research in the area of labor market problems and social norms would help us better understand why certain features, such as egalitarian pay norms and firm-size differentials, are more persistent than others.

A better theoretical understanding of the way in which institutions that function well during periods of normal or rapid growth may become liabilities when growth is stagnant is especially important. The role of the family and of state policy and their effect on female labor supply during periods of rapid social change needs to be better understood. This could be usefully looked at in an international comparative perspective, especially southern European countries where women also have had less of a role in the labor market in the past but are now increasing participation.

Although changes to overcome some of the barriers, such as the poor provision of information in the labor market, are being promoted by government and business leaders, many other changes require broader transformation of the Japanese economy. As Noguchi (1995) has pointed out, Japanese economic policy is still based to a large extent on the premise that much of the security and welfare of individuals in the economy will be provided through their employers. Japanese labor law (as developed through case law), industrial policy, and financial regulation have been based on this assumption.

Policy makers and regulators in areas other than labor will need to change their approach for the full benefits of any change in labor regulations to be realized. The large-scale restructuring that is required if Japan is to continue to shift away from manufacturing and reduce the size of its construction industry also requires a shift toward increasing provision of security through private or state-provided insurance. This in turn may have the effect of introducing a different set of inefficiencies, including an increased rate of unemployment and earlier retirement. Policies will need to be designed carefully if this kind of outcome is to be avoided.

References

Abe, Yukiko, and Fumio Ohtake. 1997. The effects of income tax and social security on the part-time labor supply in Japan. *Review of Social Policy* 6:45–64.

Ariga, Kenn, Giorgio Brunello, and Yasushi Ohkusa. 2000. *Internal labour markets in Japan.* Cambridge: Cambridge University Press.

Baron, James N. 1988. The employment relation as a social relation. *Journal of the Japanese and International Economies* 2:492–525.

Breslin, M. 1997. Japanese women want more children than their total fertility rate suggests. *Family Planning Perspectives* 29:291–92.

Brinton, Mary C. 1989. Gender stratification in contemporary Japan. *American Sociological Review* 54:549–64.

Brinton, Mary C., and Hang-Yue Ngo. 1993. Age and sex in the occupational structure: A United States-Japan comparison. *Sociological Forum* 8:93–111.

Chuma, Hiroyuki. 1997. Keizai-kankyō no henka to chūkō nensō no chōkinzokuka (The changing economic environment and the lengthening of seniority). In *Koyō kankō no henka to josei rōdō* (Changing employment customs and women's labor), ed. Hiroyuki Chuma and Terukazu Suruga, 47–114. Tokyo: Tokyo Daigaku Shuppankai.

———. 1998. Kaikoken ranyōhōri no keizaigaku (The economics of the legal principle of abuse of the right to dismissal). In *Kaishahō no keizaigaku* (The economics of company law), ed. Yoshio Miwa, Hideki Kanda, and Noriyuki Yanagawa, 425–51. Tokyo: Tokyo University Press.

Dekle, Robert. 2000. Demographic density, per-capita consumption, and the Japanese saving-investment balance. *Oxford Review of Economic Policy* 16 (2): 46–60.

Dore, Ronald. 1986. *Flexible rigidities: Industrial policy and structural adjustment in the Japanese economy, 1970–1980.* Stanford: Stanford University Press.

Genda, Yuji. 2001. *Shigoto no naka no aimai no fuan: Yureru wakamono no genzai* (Vague anxiety amidst work: the shaking world of youth today). Tokyo: Chūōkōron Shinsha.

Genda, Yuji, and Marcus Rebick. 2000. Japanese labour in the 1990s: Stagnation and stability. *Oxford Review of Economic Policy* 16 (2): 85–102.

Gordon, Andrew. 1985. *The evolution of labor relations in Japan: Heavy industry, 1853–1955.* Cambridge, Mass.: Harvard University Press.

———. 1998. *The wages of affluence: Labor and management in postwar Japan.* Cambridge, Mass.: Harvard University Press.

Granovetter, Mark S. 1974. *Getting a job: A study of contracts and careers.* Cambridge, Mass.: Harvard University Press.

Hashimoto, Masanori. 1993. Aspects of labor market adjustments in Japan. *Journal of Labor Economics* 11 (1): 136–61.

Hashimoto, Masanori, and Raisian, John. 1985. Employment tenure and earnings profiles in Japan and the United States. *American Economic Review* 75 (September): 721–35.

Hatta, Tatsuo, and Yoko Kimura. 1993. Kōteki nenkin wa sengyō shufu setai wo yūgū shiteiru (The Japanese public pension system favors households with full-time housewives). *Kikan Shakai Hoshô Kenkyû* (Quarterly of Social Security Research) 29:210–21.

Hayashi, Fumio, and Prescott, Edward. 2002. The 1990s in Japan: A lost decade. *Review of Economic Dynamics* 5:206–35.

Higuchi, Yoshio. 1995. Sengyō-shufu hogo seisaku no keizai-teki kiketsu (The economic consequences of policies to protect full-time housewives). In *Jakusha hogo seisaku no keizai bunseki* (Economic analysis of policies to protect the weak), ed. Tatsuo Hatta and Naohiro Yashiro, 185–219. Tokyo. Nihon Keizai Shimbunsha.

Higuchi, Yoshio, Masahiro Abe, and Jane Waldfogel. 1997. Nichi-bei-ou ni okeru ikuji kyūgyō shussan kyūgyō seido to josei shugyō (Childcare and maternity leave policies and women's employment in Japan, the United States, and the United Kingdom). *Jinkō Mondai Kenkyū* (Journal of Population Problems) 53:49–66.

Hill, M. Anne. 1989. Female labor supply in Japan. *Journal of Human Resources* 24:143–61.

Horioka, Charles Yuji. 1999. Japan's public pension system: What's wrong with it and how to fix it. *Japan and the World Economy* 11:293–303.

Ichinose, Tomohiro. 2001. Tenshoku ni yoru shōgai chingin no genshō to sōki taishoku yūgū seido (Early retirement plans and the decline in lifetime income resulting from job changes). *Rōsei Jihō* 3484:27–34.

Imada, Sachiko. 1998. Re-employing Japanese women: Female labor and sustained support. *Japan Labor Bulletin* 37 (June). Available at http://www.jil.go.jp.

Institute of Labor Administration. 2001. Sōki taishoku yūgū to kibō taishoku seido (Early retirement and voluntary retirement programs). *Rōsei Jihō* 3484:2–26.

International Labour Organization. 2000. *Year book of labour statistics.* Geneva: International Labour Office.

Japan Institute of Labor (JIL). 1998. Chūkōnensha no tenshoku jittai to koyō shokugyō tenbō (Employment outlook and state of job-changes among middle-age and older workers). *Japan Institute of Labour Report* 111. Tokyo: JIL.

———. 2000. 2000 survey on employment management: Managing of retiring older workers. *Japan Labor Bulletin* 39 (Oct). Tokyo: JIL.

———. 2001a. Guidelines to abolish age limits in the revised employment measures law. *Japan Labor Bulletin* 40 (November). Available at http://www.jil.go.jp.

———. 2001b. "Shitsugyō kōzō no kenkyū" (Structure of unemployment). *Japan Institute of Labour Report* 142. Tokyo: JIL.

Koike, Kazuo. 1988. *Understanding industrial relations in modern Japan.* London: Macmillan Press.

Mincer, Jacob, and Higuchi, Yoshio. 1988. Wage structures and labor turnover in the United States and Japan. *Journal of the Japanese and International Economies* 2:97–133.

Ministry of Economics, Trade, and Industry (METI) and Recruit Works Research Center. 2001. *Koyō no misumattchi no jittai bunseki* (Empirical analysis of mismatch in employment). Tokyo: METI and Recruit Works Research Center. Available at http://www.meti.go.jp/kohosys/press/0001722.remove597167316452/0/010719koyou.pdf.

Ministry of Health, Labour and Welfare (MHLW). 2001. *Kōsei rōdō hakusho* (White paper on welfare and labor). Tokyo: Gyōsei.

Ministry of Labor (MOL). 1998. *Sūji de miru koyō no ugoki* (Employment mobility survey). Tokyo: Ministry of Finance Publications.

———. 2000a. *Rōdō hakusho* (White paper on labor) Tokyo: Japan Institute of Labor.

———. 2000b. *Taishokukin seido no genjō to kadai* (The current situation and problems in the company pension system). Tokyo: Rōmu Gyōsei Kenkyusho.

———. 2000c. *Tenshokusha no jittai (heisei 10 nen chōsa)* (The current situation of job-changers—1998 survey) Tokyo: Ministry of Finance.

Morgan, S. Philip, and Kiyosi Hirosima. 1983. The persistence of extended family residence in Japan: Anachronism or alternative strategy? *American Sociological Review* 48:269–81.

Nagase, Nobuko. 1997. Wage differentials and labour supply of married women in Japan: Part-time and informal sector work opportunities. *Japanese Economic Review* 48:29–42.

———. 2001. Pāto no chingin ni 103 man en no kabe wa jūyoka (Is the upper limit of 1.03 million yen significant in determining a wage rate for part-timers?). *Japanese Journal of Labour Studies* 489:60–61.

Nakamura, Jiro, and Atsuko Ueda. 1999. On the determinants of career interruption by childbirth among married women in Japan. *Journal of the Japanese and International Economies* 13:73–89.

Nickell, Stephen J., Luca Nunziata, Wolfgang Ochel, and Glenda Quintini. 2001. The Beveridge curve, unemployment and wages in the OECD. In *Knowledge, information and expectations in modern macroeconomics: Papers in honor of Edmund S. Phelps,* ed. Phillipe Aghion, Roman Frydman, Joseph E. Stiglitz, and Michael Woodford. Princeton, N.J.: Princeton University Press.

Noguchi, Yukio. 1995. *1940 nen taisei: Saraba "senji keizai"* (The 1940 system: Japan under the wartime economy). Tokyo: Tōyō Keizai Shinpōsha.

Ogawa, Naohiro, and John F. Ermisch. 1996. Family structure, home time demands, and the employment patterns of Japanese married women. *Journal of Labor Economics* 14:677–702.

Ohta, Kiyoshi. 2000. Kokusai hikaku kara mita Nihon no shotoku kakusa (Income distribution in Japan from an international perspective). *Japanese Journal of Labour Studies* 480:33–40.

Ohtake, Fumio. 1998. The United States. In *Wage differentials: An international comparison,* ed. Toshiaki Tachibanaki, 108–144. London: Macmillan.

———. 2001. *Koyō mondai wo kangaeru* (Employment-related problems in Japan). Osaka: Osaka University Press.

Organization for Economic Cooperation and Development (OECD). 2001. *Employment outlook.* Paris: OECD.

Osawa, Machiko. 1990. Women's response to economic changes. *Japan Labor Bulletin* 29:5–8.

———. 1993. *Keizai henka to joshi rōdō* (Economic change and women's labor). Tokyo: Nihon keizai hyōronsha.

———. 1998. *Atarashii kazoku no tame no keizaigaku* (Economics for the new family). Tokyo: Chūō Kōron.

Rebick, Marcus. 1992. The persistence of firm-size earnings differentials and labor market segmentation in Japan. *Journal of the Japanese and International Economies* 7:132–56.

———. 1993. The Japanese approach to finding jobs for older workers. In *As the workforce ages: Costs, benefits, and policy challenges,* ed. Olivia Mitchell, 103–24. Ithaca, N.Y.: ILR Press.

———. 2001. Japanese labor markets: Can we expect significant change? In *Japan's new economy: Continuity and change in the twenty-first century,* ed. Magnus Blomström, Byron Gagnes and Sumner La Croix, 120–41. Oxford: Oxford University Press.

Recruit Works Institute. 2001a. *Hi-tenkei koyō rōdōsha chōsa 2001—Shufu pāto taima* (Nonstandard employment survey—Married women in part-time employment). Tokyo: Recruit.

———. 2001b. *Working persons chosa 2000—Shutoken* (Working persons survey 2000—The greater Tokyo area). Tokyo: Recruit.

Rees, Albert. 1966. Information networks in labor markets. *American Economic Review* 56:559–66.

Saso, Mary. 1990. *Women in the Japanese workplace.* London: H. Shipman.

Sato, Hiroki. 2000. The current situation of "family-friendly" policies in Japan. *Japan Labor Bulletin* 39 (February): 5–10.

Shimada, Haruo, and Yoshio Higuchi. 1985. An analysis of trends in female labor force participation in Japan. *Journal of Labor Economics* 3:S355–74.

Shirahase, Sawako. 2002. Nihon no shotoku kakusa to kōreishasetai (A study of income inequality and households with the elderly in Japan: A cross-national comparison with industrial nations). *Japanese Journal of Labour Studies* 500:72–85.

Statistics Bureau, Ministry of Public Management, Home Affairs and Posts and Telecommunications. Various years. *Labor Force Survey Annual Report.* Tokyo: Japan Statistical Association.

Tachibanaki, Toshiaki. 1998. Introduction to *Wage differentials: An international comparison,* ed. Toshiaki Tachibanaki. London: Macmillan.

Tachibanaki, Toshiaki, and Ohta, Souchi. 1994. Wage differentials by industry and the size of firms, and the labour market in Japan. In *Labour market and economic performance: Europe, Japan and the U.S.,* ed. Toshiaki Tachibanaki, 56–92. London: Macmillan.

Tsuya, Noriko O., Larry L. Bumpass, and Minja Kim Choe. 2000. Gender, employment, and housework in Japan, South Korea, and the United States. *Review of Population and Social Policy* no. 9:195–220.

Watanabe, Shin. 1992. Tenshoku hōhō (Job change methods). *Soshiki Kagaku* 25 (4): 72–84.

Yamakawa, Ryuichi. 1998. Overhaul after 50 years: The amendment of the labour standards law. *Japan Labor Bulletin* 37:11.

Yamakawa, Ryuichi, and Araki, Takashi. 2001. Rōdō hanrei kono 1 nen no sōten (Labor law precedents 1999–2000: The issues involved). *Japanese Journal of Labour Studies* 496:2–37.

Yashiro, Naohiro. 1999. *Koyō kaikaku no jidai: Hatarakikata wa dō kawaru ka?* (The age of employment reform: How will our ways of work change?). Tokyo: Chūkōshinsho.

9

An International Perspective of Corporate Groups and Their Prospects

Yishay Yafeh

Academic and popular views of the *keiretsu*, as postwar Japanese corporate groups are sometimes called, range from complete dismissal to admiration of their influence, whether it is alleged to enhance economic growth or to restrict entry into the Japanese market. During the 1990s, cross-shareholding arrangements within groups and ties between ailing financial institutions and their client firms have often been mentioned as potential impediments to structural change, especially with respect to the introduction of market-based means of corporate finance and governance.

The present chapter has three objectives. The first is to review the literature on corporate groups in Japan and elsewhere, summarizing the evidence on the economic roles (if any) corporate groups have played in the Japanese economy. The second objective is to present, for the first time, a comparison of Japanese groups and corporate groups in other developed and developing countries. The main conclusion emerging from this comparison is that Japanese groups, while similar to groups elsewhere in some respects, are different in their risk and return characteristics. The third ob-

Yishay Yafeh is senior lecturer, School of Business Administration and Department of East Asian Studies, the Hebrew University, and associate professor, Department of Economics, University of Montreal.

This essay was written during visits to the Saïd Business School and the Nissan Institute, University of Oxford, and to the Eitan Berglas School of Economics, Tel Aviv University, whose hospitality is gratefully acknowledged. I am extremely grateful to Masaharu Hanazaki of Hitotsubashi University and to Hideaki Miyajima of Waseda University for assistance in gaining access to Japanese data sources, to Colin Mayer for the industry growth data, and to Nao Saito and Anat Tamir for research assistance. I am also grateful to Larry Meissner, Sumner la Croix, the editors of this volume, and participants of the National Bureau of Economic Research (NBER) Structural Impediments to Growth in Japan conference for helpful comments and suggestions.

jective is to describe the evolution of Japan's groups since the mid-1970s and to examine whether or not groups constitute an impediment to structural change in Japan.

With some exceptions, there is limited evidence of the economic importance of corporate groups in postwar Japan. There is also little to suggest that groups have had a major impact on growth rates of particular industries, and no evidence that Japanese groups (unlike those in other countries) enjoy any particular political clout. It is therefore unlikely that corporate groups will constitute an impediment to structural change.

Powerful, family-controlled, pyramidal groups (*zaibatsu*) existed in Japan from the late nineteenth century to just after World War II. Our focus here, however, is on corporate groups in postwar Japan. These are usually divided into two types. The first consists of firms operating in many industries with large financial institutions (a city bank, a trust bank, and insurance companies) at the core. These are variously termed horizontal, financial, or bank-centered groups. There are six major groups of this type, three with *zaibatsu* roots.

The second type consists of a large manufacturer and related suppliers within the same industry or in closely related sectors. These are often described as vertical or manufacturer-centered groups. Examples include Toyota or Hitachi.

The discussion here focuses mostly on bank-centered groups. First, I review the literature on corporate groups in general, and then evaluate the empirical evidence on the economic importance of Japan's corporate groups. I then make a cross-sectional comparison between Japanese corporate groups and those in other countries, and describe the evolution of groups in Japan over time, including their prospects.

9.1   Identifying Corporate Groups

The criteria used to define the boundaries of a group and to identify members vary considerably across countries and studies (Khanna 2000). In most countries, including Japan, membership is typically informal. (Exceptions include Italy, where the law identifies "common control" [see Bianchi, Bianco, and Enriques 2001], and Chile, where groups are legal entities.)

Still, the literature has struggled to provide a definition—or at least definitions—for each country. Leff (1978, 673) put forward "a group of companies that does business in different markets under a common administrative or financial control," but this is clearly inappropriate in postwar Japan, where groups lack common control. Strachan (1976) defines a group as a long-term association of firms and the people who own and manage them, and points out that a group cannot be identified purely on the basis of a single metric. The criteria used to identify membership in

Japanese groups have mostly been based on measures of long-term relations among member firms.

9.1.1 Origins of Japanese Groups

The prewar and wartime economy of Japan was dominated by large, diversified conglomerates (*zaibatsu*). At war's end the four major *zaibatsu* represented about a quarter of paid-in capital and much larger shares in finance and heavy industries (Hoshi and Kashyap 2001, 69, box 3.5; Hadley 1970). The *zaibatsu* were family-owned conglomerates, controlled through holding companies that in turn held a large number of shares in a first tier of subsidiaries. First-tier subsidiaries controlled a second tier of companies, and so forth, forming a pyramid of firms. Horizontal ownership and personnel ties between group firms were also common.[1]

Following Japan's defeat in 1945, the U.S. occupation authorities (Supreme Commander for the Allied Powers [SCAP]) regarded the *zaibatsu* as an important part of the Japanese social and economic structure that was responsible for the war. In particular, the market power of the *zaibatsu* and the tremendous wealth of the founding families made the dissolution of the conglomerates one of the first and most important targets of the Allied Occupation reforms.

The *zaibatsu* dissolution reforms started soon after the end of the war and ended around 1950. The holding companies were dismantled and new ones prohibited by law, the founding families were stripped of their shares, and many of the incumbent managers were purged and barred from corporate office. The resulting change of ownership was of enormous scale: Some estimates suggest that over 40 percent of all corporate assets in Japan changed hands (Bisson 1954). The shares transferred were resold by the Holding Companies Liquidation Commission (HCLC) using several methods designed to guarantee dispersion of ownership structure (see Hadley 1970, 181–87). Indeed, following the conclusion of the reforms, shareholding by individuals in Japan reached an all time high of approximately 70 percent around 1949 (Aoki 1988).

Despite the hopes of the Occupation, the newly created ownership structure proved unstable. With the reopening of the Tokyo Stock Exchange in 1949, individuals who received shares during the reforms (especially company employees and residents of cities where the companies operated) began to sell, and individual shareholding began to decline. By the early 1950s a new ownership structure had emerged: Most companies were owned by other companies and by financial institutions, most notably large commercial banks ("city banks").

---

1. Okazaki (2001) argues that the *zaibatsu* were not powerful enough to dominate the Japanese economy before the start of World War II, but during the war they increased market power and played an important role in providing military equipment and supplies to the Japanese Imperial Army.

Ownership ties were sometimes part of reciprocal cross-shareholdings, often along the lines of the former *zaibatsu* and especially among what had been the three largest: Mitsui, Mitsubishi, and Sumitomo (see Hoshi 1994; Yafeh 1995). These ties were further reinforced in the late 1960s, and "new" groups centered on major (city) banks were formed (Dai-Ichi Bank and Nippon Kangyo Bank, which later merged to form the Dai-Ichi Kangyo [DKB] group; Fuji; and Sanwa).

There are several possible reasons why the period of dispersed ownership was so short. Individuals may have been too poor and too risk averse to wish to hold equity, and preferred to increase their consumption or save in the form of bank accounts rather than hold shares.

Another reason asserted by many authors (e.g., Miyajima 1994) is that the reformed firms were exposed to hostile takeovers once their *zaibatsu* shareholders were removed. Low equity prices soon after the war are posited to have made Japanese firms easy targets. To prevent this, managers sought to establish a friendly, stable ownership structure dominated by firms associated with each other in the prewar period. However, it is not clear who the potential raiders could have been.

An alternative explanation for the short life of extensive individual ownership is simply that it was inefficient. Yafeh (1995) shows that, other things equal, the greater the percentage of a firm's outstanding shares expropriated and resold by the Occupation, the worse was the firm's performance in the early 1950s. This is consistent with the view that large shareholders play an important role in corporate governance (Shleifer and Vishny 1986). Concentrated family ownership did not reappear, apparently because the old wealth of the prewar period had been destroyed by the reforms.

The efficiency argument is less likely to explain the reinforcement of cross-shareholding in the 1960s. Then, some fear of hostile takeovers was plausible as Japan opened to foreign capital.

9.1.2   Who is a Group Member?

Unlike the prewar *zaibatsu*, postwar groups in Japan have no central control, and identifying affiliation with a group is not straightforward. Core members typically take part in presidents' clubs, which are regular meetings of senior executives. Members of these clubs are easy to identify and constitute about 10 percent of all listed manufacturing firms in Japan (Weinstein and Yafeh 1995).

Beyond the presidents' club, researchers have used a variety of measures to identify group members. Commonly used definitions are those of three major publications: Keizai Chosa Kyokai's *Keiretsu no Kenkyu,* Toyo Keizai's *Kigyo Keiretsu Soran,* and Dodwell Marketing Consultants' *Industrial Groupings in Japan.* These weigh various aspects of the relationship between a firm and other group members, most notably the extent and stability of cross-shareholding arrangements, and the extent and stability of credit and equity relations maintained with the group's main financial institutions. The frequency of personnel exchange appears to be a relatively less important component.

The existing weighting schemes (and the corresponding data sources) usually concur as far as the identification of core group members is concerned, but may differ considerably in defining the boundaries of groups. Thus, Weinstein and Yafeh (1995) find the correlation between the lists of members identified by different sources to be not very high, although all commonly used definitions suggest that group-affiliated companies constitute some 40 percent to 50 percent of all listed manufacturing firms. Gibson (1995), looking at bank-firm ties in the early 1990s without reference to groups, suggests that several plausible methods agree on the identity of the main bank of most companies, although his methodology is not designed for identifying members in bank-centered groups.

While credit relationships within groups are fairly easy to interpret, the prevalence and significance of equity ties is more controversial. The extent of equity ties reported by different sources varies with the group definition used. Mitsubishi and Sumitomo presidents' club member firms had around 25 percent of their equity held by other group firms in 1990, whereas the corresponding figures for other groups hover around 15 percent to 16 percent (Sheard 1997). Figures for non-presidents' clubs firms are typically substantially lower.

Most of the equity ties within the groups involve the group's financial institutions (banks and insurance companies). By contrast, equity ties between manufacturing firms are usually low (with equity stakes that are often less than 1 percent). The meaning of these ties, which are unusually stable in spite of their small size, has been harder to interpret (see Flath 1993; Miwa and Ramseyer 2001a; and further discussion below).

The empirical literature on Japan has often treated bank-firm relations and group affiliation as one and the same. To a great extent, this is because the available definitions of group affiliation focus on ties with the group's main bank. Thus, a large number of empirical studies actually rely on group data to suggest that long term bank-firm relationships may matter for corporate governance, mitigation of informational asymmetries between the firm and its financiers, and the resolution of financial distress. (On the Japanese main bank system, see Aoki and Patrick 1994; Hoshi and Kashyap 2001, especially chap. 4).

9.2   Reasons for Groups to Exist

The literature on corporate groups has so far not reached an agreement on the most important reasons for the ubiquity of groups around the world. This section therefore begins with an evaluation of positive explanations for the existence of groups (viewing them as efficient solutions to various market imperfections) and their relevance to Japan. It then proceeds to discuss negative views of corporate groups (such as political rent-seeking and expropriation of minority shareholders) and to examine their applicability to Japan.

9.2.1   Reducing Transaction Costs

Corporate groups may be important for reducing transaction costs associated with intragroup trade. Applying this idea to Japan, Flath (1993) argues that cross-shareholding arrangements help reduce moral hazard risks among trading partners, thus facilitating transaction-specific investments. Yet empirical evidence in support of this argument is rather scarce (Flath provides some), and it appears that the volume of intragroup trade within the bank-centered groups is rather low. Sheard (1997) estimates average intragroup sales at about 2 percent, excluding the group's general trading company, which accounts for another 6+ percent. Odagiri (1992, 182) reports that in 1981, on average, 20 percent of a group firm's sales and 12 percent of its purchases were within-group transactions.

By contrast, intragroup trade and transaction-specific investments may be a major factor explaining the structure and performance of manufacturer-centered (vertical) groups, where joint development of new products and just-in-time supply of inputs are crucial. Indeed, there is substantial evidence that manufacturer-centered groups combine insurance and incentives in a way that is designed to reduce hold-up problems through long-term relations without full vertical integration (Kawasaki and MacMillan 1987; Asanuma 1989; Fujimoto 1999).

9.2.2   Coordinating Investment

Groups may facilitate major investments by providing a mechanism for coordination across firms and industries. They may therefore be of help in orchestrating a "big push." Thus, Ohkawa and Rosovsky (1973) view the *zaibatsu* as an important component in prewar Japan's ability to absorb foreign technology, which could be spread across group members.

Goto (1982) argues that the reason groups are observed in a market economy like Japan is their ability to coordinate research and development (R&D) and new investments. A weaker formulation of this hypothesis is that groups share information about investment opportunities, even if group members carry out investment decisions independently. Although this is not impossible, this conjecture is hard to test empirically and has never been formally examined.

Systematic evidence on joint investments and R&D among members of Japan's postwar groups is not available. There is little in the literature on interfirm coordination in R&D and technology absorption to suggest that the bank-centered groups have played a particularly important role in this respect (although there is some evidence on the importance of vertical groups, for which, see Branstetter 2000; Okada 2001).

Montalvo and Yafeh (1994) find that group-affiliated firms signed more licensing agreements to import foreign technology into Japan in the late 1970s. There are several possible interpretations for this result, however. It is possible that group-affiliated firms enjoyed easy access to capital from financial institutions within the group. It is also possible that group firms signed more licensing contracts because they were less involved in independent R&D activity, perhaps as a result of pressure by the group's main bank to adopt low-risk investment strategies.

Using survey data from the late 1990s, Mayer, Schoors, and Yafeh (2002) note that venture capital funds in Japan often are owned by firms related to each other, as part of one of the groups or otherwise. They do not discuss the impact of this characteristic on fund performance.

9.2.3   Substituting for Missing Institutions

Khanna and Palepu (1999) suggest groups in India and other developing countries make up for missing institutions, such as those enforcing property rights, as well as markets for skilled labor, management, and capital. This, they argue, is a plausible explanation for the evidence of superior performance of group members in India and other emerging markets, especially when groups exceed a certain size (or diversification) threshold.

This extended suggestions in the early descriptive literature that groups made up most notably for imperfect capital markets (e.g., Leff 1978). Perotti and Gelfer (2001) argue that Russian financial-industrial groups (FIGs) manage an internal capital market that may add value in the face of inefficient external capital markets in that country. In addition, there is some evidence that internal capital markets in the Korean *jaebol* (i.e., business groups) create value (Chang and Hong 2000).

Applied to skilled labor and management, the missing-institution argument could perhaps be related to *zaibatsu*, which trained a generation of prewar Japanese executives, but it is more difficult to apply it to the postwar experience, and it is not supported by any Japan-specific study.

Applied to underdeveloped capital markets, the missing-institution argument is undermined by the absence of evidence indicating efficient allocation of capital within the Japanese corporate groups, whose growth rates and other measures of performance have not been superior to those of nongroup firms. Nevertheless, some relations between the postwar corporate groups and certain aspects of capital markets (risk sharing and corporate governance) are discussed below. In addition, Hoshi, Kashyap, and Scharsfetin (1990, 1991), argue that investment decisions of group-affiliated companies are less sensitive to their cash flow positions than investment decisions of nongroup firms, and also that some unnecessary bankruptcies are prevented within the groups. This could be viewed as evidence that groups do make up for some deficiencies of imperfect capital markets in the allocation of capital.

9.2.4   Providing Mutual Insurance

One function of capital markets that has been associated with corporate groups is the provision of mutual insurance opportunities for member firms. This idea originates in the literature on Japanese groups, where several studies suggest that groups provide an organizational mechanism through which risks are shared. A theoretical formulation of this hypothesis by Aoki (1988) suggests that employees with firm-specific human capital cannot easily protect themselves against adverse shocks and therefore appreciate risk reduction through firm relations with other firms within a corporate group, and especially with the group's main bank.

Nakatani (1984) provides empirical support for the claim that Japanese corporate groups provide a low-profit and low-volatility environment. Kashyap (1989) suggests that the low volatility of profits documented by Nakatani is a result of intragroup trade relations (and therefore is not a characteristic of final-good producers within the groups).

There is evidence on a particular form of risk sharing under the auspices of the main bank within the big-six groups, namely, assistance during financial distress. For example, Sheard (1989) documents a variety of cases in which banks rescued ailing clients, typically within their group and often with the assistance of other group members. Hoshi and Kashyap (2001, chap. 5) discuss bank interventions.

Weinstein and Yafeh (1998) argue that members of bank-centered Japanese groups adopt low-risk investment strategies, although the motivation for this behavior is, in their view, related not to risk sharing but to the (excessive) influence that the group bank and other creditors exert on group firms. Khanna and Yafeh (2001) conduct a battery of risk-sharing tests among corporate groups in Japan and elsewhere, and find consistent evidence for mutual insurance among member firms of Japanese (and Korean) corporate groups, in contrast with most of the other countries they examine.

Thus, while there is limited evidence on other possible economic roles of corporate groups in Japan, the risk-sharing hypothesis does enjoy some empirical support. Furthermore, this mutual insurance feature seems to distinguish Japanese groups from most corporate groups in emerging markets. The sociological literature has also emphasized risk sharing within Japan's corporate groups (e.g., Lincoln, Gerlach, and Ahmadjian 1996). But, the evidence on risk sharing within corporate groups in Japan has not been unchallenged (see Beason 1998; Kang and Stulz 2000; Miwa and Ramseyer 2001a, b). Further discussion on risk and return within groups is included below.

9.2.5   Corporate Governance

Another capital market function that has sometimes been associated with Japanese corporate groups is corporate governance. For example, group members are viewed as important in the theoretical corporate governance model of Berglof and Perotti (1994). Yet, overall, empirical support for the special role of groups in corporate governance appears to be limited. There is much evidence on the role of main banks, typically within corporate groups, in disciplining managers of distressed firms and in restructuring their operations (Yafeh 2000; Hoshi and Kashyap 2001). There is also some evidence on the role of large shareholders (often part of the group) in corporate governance, again mostly with respect to poorly performing companies (Kang and Shivdasani 1995, 1997). Yafeh and Yosha (2003) provide some evidence for the role of large shareholders in corporate governance in companies whose performance is normal. There is very little to suggest that corporate groups contribute to corporate governance beyond the roles played by the group banks and by large shareholders (although it is perhaps possible to argue that the group provides a framework in which main banks and large shareholders operate).

9.2.6   Monopoly Power

The fear that groups with deep pockets may drive more focused (smaller) competitors out of the market is not new, and was one of the motivations for the Occupation's dissolution of the *zaibatsu* (Yafeh 1995). While groups in some countries (e.g., Korea) do appear to dominate markets, the general evidence on the relation between market power and corporate groups is weak. Encaoua and Jacquemin (1982) find little evidence of monopolization by French groups. Lawrence (1993) argues that Japanese groups constitute a barrier to entry because they prefer to purchase inputs from other group members and thus restrict competition by foreign firms. The evidence on the limited extent of intragroup trade is inconsistent with this argument and, moreover, Lawrence's empirical evidence in support of this argument is not fully convincing (Saxonhouse 1993).

Weinstein and Yafeh (1995) use an industrial organization framework to examine the relation between the intensity of competition and the market share of Japanese bank-centered groups. They suggest that, if anything, group members tend to compete more aggressively than other firms; although fierce competition may well constitute a barrier to entry, there is no evidence of collusion among group members at the expense of outsiders.

9.2.7   Political Rent Seeking

As in prewar Japan, the origins of corporate groups and their initial growth in many countries were influenced by close ties with the government. The *zaibatsu* emerged in the 1880s as part of the Matsukata privatization of government-owned assets and expanded to a large extent through government contracts and procurement. Groups in India emerged after independence when businessman with government ties acquired assets that had belonged to the British. In Korea, the *jaebol* were formed under the auspices of the government and started off by using assets left at the end of the Japanese colonial period. Such close government ties have prompted accusations that corporate groups derive benefits from rent seeking and government favors, and are therefore inefficient. Fisman (2001) finds explicit evidence for this in Indonesia.

There are no studies linking postwar Japanese groups with corruption or specific government favors and contracts. Industrial policy was notoriously conducted at the industry level and no firm-specific subsidies were given (Johnson 1982). Corruption scandals have not involved group-affiliated firms more than other corporations, and corporate groups have never been mentioned as part of any political party's constituency. (For the ruling Liberal Democratic Party (LDP), these traditionally are thought of as being farmers, small shop owners, and perhaps the construction industry).

One measure of government-business ties in Japan is the practice of *amakudari*, the transfer of bureaucrats from the government to the private sector. Van Rixtel (2002) finds that firms within corporate groups are less likely to receive *amakudari* than other firms.

9.2.8   Expropriation of Minority Shareholders

A growing amount of literature has blamed corporate groups with the expropriation of minority shareholders. Claessens et al. (1999) argue that groups are associated with minority shareholder expropriation in Asia. Similarly, Johnson et al. (2000), as well as Bertrand, Mehta, and Mullainathan (2002), view groups as institutions that are associated with poor protection of property rights and enable "tunneling" of funds from minority shareholders to the controlling party. This argument is unlikely to be particularly relevant to Japan, most notably because Japanese groups do not have a controlling shareholder and also because, according to the commonly used La Porta et al. (1998) classification, the legal protection of minority shareholders in Japan is, by international standards, not bad. Even though some cases in which unhappy Japanese shareholders sued corrupt corporations have been reported in the press, there is little systematic evidence to suggest that group-affiliated firms in Japan are particularly prone to minority shareholder expropriation.[2]

---

2. In chapter six of this volume, Ando, Christelis, and Miyagawa observe that Japanese shareholders are in a weak position relative to management, which, they argue, has been able to pursue non-profit-maximization objectives. The concern here is in the spirit of the "tunneling" literature (Johnson et al. 2000), focusing on how insider, usually majority, shareholders treat other shareholders, especially within corporate groups. According to the standard measures of statutory legal protection used in the recent finance literature, Japanese minority shareholders enjoy many of the legal protection measures of common law countries.

9.2.9   Summary

Much has been written on Japan's corporate groups, and yet concrete evidence (positive or negative) on their economic importance is surprisingly scarce. Only the groups' role in mutual risk sharing has received some empirical support. In addition, there is much evidence that large shareholders (often within a corporate group) and main bank relationships (also typically within a corporate group) are often important for corporate governance, although there is little to suggest the importance of the group structure per se. It is therefore possible to conclude that the limited evidence on Japan's corporate groups is weakly consistent with the positive views of corporate groups as substitutes for missing (capital market and other) institutions.

9.3   Comparing Groups in Japan and Elsewhere

This section compares Japan's corporate groups with groups in other countries. Of course, they may differ substantially in structure and mode of operation but, at the same time, have many common features (most notably cross-shareholding). The main thrust of the comparison is that Japanese groups are not unique in structure, but are perhaps special in their low risk and low return characteristics. Because of data constraints, and perhaps also because groups are less common in developed economies, most of the countries included in this comparison are emerging markets, although some comparisons will be made with Italian groups.

9.3.1   A First Look

Table 9.1 describes corporate groups in Japan and in a several emerging markets. The fraction of firms classified as group affiliated ranges from about a fifth in Chile and Venezuela to about two-thirds in Indonesia. In Italy, more than half of all industrial companies belong to pyramidal groups (Bianchi, Bianco, and Enriques 2001). In Japan, members of presidents' clubs account for fewer than 10 percent of listed manufacturing firms, whereas other group definitions (for example, those of Dodwell Marketing Consultants and *Keiretsu no Kenyu*) identify close to a half of all listed manufacturing firms as members. Thus, in terms of overall prevalence groups, Japan does not seem to be different.

Table 9.1 also indicates that in Japan, as well as in virtually all the other countries for which data are available (Turkey being the only exception), group-affiliated firms are larger than unaffiliated firms. Difference in median size between presidents' clubs members and other firms are somewhat bigger than differences in means—the mean size of presidents' clubs members is about seven times that of nonmembers. The mean size of firms classified as group affiliated by Dodwell is about 50 percent larger than the size of unaffiliated firms.

Table 9.1   Corporate Groups: Japan and Emerging Markets

Country and Period	Percent in Group[a]	Relative Size[b]
Argentina 1990–1997	44	5.5
Brazil 1990–1997	47	2.5
Chile 1989–1996	22	18.7
India 1990–1997	33	4.4
Indonesia 1993–1995	65	2.8
Israel 1993–1995	23	5.0
Italy, early 1990s	>50	n.a.[c]
Korea 1991–1995	51	3.9
Mexico 1988–1997	35	2.3
Philippines 1992–1997	25	3.4
Taiwan 1990–1997	44	2.0
Thailand 1992–1997	62	2.3
Turkey 1988–1997	52	1.0
Prewar Japan (largest three groups) 1932–1943	29	6.8
Postwar Japan (presidents' clubs) 1977–1992	9	8.5
Postwar Japan (Dodwell definition) 1977–1992	39	2.0

Sources: Khanna and Yafeh (2001), except Italy, which is from Bianchi, Bianco, and Enriques (2001).

Note: n.a. = not available.

[a]Percentage of firms affiliated with groups.

[b]Median size of group-affiliated firms divided by median size of unaffiliated firms.

[c]Group firms are much larger.

This pattern is very pronounced in Italy as well, where large firms are predominantly group affiliated: Over 99 percent of firms with over 1,000 employees are group members, as are about 89 percent of the firms with 500 to 1,000 employees. By contrast, less than 40 percent of small firms (fewer than 100 employees) are group members (Bianchi, Bianco, and Enriques 2001).

9.3.2   Group Organization and Location Across Industries

Japan's postwar corporate groups are different from groups in many other countries in the conspicuous absence of a centralized decision-making mechanism. Without holding companies (legally banned between the end of World War II and 1998) or other formal joint control mechanism, it is hard to expect groups to coordinate their activities very extensively. This is in sharp contrast with Italian groups, where an elaborate pyramid structure guarantees centralized control; Indeed, Bianchi, Bianco, and Enriques (2001) argue that the very reason for the prevalence of groups in Italy is to generate a wedge between control and cash flow rights.

Although the degree of cohesiveness of groups varies across countries and across groups, in many emerging markets, including Korea, groups seem to be far more centrally controlled than they are in Japan. Thus, the loose structure of Japan's postwar groups appears to be distinctly different than the structure of groups in many emerging markets (and also in sharp contrast with the prewar period).

The spread of groups across manufacturing industries is displayed in table 9.2. (There are insufficient data to include services). Perhaps the most notable pattern is the absence of a clear pattern of group location across industries, although there is some evidence that groups in several countries tend to locate in somewhat more capital-intensive industries. This pattern is reminiscent of the *zaibatsu* in prewar Japan, although it is far from universally true.

Postwar Japanese group firms seem to be evenly spread across many sectors (the so-called one set policy). This pattern is not unique to Japan; for example, Chilean groups also seem to exhibit this tendency, although their structure appears to be less complete than that of the Japanese groups. In terms of sales, relatively more capital-intensive sectors, such as metals and chemicals, seem to be particularly important for Japan's corporate groups in terms of both the fraction of total group assets and group firms' market shares. These sectors are generally important for the Japanese economy as a whole, so this finding is hardly surprising.

The importance of services, most notably financial services, varies tremendously among groups in different countries. Whereas in some countries groups' entry into the financial services industry has been restricted (e.g., Korea), in other countries services constitute the bulk of group activity. Thus, it appears that, aside from the loose control, the structure and organization of Japan's corporate groups is not unique.

9.3.3   Risk and Return

Table 9.3 displays simple profit rates and profit volatility statistics for group and nongroup member firms in Japan and elsewhere. In six of twelve countries in the table, profit rates and profit volatility are lower for group-affiliated firms, although not always in a statistically significant manner.

Japanese corporate groups are among those characterized by low risk and low profitability, although differences in medians appear to be small and not statistically significant. Differences in mean profitability (3.7 percent for members of presidents' clubs versus 4.0 percent for other firms) are also statistically insignificant, although differences in mean standard deviation of profitability are statistically significant (standard deviation of operating profitability of 2.4 for presidents' clubs members versus 2.9 for other firms). Using the Dodwell definition, group firms exhibit significantly lower mean profitability, as well as significantly lower mean and median standard deviation of profitability relative to other firms.

The characterization of the Japanese groups as providing a low-risk and

Table 9.2   Group Location Across Manufacturing Industries

Country	Groups' Most Important Industries	Industries in Which Group Market Share is Largest
Argentina	Oil refining and natural resource extraction; metals	Oil refining and natural resource extraction; textiles; metals
Brazil	Chemicals; oil refining and natural resource extraction; metals	Food; lumber and wood; metals
Chile	Firms spread across sectors (lumber and wood important)	Food and tobacco; lumber and wood; rubber and plastic
Indonesia	Firms spread across sectors; lumber and wood; construction; (transportation equipment important)	Construction; machinery; transportation equipment
Israel	Metals; electronics; chemicals	Metals; electronics; chemicals
Korea	Machinery; metals; transportation equipment	Oil refining and natural resource extraction; transportation equipment; rubber; many sectors
Mexico	Food and tobacco; mining	Food and tobacco; construction; textile; mining
The Philippines	Food and tobacco; oil refining and natural resource extraction	Food and tobacco; lumber and wood
Taiwan	Machinery; textile; chemicals	Miscellaneous; oil refining and natural resource extraction; lumber and wood
Thailand	Firms spread across sectors	Metals; oil refining and natural resource extraction; chemicals
Turkey	Firms spread across sectors	Construction; food and tobacco; chemicals
Prewar Japan	Heavy industry[a]	Heavy industry[a]
Postwar Japan (1987)	One set policy—firms evenly spread across sectors; a bit more weight in chemicals, electronics and transportation equipment	Metals; chemicals

Note: The sample periods, division between group and nongroup firms, and sources are the same as in table 9.1.

[a]See Hadley (1970).

Table 9.3   **Risk and Return Characteristics of Corporate Groups**

Country	ROA[a]	Standard Deviation[b]
Argentina	–3.9*	–1.2*
Brazil	1.5*	–1.0
Chile	3.7**	0.3
India	2.1**	0.2**
Indonesia	–0.5	–0.6**
Israel	2.4**	–0.5
Korea	–0.3	–0.7**
Mexico	2.1	0.5
Philippines	3.3	–0.4
Taiwan	–1.1	–0.6*
Thailand	–1.5**	–0.6*
Turkey	–1.7	–2.9
Prewar Japan (three largest *zaibatsu*)	–0.9	–2.7
Postwar Japan (presidents' clubs)	–0.2	–0.1
Postwar Japan (Dodwell)	–0.2	–0.2**

Source: See Khanna and Yafeh (2001).

Note: Data are for the year of maximal coverage for each country (for Japan, 1987 profitability, and standard deviation based on 1977–1992) and exclude firms with profit rates above 100 percent or below –100 percent. Significance levels for the comparisons of medians are based on Wilcoxon signed-rank tests.

[a]Difference in median ROA between group and nongroup firms.
[b]Difference in median of standard deviation of ROA between group and nongroup firms.
**Statistically significant at the 5 percent level.
*Statistically significant at the 10 percent level.

low-return environment is borne out in more sophisticated econometric tests of the mutual insurance hypothesis conducted in Khanna and Yafeh (2001). They report that Japanese corporate groups (members of presidents' clubs) seem to provide mutual insurance for members' firms according to five of the six tests they conducted.[3]

This is hardly true for most groups around the world: Although groups in Korea and a few other countries also seem to provide a low-risk envi-

3. There are six tests: (a) A benchmark ordinary least squares (OLS) regression where the standard deviation of operating profitability is regressed on a number of control variables and a group affiliation dummy; (b) A test of the relation between the squared residuals from a regression with profitability as a dependent variable, and a group affiliation dummy; (c) Tests of first order stochastic dominance comparing the distributions of profit volatility among group-affiliated and nonaffiliated firms; (d) A test comparing whether the distribution of profitability among group firms is more skew than among nongroup firms because groups bail out member firms in financial distress and should therefore include fewer poorly performing members; (e) A test derived from Asdrubali, Sorensen, and Yosha (1996) of the extent to which shocks to profitability are smoothed through changes in dividends received; (f) A two-dimensional stochastic dominance test of the hypothesis that group-affiliated firms exhibit both low profitability and low profit volatility relative to nongroup firms. For Japanese groups, evidence of risk sharing (low profit volatility) was found in all of the tests except the last.

ronment according to these tests, groups in most emerging markets do not. Furthermore, there seems to be little relation between the extent of development of a country's financial system and the extent of mutual insurance provided by groups. In Japan too, there is little difference between measures of mutual insurance within corporate groups before and after the liberalization of Japan's financial markets in the 1980s.

The simple profitability statistics reported in table 9.3 suggest that in many cases, group-affiliated firms outperform their unaffiliated counterparts. More detailed econometric studies (controlling for various firm and group characteristics) also confirm that group membership is often associated with superior performance (See Chang and Choi 1988 for Korea; Keister 1998 for China; Khanna and Palepu 1999, 2000 for Chile and India).

By contrast, the raw figures for Japan, suggesting lower profit rates for group-affiliated firms, are confirmed by a long list of empirical studies. Caves and Uekusa (1976), Nakatani (1984), Odagiri (1992), Weinstein and Yafeh (1995, 1998), and Kang and Shivdasani (1999) all find that members of bank-centered Japanese groups underperform otherwise comparable unaffiliated firms. Weinstein and Yafeh (1998) also point out that growth rates among group-affiliated companies were never higher than growth rates of corresponding unaffiliated companies.

A plausible explanation for this phenomenon is that Japanese group firms do something other than profit maximization, perhaps in accordance with the interests of influential creditors (banks) within the group. We conclude that, in terms of risk and return trade-offs, Japanese corporate groups appear to differ from most of the corporate groups elsewhere.

For further discussion of the reasons for low profit rates among group firms see Hoshi and Kashyap (2001, 200–03). Okazaki (2001) finds that, in the prewar period, firms affiliated with *zaibatsu* exhibited higher profit rates than comparable unaffiliated firms, in contrast to the postwar period.

9.4   Long-Term Changes and Prospects

This section begins with an evaluation of the impact of corporate groups on the development of the Japanese economy in the long run. It then proceeds to a discussion of the evolution of the groups over time, continues to discuss the relative performance of group members in the 1990s, and concludes with an examination of the weakening of cross-shareholding and banking ties.

9.4.1   Long-Run Development of Industries

One (admittedly rough) way to evaluate the impact of corporate groups on the development of industries is to compare the growth rates of industries in Japan and the United States, and to relate the differences to group presence. Using industry-level growth rates (drawn from Carlin and Mayer 1999), table 9.4 displays the fastest growing and declining industries in the United States and Japan for the period 1970–1995.

In terms of capital formation, the same industries lead the list in both countries; in terms of growth of value added, there are some differences. Declining industries in the two countries also are quite similar. For the purpose of the present discussion, there is nothing to suggest that the growth rates of Japanese industries where group presence is more pronounced is substantially different than in the United States. Note that it is difficult to calculate the correlation between industry growth and group market share because the industry definitions Carlin and Mayer used are somewhat different than the 2-digit Standard Industrial Classification (SIC) used in table 9.2.

9.4.2   Industry Location

Group affiliation data drawn from the 1994 *Keiretsu no Kenkyu* suggest that group members were spread across many sectors, with their presence more pronounced in the chemicals, machinery, and electronics industries, much as in earlier periods. The differences in size between group and nongroup firms documented earlier seem to have persisted into the 1990s, and, much as in earlier periods, group firms are still somewhat more leveraged (table 9.5). There is no reason to believe groups have reorganized so as to focus more on certain industries, and there is little evidence that the structure of Japan's corporate groups has changed significantly in other ways, at least until the mid-1990s.

Table 9.4   **Growth of Industries in Japan and the United States, 1970–1995**

	Japan	United States
Fastest growing industries		
Measured by capital formation	Electrical machinery; transportation equipment; nonelectrical machinery; metals; chemicals (nonindustrial)	Plastic; electrical machinery; nonelectrical machinery; chemicals (nonindustrial); chemicals (industrial)
Measured by growth of value added	Tobacco; plastic; printing; electrical machinery; chemicals (nonindustrial)	Electrical machinery; professional goods; transportation equipment; machinery; metals
Slowest growing industries		
Measured by capital formation	Wood; footwear; leather; apparel; shipbuilding	Iron; shipbuilding; tobacco; footwear; leather
Measured by growth of value added	Iron; wood; shipbuilding; textile; furniture	Wood; footwear; leather; apparel; shipbuilding

Source: Carlin and Mayer (1999).

Table 9.5   Corporate Groups, 1991–2000

	Group Firms		Other Firms	
	Mean	SD[a]	Mean	SD[a]
Number of observations[b]	4150		2883	
Total assets (¥ billions)	287**	566	191	494
Debt assets	0.57**	0.17	0.54	0.26
ROA (%)	3.8**	3.5	4.0	4.5
Standard deviation of ROA (%)[c]	2.0**	1.2	2.4	1.5
Operating profit (% assets)	3.0	3.3	3.2	4.6
Ordinary profit (% assets)[d]	2.9	3.5	3.1	5.4

Note: Group affiliation is based on the 1994 *Keiretsu no Kenkyu* definition. Note that the percentage of group-affiliated companies in this sample is somewhat higher than in earlier studies.

[a]Standard deviation.

[b]Total number of observations over the entire period.

[c]Mean (within firm) standard deviation of ROA.

[d]Ordinary profit is total profit (operating and other income, including capital gains, losses, and depreciation) after interest expenses.

**Statistically significant at the 5 percent level.

9.4.3 Performance in the 1990s

Table 9.5 suggests that small differences in returns on assets (ROA) are still present in the 1990s, with group-affiliated companies being somewhat less profitable than unaffiliated firms. The table also suggests that the characterization of group members as less volatile appears to hold for the 1990s as well.

Differences in profitability between group members and unaffiliated firms are clearly observed in the multivariate regressions displayed in table 9.6. It is also interesting to note that while the average group-affiliated company experienced (nominal) asset growth of about 10 percent between 1991 and 2000, the assets of nongroup companies grew, on average, at about 17 percent during the same period. Thus, risk and return differences between group members and other companies seem to hold in the 1990s as well.

To the extent that performance differences in earlier years were due to bank monopoly power, leading to non-profit-maximization among group firms (see Weinstein and Yafeh 1998), the evidence from the 1990s may attest to continued influence of banks on remaining clients, despite ongoing liberalization. Low profitability of group members as a result of low risk strategies may still explain some of the differences in the 1990s, as the low volatility of profits suggests. The banking crisis may have had a negative effect on firms with ties to ailing banks and is another possible explanation for these findings (see Kang and Stulz 2000). Finally, it is quite possible that

Table 9.6   **Profitability Regressions, 1991–2000**

	ROA		Operating Profits/Assets		Ordinary Profits/Assets	
Group dummy	−0.38**	(0.09)	−0.30**	(0.08)	−0.24**	(0.09)
Debt/assets	−5.75**	(0.51)	−6.19**	(0.35)	−10.37**	(1.48)
Fixed assets/total assets	−5.64**	(0.39)	−5.35**	(0.40)	−6.62**	(0.40)
Log (sales)	0.56**	(0.06)	0.57**	(0.06)	0.69**	(0.10)
Standard deviation of ROA	−0.14**	(0.06)	−0.24**	(0.06)	−0.24**	(0.07)
Percentage of shares held by						
Top 12 shareholders	0.011	(0.004)	0.015**	(0.005)	0.017**	(0.005)
Individuals	0.05**	(0.01)	0.03**	(0.01)	0.02**	(0.01)
Financial institutions	0.004	(0.005)	0.002	(0.004)	0.004	(0.006)
Nonfinancial firms	−0.09**	(0.03)	−0.06	(0.03)	−0.09	(0.04)
R^2	0.29		0.28		0.41	

Note: The dependent variables are measures of profitability and the regressions are OLS using pooled data with heteroskedasticity-consistent standard errors reported in parentheses. The group affiliation dummy equals 1 for firms that are classified as group members using the 1994 *Keiretsu no Kenkyu* definition. In all three cases N is 7,033, and year dummies and industry dummies are used.

**Statistically significant at the 5 percent level.

some of the relatively poor performance of group members in the 1990s is due to the phenomenon of good firms ending their long-term ties with their main bank and possibly with their bank-centered group (see Hoshi and Kashyap 2001, 241–48, and further discussion below).

9.4.4   Cross-Shareholding

The ongoing recession in Japan and the decline in share prices may have made cross-shareholding arrangements costly to maintain, and the weakness of the group's main banks may have also contributed to the disintegration of the groups. At the same time, it is possible to argue that mutual risk-sharing arrangements within the groups are particularly valuable in the present economic conditions.

Suzuki (1998) reports that the sale of equity stakes held by corporations for long periods of time had not been a widespread phenomenon at the time he conducted his research. However, Okabe (2001) shows that substantial divestment of shares has been going on within the corporate groups since the late 1990s, especially by nonfinancial corporations. His main finding is that nonfinancial corporations have reduced cross-shareholding ties with financial institutions substantially, whereas other forms of cross-shareholding within groups (among financial institutions, between financial institutions and nonfinancial corporations, and among nonfinancial corporations) have remained virtually unchanged. For example, shares held by financial institutions as part of cross-shareholding arrangements remained roughly unchanged between 1987 and 1997, and

Table 9.7   Trends in Cross-Shareholding of Major Groups (%)

Group[b]	1987	1997	2000	Change 1997–2000[a]
Mitsubishi	14.8	14.0	11.3	–19.3
Sumitomo	13.4	11.3	8.9	–21.3
Mitsui	10.2	7.6	5.1	–32.9
Fuji	11.2	7.7	4.6	–40.3
DKB	9.1	7.9	6.2	–21.5
Sanwa	9.3	7.3	4.9	–32.9

Source: Nippon Life Insurance (2001), table 5.

Note: Average percentage of shares of a member firm cross-held by other group firms. The figures refer to cross-shareholding only, as identified by Nippon Life Insurance, as opposed to all stable shareholding within the group.

[a]Percentage change in cross shareholding from 1997 to 2000.

[b]Group firms as identified by Nippon Life Insurance.

then declined from about 8 percent of all shares to 6 percent in 1999. This reflects a decrease of similar magnitude in shareholding by financial institutions in both financial and nonfinancial companies. By contrast, shareholding by nonfinancial corporations declined somewhat in the early 1990s and then, during 1995–1999, declined from about 9 percent of total market value to 4.5 percent. This is accounted for primarily by a 4.1 percentage-point fall in shares held by corporations in financial institutions (Okabe 2001, table 2). A Nippon Life Insurance (2001) study, which is the source of Okabe's figures, confirms more broadly that the reduction in cross-shareholding is a phenomenon of the second half of the 1990s and that it is common to all major corporate groups. Some data are in table 9.7.

In spite of these trends, comparisons of membership in presidents' clubs show little evidence of group disintegration between 1989 and 1999. It is important to note also that these figures are somewhat sensitive to the definition of group affiliation and cross- or stable shareholding ties.

9.4.5   Banking Ties and Mergers

The trend of decreasing cross-shareholding ratios, especially between nonfinancial corporations and banks, is likely to be exacerbated by firms deciding to discontinue their long-term relations with the group's main banks. There is now no doubt that this phenomenon, documented initially by Hoshi, Kashyap, and Scharfstein (1993), and more recently in Anderson and Makhija (1999) and in Miyajima and Arikawa (2001), is of large magnitude.

The merger wave among financial institutions that cuts across traditional group lines is another factor that is likely to destabilize the existing group structure. For example, mergers between DKB and Fuji banks (together with the Industrial Bank of Japan), and between Sakura (Mitsui) and Sumitomo banks, could potentially lead to mergers of their clients' firms. An early-2002 example of this is the merger talks between the marine and fire insurance companies of the Mitsui and Sumitomo groups. Mitsui Chemical and Sumitomo Chemical merged in 1998, and NKK, part of the Fuji group, formed a strategic alliance with Kawasaki Steel of the DKB group. It will certainly alter the previous situation in which no group contains two competing firms, and no bank serves as main bank to competing companies.

9.4.6 Summary

It is clear that Japan's corporate groups have been changing, and that the bank-firm (equity and debt) ties which were at their core, have been substantially weakened. One telling indicator of a declining importance of groups is the cessation of publication of two main data sources on groups (*Keiretsu no Kenkyu* ceased publication in 1998 and *Kigyo Keiretsu Soran* in 2000). This decline in corporate groups appears to be associated with a general move towards a more market-based financial system in Japan (Hoshi and Kashyap 1999) and may even have contributed to the decline in Japanese stock prices. Yet it would be ridiculous to argue that the miserable stock returns are simply due to dumping of shares formerly held within corporate groups. The unwinding of cross-shareholdings should contribute to market liquidity, although this effect is hard to assess given the deteriorating macroeconomic conditions.

A decrease in stable shareholding within corporate groups is likely to increase the likelihood of hostile takeovers. Indeed, a few takeovers were observed in Japan in the late 1990s (Yafeh 2000), but none involved a core group company.

9.5 Conclusion

Corporate groups in Japan are undergoing significant change reflected in declining cross-shareholding, as well as in weakened main bank relationships. The consolidation of banks across groups is likely to accelerate this trend, making former main bank relationships obsolete. If groups were ever an impediment to structural change, perhaps most notably as hindrances to hostile takeovers and market-based corporate governance, they are unlikely to constitute a major obstacle in the future.[4]

For all the attention Japanese groups attracted in the last third of the twentieth century, not much is going to be missed from their demise, at least in terms of the economic roles they played. Even the mutual insurance

---

4. Peek and Rosengren (2002) express a different view, arguing that loans by financial institutions within groups impede "creative destruction" by prolonging the life of weak corporate borrowers. Although long-term bank-firm relations may prevent some bankruptcies of firms that are no longer viable, it is not clear that corporate groups substantially exacerbate this tendency.

provided within corporate groups is likely to decline in importance, as firm-specific human capital will lose some of its value and financial markets become ever more developed.

Similarly, the corporate governance roles allegedly played by large shareholders and financial institutions within the corporate groups are likely to be replaced by new, perhaps more market-oriented mechanisms, guaranteeing the efficient operations of firms. Thus, limited economic importance, combined with little political clout, suggest that Japan's corporate groups are unlikely to constitute an impediment to future changes in financial markets and corporate strategy.

Despite the large literature on corporate groups in Japan and elsewhere, the phenomenon of business groups still has many unanswered questions. Why is it that groups are observed in so many countries in early stages of their economic development? What is the most important reason for their existence? Why is the mutual insurance function of groups more important in Japan and a few other countries than in most emerging markets? How do groups evolve over time, and does their development pattern provide any evidence on their raison d'être? Will the Japanese groups provide the first example of groups that end their lives peacefully, or will government intervention be needed? These are only some of the questions on corporate groups that await further research.

References

Anderson, Christopher, and Anil Makhija. 1999. Deregulation, disintermediation, and agency costs of debt: Evidence from Japan. *Journal of Financial Economics* 51:309–39.

Aoki, Masahiko. 1988. *Information, incentives and bargaining in the Japanese economy.* Cambridge: Cambridge University Press.

Aoki, Masahiko, and Hugh Patrick, eds. 1994. *The Japanese main bank system: Its relevance for developing and transforming economies.* Oxford: Oxford University Press.

Asanuma, Banri. 1989. Manufacturer-supplier relationships in Japan and the concept of a relation-specific skill. *Journal of the Japanese and International Economies* 3:1–30.

Asdrubali, Pierfederico, Bent Sorensen, and Oved Yosha. 1996. Channels of interstate risk sharing: United States, 1963–1990. *Quarterly Journal of Economics* 111:1081–10.

Beason, Richard. 1998. *Keiretsu* affiliation and share price volatility in Japan. *Pacific Basin Finance Journal* 6:27–43.

Berglof, Erik, and Enrico Perotti. 1994. The governance structure of the Japanese financial *keiretsu. Journal of Financial Economics* 36:259–84.

Bertrand, Marianne, Paras Mehta, and Sendhil Mullainathan. 2002. Ferreting out tunneling. *Quarterly Journal of Economics* 117:121–48.

Bianchi, Marcello, Magda Bianco, and Luca Enriques. 2001. Ownership, pyramidal groups, and the separation between ownership and control in Italy. In *The control of corporate Europe,* ed. Fabrizio Barca and Marco Becht, 154–87. Oxford: Oxford University Press.

Bisson, Thomas. 1954. *Zaibatsu dissolution in Japan.* Berkeley, Cal.: University of California Press.

Branstetter, Lee. 2000. Vertical *keiretsu* and knowledge spillovers in Japanese manufacturing: An empirical assessment. *Journal of the Japanese and International Economies* 14:73–104.

Carlin, Wendi, and Colin Mayer. 1999. Finance, investment, and growth. *Journal of Financial Economics,* forthcoming.

Caves, Richard, and Masu Uekusa. 1976. *Industrial organization in Japan.* Washington, D.C.: Brookings Institution.

Chang, Sea-jin, and Unghwan Choi. 1988. Strategy, structure, and performance of Korean business groups: A transaction cost approach. *Journal of Industrial Economics* 37:141–58.

Chang, Sea-jin, and Jaebum Hong. 2000. The economic performance of the group affiliated companies in Korea: Groupwise resource sharing and internal transactions. *Academy of Management Journal* 43:429–48.

Claessens, Stijn, Simon Djankov, Joseph Fan, and Larry Lang. 1999. The rationale for groups: Evidence from East Asia. Washington, D.C.: World Bank. Unpublished Manuscript.

Encaoua, David, and Alexis Jacquemin. 1982. Organizational efficiency and monopoly power: The case of French industrial groups. *European Economic Review* 19:25–51.

Fisman, Raymond. 2001. Estimating the value of political connections. *American Economic Review* 91:1095–1102.

Flath, David. 1993. Shareholding in the *keiretsu*: Japan's corporate groups. *Review of Economics and Statistics* 75:249–57.

Fujimoto, Takahiro. 1999. *The evolution of a manufacturing system at Toyota.* Oxford: Oxford University Press.

Gibson, Michael. 1995. Can bank health affect investment? Evidence from Japan. *Journal of Business* 68:281–308.

Goto, Akira. 1982. Business groups in a market economy. *European Economic Review* 19:53–70.

Hadley, Eleanor. 1970. *Antitrust in Japan.* Princeton, N.J.: Princeton University Press.

Hoshi, Takeo. 1994. Evolution of the main bank system in Japan. In *The structure of the Japanese economy,* ed. Mitsuaki Okabe, 287–322. London: Macmillan.

Hoshi, Takeo, and Anil Kashyap. 1999. The Japanese banking crisis: Where did it come from and how will it end? *NBER Macroeconomics Annual* 14:121–201.

———. 2001. *Corporate financing and governance in Japan: The road to the future.* Cambridge, Mass.: MIT Press.

Hoshi, Takeo, Anil Kashyap, and David Scharfstein. 1990. The role of banks in reducing the costs of financial distress in Japan. *Journal of Financial Economics* 27:67–88.

———. 1991. Corporate structure, liquidity and investment: Evidence from Japanese industrial groups. *Quarterly Journal of Economics* 106:33–60.

———. 1993. The choice between public and private debt: An analysis of post deregulation corporate financing in Japan. NBER Working Paper no. 4421. Cambridge, Mass.: National Bureau of Economic Research, August.

Johnson, Chalmers. 1982. *MITI and the Japanese miracle: The growth of industrial policy, 1925–1975.* Stanford, Cal.: Stanford University Press.

Johnson, Simon, Peter Boone, Alasdair Breach, and Eric Friedman. 2000. Corporate governance in the Asian financial crisis. *Journal of Financial Economics* 58:141–86.

Kang, Jun-Koo, and Anil Shivdasani. 1995. Firm performance, corporate governance, and top executive turnover in Japan. *Journal of Financial Economics* 38:29–58.

———. 1997. Corporate restructuring during performance declines in Japan. *Journal of Financial Economics* 46:29–65.

———. 1999. Alternative mechanisms of corporate governance in Japan: An analysis of independent and bank-affiliated firms. *Pacific Basin Finance Journal* 7:1–22.

Kang, Jun-Koo, and René Stulz. 2000. Do banking shocks affect firm performance? An analysis of the Japanese experience. *Journal of Business* 73:1–23.

Kashyap, Anil. 1989. Empirical evidence on the insurance aspects of Japanese industrial alliances. Chap. 4 in *Price setting and investment: Models and evidence* Ph.D. diss., 172–208. MIT, Department of Economics.

Kawasaki, Seiichi, and John McMillan. 1987. The design of contracts: Evidence from Japanese subcontracting. *Journal of the Japanese and International Economies* 1:327–49.

Keister, Lisa. 1998. Engineering growth: Business group structure and firm performance in China's transition economy. *American Journal of Sociology* 10:404–40.

Khanna, Tarun. 2000. Business groups and social welfare in emerging markets: Existing evidence and unanswered questions. *European Economic Review* 44:748–61.

Khanna, Tarun and Krishna Palepu. 1999. Policy shocks, market intermediaries, and corporate strategy: The evolution of business groups in Chile and India. *Journal of Economics and Management Strategy* 8:271–310.

———. 2000. Is group membership profitable in emerging markets? An analysis of diversified Indian business groups. *Journal of Finance* 55:867–91.

Khanna, Tarun and Yishay Yafeh. 2001. Business groups and risk sharing around the world. Harvard University: Harvard Business School. Unpublished Manuscript.

La Porta, Rafael, Florencio Lopez de Silanes, Andrei Shleifer, and Robert Vishny. 1998. Law and Finance. *Journal of Political Economy* 106:1113–55.

Lawrence, Robert. 1993. Japan's different trade regime: An analysis with particular reference to *keiretsu*. *Journal of Economic Perspectives* 7:3–19.

Leff, Nathaniel. 1978. Industrial organization and entrepreneurship in the developing countries: The economic groups. *Economic Development and Cultural Change* 26:661–75.

Lincoln, James, Michael Gerlach, and Christina Ahmadjian. 1996. *Keiretsu* networks and corporate performance in Japan. *American Sociological Review* 61:67–88.

Mayer, Colin, Koen Schoors, and Yishay Yafeh. 2002. Sources of funds and investment strategies of venture capital funds: Evidence from Germany, Israel, Japan and the U.K. CEPR Discussion Paper no. 3340. London: Center for Economic Policy and Research.

Miwa, Yoshiro, and Mark Ramseyer. 2001a. The fable of the *keiretsu*. Harvard Law School Discussion Paper no. 316. Cambridge, Mass.: Harvard University.

———. 2001b. The myth of the main bank: Japan and comparative corporate governance. University of Tokyo, CIRJE Discussion Paper no. F-131. Tokyo: Center for Economic Research on the Japanese Economy.

Miyajima, Hideaki. 1994. The transformation of *zaibatsu* to postwar corporate groups—From hierarchically integrated groups to horizontally integrated groups. *Journal of the Japanese and International Economies* 8:293–328.

Miyajima, Hideaki, and Yasuhiro Arikawa. 2001. Relationship banking and debt choice: Evidence from the liberalization in Japan. Waseda University, Institute of Financial Studies, Working Paper no. 01-003. Tokyo: Waseda University.

Montalvo, Jose, and Yishay Yafeh. 1994. A micro-econometric analysis of technology transfer: The case of licensing agreements of Japanese firms. *International Journal of Industrial Organization* 12:227–44.

Nakatani, Iwao. 1984. The economic role of financial corporate grouping. In *The economic analysis of the Japanese firm,* ed. Masahiko Aoki, 227–58. New York, N.Y.: North Holland.

Nippon Life Insurance. 2001. *The year 2000 survey on the state of cross shareholding* (in Japanese). http://www.nli-research.co.jp.

Odagiri, Hiroyuki. 1992. *Growth through competition, competition through growth.* Oxford: Oxford University Press.

Ohkawa, Kazushi, and Henry Rosovsky. 1973. *Japanese economic growth: Trend acceleration in the twentieth century.* Stanford, Cal.: Stanford University Press.

Okabe, Mitsuaki. 2001. *Are cross shareholdings of Japanese corporations dissolving? Evolution and implications.* University of Oxford, Nissan Institute. Occasional Paper no. 33.

Okada, Yoshitaka. 2001. Cooperative learning and Japan's techno-governance structure: Exploratory case studies. *Sophia International Review* 23 (1): 19–42.

Okazaki, Tetsuji. 2001. The role of holding companies in prewar Japanese economic development: Rethinking *zaibatsu* in perspective of corporate governance. *Social Science Japan* 4:243–68.

Peek, Joe, and Eric Rosengren. 2002. Corporate affiliation and the (mis) allocation of credit. Paper presented at the NBER Japan Project Meeting. 13–14 September 2002, Tokyo.

Perotti, Enrico, and Stanislav Gelfer. 2001. Red barons or robber barons? Governance and financing in Russian financial-industrial groups. *European Economic Review* 45:1601–17.

Saxonhouse, Gary. 1993. What does Japanese trade structure tell us about Japanese trade policy? *Journal of Economic Perspectives* 7:21–43.

Sheard, Paul. 1989. The main bank system and corporate monitoring and control in Japan. *Journal of Economic Behavior and Organization* 11:399–422.

———. 1997. *Keiretsu,* competition and market access. In *Global economic policy,* ed. Edward Graham and David Richardson, 501–46. Washington, D.C.: Institute of International Economics.

Shleifer, Andrei, and Robert Vishny. 1986. Large shareholders and corporate control. *Journal of Political Economy* 94:461–88.

Strachan, Harry. 1976. *Family and other business groups in economic development: The case of Nicaragua.* New York, N.Y.: Praeger Press.

Suzuki, Kazunori. 1998. Inter-corporate shareholding in Japan: Their significance and impact of sales of stakes. University of London: London Business School. Unpublished Manuscript.

van Rixtel, Adrian. 2002. *Informality and monetary policy in Japan: The political economy of bank performance.* Cambridge: Cambridge University Press.

Weinstein, David, and Yishay Yafeh. 1995. Collusive or competitive? An empirical investigation of *keiretsu* behavior. *Journal of Industrial Economics* 43:359–76.

———. 1998. On the costs of a bank-centered financial system: Evidence from the changing main bank relations in Japan. *Journal of Finance* 53:635–72.

Yafeh, Yishay. 1995. Corporate ownership, profitability, and bank-firm ties: Evidence from the American occupation reforms in Japan. *Journal of the Japanese and International Economies* 9:154–73.

———. 2000. Corporate governance in Japan: Past performance and future prospects. *Oxford Review of Economic Policy* 16:74–84.

Yafeh, Yishay, and Oved Yosha. 2003. Large shareholders and banks: Who monitors and how. *Economic Journal* 113:128–46.

Contributors

Albert Ando, deceased
Department of Economics
McNeil Building, Room 412
University of Pennsylvania
3718 Locust Walk
Philadelphia, PA 19104-6297

Kenn Ariga
Institute of Economic Research
Kyoto University
Yoshida-honmachi, Sakyo-ku
Kyoto 6068501
JAPAN

Magnus Blomström
European Institute of Japanese Studies
Stockholm School of Economics
Post Office Box 6501, Sveavagen 65
S-113 83 Stockholm
SWEDEN

Lee Branstetter
Columbia Business School
813 Uris Hall
3022 Broadway
New York, NY 10027

Dimitrios Christelis
Department of Economics
University of Pennsylvania
3718 Locust Walk
Philadelphia, PA 19104-6297

Jennifer Corbett
Japan Centre
Asian Studies Faculty and APSEM
Australian National University
Canberra ACT 0200
AUSTRALIA

Robert Dekle
Department of Economics
University of Southern California
Los Angeles, CA 90089

Takero Doi
Faculty of Economics
Keio University
2-15-45 Mita
Minato-ku, Tokyo 108-8345
JAPAN

David Flath
Department of Economics
322 Nelson
North Carolina State University
Hillsborough Street and Brooks Avenue
Raleigh, NC 27695-8614

Mitsuhiro Fukao
Faculty of Business and Commerce
Keio University
2-15-45 Mita, Minato-ku
Tokyo 108-8345
JAPAN

Fumio Hayashi
Department of Economics
University of Tokyo
Tokyo 113-0033
JAPAN

Takeo Hoshi
Graduate School of International
    Relations & Pacific Studies
IR/PS, Office #1319
University of California,
    San Diego
9500 Gilman Drive
La Jolla, CA 92093-0519

Anil Kashyap
Graduate School of Business
The University of Chicago
1101 East 58th Street
Chicago, IL 60637

Kenji Matsui
Faculty of Business Administration
Yokohama National University
79-4 Tokiwa-dai, Hodogaya-ku
Yokohama, Kanagawa 2408501
JAPAN

Tsutomu Miyagawa
Faculty of Economics
Gakushuin University
1-5-1 Mejiro, Toshima-ku
Tokyo 171-8588
JAPAN

Yoshiaki Nakamura
Director for General Affairs Division
Kanto Bureau of Economy, Trade and
    Industry
METI (Ministry of Economy, Trade
    and Industry)
2-11, Kamiochiai, Saitama-shi
Saitama-ken 330-9715
JAPAN

Hiroshi Ono
The European Institute of Japanese
    Studies
Stockholm School of Economics
P.O. Box 6501
S-113 83, Stockholm
SWEDEN

Marcus E. Rebick
St. Antony's College
Oxford University
Oxford, OX2 6JF
ENGLAND

Yishay Yafeh
School of Business Administration
Hebrew University
Jerusalem 91905
ISRAEL
and Economics Department
University of Montreal
C.P. 6128, Succursale Centre-ville
Montreal, Quebec H3C 3J7
CANADA

Author Index

Subject Index

Age-based discrimination, 235–36
Aggregation biases: CPI and, 104–15; within items, 107–8; substitution across brands and, 108–11; substitution across stores and, 111–15. *See also* Biases
Alliances, research, 213–14; promotion of knowledge flows and, 214–16
Amakudari, 268
Asahi Life, 29
Automobile ownership, 143–44, 151–52

Banking sector, 2; causes of unprofitability of, 20–25; corporate groups and, 278–79; deflation and, 9; deregulation and, 20–23; deteriorating condition of, 15–18; loan loss reserves in, 12–15; mergers in, 278–79; nationalization of, 9; problem loans and, 10–12; unprofitability of, 18–20. *See also* Government financial institutions (GFIs); Insurance companies
Bank of Japan, 9. *See also* Banking sector
Benefit systems, effect of, on labor supply, 244–45
Biases: commodity, in CPI, 118–20; sources of, in CPI, 100–104. *See also* Aggregation biases
Bonds: Japanese government, 63; yields, of FILP, 63
Brands: selection procedures, for CPI, 100–

102; substitution across, and aggregation biases, 108–11
Business groups, Japanese, 7

Capital stock: adjusting depreciation and, 187–88; calculating, for Japanese corporate sector, 182–87
Car ownership, 143–44, 151–52
Carry, 10
Child care leave, 245–46
Child Care Leave and Family Care Leave Law, 245
Chiyoda Life, 10, 27, 29, 31
Classified loans, 12
COGI. *See* Cost of goods index (COGI)
COLI. *See* Cost of living index (COLI)
Commodity biases, in CPI, 118–20
Compensation arrangements, 227–28; managerial, 228. *See also* Pay structure, seniority and
Competition, structure of, and growth, 7
Consumer behavior, changes in, 4
Consumer Price Index (CPI), 4, 89–92, 90–91, 97; aggregation biases in, 104–15; alternative inflation measures and, 97–98; brand selection procedures and, 100–102; commodity biases in, 118–20; as cost of goods index, 98–100; as cost of living index, 98–100; medical and health care expenditures and, 102; new products and, 103–4; quality changes